# LONGMAN
# KEYSTONE

## F

**Anna Uhl Chamot**

**John De Mado**

**Sharroky Hollie**

PEARSON
Longman

Pearson Education, 10 Bank Street, White Plains, NY 10606

**Staff credits:** The people who made up the Longman Keystone team, representing editorial, production, design, manufacturing, and marketing, are John Ade, Rhea Banker, Liz Barker, Danielle Belfiore, Don Bensey, Virginia Bernard, Kenna Bourke, Anne Boynton-Trigg, Johnnie Farmer, Maryann Finocchi, Patrice Fraccio, Geraldine Geniusas, Charles Green, Henry Hild, David L. Jones, Lucille M. Kennedy, Ed Lamprich, Emily Lippincott, Tara Maceyak, Maria Pia Marrella, Linda Moser, Laurie Neaman, Sherri Pemberton, Liza Pleva, Joan Poole, Edie Pullman, Monica Rodriguez, Tania Saiz-Sousa, Donna Schaffer, Chris Siley, Lynn Sobotta, Heather St. Clair, Jennifer Stem, Siobhan Sullivan, Jane Townsend, Heather Vomero, Marian Wassner, Lauren Weidenman, Matthew Williams, and Adina Zoltan.

**Smithsonian American Art Museum contributors:** Project director and writer: Elizabeth K. Eder, Ph.D.; Writer: Mary Collins; Image research assistants: Laurel Fehrenbach, Katherine G. Stilwill, and Sally Otis; Rights and reproductions: Richard H. Sorensen and Leslie G. Green; Building photograph by Tim Hursley.

**Text design and composition:** Kirchoff/Wohlberg, Inc.

**Text font:** 11.5/14 Minion
**Acknowledgments:** See page 468.
**Illustration and Photo Credits:** See page 470.

**Library of Congress Cataloging-in-Publication Data**
Chamot, Anna Uhl.
   Longman keystone / Anna Uhl Chamot, John De Mado, Sharroky Hollie.
      p. cm. -- (Longman keystone ; F)
   Includes index.
   ISBN 0-13-158259-3 (v. F)
   1. Language arts (Middle school)--United States. 2. Language arts (Middle school)--Activity programs. 3. Language arts (Secondary)--United States. 4. English language--Study and teaching. I. Demado, John II. Hollie, Sharroky III. Title.
   LB1631.C4466 2008
   428.0071'2--dc22
                                 2007049279

ISBN-13: 978-0-13-158259-0
ISBN-10: 0-13-158259-3

**PEARSON LONGMAN** ON THE WEB

**Pearsonlongman.com** offers online resources for teachers and students. Access our Companion Websites, our online catalog, and our local offices around the world.

Visit us at **www.pearsonlongman.com**.

Printed in the United States of America
4 5 6 7 8 9 10 11 12—DWL—12 11 10 09

# About the Authors

**Anna Uhl Chamot** is a professor of secondary education and a faculty advisor for ESL in George Washington University's Department of Teacher Preparation. She has been a researcher and teacher trainer in content-based second-language learning and language-learning strategies. She co-designed and has written extensively about the Cognitive Academic Language Learning Approach (CALLA) and spent seven years implementing the CALLA model in the Arlington Public Schools in Virginia.

**John De Mado** has been an energetic force in the field of Language Acquisition for several years. He is founder and president of John De Mado Language Seminars, Inc., an educational consulting firm devoted exclusively to language acquisition and literacy issues. John, who speaks a variety of languages, has authored several textbook programs and produced a series of music CD/DVDs designed to help students acquire other languages. John is recognized nationally, as well as internationally, for his insightful workshops, motivating keynote addresses, and humor-filled delivery style.

**Sharroky Hollie** is an assistant professor in teacher education at California State University, Dominguez Hills. His expertise is in the field of professional development, African-American education, and second-language methodology. He is an urban literacy visiting professor at Webster University, St. Louis. Sharroky is the Executive Director of the Center for Culturally Responsive Teaching and Learning (CCRTL) and the co-founding director of the nationally acclaimed Culture and Language Academy of Success (CLAS).

# Reviewers

# Dear Student,

## *Welcome to* LONGMAN

# KEYSTONE

*Longman Keystone* has been specially designed to help you succeed in all areas of your school studies. This program will help you develop the English language skills you need for language arts, social studies, math, and science. You will discover new ways to use and build upon your language skills through your interactions with classmates, friends, teachers, and family members.

*Keystone* includes a mix of many subjects. Each unit has four different reading selections that include literary excerpts, poems, and nonfiction articles about science, math, and social studies. These selections will help you understand the vocabulary and organization of different types of texts. They will also give you the tools you need to approach the content of the different subjects you take in school.

As you use this program, you will discover new words, use your background knowledge of the subjects presented, relate your knowledge to the new information, and take part in creative activities. You will learn strategies to help you understand readings better. You will work on activities that help you improve your English skills in grammar, word study, and spelling. Finally, you will be asked to demonstrate the listening, speaking, and writing skills you have learned through fun projects that are incorporated throughout the program.

Learning a language takes time, but just like learning to skateboard or learning to swim, it is fun! Whether you are learning English for the first time, or increasing your knowledge of English by adding academic or literary language to your vocabulary, you are giving yourself new choices for the future, and a better chance of succeeding in both your studies and in everyday life.

We hope you enjoy *Longman Keystone* as much as we enjoyed writing it for you!

Good luck!

Anna Uhl Chamot
John De Mado
Sharroky Hollie

# *Learn about* *Art* *with the*
# Smithsonian American Art Museum

## *Dear Student,*

At the end of each unit in this book, you will learn about some artists and artworks that relate to the theme you have just read about. These artworks are all in the Smithsonian American Art Museum in Washington, D.C. That means they belong to you, because the Smithsonian is America's collection. The artworks were created over a period of 300 years by artists who responded to their experiences in personal ways. Their world lives on through their artworks and, as viewers, we can understand them and ourselves in new ways. We discover that many of the things that concerned these artists still engage us today.

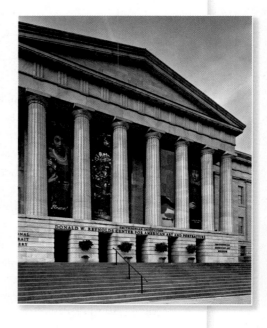

Looking at an artwork is different from reading a written history. Artists present few facts or dates. Instead, they offer emotional insights that come from their own lives and experiences. They make their own decisions about what matters, without worrying if others agree or disagree. This is a rare and useful kind of knowledge that we can all learn from. Artists inspire us to respond to our own lives with deeper insight.

There are two ways to approach art. One way is through the mind—studying the artist, learning about the subject, exploring the context in which the artwork was made, and forming a personal view. This way is deeply rewarding and expands your understanding of the world. The second way is through the senses—letting your imagination roam as you look at an artwork, losing yourself in colors and shapes, absorbing the meaning through your eyes. This way is called "aesthetic." The great thing about art is that an artwork may have many different meanings. You can decide what it means to you.

This brief introduction to American art will, I hope, lead to a lifetime of enjoyment and appreciation of art.

**Elizabeth Broun**
The Margaret and Terry Stent Director
Smithsonian American Art Museum

# Glossary of Terms

You will find the following words useful when reading, writing, and talking about art.

abstract  a style of art that does not represent things, animals, or people realistically

acrylic  a type of paint that is made from ground pigments and certain chemicals

background  part of the artwork that looks furthest away from the viewer

brushstroke  the paint or ink left on the surface of an artwork by the paintbrush

canvas  a type of heavy woven fabric used as a support for painting; another word for a painting

composition  the way in which the different parts of an artwork are arranged

detail  a small part of an artwork

evoke  to produce a strong feeling or memory

figure  the representation of a person or animal in an artwork

foreground  part of the artwork that looks closest to the viewer

geometric  a type of pattern that has straight lines or shapes such as squares, circles, etc.

mixed media  different kinds of materials such as paint, fabric, objects, etc. that are used in a single artwork

oil  a type of paint that is made from ground pigments and linseed oil

paintbrush  a special brush used for painting

perception  the way you understand something you see

pigment  a finely powdered material (natural or man-made) that gives color to paint, ink, or dye

portrait  an artwork that shows a specific person, group of people, or animal

print  an artwork that has been made from a sheet of metal or a block of wood covered with a wet color and then pressed onto a flat surface like paper. Types of prints include lithographs, etchings, aquatints, etc.

symbol  an image, shape, or object in an artwork that represents an idea

texture  the way that a surface or material feels and how smooth or rough it looks

tone  the shade of a particular color; the effect of light and shade with color

watercolor  a type of paint that is made from ground pigments, gum, and glycerin and/or honey; another word for a painting done with this medium

# Contents

# Contents

# How do generations differ from one another?

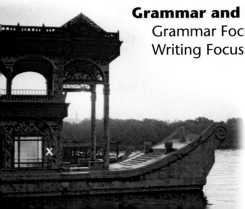

# UNIT 4

# Contents

## How does the sea affect our lives?

## **H**ow do struggles build character? ................................................ **262**

# UNIT 6

# Contents

**W**hy are ideals important? ...................................... **326**

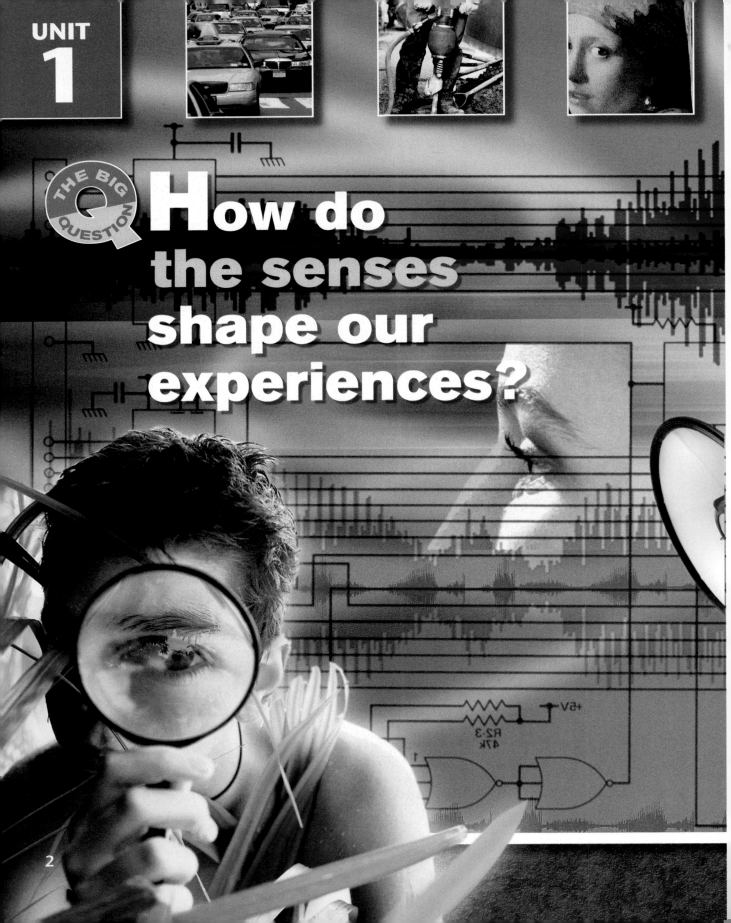

THE BIG Q QUESTION

# How do the senses shape our experiences?

This unit is about the senses. You will read literature about sounds and colors and articles about how you hear and see. Reading, writing, and talking about these topics will make you more aware of the world around you and will help you become a better student.

## READING 1:

**Two Personal Narratives**

■ "The Sounds of the City" by James Tuite

■ "The Sounds of the Desert" by Sandra Day O'Connor and H. Alan Day

## READING 2: Science Article

■ "How We Hear"

## READING 3: Novel Excerpt

■ From *Girl with a Pearl Earring* by Tracy Chevalier

## READING 4: Science Article

■ "How We See"

### Listening and Speaking

At the end of this unit, you will make a **group presentation** about a person, place, or experience you want to share.

### Writing

In this unit you will practice **descriptive writing**. Describing means telling what things look, sound, feel, smell, or taste like. After each reading you will learn a skill to help you write a descriptive paragraph. At the end of the unit, you will use these skills to help you write a descriptive essay.

### QuickWrite

In your notebook, list two or three experiences that each sense brings to your life. Then share your ideas with a partner.

## What You Will Learn

**Reading**
- Vocabulary building: *Literary terms, word study*
- Reading strategy: *Predict*
- Text type: *Literature (personal narrative)*

**Grammar, Usage, and Mechanics**
Prepositions of location and direction

**Writing**
Describe a place

### THE BIG QUESTION

**How do the senses shape our experiences?** Sounds are all around us. Every place has its own distinctive sounds. First, imagine that you are walking through a busy city street. Then imagine you are walking through a desert. What kinds of sounds might you hear in each place? Make a list with a partner.

### BUILD BACKGROUND

In this section you will read two personal narratives. A personal narrative tells a story about a writer's personal experience. **"The Sounds of the City"** describes the experience of life in New York City. There people, traffic, and other activity create an environment full of different sounds. **"The Sounds of the Desert"** describes the much more quiet life in a desert in the southwestern part of the United States. But the natural world is also rich in sounds.

▲ A city street          ▲ A desert

## VOCABULARY

### Learn Literary Words

Writers have different ways of creating vivid descriptions. **Onomatopoeia** is the use of a word whose sound is related to the word's meaning. In the example below, the word *rat-a-tat-tat* makes a sound like a drill pounding on the street.

> A pneumatic drill frays countless nerves with its rat-a-tat-tat, for dig they must to perpetuate the city's dizzy motion.

Another way writers make descriptions come alive is with **imagery**. Imagery is the use of words to create word pictures. These pictures, or images, help the reader imagine how something looks, sounds, smells, feels, or tastes. The example below paints a vivid picture of what a river looks like after it rains.

> . . . the river becomes an angry, rushing, mud-colored flood . . .

Giving human qualities to a nonhuman thing is called **personification**. In the following example, the writer personifies a sanitation truck by comparing it to a person eating a huge meal.

> Metallic jaws on sanitation trucks gulp and masticate . . . then digest it with a satisfied groan of gears.

### Practice  **Workbook** Page 1

With a partner, take turns reading aloud the examples of personification below. Identify the object and say how it is personified. Then, in your notebook, write three sentences of your own that use personification.

▲ **A sanitation truck**

> The delicious breath of rain was in the air.   *(Kate Chopin)*
>
> In November a cold, unseen stranger, whom the doctors called Pneumonia, stalked about the colony, touching one here and there with his icy finger.   *(O. Henry)*
>
> It was afternoon: great clouds stumbled across the sky.   *(H. E. Bates)*
>
> Arise, fair sun, and kill the envious moon,
> Who is already sick and pale with grief.   *(William Shakespeare)*

## Learn Academic Words

Study the **red** words and their meanings. You will find these words useful when reading and writing about literature. Write each word and its meaning in your notebook. After you read "The Sounds of the City" and "The Sounds of the Desert," try to use these words to respond to the texts.

**Academic Words**

contrast
identify
similar
specific

| | | |
|---|---|---|
| **contrast** = compare two people, ideas, or things to show how they are different from each other | ➡ | The poems **contrast** life in the mountains with life by the seashore. |
| **identify** = recognize and name someone or something | ➡ | I can **identify** the source of that noise. It's a dove. |
| **similar** = almost the same but not exactly the same | ➡ | The sound a dog makes is **similar** to the sound a coyote makes. |
| **specific** = used when talking about a particular person, place, or thing | ➡ | Some of the **specific** sounds of the city include sirens, auto horns, and shouts. |

**Practice**  **Workbook** Page 2

Work with a partner to answer these questions. Try to include the **red** word in your answer. Write the sentences in your notebook.

1. How does the sound a mouse makes compare and **contrast** to the sound an elephant makes?

2. What clues help you **identify** where a sound is coming from?

3. Which animals are **similar** in appearance?

4. What are some **specific** sounds you hear in your classroom?

▲ A coyote

◀ A dove

6

## Word Study: Spelling Long Vowels

Long vowel sounds are spelled in different ways. Read the words in the chart below to see the spelling patterns that are common for each vowel sound.

| Long *a* | Long *e* | Long *i* | Long *o* | Long *u* |
|----------|----------|----------|----------|----------|
| brakes | sleepless | spine | lonely | mute |
| strains | beat | high | moan | youth |
| day | believe | mind | shows | view |
| break | story | why | cold | cue |
|  | key |  |  | community |

**Practice**  Workbook Page 3

Work with a partner. Copy the chart into your notebook. Take turns asking each other the words from the chart and spelling them aloud. Continue until you can spell all these words correctly. Then work with your partner to spell the following words.

| | | | | |
|---|---|---|---|---|
| flight | trace | groan | rescue | creaking |
| music | whine | rains | beetle | smoke |

## READING STRATEGY   PREDICT

Predicting helps you understand a text better and focus on the information in it. Before you read, predict, or guess, what the text will be about. You can also make new predictions as you're reading. To predict, follow these steps:

- Look at the headings and ask yourself, "What will this section be about?"
- Look for clues in the illustrations.
- Think about what you already know and your own experiences.
- As you read, check to see if your prediction is correct. If it isn't, make a new prediction.

As you read "The Sounds of the City" and "The Sounds of the Desert," stop from time to time and check to see if your prediction was correct. Did you learn anything new that made you want to change your prediction? Make a new prediction if necessary.

 Workbook Page 4

**Set a purpose for reading** Look at the titles of the two readings. What kinds of sounds do you expect to read about in each one? Look for words that give you clues.

# The Sounds of the City

*James Tuite*

New York is a city of sounds: muted sounds and shrill sounds; shattering sounds and soothing sounds; urgent sounds and aimless sounds. The cliff dwellers of Manhattan—who would be racked by the silence of the lonely woods—do not hear these sounds because they are constant and eternally urban. The visitor to the city can hear them, though, just as some animals can hear a high-pitched whistle inaudible to humans. To the casual caller to Manhattan, lying restive and sleepless in a hotel twenty or thirty floors above the street, they tell a story as fascinating as life itself. And back of the sounds broods the silence.

## Strains of Music

Night in midtown is the noise of tinseled honky-tonk and violence. Thin strains of music, usually the firm beat of rock-and-roll or the frenzied outbursts of the discotheque, rise from ground level. This is the cacophony, the discordance of youth, and it comes on strongest when nights are hot and young blood restless.

---

**cliff dwellers**, people who live in tall apartment
   buildings
**broods**, thinks and worries about something for
   a long time
**honky-tonk**, type of loud, cheap nightclub music
**frenzied outbursts**, sudden, uncontrolled increase
   of music
**cacophony**, loud mixture of unpleasant sounds
**discordance**, musical notes that do not go together

Somewhere in the canyons below there is shrill laughter or raucous shouting. A bottle shatters against concrete. The whine of a police siren slices through the night, moving ever closer, until an eerie Doppler effect brings it to a guttural halt.

## Imagination Takes Flight

There are few sounds so exciting in Manhattan as those of fire apparatus dashing through the night. At the outset there is the tentative hint of the first-due company bullying its way through midtown traffic. Now a fire whistle from the opposite direction affirms that trouble is, indeed, afoot. In seconds, other sirens converging from other streets help the skytop listener focus on the scene of excitement.

But he can only hear and not see, and imagination takes flight. Are the flames and smoke gushing from windows not far away? Are victims trapped there, crying out for help? Is it a conflagration, or only a trash-basket fire? Or, perhaps, it is merely a false alarm.

The questions go unanswered and the urgency of the moment dissolves. Now the mind and the ear detect the snarling, arrogant bickering of automobile horns. People in a hurry. Taxicabs blaring, insisting on their checkered priority.

Even the taxi horns dwindle down to a precocious few in the gray and pink moments of dawn. Suddenly there is another sound, a morning sound that taunts the memory for recognition. The growl of a predatory monster? No, just garbage trucks that have begun a day of scavenging.

Trash cans rattle outside restaurants. Metallic jaws on sanitation trucks gulp and masticate the residue of daily living, then digest it with a satisfied groan of gears.

The sounds of the new day are businesslike. The growl of buses, so scattered and distant at night, becomes a demanding part of the traffic bedlam. An occasional jet or helicopter injects an exclamation point from an unexpected quarter. When the wind is right, the vibrant bellow of an ocean liner can be heard.

---

**fire apparatus**, fire engine or fire truck
**bullying**, pushing rudely or forcefully
**conflagration**, huge fire
**bickering**, arguing about something that is not important
**dwindle**, gradually become fewer
**scavenging**, searching for things to eat

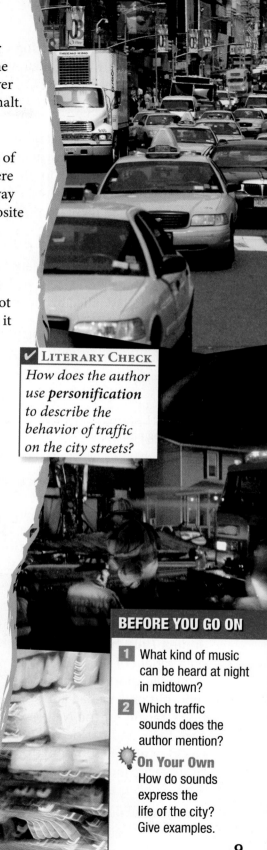

✔ **LITERARY CHECK**
*How does the author use **personification** to describe the behavior of traffic on the city streets?*

**BEFORE YOU GO ON**

**1** What kind of music can be heard at night in midtown?

**2** Which traffic sounds does the author mention?

💡**On Your Own**
How do sounds express the life of the city? Give examples.

9

The sounds of the day are as jarring as the glare of a sun that outlines the canyons of midtown in drab relief. A pneumatic drill frays countless nerves with its rat-a-tat-tat, for dig they must to perpetuate the city's dizzy motion. After each screech of brakes there is a moment of suspension, of waiting for the thud or crash that never seems to follow.

The whistles of traffic policemen and hotel doormen chirp from all sides, like birds calling for their mates across a frenzied aviary. And all of these sounds are adult sounds, for childish laughter has no place in these canyons.

## Farewell to Day

Night falls again, the cycle is complete, but there is no surcease from sound. For the beautiful dreamers, perhaps, the "sounds of the rude world heard in the day, lulled by the moonlight have all passed away," but this is not so in the city.

Too many New Yorkers accept the sounds about them as bland parts of everyday existence. They seldom stop to listen to the sounds, to think about them, to be appalled or enchanted by them. In the big city, sounds are life.

---

**jarring**, shocking and unpleasant
**frays**, tears
**perpetuate**, continue
**moment of suspension**, moment when everything stops
**aviary**, large cage where birds are kept
**surcease**, rest; relief

✔ **LITERARY CHECK**
*What **imagery** does the author use to describe the sounds made by the policemen and the doormen? What do you hear? What do you see?*

## ABOUT THE AUTHOR

**James Tuite** has written on a variety of subjects, especially sports. Tuite has reported on baseball and horse-racing for the *New York Times* and has delved further into the world of athletics in books on a wide range of subjects, including *Snowmobiles and Snowmobiling* and *How to Enjoy Sports on TV*.

10

# THE SOUNDS OF THE DESERT

*Sandra Day O'Connor and H. Alan Day*

The earliest memory is of sounds. In a place of all-encompassing silence, any sound is something to be noted and remembered. When the wind is not blowing, it is so quiet you can hear a beetle scurrying across the ground or a fly landing on a bush. Occasionally an airplane flies overheard—a high-tech intrusion penetrating the agrarian peace.

When the wind blows, as it often does, there are no trees to rustle and moan. But the wind whistles through any loose siding on the barn and causes any loose gate to bang into the fence post. It starts the windmills moving, turning, creaking.

✔ **LITERARY CHECK**

*Find an example of **onomatopoeia** on this page. What makes the sound?*

---

**all-encompassing**, total
**scurrying**, moving very quickly
**intrusion**, unwanted interruption
**agrarian**, relating to farming
**moan**, make a long low sound expressing pain
**creaking**, making a long high noise

**High desert country near the Gila River in Arizona** ▼

**BEFORE YOU GO ON**

**1** What are some unpleasant sounds that can be heard in the city during the day?

**2** What can you hear when the wind is not blowing in the desert?

💡**On Your Own**
Which sounds do you find jarring? Which ones do you find soothing?

11

At night the sounds are magnified. Coyotes wait on the hillside, calling to each other or to the moon—a sound that sends chills up the spine. We snuggle deeper in our beds. What prey have the coyotes spotted? Why are they howling? What are they doing? Just before dawn the doves begin to call, with a soft cooing sound, starting the day with their endless search for food. The cattle nearby walk along their trail near the house, their hooves crunching on the gravel. An occasional *moo* to a calf or to another cow can be heard, or the urgent bawl of a calf that has lost contact with its mother, or the low insistent grunt, almost a growl, of a bull as it walks steadily along to the watering trough or back out to the pasture. The two huge windmills turn in the wind, creaking as they revolve to face the breeze, and producing the clank of the sucker rods as they rise and fall with each turn of the huge fan of the mill.

The Lazy B Ranch straddles the border of Arizona and New Mexico along the Gila River. It is high desert country—dry, windswept, clear, often cloudless. Along the Gila the canyons are choked with cottonwoods and willows. The cliffs rise up sharply and are smooth beige sandstone.

A windmill turning
in the wind ▼

---

**magnified**, made louder
**pasture**, land covered with grass
**straddles**, sits on both sides of
**choked**, filled
**cottonwoods and willows**, types of trees

▲ Cattle in a desert pasture

The water flowing down the riverbed from the Gila Wilderness to the northeast is usually only a trickle. But sometimes, after summer rains or a winter thaw in the mountains, the river becomes an angry, rushing, mud-colored flood, carrying trees, brush, rocks, and everything else in its path. Scraped into the sandstone bluffs are petroglyphs of the Anasazi of centuries past. Their lives and hardships left these visible traces for us to find, and we marvel at their ability to survive as long as they did in this harsh environment. High up on one of the canyon walls is a small opening to a cave. A few ancient steps are cut out of the bluff leading to it. To reach it now requires climbing apparatus—ropes and pitons. The cave's inner walls have been smoothed with mud plaster, and here and there is a handprint, hardened when the mud dried, centuries ago.

▲ The location of the Lazy B Ranch

---

**trickle**, thin slow flow of water
**scraped**, cut
**petroglyphs of the Anasazi**, pictures cut into the rocks by ancient Native American people

▲ A petroglyph of a sheep

## ABOUT THE **AUTHORS**

**Sandra Day O'Connor** was appointed to the Supreme Court in 1981 after a distinguished career in law and politics in Arizona. She was the first woman to receive this honor. She served on the Court until her retirement in 2006. In addition to her legal writings and the childhood memoir from which this excerpt is taken, O'Connor has written a children's book, *Chico*.

**H. Alan Day** ran the Day family ranch, the Lazy B, for thirty years. He also ranched in Nebraska and South Dakota, where he helped run a sanctuary for wild horses.

**BEFORE YOU GO ON**

1 What animals can be heard at night in the desert? What sounds do they make?

2 Where is the Lazy B Ranch located?

**On Your Own**
Why do you think sounds seem to be magnified at night?

# Review and Practice

## DRAMATIC READING

In small groups, read aloud the text under the heading "Strains of Music," on pages 8–9. Assign one or more sentences of this text to each member of the group. Identify each specific sound in the text and create vocal sound effects to go along with the reading. For example, one group member mimics the sound of a siren; another, a disco beat. Have members of the group add their sound effects at the appropriate moments to support the dramatic reading.

**Speaking TIP**

Vary the volume of your voice.

## COMPREHENSION

**Workbook**
**Page 5**

**Right There**

1. According to the author, what is one of the most exciting sounds in New York City?
2. In the desert, what happens when the wind blows?

**Think and Search**

3. What are some sounds that can be heard in the city at night? What are some examples of day sounds? How do these sounds contrast?
4. What types of things cause sounds in the desert? How are desert sounds different from city sounds?

**Author and You**

5. Do you think the author of "The Sounds of the City" likes New York? Find examples in the text to support your answer.
6. The authors of "The Sounds of the Desert" create a mood. How would you describe this mood? Give examples.

**On Your Own**

7. Would you prefer to live in a place that is similar to New York City or to the desert? Explain.
8. The author of "The Sounds of the City" believes that New Yorkers no longer hear certain sounds. What specific sounds do you no longer notice in the place where you live? Why does this happen?

▲ **New York City at night**

## DISCUSSION

Discuss in pairs or small groups.

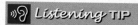
Look at each speaker as he or she speaks.

1. When you read the heading, "Strains of Music," what did you expect to learn? When you read the text below this heading, what did you find out? Were your predictions about this text similar to the actual content?

2. Which reading gave you the most vivid mental pictures? What images do you recall? What specific language do you remember from that reading?

3. Do you think it would be more difficult to identify a sound in the desert or in a busy city? Why?

**Q** **How do the senses shape our experiences?** What are some places you've been to that had particular sounds? How does our sense of hearing shape our experiences of those places?

## RESPONSE TO LITERATURE

**Workbook**
**Page 5**

A poem can appeal directly to our senses by evoking the sights, sounds, tastes, feelings, and smells of life. Write a simple poem describing your favorite place at your favorite time of day. Try to recall what you see, hear, and smell there. Concentrate on capturing specific sensory details of your own experience in vivid imagery. Use personification and onomatopoeia. A thesaurus and a dictionary can help you find the specific words to express yourself.

▲ Every place has its own distinctive sights, sounds, and smells.

# Grammar and Writing

### Prepositions of Location and Direction

Prepositions of location can be used to indicate where something is located. Look at the chart below.

| Where | Examples |
|-------|----------|
| at | They stayed **at** a big hotel. |
| in | Trees grow **in** the canyons. |
| on | Coyotes wait **on** the hillside. |
| above | His hotel room was thirty floors **above** the street. |
| by | A cow stood **by** the fence. |
| outside | Trash cans rattle **outside** restaurants. |

Prepositions of direction can be used to indicate in what direction something is moving. Look at the chart below.

| In What Direction | Examples |
|-------------------|----------|
| down | The water flows **down** the riverbed. |
| into | Cattle are walking **into** the pasture. |
| across | A beetle is scurrying **across** the ground. |
| from | The sound of music came **from** the opposite direction. |
| to | The dog ran **to** the barn. |
| toward | A jet plane was flying **toward** the city. |

**Practice**  Workbook Page 6

Work with a partner. Write sentences in your notebook using the phrases below to indicate where something is located or in what direction something is moving. Then read your sentences aloud.

| | | |
|---|---|---|
| in the restaurant | outside the park | from the barn |
| on the mountain | down the street | to the corner |
| toward the border | above the building | into the hotel |
| by the gate | across the desert | at the ranch |

# WRITING A DESCRIPTIVE PARAGRAPH

## Describe a Place

At the end of this unit, you will write a descriptive essay. To do this, you'll need to learn some of the skills authors use in descriptive writing. When you describe, you use sensory details. Sensory details help the reader see, hear, feel, smell, or taste what you are describing. They appeal to the reader's five senses. For example, the words *shrill car alarm* appeal to the sense of hearing, whereas the words *sparkling lights* appeal to the sense of sight.

Here is a model of a descriptive paragraph about a video arcade. The writer has included sensory details. Before writing, she listed her ideas in a sensory details chart.

| Sensory details | |
| --- | --- |
| Sight | |
| Hearing | |
| Touch | |
| Smell | |
| Taste | |

*Sophie Haas*

### Video Arcades

Video arcades are popular spots for young adults. You can find them in malls, in airports, and sometimes even in roadside rest areas. There is usually a wide variety of games. Some games require players to shoot at aliens, while in other games, players might drive race cars. Video arcades are usually quite dark so that players can see the illuminated game screens. Game screens have bright flashing lights, and some games even have loud sound effects, such as the screech of car tires or the whistles and shouts of a sports game. This, combined with the constant ringing of the games and the groans or elated cheers of players, makes video arcades very noisy places. Most video arcades sell snack foods, such as French fries or popcorn, and because of this, the controls on many games are greasy to the touch.

## Practice

**Workbook**
Page 7

Write a paragraph describing a place that is familiar to you, such as the school lunchroom, a museum, a train station, a library, or a gym. In your description, use words that appeal to as many of the five senses as you can. List your ideas in a sensory details chart. Be sure to use prepositions of location and direction correctly.

### Writing Checklist

**IDEAS:**
☑ I described a place clearly.

**WORD CHOICE:**
☑ I chose words to create vivid sensory details.

17

## What You Will Learn

**Reading**

- Vocabulary building: *Context, dictionary skills, word study*

- Reading strategy: *Preview*

- Text type: *Informational text (science)*

**Grammar, Usage, and Mechanics**
Subject-verb agreement

**Writing**
Describe an event or experience

### THE BIG QUESTION

**How do the senses shape our experiences?** What do you know about hearing? How is sound important in your life? How do sounds affect you?

Make a K-W-L-H chart like the one below in your notebook. Work in small groups. Complete the first column with information you know about sound and hearing. Then complete the second column with what you want to know about sound and hearing. When you've finished reading the text, complete the third column with the new information you've learned. Complete the fourth column by telling how you learned the new information.

| K<br>What do I **know**? | W<br>What do I **want** to know? | L<br>What did I **learn**? | H<br>**How** did I learn it? |
|---|---|---|---|
|  |  |  |  |

### BUILD BACKGROUND

**"How We Hear"** is a science article that explains how sounds are made and why they can be different. The article also identifies the parts of the ear that allow us to hear sounds and describes how these parts work. Many things can cause people to lose their hearing. The article explains why people develop hearing problems and how some of these problems can be prevented.

French horn players ▶

### Learn Key Words

Read these sentences. Use the context to figure out the meaning of the **red** words. Use a dictionary to check your answers. Then write each word and its meaning in your notebook.

**Key Words**

amplify
impulses
membrane
molecules
produced
stimulate
volume

1. Bullhorns are helpful because they **amplify** the voices of workers during an emergency.

2. Nerve **impulses** carry information from any part of the body to the brain.

3. A **membrane** is a very thin skin that covers or connects parts of the body.

4. **Molecules** of water are tiny particles that are too small to be seen.

5. When the strings of a guitar vibrate, musical sounds are **produced**.

6. Vibrations **stimulate** nerve cells, causing them to send messages to the brain.

7. Listening to very loud music can damage your hearing. Turn down the **volume** a little to be safe.

**Practice**  Workbook Page 8

Write the sentences in your notebook. Choose a **red** word from the box above to complete each sentence. Then take turns reading the sentences aloud with a partner.

1. Smells of food can _____ a person's appetite.

2. Loudspeakers _____ music at rock concerts.

3. A single drop of water contains millions of tiny _____.

4. She couldn't hear the music when the police sirens started wailing, so she turned the _____ up.

5. A sheet of plastic wrap is a kind of man-made _____.

6. An extremely loud sound is _____ when a jet airplane flies overhead.

7. Nerve cells in the ear send _____ to the brain, enabling us to hear.

▲ A guitar produces musical sounds.

## Learn Academic Words

Study the red words and their meanings. You will find these words useful when talking and writing about informational texts. Write each word and its meaning in your notebook. After you read "How We Hear," try to use these words to respond to the text.

| | | |
|---|---|---|
| **function** = the natural purpose or action of a body part | ➡ | The **function** of the ear is to allow people to hear. |
| **injury** = damage or harm to someone or something | ➡ | A twisted ankle is not a serious **injury**. |
| **interpret** = explain the meaning of something, such as an event or a text | ➡ | Readers often **interpret** a story according to personal experience. |
| **reverse** = undo the effect of something | ➡ | There is no way to **reverse** hearing loss due to old age. This kind of hearing loss is permanent. |
| **structure** = the way a thing is made or the arrangement of its parts | ➡ | The **structure** of the ear is complex; there are many different parts that work together. |
| **transmit** = send a signal | ➡ | The body's nerves **transmit** messages to the brain. |

## Practice

Workbook
Page 9

Work with a partner to answer these questions. Try to include the red word in your answer. Write the sentences in your notebook.

1. What do you think is more important, the **function** of the ears or the **function** of the eyes?

2. How can you avoid **injury** to your ears?

3. Why do you think people **interpret** the same event in different ways?

4. How can we **reverse** the effects of pollution?

5. How is the **structure** of your hand similar to the **structure** of your foot?

6. If you were hungry, which body part do you think would **transmit** that impulse to the brain?

A violinist interprets the music he plays. ▶

## Word Study: Antonyms

Antonyms are words that have opposite or nearly opposite meanings. Word pairs such as *above/below, noisy/quiet,* and *night/day* are examples of antonyms. As you read, you can use antonyms as context clues to help you figure out the meaning of unfamiliar words. Look at the sentence below.

> Some sounds, like bird songs, are **pleasing**, but other sounds can be very **annoying**.

Suppose you knew the word *pleasing* but not the word *annoying*. The context of the sentence tells you that *annoying* means nearly the opposite of *pleasing*.

**Practice**  Workbook Page 10

Work with a partner. Find the following words in the article "How We Hear." Try to figure out what each word means from the context. Write an antonym for each word, using a dictionary if necessary. Then write a sentence for each word.

| | | | |
|---|---|---|---|
| loud | permanent | protect | tight |
| outer | prevents | rapidly | tiny |

## READING STRATEGY | PREVIEW

Previewing a text helps you understand the content more quickly. It also helps you establish a purpose for reading. To preview, follow these steps:

- Look at the title and headings. Look at the visuals and read the captions or labels.
- Think about what you already know about the subject.
- Think about your purpose for reading the text and the author's purpose for writing.

Before you read "How We Hear," look at the title, visuals, and captions. Think about what you already know about this subject. What more would you like to know?

 Workbook Page 11

**Set a purpose for reading** As you read, think about how important your sense of hearing is. What are some sounds that you hear every day that you might not even think about? Discuss with a partner.

# How We Hear

Did you hear that? You live in a world of sound, and the sounds of that world enter your ears all the time. Some of those sounds can bring you great pleasure, like the rustling of autumn leaves, your best friend's giggle, or your favorite song. Other sounds are much less enjoyable, like the shrill alarm of the clock that wakes you in the morning, the loud roar of a lawnmower, or the wail of a fire engine's siren.

In order to understand how you hear, you first need to understand the anatomy, or structure, of the ear as well as what sound is and how it is produced.

## Anatomy of the Ear

The ear is divided into three parts: the outer ear, the middle ear, and the inner ear. The outer ear includes the part of the ear that we can see. It also includes the ear canal, which is a short passage that reaches to the eardrum. The eardrum is a thin membrane that is stretched tight, like the head of a drum. Behind the eardrum, in the middle ear, are three tiny bones, called the hammer, the anvil, and the stirrup. They are the smallest bones in the body. Behind these bones, within the inner ear, is the cochlea, a small, curled

Outer Ear     Middle Ear     Inner Ear

Hammer

Anvil

Auditory nerve

Ear canal

Stirrup

Eardrum

Cochlea

▲ **Structures of the ear**

---

**rustling**, light sound made by leaves as they rub together
**shrill**, unpleasant because it is too loud and high
**wail**, long, high, loud sound

22

tube that is shaped like a snail. The cochlea is filled with fluid and also contains numerous tiny hair cells. At the base of each hair cell is a nerve cell that sends impulses along the auditory nerve to the brain.

## What Is Sound and How Is It Produced?

Every sound is caused by a vibration, or continuous movement back and forth. For example, when a bell is rung, the metal vibrates. When an object vibrates, the air molecules around it also vibrate. As the molecules move back and forth rapidly, they bump into each other and then push apart, moving outward, away from the object. This bumping, pushing, and moving of molecules is called a sound wave. Sound waves can travel through air, water, or solid objects, like wood and steel.

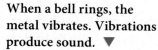

**When a bell rings, the metal vibrates. Vibrations produce sound.** ▼

If all sounds are waves of vibrating air particles, why do they sound different? One reason is that different sounds are produced according to the number of times the air vibrates. This is called the frequency of the sound. Frequency determines pitch, that is, how high or low a sound is. Another reason for differences in sounds has to do with the size of the vibrations. Large vibrations make loud sounds and smaller vibrations make softer sounds. This is called the volume or amplitude of the sound. The amplitude of a sound is measured in decibels.

## The Act of Hearing

Sound waves enter the outer ear, which is shaped to collect the waves and funnel them through the ear canal to the eardrum. The sound waves cause the eardrum to vibrate, like a drum head being hit by a drumstick. The vibrating eardrum in turn causes the three tiny ear bones to vibrate. One of these bones vibrates against the cochlea. This causes the fluid inside the cochlea to move and the hair cells to vibrate. The nerve cells at the base of the hair cells then send impulses along the auditory nerve to the brain, where they are interpreted as sounds.

---

**tube**, hollow pipe
**fluid**, liquid
**base**, bottom
**collect**, bring together
**funnel**, send through a narrow space

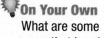

**BEFORE YOU GO ON**

**1** What are sound waves?

**2** What is the function of the outer ear?

**On Your Own**
What are some ways that hearing connects us to the world?

## Hearing Problems

People can develop hearing problems related to age, illness, or injury. A person with hearing loss may not be able to hear some sounds or may have particular difficulty when there is background noise. Here are some common types of problems that may result in hearing loss.

**Blocked ear canals.** Anything that blocks the ear canal can keep sound waves from traveling into the middle and inner ear. Earwax is a sticky substance produced inside the ear canals of some people. If earwax builds up and hardens, it blocks the ear canal. Once the accumulated wax is removed, sound waves can reach the eardrum, and the hearing loss is reversed.

**Abnormal function of middle ear bones.** A disease called otosclerosis occurs when the stirrup bone is prevented from vibrating because of abnormal bone growth. This prevents sound waves from moving through the middle ear to the inner ear. Doctors can often replace the stirrup bone with an artificial bone. This allows the sound waves to travel normally and reverses the hearing loss.

**Deterioration of the cochlea due to age.** All adults develop some gradual hearing loss as they age. Over time, parts of the cochlea begin to wear down from a lifetime of noise exposure. Changes in the blood supply to the inner ear can also contribute to hearing loss. Hearing aids, electronic devices worn behind the ear or inside the ear canal, can often help people who have some hearing loss. Hearing aids amplify sounds. The louder sounds in turn stimulate the nerve cells in the cochlea.

**Injury to the cochlea due to noise.** When loud noise causes the hair cells in the cochlea to vibrate too forcefully, they can bend or break. This damage can occur at any age and is permanent. Since a damaged hair cell cannot send nerve impulses to the brain efficiently, this will result in some hearing loss.

▲ A jackhammer produces extremely loud sounds.

▲ The volume of music at a rock concert can damage your ears.

---

**blocks**, stops something from moving through a place
**substance**, a liquid or solid material
**prevented**, stopped
**artificial**, not natural, but made by people
**exposure**, contact with something with no protection
**devices**, small machines that do a special job

## Preventing Hearing Problems

There is no way to reverse hearing loss due to old age or noise damage. But there are ways to protect yourself in order to prevent hearing loss due to noise damage.

**Turn down the volume.** When you listen to music, turn down the volume. Every loud drumbeat, horn blare, or other sound can easily damage or destroy one or more of the hair cells in the cochlea. If you have a portable music device, do not use the ear buds that sit inside your ears, unless you turn the music volume down low. Experts caution that ear buds should never be worn for more than two hours at a time.

**Wear earplugs.** Soft earplugs fit right into the front of the ear canal to protect the ears from loud sounds. Wear earplugs during any activity that exposes you to loud noise, such as when you go to a concert, mow your lawn, or walk by a construction site with loud jackhammers and drills.

## Decibel Levels in the Environment

The loudness of a sound is measured in decibels. Each ten-point increase on the decibel scale represents a tenfold increase in sound intensity over the previous level. Even some everyday noises can be hazardous to hearing if exposure goes on for too long a time.

| Decibels | Example | Dangerous Exposure |
|---|---|---|
| 0 | Lowest sound we can hear | |
| 30 | Quiet library, soft whisper | |
| 40 | Quiet office, living room | |
| 50 | Light traffic, refrigerator | |
| 60 | Air conditioner, conversation | |
| 70 | Busy traffic, noisy restaurant | |
| 80 | Subway, heavy city traffic | More than 8 hours |
| 90 | Truck traffic, noisy home appliances | Less than 8 hours |
| 100 | Chain saw, jackhammer | Less than 2 hours |
| 120 | Rock concert in front of speakers, auto horn | More than 15 minutes |
| 140 | Gunshot blast, jet plane at 50 feet | Any exposure time is dangerous. |
| 180 | Rocket launching pad | Hearing loss is inevitable. |

**ear buds**, devices you put into your ear to listen to music
**intensity**, quality of having a strong effect
**hazardous**, dangerous
**inevitable**, certain to happen

**BEFORE YOU GO ON**

1 What are some noises that can damage your hearing?

2 What are some ways to protect your hearing?

**On Your Own**
How is sound important in your everyday experience? Give examples.

25

# Review and Practice

## COMPREHENSION  Workbook Page 12

**Right There**

1. What are the three parts of the ear?

2. What causes a sound?

**Think and Search**

3. Give two reasons for differences in sounds.

4. Which hearing problem is the most serious? Why?

**Author and You**

5. Is any one part of the process of hearing more important than the other parts? Why or why not?

6. Is the author neutral about the use of safety measures to protect your hearing? Is the author trying to persuade you to try them? Find specific language in the article to support your answer.

**On Your Own**

7. Have you ever been to a rock concert or sporting event? Did the volume of the sound affect your hearing afterward? Explain.

8. Think about the sounds you hear every day. Which is the loudest? The softest? Find the name for this measurement in the text.

▲ The sound volume at sporting events can be very high.

## IN YOUR OWN WORDS

Work with a partner. Imagine you are describing the process of hearing to a younger student. First make a list of the important ideas in the article, "How We Hear." You may want to use the subheads as a guide. Then take turns explaining the information you remember from the article.

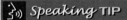 Speaking TIP

Speak slowly and clearly.

## DISCUSSION

Discuss in pairs or small groups.

1. How do the structures of the ear function? Explain the process of hearing step by step.
2. What do you think of the author's warnings about loud noise? Do you think it is possible to reduce noise in the environment?
3. What different sounds do you hear every day? What are some of your favorite sounds? Why? What are some of your least favorite sounds? Why?

**Q** **How do the senses shape our experiences?** How does our sense of hearing shape our most common experiences? What would your life be like if you could not hear the sounds that are part of your everyday life?

**Listening TIP**

If you can't hear a speaker, you may say "Excuse me, could you speak louder, please?"

▲ Birds singing

## READ FOR FLUENCY

It is often easier to read a text if you understand the difficult words and phrases. Work with a partner. Choose a paragraph from the reading. Identify the words and phrases you do not know or have trouble pronouncing. Look up the difficult words in a dictionary.

Take turns pronouncing the words and phrases with your partner. If necessary, ask your teacher to model the correct pronunciation. Then take turns reading the paragraph aloud. Give each other feedback.

▲ Rain falling

▲ A jet plane flying

## EXTENSION

Workbook Page 12

Use the Internet or go to the library and research the effects of unnecessary noise, or noise pollution, on our health and well-being. Find specific health and quality-of-life problems that have been connected to noise pollution. Then investigate your own neighborhood. Document the unnecessary, irritating, or stressful noises you are exposed to every day.

# Grammar and Writing

## GRAMMAR, USAGE, AND MECHANICS

### Subject-Verb Agreement

Subjects and verbs agree in number. A singular subject takes a singular verb. A plural subject takes a plural verb. When the subject of a sentence is a singular noun or pronoun (*he*, *she*, or *it*), add *-s* or *-es* to the verb.

> The **outer ear** **includes** the part of the ear that we can see.

When the subject is a plural noun or the subject pronoun *I*, *we*, *you*, or *they*, do not add *-s* or *-es* to the verb.

> Sound **waves** **enter** the outer ear. **They** **travel** to the eardrum.

Two or more subjects connected with *and* take a plural verb.

> **Age**, **illness**, and **injury** **cause** hearing problems.

### Practice

**Workbook Page 13**

Work with a partner. Write the subjects listed in the chart below in your notebook. Then, for each subject, choose a verb form and a sentence ending to produce a correct and true sentence. More than one sentence may be possible. Choose verb forms that agree with their subjects.

| Subject | Verb | Sentence Ending |
|---|---|---|
| Vibrations | produce / produces | amplitude. |
| Sound waves | travel / travels | the school song. |
| The cochlea | transmit / transmits | loud noises. |
| Loud noise | damage / damages | through solid objects. |
| A siren and a fire alarm | produce / produces | sound waves. |
| Decibels | measure / measures | nerve impulses. |
| The band | play / plays | your hearing. |

## WRITING A DESCRIPTIVE PARAGRAPH

### Describe an Event or Experience

You have learned to use sensory details in your descriptive writing about a place. When you describe an event or an experience, it is important to make the order in which things happen clear. You do this by using sequence words such as *first, then, next, finally,* and *after.* When you describe an event or experience in the order in which things happen, you are using chronological order.

Here is a model of a descriptive paragraph about a concert. The writer has organized the paragraph in chronological order. Before writing, she listed her ideas in a sequence-of-events chart.

| First |
|:---:|
| Next |
| Finally |

---

*Olivia Kefauver*

#### An Unforgettable Performance

My last orchestra concert was one that I will never forget. We had rehearsed for months and were well prepared and confident. Then the unexpected happened. The cello soloist fell ill on the day of the concert, and I was expected to play all of her solos without having seen them before! At first, when the conductor gave me this news, my heart started racing and I was filled with apprehension. But then I sat down with my teacher to learn the parts. As I focused on the music, I began to calm down. That night at the performance, I sat down to play and wiped my damp palms on my black skirt. Once I felt the heat of the stage lights beating down on my face and heard the hushed whispers from the audience, I began to play. When I finished, I was smiling from ear to ear. I knew that I had met this challenge and had pushed myself to a new height.

### Practice

Workbook Page 14

Write a paragraph describing an enjoyable event or experience in your life, such as a performance you went to, a party, or a sports event. Include sensory details and describe your experience using chronological order. Before you write, list the events in a sequence-of-events chart. Use sequence words to make your descriptions easy to follow. Be sure that the subject of each sentence agrees with the verb.

**Writing Checklist**

**ORGANIZATION:**
- ✔ My paragraph is in chronological order and uses sequence words.

**WORD CHOICE:**
- ✔ I chose words that create vivid sensory details.

29

# Prepare to Read

## What You Will Learn

**Reading**
- Vocabulary building: *Literary terms, context, word study*
- Reading strategy: *Visualize*
- Text type: *Literature (novel excerpt)*

**Grammar, Usage, and Mechanics**
Adjectives with and without commas

**Writing**
Describe a person

## THE BIG QUESTION

**How do the senses shape our experiences?** When you look at a painting, what catches your attention? Have you ever seen paintings by Jan Vermeer or other artists who lived in Holland during the seventeenth century? What kinds of settings and people did they paint? How would you describe Vermeer's painting, *Girl with a Pearl Earring*?

## BUILD BACKGROUND

In this section, you will read an excerpt from the historical novel **Girl with a Pearl Earring**. This novel takes place in Holland in the 1660s. During this time, the people of Holland, the Dutch, controlled world trade and made Holland a center of great wealth. As a result, there was a new appreciation of art. Many artists became very successful by painting the portraits of rich merchants and their families. One of the most extraordinary Dutch artists was Jan Vermeer, who is a main character in *Girl with a Pearl Earring*. The novel gets its title from an actual Vermeer painting. Although the painting is real, the story of the novel is not. It focuses on a fictional sixteen-year-old girl named Griet, who becomes a maid for the Vermeer family.

▲ *Girl with a Pearl Earring* by Jan Vermeer

### Learn Literary Words

When authors use figurative language, they create vivid
impressions by making comparisons between different things.
Similes and metaphors are types of figurative language.

A simile uses *like* or *as* to compare two different things in an
unusual way. This makes the reader see them in a new way.

| |
|---|
| He sounded like a cricket in the grass, a little one. (*William Faulkner*) |
| Even as a little girl she hungered for learning as a child does for cookies in the late afternoon. (*John Steinbeck*) |

There are many similes in everyday language, such as *busy as a bee* or
*swim like a fish*. They have been used too often, so they have lost the
power to make us see things in a fresh way.

A metaphor compares two things without using *like* or *as*. A
metaphor often describes something by using a word or phrase
normally used to describe something else.

| | |
|---|---|
| A curtain of rain fell on the fields. | The man waded through the crowd. |

The first example compares the rain to a curtain that falls on a
window. The second example compares the crowd to a body of water
that the man wades through.

**Practice**  **Workbook Page 15**

Work with a partner. Take turns reading the examples below. Identify
each one as a simile or a metaphor. Identify the things that are
being compared or linked together. Discuss the ways in which these
examples of figurative language create powerful images.

| |
|---|
| All the world's a stage. (*William Shakespeare*) |
| I wandered lonely as a cloud. (*William Wordsworth*) |
| The road was a ribbon of moonlight. (*Alfred Noyes*) |
| Her hair hung in little rolled clusters, like sausages. (*John Steinbeck*) |
| She is the red rose of the family and I am the green thorn. (*Longhang Nguyen*) |

Write a simile and a metaphor of your own in your notebook. As a
class, take turns reading your similes and metaphors aloud.

## Learn Academic Words

Study the **red** words and their meanings. You will find these words useful when talking and writing about literature. Write each word and its meaning in your notebook. After you read the excerpt from *Girl with a Pearl Earring*, try to use these words to respond to the text.

| | | |
|---|---|---|
| **analyze** = examine or think about something carefully in order to understand it | ➡ | She tried to **analyze** the way he used colors so she could learn how he created his paintings. |
| **component** = one part of something | ➡ | Lighting is an important **component** of a good photograph. |
| **create** = make something exist or invent something new | ➡ | He will **create** a portrait of the baker's daughter. |
| **demonstrate** = show or describe how to do something | ➡ | The painter wanted to **demonstrate** a new way to mix colors. |
| **proceed** = begin and carry on an activity | ➡ | Artists sometimes make a drawing before they **proceed** to paint. |

**Practice**  Workbook Page 16

Work with a partner to answer these questions. Try to include the **red** word in your answer. Write the sentences in your notebook.

1. When have you had to **analyze** a problem in order to come up with a solution?

2. What is one **component** of a good story?

3. When have you tried to **create** something new?

4. What skill have you asked someone to **demonstrate** for you?

5. How do you **proceed** to prepare a writing assignment?

## Word Study: Inflections *-ed*, *-ing*, *-er*, and *-est*

When an inflection is added to a word, the form and meaning of the word changes. When adding the inflections *-ed*, *-ing*, *-er*, or *-est* to a word ending in *e*, drop the *e* and add the inflection.

| Base word | Inflection *-ed* | Inflection *-ing* |
|---|---|---|
| surpris**e** | surpris**ed** | surpris**ing** |
| wip**e** | wip**ed** | wip**ing** |
| arriv**e** | arriv**ed** | arriv**ing** |

| Base word | Inflection *-er* | Inflection *-est* |
|---|---|---|
| gentl**e** | gentl**er** | gentl**est** |
| wis**e** | wis**er** | wis**est** |
| fin**e** | fin**er** | fin**est** |

**Practice**  **Workbook** Page 17

Work with a partner. Find five verbs in the reading that end with *e*. Make a chart like the one above in your notebook. Add the inflections *-ed* and *-ing* to each verb to make different forms of the verb.

## READING STRATEGY    VISUALIZE

Visualizing helps you understand what the author wants you to see. When you visualize, you make pictures in your mind of what you are reading. To visualize, follow these steps:

- Think about what the author wants you to see in your mind.
- Pay special attention to descriptive words and figurative language.
- Stop from time to time and visualize the characters, places and events.
- Think about how the author helps you visualize the characters and setting.

As you read the excerpt from *Girl with a Pearl Earring,* notice the words that the author uses to describe the characters. How does visualizing them help you understand the rest of the story?

 **Workbook** Page 18

**Set a purpose for reading** As you read, try to visualize the characters. Notice how the author uses color to describe things. Why do you think she does that? How does the character of Vermeer teach Griet to "see" color?

*from*

# Girl with a Pearl Earring

*Tracy Chevalier*

*In the first scene of the novel, the artist Vermeer and his wife Catharina have come to Griet's home to meet her for the first time.*

My mother did not tell me they were coming. Afterwards she said she did not want me to appear nervous. I was surprised, for I thought she knew me well. Strangers would think I was calm. I did not cry as a baby. Only my mother would note the tightness along my jaw, the widening of my already wide eyes.

I was chopping vegetables in the kitchen when I heard voices outside our front door—a woman's, bright as polished brass, and a man's, low and dark like the wood of the table I was working on. They were the kind of voices we heard rarely in our house. I could hear rich carpets in their voices, books and pearls and fur.

I was glad that earlier I had scrubbed the front steps so hard.

My mother's voice—a cooking pot, a flagon—approached from the front room. They were coming to the kitchen. I pushed the leeks I had been chopping into place, then set the knife on the table, wiped my hands on my apron, and pressed my lips together to smooth them.

My mother appeared in the doorway, her eyes two warnings. Behind her the woman had to duck her head because she was so tall, taller than the man following her.

All of our family, even my father and brother, were small.

The woman looked as if she had been blown about by the wind, although it was a calm day. Her cap was askew so that tiny blond curls escaped and hung about her forehead like bees which she swatted at impatiently several times. Her collar needed straightening and was not as crisp as it could be.

> ✔ **LITERARY CHECK**
>
> *What **similes** and **metaphors** does the author use to describe the voices of the artist Vermeer, his wife, Catharina, and Griet's mother? How are the metaphors different from the similes?*

---

**chopping,** cutting into small pieces
**polished,** shiny
**brass,** bright yellow metal
**scrubbed,** rubbed hard with a brush to clean
**crisp,** fresh, clean, and stiff

She pushed her grey mantle back from her shoulders, and I saw then that under her dark blue dress a baby was growing. It would arrive by the year's end, or before.

The woman's face was like an oval serving plate, flashing at times, dull at others. Her eyes were two light brown buttons, a color I had rarely seen coupled with blond hair. She made a show of watching me hard, but could not fix her attention on me, her eyes darting about the room.

"This is the girl, then," she said abruptly.

"This is my daughter, Griet," my mother replied. I nodded respectfully to the man and woman.

"Well. She's not very big. Is she strong enough?" As the woman turned to look at the man, a fold of her mantle caught the handle of the knife, knocking it off the table so that it spun across the floor.

The woman cried out.

"Catharina," the man said calmly. He spoke her name as if he held cinnamon in his mouth. The woman stopped, making an effort to quiet herself.

I stepped over and picked up the knife, polishing the blade on my apron before placing it back on the table. The knife had brushed against the vegetables. I set a piece of carrot back in its place.

---

**flashing**, shining brightly for a moment
**coupled**, joined
**cinnamon**, sweet-smelling brown spice
**brushed**, touched lightly

**BEFORE YOU GO ON**

**1** How does Griet feel when the two visitors arrive? How does she behave?

**2** What does Catharina want to know about Griet?

**On Your Own**
How do you feel when people you don't know come to your house? How do you behave?

35

The man was watching me, his eyes grey like the sea. He had a long, angular face, and his expression was steady, in contrast to his wife's, which flickered like a candle. He had no beard or moustache, and I was glad, for it gave him a clean appearance. He wore a black cloak over his shoulders, a white shirt, and a fine lace collar. His hat pressed into hair the red of brick washed by rain.

"What have you been doing here, Griet?" he asked.

I was surprised by the question but knew enough to hide it. "Chopping vegetables, sir. For the soup."

I always laid vegetables out in a circle, each with its own section like a slice of pie. There were five slices: red cabbage, onions, leeks, carrots and turnips. I had used a knife edge to shape each slice, and placed a carrot disk in the center.

The man tapped his finger on the table. "Are they laid out in the order in which they will go into the soup?" he suggested, studying the circle.

"No, sir." I hesitated. I could not say why I had laid out the vegetables as I did. I simply set them as I felt they should be, but I was too frightened to say so to a gentleman.

---

**angular**, thin and bony
**steady**, firmly in one place without moving
**flickered**, moved in a quick and unsteady way

✔ **LITERARY CHECK**
*What type of figurative language does the author use in this paragraph?*

"I see you have separated the whites," he said, indicating the turnips and onions. "And then the orange and the purple, they do not sit together. Why is that?" He picked up a shred of cabbage and a piece of carrot and shook them like dice in his hand.

I looked at my mother, who nodded slightly.

"The colors fight when they are side by side, sir."

He arched his eyebrows, as if he had not expected such a response. "And do you spend much time setting out the vegetables before you make the soup?"

"Oh, no, sir," I replied, confused. I did not want him to think I was idle.

From the corner of my eye I saw a movement. My sister, Agnes, was peering round the doorpost and had shaken her head at my response. I did not often lie. I looked down.

The man turned his head slightly and Agnes disappeared. He dropped the pieces of carrot and cabbage into their slices. The cabbage shred fell partly into the onions. I wanted to reach over and tease it into place. I did not, but he knew that I wanted to. He was testing me.

"That's enough prattle," the woman declared. Though she was annoyed with his attention to me, it was me she frowned at. "Tomorrow, then?" She looked at the man before sweeping out of the room, my mother behind her. The man glanced once more at what was to be the soup, then nodded at me and followed the women.

When my mother returned I was sitting by the vegetable wheel. I waited for her to speak. She was hunching her shoulders as if against a winter chill, though it was summer and the kitchen was hot.

"You are to start tomorrow as their maid. If you do well, you will be paid eight stuivers a day. You will live with them."

I pressed my lips together.

"Don't look at me like that, Griet," my mother said. "We have to, now your father has lost his trade."

"Where do they live?"

"On the Oude Langendijck, where it intersects with the Molenpoort."

"Papists' Corner? They're Catholic?"

"You can come home Sundays. They have agreed to that." My mother cupped her hands around the turnips, scooped them up along with some of the cabbage and onions and dropped them into the pot of water waiting on the fire. The pie slices I had made so carefully were ruined. . . .

\* \* \*

---

**dice**, small cubes with a different number of spots on each side, used to play games
**tease**, push gently
**prattle**, talk about silly or unimportant things
**sweeping**, moving quickly
**hunching**, bending forward
**scooped**, picked

**BEFORE YOU GO ON**

1 Why does Griet arrange the vegetables in a special order?

2 What will Griet do tomorrow? Why?

**On Your Own**
Have you ever had to do something for your family that was difficult for you or that you did not want to do? Explain.

*Griet has been a servant in the Vermeer household for several months. One of her responsibilities is to put out the colors Vermeer will use to paint each day. She watches and learns as he creates his paintings.*

I had never seen a painting made from the beginning. I thought that you painted what you saw, using the colors you saw.

He taught me.

He began the painting of the baker's daughter with a layer of pale grey on the white canvas. Then he made reddish-brown marks all over it to indicate where the girl and the table and pitcher and window and map would go. After that I thought he would begin to paint what he saw—a girl's face, a blue skirt, a yellow and black bodice, a brown map, a silver pitcher and basin, a white wall. Instead he painted patches of color— black where her skirt would be, ocher for the bodice and the map on the wall, red for the pitcher and the basin it sat in, another grey for the wall. They were the wrong colors—none was the color of the thing itself. He spent a long time on these false colors, as I called them.

---

**layer**, amount of a substance that covers all of a surface
**bodice**, part of a woman's dress above her waist
**patches**, small areas
**ocher**, reddish-yellow color

Sometimes the girl came and spent hour after hour standing in place, yet when I looked at the painting the next day nothing had been added or taken away. There were just areas of color that did not make things, no matter how long I studied them. I only knew what they were meant to be because I cleaned the objects themselves, and had seen what the girl was wearing when I peeked at her one day as she changed into Catharina's yellow and black bodice in the great hall.

I reluctantly set out the colors he asked for each morning. One day I put out a blue as well. The second time I laid it out he said to me, "No ultramarine, Griet. Only the colors I asked for. Why did you set it out when I did not ask for it?" He was annoyed.

"I'm sorry, sir. It's just—" I took a deep breath—"she is wearing a blue skirt. I thought you would want it, rather than leaving it black."

"When I am ready, I will ask."

I nodded and turned back to polishing the lion-head chair. My chest hurt. I did not want him to be angry at me.

He opened the middle window, filling the room with cold air.

"Come here, Griet."

I set my rag on the sill and went to him.

"Look out the window."

I looked out. It was a breezy day, with clouds disappearing behind the New Church tower.

"What color are those clouds?"

"Why, white, sir."

He raised his eyebrows slightly. "Are they?"

I glanced at them. "And grey. Perhaps it will snow."

"Come, Griet, you can do better than that. Think of your vegetables."

"My vegetables, sir?"

He moved his head slightly. I was annoying him again. My jaw tightened.

"Think of how you separated the whites. Your turnips and your onions—are they the same white?"

Suddenly I understood. "No. The turnip has green in it, the onion yellow."

"Exactly. Now, what colors do you see in the clouds?"

---

**reluctantly,** unwillingly
**ultramarine,** very bright blue color
**annoyed,** slightly angry
**rag,** small piece of old cloth used for cleaning

**BEFORE YOU GO ON**

**1** Why does Griet say that Vermeer used "the wrong colors" to begin his painting?

**2** Why does Griet set out the blue paint? Why is Vermeer annoyed?

**On Your Own**
What are some ways color is used to affect people? How do different colors affect you?

39

"There is some blue in them," I said after studying them for a few minutes. "And—yellow as well. And there is some green!" I became so excited I actually pointed. I had been looking at clouds all my life, but I felt as if I saw them for the first time at that moment.

He smiled. "You will find there is little pure white in clouds, yet people say they are white. Now do you understand why I do not need the blue yet?"

"Yes, sir." I did not really understand, but did not want to admit it. I felt I almost knew.

When at last he began to add colors on top of the false colors, I saw what he meant. He painted a light blue over the girl's skirt, and it became a blue through which bits of black could be seen, darker in the shadow of the table, lighter closer to the window. To the wall areas he added yellow ocher, through which some of the grey showed. It became a bright but not a white wall. When the light shone on the wall, I discovered, it was not white, but many colors.

The pitcher and basin were the most complicated—they became yellow, and brown, and green, and blue. They reflected the pattern of the rug, the girl's bodice, the blue cloth draped over the chair—everything but their true silver color. And yet they looked as they should, like a pitcher and a basin.

After that I could not stop looking at things.

---

**draped**, lying loosely

▲ *Young Woman with a Water Pitcher* by Jan Vermeer

## ABOUT THE **AUTHOR**

**Tracy Chevalier** was born in Washington, D.C., in 1962 and now lives in the United Kingdom. As in *Girl with a Pearl Earring*, her latest novel, *Burning Bright*, includes an actual artist, the poet William Blake, as a central character. Much of her work is based on artistic themes. Chevalier's 2003 novel, *The Lady and the Unicorn*, for example, explored the lives of weavers of medieval tapestries. *Girl with a Pearl Earring* was made into a motion picture in 2004.

## BEFORE YOU GO ON

**1** What does Griet learn from Vermeer about color?

**2** How does Vermeer create colors when he paints? For example, how does he paint the girl's skirt?

**On Your Own**
Describe Vermeer's painting, *Young Woman with a Water Pitcher*.

**41**

# Review and Practice

## READER'S THEATER

Act out the following conversation between Griet and her mother.

**Mother:** Griet, you will begin working for them tomorrow. You will live with them as well.

**Griet:** [*sadly*] All right, Mother.

**Mother:** What is the matter with you?

**Griet:** Nothing.

**Mother:** It isn't like you to mope. What's wrong?

**Griet:** You didn't even tell me they were coming. I didn't know this might happen.

**Mother:** It was better that way. I didn't want you to worry.

**Griet:** I don't want to live with strangers.

**Mother:** You have to. We have no choice. We need the money now that your father can no longer work.

**Griet:** Where do they live?

**Mother:** They have a very nice house on the Oude Langendijck.

**Griet:** When can I come home?

**Mother:** They have agreed to let you come home every Sunday. But work hard when you are there. If they like you, they will pay you well.

**Griet:** All right, Mother. If I must.

**Mother:** You must. And you must always be respectful. Now go get your things together so you will be ready tomorrow.

**Griet:** I will miss you and Agnes.

**Mother:** We will miss you, too, but our family needs your help now.

## COMPREHENSION

**Workbook**
Page 19

**Right There**

1. How does Griet arrange the vegetables when she prepares a soup?

2. What are the first two steps the artist completes as he begins his painting of the baker's daughter?

### Think and Search

**3.** Describe the interaction between Griet and her mother. Explain the mother's behavior toward her daughter.

**4.** Why does the artist want Griet to look at the clouds? What connection does he make between the clouds and the vegetables Griet cut for the soup?

### Author and You

**5.** Why do you think the artist is interested in the way that Griet has arranged the vegetables? Does his wife understand? Look for clues in the text.

**6.** What does the author suggest about Griet's character from the way she behaves and tells her story? Support your answers.

### On Your Own

**7.** What is your opinion of the characters in the selection? Do you like or dislike them? Do they seem real to you? Support your answers.

**8.** Think of a person you know who has talent. It might be in drawing, doing math, or any other area. Is the person proud, confident, or shy? How does the person's talent affect his or her personality?

## DISCUSSION

**1.** Discuss the relationship between Griet and the artist. How do you think they feel about each other? Based on what you have read, predict what you think will happen.

**2.** Discuss the components of painting that are described in the story. How does this description compare to the knowledge you had of painting before you read?

**Q** **How do the senses shape our experiences?** Griet notices that the clouds have very little white in them. Think about the "true" colors of everyday objects around you. Discuss with a partner.

**Listening TIP**

Be quiet and pay attention while others are speaking. Open your eyes and ears.

## RESPONSE TO LITERATURE

**Workbook Page 19**

Write the first paragraph of a first-person fictional story about meeting your personal hero. It can be anyone you greatly admire— a world leader, sports figure, or a music or movie star. Use your imagination to visualize what such a meeting would really be like. How would your hero behave? What would you feel? Use sensory images to create a sense of reality in an imaginary encounter.

# Grammar and Writing

## Adjectives with and without Commas

We often use more than one adjective to describe a noun, as in *fine lace collar*. When adjectives are in different categories, they must appear in order according to category, as in the chart below. We do not separate these adjectives with a comma.

| Adjectives by Category | | | | | Noun |
|---|---|---|---|---|---|
| **Opinion** | **Size** | **Age** | **Color** | **Material** | |
| fine | | | | lace | collar |
| | tiny | | blond | | curls |
| | | old | | wooden | table |
| kind | | young | | | man |

Adjectives that are in the same category do not have to appear in a specific order, as in the examples below. We separate them with a comma.

> The artist used a **long, thin** paintbrush.
> The servant is an **intelligent, hardworking, honest** woman.

**Practice**

Work with a partner. Use each group of words below to write sentences with more than one adjective. Use the chart above to help you place the adjectives in the correct order. Use a comma to separate adjectives that are in the same category.

1. eyes / huge / blue / unusual
2. quiet / shy / child / polite
3. lazy / person / cruel / silly
4. wool / red / skirt / short
5. long / hair / beautiful / black

▲ A long, thin paintbrush

44

# WRITING A DESCRIPTIVE PARAGRAPH

## Describe a Person

You have learned to use sensory details and chronological order to describe places and events. When you describe a person, include details that tell what the person looks like and how he or she behaves.

Details that tell what a person looks like are called physical traits. For example, in the reading, the artist's wife has "tiny blond curls" and eyes like "light brown buttons." Details that tell how a person behaves are called character traits. For example, Griet describes her own character traits when she says, "I did not often lie."

The writer of the paragraph below has described her aunt, including both physical traits and character traits. Before writing, the writer listed her ideas in a T-chart.

| Physical traits | Character traits |
|---|---|
|  |  |

*Kim Kirschenbaum*

### My Aunt Rose

My Aunt Rose is a truly talented artist. She has painted hundreds of beautiful, detailed portraits. Her portraits are so vivid and realistic that I often feel as though I am looking at real people. I love watching Aunt Rose at work; her lively approach to painting is so interesting to observe. Her delicate, graceful movements make her appear like a ballerina, as her tall, slender body moves with each stroke of her paintbrush. Her long, thin fingers control the paintbrush as it glides across the large canvas. Her deep, intense brown eyes move in every direction. Occasionally, a strand of her long blond hair falls in front of her face, and she immediately tucks it back behind her ears. After many long, grueling hours of work, Aunt Rose lets out a quiet, relieved sigh and proudly smiles at her masterpiece.

## Practice

Workbook Page 21

Write a paragraph describing a person you know, such as a family member, a friend, or someone in your neighborhood. List the person's physical traits and character traits in a T-chart. Then decide which traits you want to include in your paragraph. Be sure to use adjectives in the correct order and with correct punctuation.

### Writing Checklist

**VOICE:**
- ☑ I described physical traits and character traits.

**SENTENCE FLUENCY:**
- ☑ My adjectives are in the correct order.

45

# Prepare to Read

## What You Will Learn

**Reading**

- Vocabulary building: *Context, dictionary skills, word study*

- Reading strategy: *Skim*

- Text type: *Informational text (science)*

**Grammar, Usage, and Mechanics**
More prepositions of location and direction

**Writing**
Describe an object

 **THE BIG QUESTION**

**How do the senses shape our experiences?** What do you know about vision? What common problems do people have with their vision? How is your sense of sight important in your life?

Make a K-W-L-H chart like the one below in your notebook. Work in small groups. Complete the first column with information you know about vision. Use the questions above as a guide. Then complete the second column with what you want to know about vision. When you've finished reading the text, complete the third column with the new information you've learned. Complete the fourth column by telling how you learned the new information.

| **K**<br>What do I **know**? | **W**<br>What do I **want** to know? | **L**<br>What did I **learn**? | **H**<br>**How** did I learn it? |
|---|---|---|---|
|  |  |  |  |

**BUILD BACKGROUND**

**"How We See"** is a science article that contains facts about the eye and explains how you see. The eye is made up of many parts. These parts work together with the brain to allow you to see. The article also explains what causes certain types of vision problems and how they are corrected. Special structures in the eye enable you to perceive colors. The article describes how these structures work.

A painter explores the world of color. ▶

46

## VOCABULARY

### Learn Key Words

Read these sentences. Use the context to figure out the meaning of the red words. Use a dictionary to check your answers. Then write each word and its meaning in your notebook.

1. Use a sponge to **absorb** the spilled water.

2. The artist will **blend** blue and yellow paint to make green.

3. Sometimes only an expert can **distinguish** an original painting from a copy.

4. If you **focus** a telescope on the moon, you'll be able to see the craters on the moon's surface.

5. **Muscles** are attached to bones and enable us to move.

6. Shiny surfaces, like polished steel, **reflect** more light than dull surfaces, like velvet.

**Key Words**

absorb
blend
distinguish
focus
muscles
reflect

### Practice

Workbook
Page 22

Write the sentences in your notebook. Choose a red word from the box above to complete each sentence. Then take turns reading the sentences aloud with a partner.

1. _____ in your arm enable you to raise and lower your arm.

2. In dim light, objects _____ less light. As a result, it is more difficult to see them.

3. If you _____ red and yellow paint, you will make the color orange.

4. The artist used a piece of cloth to _____ the paint that splashed on the table.

5. In order to take a clear picture, you need to _____ the camera on your subject.

6. A cat can _____ many more objects in the dark than a human being can.

▲ You can blend blue and yellow paint to make green paint.

▲ When you focus a telescope on a star, you can see it clearly.

## Learn Academic Words

Study the **red** words and their meanings. You will find these words useful when talking and writing about informational texts. Write each word and its meaning in your notebook. After you read "How We See," try to use these words to respond to the text.

| | | |
|---|---|---|
| **adjust** = change or move something slightly in order to make it better or more effective | → | The photographer will **adjust** the lens of the camera in order to get a good picture. |
| **consist** = be made of | → | Our bodies **consist** of bones, muscles, blood, and organs. |
| **image** = a picture that you can see through a camera, on television, or in a mirror | → | The **image** we see of ourselves in a mirror is a reflection. |
| **perceive** = become aware of something through the senses | → | We **perceive** light with our eyes. |
| **project** = cause something to fall upon a surface | → | We use a flashlight to **project** light onto objects in the dark. |

**Practice**  **Workbook** Page 23

Work with a partner to answer these questions. Try to include the **red** word in your answer. Write the sentences in your notebook.

1. Why do you need to **adjust** the mirrors in a car?
2. What colors does a rainbow **consist** of?
3. What is the **image** made by a camera called?
4. What part of our bodies do we use to **perceive** sound?
5. Why would you **project** light onto an object in the dark?

▲ You use a flashlight to project light.

## Word Study: Homographs

Some words in English are spelled alike but have different meanings. These words are called homographs. Here are some ways to figure out the meaning of a homograph.

- Check to see how the word is used in the sentence. What part of speech is it?
- Look for context clues. Do any of the other words in the sentence give you a hint?
- Use a dictionary to find the correct definition.

Look at the examples of homographs in the chart below.

| Homograph | Part of speech | Meaning |
|-----------|----------------|---------|
| watch | noun | small clock that you wear on your wrist |
| watch | verb | look at and pay attention to something |
| processes | noun | series of actions that happen naturally |
| processes | verb | examines |

**Practice**  Workbook Page 24

Work with a partner. Find the following words in the article "How We See": *pupil, light, focus, objects, close*. Try to figure out their meaning from the context. Then use a dictionary to find a homograph for each word. Write sentences with the words in your notebook. Then try to find other homographs in the reading.

## READING STRATEGY | SKIM

Skimming a text helps you get a general understanding of what the text is about. To skim a text, follow these steps:

- Look at the title and the visuals. What do they tell you about the text?
- Read the first paragraph quickly. Then read the first sentence of each paragraph that follows.
- Now read all the paragraphs quickly. Skip over words you don't know.
- After you skim the text, try to summarize what you learned before you go back and read it again more carefully.

Before you read "How We See," skim the text quickly to see what it's about. Think about the subject and what you already know about it. What more do you think you will learn?

 Workbook Page 25

**Set a purpose for reading** What are the most important structures of the eye? How do these structures work to make vision possible?

# How We See

As you read these words, the complicated structure and inner workings of your eyes are continually sending messages to your brain. Your eyes perform all kinds of amazing jobs every day. They enable you to find the shiniest red apple in the bunch, gaze at a beautiful rainbow after a rainstorm, and watch glowing meteors as they shoot across a night sky.

In order to understand how your eyes enable you to see light, movement, shapes, color, and depth, you first need to understand the anatomy, or structure, of the eye.

## Anatomy of the Eye

The eye is shaped like a very small, round ball—about one inch in diameter. It sits in a cup-shaped eye socket made of bone. Six small muscles hold the eyeball in place inside the socket and enable it to move in all directions.

The structures of the eye that enable you to see are the cornea, iris, pupil, lens, retina, and optic nerve. The cornea is a clear, curved structure that helps protect the front of the eye and allows light to enter. Behind the cornea is the iris, which is the colored (brown, blue, green, etc.) part of the eye. The small hole in the middle of the iris, which looks like a black dot, is the pupil.

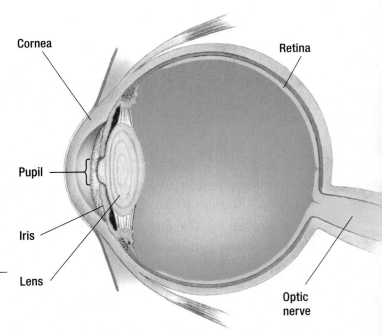

Cornea

Retina

Pupil

Iris

Lens

Optic nerve

▲ **Structures of the eye**

---

**complicated**, not simple
**gaze**, look for a long time
**diameter**, line from one side of a circle to the other that passes through the center
**curved**, bent like part of a circle

Behind the pupil is the lens, a curved, clear part of the eye that can change its shape to focus light. At the back of the eye is the retina, which is made up of a layer of light-sensitive cells called rods and cones. Rods enable us to see in dim light, and they help us see things that are moving. Cones enable us to see in moderate or bright light, and they allow us to see colors. The retina's rods and cones capture light and change it into nerve, or electrical, impulses. These impulses travel along the optic nerve to the brain, which interprets them as visual images.

## The Act of Seeing

So, how do we see? First, light reflects from objects and travels in a straight line until it passes through the curved cornea, where it bends a little. This bending enables the cornea to adjust and focus the light to travel through to the iris and into the pupil. The muscles in the iris control the amount of light that enters the pupil. For example, on a very bright, sunny day, the muscles in the iris will tighten to make the pupil smaller. This protects the eye from too much light. When it is dark, however, the muscles will relax to enlarge the pupil so that it can take in more light.

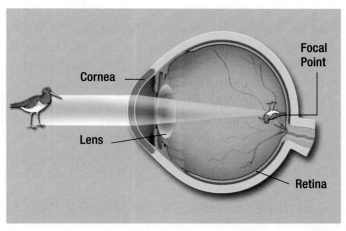

▲ In normal vision, light is focused directly on the retina.

After moving through the pupil, light continues traveling to the lens. Eye muscles surrounding the lens tighten or relax to help the lens change shape. When the muscles tighten, the lens becomes rounder and shorter. This helps the eye see objects clearly when they're close. When the muscles relax, the lens becomes flatter and longer. This helps the eye see objects clearly when they're farther away. When the lens changes shape, it bends the light that is hitting it, and this determines the sharpness of our vision.

The light then travels to the retina. When you look at an object, the visual image is projected, upside down, on the retina. The retina then sends out this information in the form of tiny nerve impulses along the optic nerve, all the way to the brain. Once it reaches the brain, the image turns right-side-up, and you can see the object you're looking at. So, the act of seeing is really a team effort between your eyes and your brain!

light-sensitive, able to react to small changes in light
surrounding, that are all around
flatter, smooth and level, without any raised areas
sharpness, ability to see and notice details very well
upside down, with the top at the bottom and the bottom at the top

**BEFORE YOU GO ON**

**1** What do the muscles of the iris control? Why?

**2** What happens when light reflected from an image reaches the retina?

**On Your Own**
Describe the ways in which you depend on your sight in an everyday situation, such as walking down the street or attending a class.

**51**

## Vision Problems

Very few people have perfect vision. Many people's eyeballs do not have a perfectly round shape. Some people don't have perfectly curved corneas and others might have a lens in one or both eyes that doesn't focus the light the way it should. All of these things make for less than perfect vision, unless corrective lenses (eyeglasses or contact lenses) are worn. Corrective lenses bend light in different ways in order for the eyes to focus sharply.

Two common vision problems are nearsightedness and farsightedness. Nearsightedness occurs when the eye focuses incoming light in front of the retina instead of directly on it. When this happens, objects that are distant appear blurred, but objects that are close appear clear. Corrective lenses bend the light outward so that it focuses directly onto the retina. Farsightedness occurs when the eye focuses incoming light behind the retina, not directly on it. When this happens, objects that are close appear blurred, but objects that are distant appear clear. Corrective lenses bend the light inward so that it focuses directly onto the retina.

## How Do We See Colors?

When English scientist Isaac Newton looked through a prism in 1666, he discovered that pure light, such as sunlight, is not white. It is composed of many colors. Scientists now know that all objects reflect some colors and absorb the remaining colors, and that our eyes and brains work together to see *only* the reflected colors. For example, a red strawberry is red because its surface reflects red light and absorbs all the rest of the light. What about the colors black and white? An object appears white when it reflects all light and appears black when it absorbs all light.

As you learned, the retina is made up of millions of rods and cones. Only the cones are sensitive to color. When light enters the eyes, the cones detect only three colors:

---

**blurred**, not clear in shape
**surface**, top layer

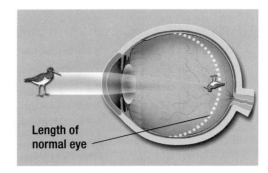

Length of normal eye

▲ **Nearsightedness occurs when light is focused in front of the retina.**

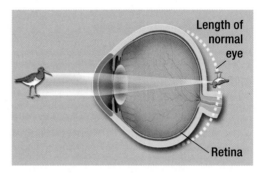

Length of normal eye

Retina

▲ **Farsightedness occurs when light is focused behind the retina.**

A prism separates pure light into the colors of the rainbow. ▶

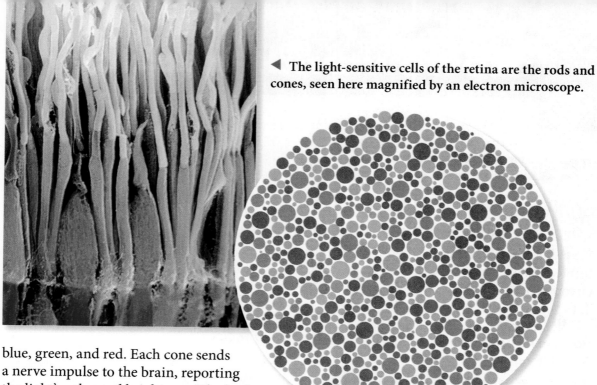

◀ The light-sensitive cells of the retina are the rods and cones, seen here magnified by an electron microscope.

▲ A person with red-green color blindness will be unable to detect the number on this chart.

blue, green, and red. Each cone sends a nerve impulse to the brain, reporting the light's color and brightness. The brain then processes the information by blending individual colors to make more colors. For example, if only the red-sensitive cone sends an impulse, the brain interprets the color as red. But if the red-sensitive cone and the green-sensitive cone both send impulses, the brain mixes the colors and interprets those impulses to mean that the color must be yellow. In fact, the brain blends colors in the same way we mix colors of paint to get new colors. The brain's ability to blend colors is what enables us to see the full spectrum of colors, made up of different combinations and intensities of blue, green, and red.

Some people's retinas are missing one or more cones, causing color blindness. The most common cones that are missing are those that detect red and green. Most people who are color-blind can see some colors, but they often confuse one color with another. There is no way to correct color blindness. People who are color-blind often ask friends to help them distinguish colors so that they can match socks, buy wall paint, and do other things that require good color perception.

processes, examines
combinations, two or more different things that are put together
intensities, degrees of brightness

Red strawberries absorb all colors of light except red. ▶

## BEFORE YOU GO ON

1 Why do objects have colors? For example, why do leaves appear green?

2 What are cones? How do they work?

On Your Own
In what ways would your life be different if you could not see?

53

# Review and Practice

### Right There

1. What are the structures of the eye that enable us to see?

2. What happens to the lens when the eye muscles surrounding it tighten? What happens when these muscles relax? Why do these changes occur?

### Think and Search

3. How are nearsightedness and farsightedness similar? How are they different?

4. Why do we perceive colors when we look at things? What is the cause of color blindness?

### Author and You

5. Why does the author say that the act of seeing is a "team effort between your eyes and your brain"? Do you think this is a good metaphor for the way seeing works? Explain.

6. What is the role of the brain in perceiving color? What does the author suggest about how the brain helps us see colors?

### On Your Own

7. Do you think that vision is more important than the other senses? Why or why not?

8. How is color important in everyday life? How is it important to you? How would life be different if there were no colors, only black, white, and different shades of gray?

## IN YOUR OWN WORDS

Work with a partner. Imagine you are describing the process of seeing to a younger student. First make a list of the important ideas in the article, "How We See." You may want to use the subheads as a guide. Then take turns explaining the information you remember from the article.

**🔊 Speaking TIP**

Look at your partner as you speak.

## DISCUSSION

Discuss in pairs or small groups.

1. In what ways is the process of seeing similar to the process of hearing? In what ways are these processes different?

2. How can problems in the structure of the eye affect what we see?

3. If you had to give up your ability to hear or your ability to see, which one would you give up and why?

**Q How do our senses shape our experiences?** Many animals do not have as strong a sense of sight as humans. In some animals, for example, the sense of smell is stronger. How do you think our social world would be different if the sense of sight in humans were weaker than other senses?

»)) **Listening TIP**

Give each speaker a chance to make a statement. Wait until someone has finished speaking before you speak.

## READ FOR FLUENCY

When we read aloud to communicate meaning, we group words into phrases, pause or slow down to make important points, and emphasize important words. Pause for a short time when you reach a comma and for a longer time when you reach a period. Pay attention to rising and falling intonation at the end of sentences.

   Work with a partner. Choose a paragraph from the reading. Discuss which words seem important for communicating meaning. Practice pronouncing difficult words. Give each other feedback.

## EXTENSION  Workbook Page 26

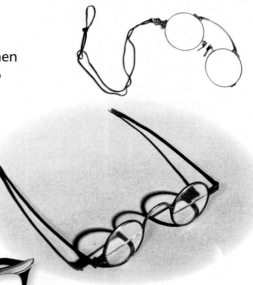

Research the history of eyeglasses. Find out when and where human beings first started trying to improve poor eyesight. What did people do before there were eyeglasses? Who were the inventors that developed improvements in eyeglasses? What were the different materials used to make lenses throughout history? Then make a timeline and put your findings in their proper time period.

# Grammar and Writing

## More Prepositions of Location and Direction

Earlier in the unit, you learned about prepositions of location and direction. Remember that prepositions of location tell where something is located and prepositions of direction tell in what direction something is moving. Look at the illustrations of the eye (page 50) and the ear (page 22) as you study the examples in the charts below.

Here are more prepositions of location.

| Where | Examples |
|---|---|
| **in front of** | The cornea is **in front of** the iris. |
| **behind** | The lens is **behind** the pupil. |
| **in the middle of** | The small hole **in the middle of** the iris is the pupil. |
| **at the back of** | The retina is **at the back of** the eye. |
| **next to** | Three tiny bones **are next to** the eardrum. |
| **between** | The middle ear is **between** the outer ear and the inner ear. |

Here are more prepositions of direction.

| In What Direction | Examples |
|---|---|
| **along** | Impulses travel **along** the optic nerve. |
| **through** | Light passes **through** the cornea. |

**Practice**

Work with a partner. Copy the words and phrases in the left column of the first chart above into your notebook. Write as many sentences as you can about the structure of the eye and ear using each word or phrase. Check a dictionary if you need help defining a word.

## WRITING A DESCRIPTIVE PARAGRAPH

### Describe an Object

When you describe an object, you can organize the details by using order of importance and spatial order.

When you organize details according to their importance, you describe the most important detail first and the least important last. For example, if you were describing a car, you might mention its color first, then the model name, and then other features.

When you use spatial order, you describe details from left to right, bottom to top, near to far, and so on. For example, if you were describing a sculpture, you might walk around it and give details describing what you see from the front, the side, the back, and the other side.

Here is a model of a paragraph describing a bowl of fruit. This writer has organized the details using spatial order. Before writing, she listed her ideas in a graphic organizer.

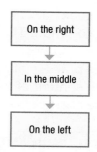

| On the right |
| In the middle |
| On the left |

*Julitza Garcia*

**A Bowl of Fruit**

A bowl of fruit sits on my kitchen counter. The bowl is made of smooth ceramic and is painted light blue with a narrow white band along the bottom. Three bright yellow bananas lie in the bowl, on the right side. Two apples sit in the middle. One apple is a light red color and rests on top of a green apple. Each apple has a short, brown stem that sticks out of the top. An orange, partially visible behind the red apple, gives off a sweet, flowery aroma. Unlike the smooth, shiny surface of the apples, the orange peel is bumpy and a bit dull. To the left of the apples and orange is a cluster of plump, dark purple grapes that look incredibly juicy.

**Practice**  **Workbook Page 28**

Write a paragraph describing an object—something you find interesting to look at—such as an arrangement of flowers, a sleek sports car, a piece of sculpture, or another work of art. Before you begin writing, use a graphic organizer to list your ideas in order of importance or in spatial order. Be sure to use prepositions of location and direction correctly.

**Writing Checklist**

**WORD CHOICE:**
☑ I used adjectives and provided sensory details.

**ORGANIZATION:**
☑ I used spatial order or order of importance.

57

# Link the Readings

## Critical Thinking

Look back at the readings in this unit. Think about what they have in common. They all tell about the senses. Yet they do not all have the same purpose. The purpose of one reading might be to inform, while the purpose of another might be to entertain or persuade. In addition, the content of each reading relates to the senses differently. Now copy the chart below into your notebook and complete it.

| Title of Reading | Purpose | Big Question Link |
|---|---|---|
| "The Sounds of the City" "The Sounds of the Desert" | | |
| "How We Hear" | *to inform* | |
| From *Girl with a Pearl Earring* | | |
| "How We See" | | *It discusses the sense of sight.* |

## Discussion

Discuss in pairs or small groups.

- How is the article "How We See" different in purpose from the excerpt from *Girl with a Pearl Earring*? What does *Girl with a Pearl Earring* bring to the reader that "How We See" cannot? "The Sounds of the City" is nonfiction; *Girl with a Pearl Earring* is fiction. How are these texts similar? How are they different?

- **Q How do the senses shape our experiences?** The act of seeing and the act of hearing are physical experiences. How does seeing things, like works of art, and hearing things, like music, affect us emotionally and spiritually?

## Fluency Check

Work with a partner. Choose a paragraph from one of the readings. Take turns reading it for one minute. Count the total number of words you read. Practice saying the words you had trouble reading. Take turns reading the paragraph three more times. Did you read more words each time? Copy the chart below into your notebook and record your speeds.

| | 1st Speed | 2nd Speed | 3rd Speed | 4th Speed |
|---|---|---|---|---|
| Words Per Minute | | | | |

# Projects

Work in pairs or small groups. Choose one of these projects.

**1** Create a model of the human ear or human eye. Label the model to show the important structures and details. Present the model to the class and explain why this organ is important.

**2** Draw or paint a picture of an object or scene that you see as beautiful. Analyze why this object or scene is beautiful. Then present and explain your drawing or painting to the class.

**3** Write a poem about your favorite musical group or performer. Include sensory details that describe your feelings when you listen to the music. Then read your poem to the class.

**4** If you have access to a portable tape recorder, take it to a place that has a lot of interesting sounds and record them. Play your tape for the class and let them try to identify the sounds.

# Further Reading

To find out more about the theme of this unit, choose from these reading suggestions.

**The Fall of the House of Usher and Other Stories,** Edgar Allan Poe
This Penguin Reader® adaptation features a collection of Poe's most intriguing stories.

**The Sculptor's Eye,** Jan Greenberg
Intriguing artwork—including pieces by George Segal, Louise Nevelson, and others—is displayed in a way that opens the viewer's eye to seeing art in a variety of settings.

**Vision and Art: The Biology of Seeing,** Margaret Livingstone
The author describes the role the sense of sight plays in making the artwork of Monet, van Gogh, da Vinci, and Warhol so appealing. She also gives fascinating bits of trivia, such as why purple dyes are so rare.

# Put It All Together

## LISTENING & SPEAKING WORKSHOP
### Group Presentation

You will give a group presentation describing a person, place, event, or experience you want to share with the class.

**1** **THINK ABOUT IT** Reread the "Imagination Takes Flight" section of "The Sounds of the City." Then reread Griet's description of the artist's wife, Catharina, in the excerpt from *Girl with a Pearl Earring*. In small groups, discuss what makes these two descriptions effective.

With your group, talk about people, places, events, or experiences you would like to describe. Work together to develop a list of topics you're all familiar with. For example:

- An interesting teacher at your school
- An unusual neighborhood in your city
- A street, state, or county fair
- A visit to an amusement park, a circus, or a zoo
- A day at the beach

**2** **GATHER AND ORGANIZE INFORMATION** As a group, choose a topic from your list. Write down sensory details about it. Include sights, sounds, smells, and feelings that will help listeners picture your subject. Use a sensory details chart or other graphic organizer to record your information.

**Research** Use the library and the Internet to find more information about your topic. Use a dictionary or thesaurus to find words that create powerful sensory images. Take notes on what you find.

**Order Your Notes** As a group, discuss which details to include in your presentation. Put these in a logical order: Make an outline if you are describing a person or place. Make a timeline if your topic is an event or experience. Create an interesting introduction that tells the audience what your topic is. Decide which part of the outline or timeline each group member will present.

**Use Visuals** Collect photos and pictures that illustrate your person, place, event, or experience. You may also wish to find appropriate music or sound effects to use in your presentation.

**3 PRACTICE AND PRESENT** Practice your presentation as a group, following your outline or timeline. Use your visual aids and music or sound effects to support key ideas. If a classmate is operating a CD player for you, practice together so that the sounds will come in "on cue." Keep practicing until all group members know their parts well. Work on making smooth transitions between speakers. Remember to talk to your listeners instead of reading to them.

**Deliver Your Group Presentation** Before you begin, visualize the person, place, event, or experience you want to describe. As you speak, look at your listeners and try to help them see what you see. Speak clearly and loudly enough to be heard at the back of the room. Use your visual aids and music or sound effects at the appropriate times.

**4 EVALUATE THE PRESENTATION**
You will improve your skills as a speaker and a listener by evaluating each group presentation you give and hear. Use this checklist to help you judge your group's presentation and the presentations of other groups.

☑ Was the group's topic clear?

☑ Did the speakers use sensory details to help listeners create a picture in their minds?

☑ Could you hear and understand each speaker easily?

☑ Were the transitions between speakers smooth and logical?

☑ What suggestions do you have for improving the group presentation?

### Speaking TIPS

You may wish to use note cards as a memory aid. Write a key word or phrase on each card, and number them in the proper order.

Take your time. There's no need to rush. Keep your purpose in mind as you speak.

### Listening TIPS

Listen carefully to your fellow group members, and learn your *cues*—words or actions that signal it is your turn to speak.

Take notes or make drawings as you listen. Try to picture what each speaker is describing.

# WRITING WORKSHOP
## Descriptive Essay

In this workshop you will write a descriptive essay. An essay is a piece of writing that develops a specific idea. A descriptive essay is similar to a descriptive paragraph but describes someone or something in greater depth. The writer begins with a paragraph that tells what the essay is about. Two or more body paragraphs present descriptive details in a logical order. In a descriptive essay, the writer chooses precise details to help readers form a vivid picture in their minds of the person, place, thing, or event being described. Sensory words and images appeal to a reader's senses. A concluding paragraph sums up the essay's main points in a lively and memorable way.

Your assignment for this workshop is to write a five-paragraph essay describing a person or an experience that has had an important impact on your life.

**1 PREWRITE** Close your eyes briefly and see what images come to mind. Is there an experience you will never forget? Is there an individual who means a lot to you? Brainstorm a list of possible topics for your essay in your notebook. Choose a person or an experience that you can describe vividly and enthusiastically.

**List and Organize Ideas and Details** Use a graphic organizer such as a sensory details chart or a word web to organize your ideas. A student named Julitza decided to write about her visit to a famous site in Puerto Rico. Here is her sensory details chart:

| Sight | Hearing | Touch | Smell |
|-------|---------|-------|-------|
| green island turquoise sea | waves against shore | ocean breeze warmth of sun | sweet tropical flowers |

**2 DRAFT** Use the model on page 65 and your graphic organizer to help you write a first draft. Remember to include an introductory paragraph, three body paragraphs, and a concluding paragraph.

**3 REVISE** Read over your draft. As you do so, ask yourself the questions in the writing checklist. Use the questions to help you revise your essay.

## SIX TRAITS OF WRITING CHECKLIST

- ☑ **IDEAS:** Will my topic be interesting to readers?
- ☑ **ORGANIZATION:** Do I present details in an order that makes sense?
- ☑ **VOICE:** Does my writing express my personality?
- ☑ **WORD CHOICE:** Do I use precise, colorful words?
- ☑ **SENTENCE FLUENCY:** Do my sentences flow smoothly?
- ☑ **CONVENTIONS:** Does my writing follow the rules of grammar, usage, and mechanics?

Here are the changes Julitza plans to make when she revises her first draft:

---

An Unforgettable Visit

Have you ever visited a place and loved it so much you couldn't wait to go back? I've had that experience! When my class visited El Castillo Serrallés, the castle was so beautiful and the views ~~was~~ *were* so breath taking that all of us wanted to return.

The castle, which overlooks the sea, was built for a wealthy family about eighty years ago. *Although* Called a castle, El Castillo Serrallés is *actually* a magnificent villa *perched* high on a rolling hilltop in Puerto Rico. The first sight to greet you is the *lush* garden in front of the villa. The sweet pungent smell of bright tropical flowers seems to be everywhere.

---

*Inside,*
^One of the first things you notice is a huge painting of how the

*in*
castle use to look. The castle's appearance ^on the painting is very

different from its appearance now. The structure looks dark, like

a medieval castle might have looked centuries ago. As I examined

the painting, I could imagine a musty, damp smell, as if I had been

carried back into the past.

*outside*
The tour guide also took us ^to the spacious grounds behind the

*wooden*
castle. Here, you cross an old ^bridge to reach La Cruceta del Vigía,

a look-out tower in the form of a cross. From this spot, you can see

*emerald green*
much of the island beneath you. The turquoise ocean *caresses* ^is at the island's

shores. You can almost hear the soft roar of the waves far below. To

me, the warmth of the sun and the breezey ocean air made El Castillo

Serrallés feel like paradise.

The trip to El Castillo Serrallés was very exciting for me. Thinking

about it bring back wonderful memories of when I lived in Puerto Rico.

In some ways, this trip changed my life by changing how I perceive

the world and making me aware of how much I appreciate its beauty.

## 4 EDIT AND PROOFREAD

**Workbook**
Page 29

Copy your revised draft onto a clean sheet of paper. Read it again. Correct
any errors in grammar, word usage, mechanics, and spelling. Here are the
additional changes Julitza plans to make when she prepares her final draft.

Julitza Garcia

## An Unforgettable Visit

Have you ever visited a place and loved it so much you couldn't wait to go back? I've had that experience! When my class visited El Castillo Serrallés, the castle was so beautiful and the views were so breath taking that all of us wanted to return.

Although called a castle, El Castillo Serrallés is actually a magnificent villa perched high on a rolling hilltop in Puerto Rico. The castle, which overlooks the sea, was built for a wealthy family about eighty years ago. The first sight to greet you is the lush garden in front of the villa. The sweet pungent smell of bright tropical flowers seems to be everywhere.

Inside, one of the first things you notice is a huge painting of how the castle use to look. The castle's appearance in the painting is very different from its appearance now. The structure looks dark, like a medieval castle might have looked centuries ago. As I examined the painting, I could imagine a musty, damp smell, as if I had been carried back into the past.

The tour guide also took us outside to the spacious grounds behind the castle. Here, you cross an old wooden bridge to reach La Cruceta del Vigía, a look-out tower in the form of a cross. From this spot, you can see much of the emerald green island beneath you. The turquoise ocean caresses the island's shores. You can almost hear the soft roar of the waves far below. To me, the warmth of the sun and the breezey ocean air made El Castillo Serrallés feel like paradise.

The trip to El Castillo Serrallés was very exciting for me. Thinking about it bring back wonderful memories of when I lived in Puerto Rico. In some ways, this trip changed my life by changing how I perceive the world and making me aware of how much I appreciate its beauty.

**5** **PUBLISH** Prepare your final draft. Share your essay with your teacher and classmates.

Workbook
Page 30

# Technology's Impact on the Senses

*T*hroughout U.S. history, artists have tried to capture the relationship between our senses and our environment. Cars, computers, cell phones, and many other inventions have changed how we experience time and space in the modern world. What does it mean to "see" something from the window of a moving car, or to "hear" a podcast of a concert when the music is actually being performed hundreds or even thousands of miles away?

### Theodore Roszak, *Recording Sound* (1932)

In *Recording Sound*, Theodore Roszak was one of the first artists to try to capture what it feels like to listen to music through an electric machine— a phonograph—in a place and time separate from the performance itself.

Roszak felt limited by paint, so he built a miniature stage with a solo performer made out of plaster, and attached it to the canvas. The horn of the phonograph (used to magnify sound) resembles an ear. Geometric images of circles and spirals evoke the motion of sound waves. A small balloon in the upper-right corner suggests the escape that music can provide. By mixing media, that is, by using both paint and plaster in a single work, Roszak tried to capture the whole experience of listening to music: the performance, the listener's experience of the live performance, and the listener's experience of the recording replaying the real event from the phonograph.

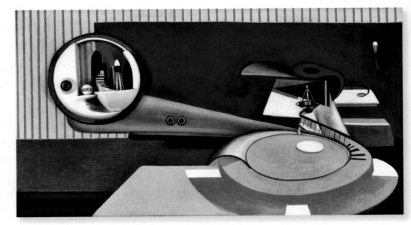

▲ Theodore Roszak, *Recording Sound*, 1932, plaster and oil, 32 × 48 × 6¾ in., Smithsonian American Art Museum

▲ David Hockney, *Snails Space with Vari-Lites, "Painting as Performance,"* 1995–96, mixed media, 84 x 260 x 135 in., Smithsonian American Art Museum

## David Hockney, *Snails Space with Vari-Lites,* *"Painting as Performance"* (1995–96)

David Hockney also explores how technology can change the way our senses shape our experience of the world. During the 1980s, he drove at varying speeds up and down a street near his home in California to see how the different speeds changed his perception of his surroundings. He created a series of paintings based on his drive-by experiences.

In his multimedia work *Snails Space*, Hockney painted two attached canvases and a floor piece to look like an enormous tangled world. The patterns and shapes appear to advance and recede with the changing colors provided by a nine-minute computer program. Viewers watch the light and mood change from serene to tragic, like the scenes in a play. Viewers feel as though they are in a new space again and again, even though they never move. The overall effect of *Snails Space* is like watching an opera, even though there is no sound, a remarkable achievement since Hockney had lost much of his hearing. So, to compensate for the loss of one sense, Hockney found ways to convey sound through his other senses.

### Apply What You Learned

**1** How does Roszak's *Recording Sound* capture the experience of listening to music?

**2** How does Hockney's *Snails Space* recreate the experience of moving at different speeds?

 **Big Question**
What technological innovation would you include in an artwork to show technology's impact on the senses? Why?

 **Workbook**
Pages 31–32

# How do generations differ from one another?

**T**his unit is about generations. You'll read texts that describe relationships between children, their parents, and their grandparents. Reading, writing, and talking about this topic will give you practice using academic language and help you become a better student.

### READING 1: Science Article and Legend

- "Mendel and the Laws of Heredity"
- "A Son Searches for His Father" by Daniel Comstock

### READING 2: Three Poems

- "My Father and the Figtree" by Naomi Shihab Nye
- "I Ask My Mother to Sing" by Li-Young Lee
- "Mother to Son" by Langston Hughes

### READING 3: Social Studies Article

- "That Older Generation" by Barbara Weisberg

### READING 4: Short Story

- "An Hour with Abuelo" by Judith Ortiz Cofer

## Listening and Speaking

At the end of this unit, you will write and perform a **skit** about people in a family.

## Writing

In this unit you will practice **narrative writing**. This type of writing tells a story. After each reading you will learn a skill to help you write a narrative paragraph. At the end of this unit, you will use these skills to write a fictional narrative.

## QuickWrite

How are you similar to and different from your parents and grandparents?

## What You Will Learn

**Reading**

- Vocabulary building: *Context, dictionary skills, word study*

- Reading strategy: *Use visuals*

- Text type: *Informational text (science) Literature (legend)*

**Grammar, Usage, and Mechanics**
Infinitives of purpose

**Writing**
Write a story from a different point of view

### THE BIG QUESTION

**How do generations differ from one another?** Do you look like anyone in your family? Do you have anything in common with your family members? Do you have similar habits, or are yours different? Do you share similar tastes and views on topics, or are your tastes and views different? How would you explain these similarities and differences? Discuss with a partner.

### BUILD BACKGROUND

**"Mendel and the Laws of Heredity"** is an informational article from a science textbook. It contains facts about the life and work of Gregor Mendel. In the middle of the nineteenth century, when Mendel lived, much of the science we know and practice today was still undiscovered. The article describes Mendel's discovery of the way in which physical characteristics are passed from parents to their children. You will also read **"A Son Searches for His Father,"** a legend from *The Odyssey* about a young man who goes in search of news about a father he has never known.

▲ A mother and her daughter

▲ A father and his sons

## VOCABULARY

### Learn Key Words

Read these sentences. Use the context to figure out the meaning of the **red** words. Use a dictionary to check your answers. Then write each word and its meaning in your notebook.

**Key Words**

contributes
control
dominant
generation
heredity
offspring

1. Each parent **contributes** a set of genes to a child. As a result, there are often similarities between parents and children.

2. Genes **control** physical traits that are passed from parents to children.

3. The gene for brown eyes is **dominant**, or strong. If a gene for brown eyes is present, a child is more likely to have brown eyes than blue eyes.

4. Physical characteristics in the parents' **generation** are often, but not always, passed to the children.

5. Many people believe that environment and education are just as important as **heredity** in determining intelligence.

6. The **offspring** of cats are called kittens. The offspring of lions are called cubs.

### Practice

**Workbook**
**Page 33**

Write the sentences in your notebook. Choose a **red** word from the box above to complete each sentence. Then take turns reading the sentences aloud with a partner.

1. Mendel explained the factors that _____ how physical traits are passed from parents to children.

2. You probably look like your parents in some ways because of _____.

3. Traits that are controlled by _____ genes have a greater chance of being passed from parents to children.

▲ A lioness and her offspring

4. Physical traits can be passed from either parent to a child. This is because each parent _____ genes to the child.

5. Sometimes there is little or no physical resemblance between one _____ and the next.

6. Puppies are the _____ of dogs.

## Learn Academic Words

Study the red words and their meanings. You will find these words useful when talking and writing about informational texts. Write each word and its meaning in your notebook. After you read "Mendel and the Laws of Heredity," try to use these words to respond to the text.

| | | |
|---|---|---|
| **conclude** = decide after considering all of the information | ➡ | After completing his experiments, Mendel had to **conclude** that parents passed physical traits to their children. |
| **factor** = one of several things that influence or cause a situation | ➡ | A high-fat diet is one **factor** that causes heart disease. |
| **identical** = exactly the same | ➡ | Twins with the same genetic makeup are called **identical**. |
| **investigate** = try to find out the truth | ➡ | Scientists **investigate** the causes of a disease in order to discover a cure for it. |
| **research** = serious study of a subject that is intended to discover new facts about it | ➡ | The **research** of many scientists has led to more effective treatments for cancer. |

**Practice**  **Workbook Page 34**

Work with a partner to answer these questions. Try to include the red word in your answer. Write the sentences in your notebook.

1. How much do you study for a test before you **conclude** that you are well prepared?

2. What is one **factor** that is important for good health?

3. Have you ever had a problem that was **identical** to someone else's problem?

4. What does a reporter do to **investigate** the facts of a story?

5. When have you done **research**? Explain.

▲ Identical twins

## Word Study: Levels of Specificity

In English more than one word can often be used to refer to the same thing. Choosing a specific word makes what we say and write clear. For example, the word *animal* is general. The word *cat* is more specific than *animal* and better indicates which animal is being referred to.

**Practice**  Workbook Page 35

Write the words in the box below in your notebook. Work with a partner. Take turns trying to find a more specific word for each word. For example: *animal—feline*. If you need to check the meaning of a word, use a dictionary.

| | | |
|---|---|---|
| clothing | plant | sound |
| food | means of transportation | sport |
| furniture | musical instrument | |

▲ All cats are felines. Here are a Maine Coon cat, a Siamese cat, an Abyssinian cat, and a Persian cat.

## READING STRATEGY    USE VISUALS

Using visuals helps you understand a text better. Visuals include illustrations, photographs, diagrams, charts, and maps. To use visuals, follow these steps:

- Look at each visual. Ask yourself what it shows and how it will help you understand the text.
- Read the titles, headings, labels, and captions carefully.
- Review the visuals as you read each section.
- If you come across a difficult word or idea, it may be represented in a visual. This will help your comprehension.

As you read "Mendel and the Laws of Heredity," look at the illustrations. In what ways are they as important as the text?

 Workbook Page 36

**Set a purpose for reading** Why did the results of Mendel's first two experiments surprise him? What did these experiments show about the similarities and differences between generations?

# MENDEL and the Laws of Heredity

The year was 1851. Gregor Mendel, a young priest from a monastery in Central Europe, entered the University of Vienna to study mathematics and science. Two years later, Mendel returned to the monastery and began teaching at a nearby high school.

Mendel also cared for the monastery's garden, where he grew hundreds of pea plants. He became curious about why some of the plants had different physical characteristics, or traits. Some pea plants grew tall while others were short. Some plants produced green seeds, while others had yellow seeds.

Mendel observed that the pea plants' traits were often similar to those of their parents. Sometimes, however, the pea plants had different traits than their parents. The passing of traits from parents to offspring is called heredity. For more than ten years, Mendel experimented with thousands of pea plants to understand the process of heredity. Mendel's work formed the foundation of genetics, the scientific study of heredity.

## Mendel's Peas

Mendel made a wise decision when he chose to study peas rather than other plants in the monastery garden. Pea plants are easy to study because they have many traits that exist in

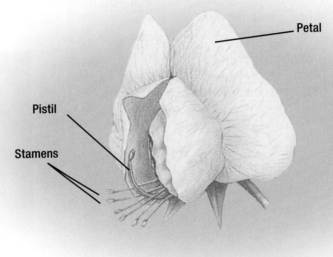

▲ **Figure 1. A flowering pea plant**

only two forms. For example, pea plant stems are either tall or short, but not medium height. Also, garden peas produce a large number of offspring in one generation. Thus, it is easy to collect large amounts of data to analyze.

Figure 1 shows a flowering pea plant. Notice that the flower's petals surround the pistil and the stamens. The pistil produces female sex cells, or eggs, while the stamens produce pollen, which contains the male sex cells.

---

**experimented,** did scientific tests

**data,** information

In nature, pea plants are usually self-pollinating. This means that pollen from one flower lands on the pistil of the same flower. Mendel developed a method by which he could cross-pollinate or "cross" pea plants. To cross two plants, he removed pollen from a flower on one plant and brushed it onto a flower on a second plant. To prevent the pea plants from self-pollinating, he carefully removed the stamens from the flowers on the second plant.

## Mendel's Experiments

In order to study the inheritance of traits, Mendel decided to cross plants with opposite forms of a trait, for example, tall plants and short plants. He started his experiments with purebred plants. A purebred plant is one that always produces offspring with the same form of a trait as the parent. For example, purebred short pea plants always produce short offspring. Purebred tall pea plants always produce tall offspring. To produce purebred plants, Mendel allowed peas with one particular trait to self-pollinate for many generations. By

---

**cross-pollinate**, transfer pollen from one flower to another
**inheritance**, the process of passing physical traits or qualities from one generation to another

using purebred plants, Mendel knew that the offspring's trait would always be identical to that of the parents.

In his first experiment, Mendel crossed purebred tall plants with purebred short plants. He called these parent plants the parental generation, or P generation. He called the offspring from this cross the first filial (FIL ee ul) generation, or the $F_1$ generation. The word *filial* means "son" in Latin.

You can see the results of Mendel's first cross in Figure 2. To Mendel's surprise, all of the offspring in the $F_1$ generation were tall. Despite the fact that one of the parent plants was short, none of the offspring were short. The shortness trait had disappeared!

Mendel let the plants in the $F_1$ generation grow and allowed them to self-pollinate. The results of this experiment also surprised Mendel. The plants in the $F_2$ (second filial) generation were a mix of tall and short plants. This occurred even though none of the $F_1$ parent plants were short. The shortness trait had reappeared. Mendel counted the number of tall and short plants in the $F_2$ generation. He found that about three fourths of the plants were tall, while one fourth of the plants were short.

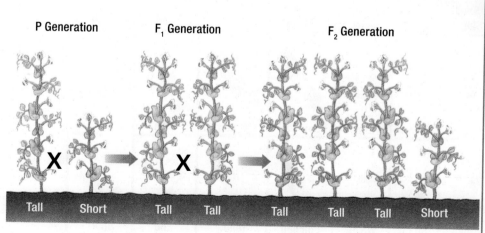

| P Generation | $F_1$ Generation | $F_2$ Generation |

Tall  Short     Tall  Tall     Tall  Tall  Tall  Short

▲ **Figure 2. Mendel's first experiment**

**BEFORE YOU GO ON**

1  What is a purebred plant? How did Mendel produce purebred plants?

2  How did Mendel cross-pollinate two plants? Why did he do this?

**On Your Own**
Have you ever conducted an experiment? What did you do? What did you learn?

## Other Traits

In addition to stem height, Mendel studied six other traits in garden peas: seed shape, seed color, seed coat color, pod shape, pod color, and flower position. Compare the two forms of each trait in Figure 3. Mendel crossed plants with these traits in the same manner as he did for stem height. The results in each experiment were similar to those that he observed with stem height. Only one form of the trait appeared in the $F_1$ generation. However, in the $F_2$ generation the "lost" form of the trait always reappeared in about one fourth of the plants.

## Dominant and Recessive Alleles

From his results, Mendel reasoned that individual factors must control the inheritance of traits in peas. The factors that control each trait exist in pairs. The female parent contributes one factor, while the male parent contributes the other factor.

Mendel went on to reason that one factor in a pair can mask, or hide, the other factor. The tallness factor, for example, masked the shortness factor in the $F_1$ generation.

Today, scientists call the factors that control traits genes. They call the different forms of a gene alleles (uh LEELZ). The gene that controls stem height in peas, for example, has one allele for tall stems and one allele for short stems. Each pea plant inherits a combination of two alleles from its parents—either two alleles for tall stems, two alleles for short stems, or one of each.

Individual alleles control the inheritance of traits. Some alleles are dominant, while other alleles are recessive. A dominant allele is one whose trait always shows up in the organism when the allele is present. A recessive allele, on the other hand, is masked, or covered up, whenever the dominant allele is present. A trait controlled by a recessive allele will show up only if the organism does not have the dominant allele.

In pea plants, the allele for tall stems is dominant over the allele for short stems. Pea plants with one allele for tall stems and one allele for short stems will be tall. The allele for tall stems masks the allele for short stems. Only pea plants that inherit two recessive alleles for short stems will be short.

---

**combination**, two or more different things that are put together
**organism**, living thing

| Traits | Seed Shape | Seed Color | Seed Coat Color | Pod Shape | Pod Color | Flower Position | Stem Height |
|---|---|---|---|---|---|---|---|
| Controlled by Dominant Allele | Round | Yellow | Gray | Smooth | Green | Side | Tall |
| Controlled by Recessive Allele | Wrinkled | Green | White | Pinched | Yellow | End | Short |

▲ Figure 3. Traits of pea plants

76

**TT x tt ➡ Tt x Tt ➡ TT   Tt   Tt   tt**

▲ Figure 4. Symbols describing Mendel's first experiment

## Understanding Mendel's Crosses

You can understand Mendel's results by tracing the inheritance of alleles in his experiments. The purebred plants in the P generation had two identical alleles for stem height. The purebred tall plants had two alleles for tall stems. The purebred short plants had two alleles for short stems. In the $F_1$ generation, all of the plants received one allele for tall stems from the tall parent. They received one allele for short stems from the short parent. The $F_1$ plants are called hybrids (HY bridz) because they have two different alleles for the trait. All the $F_1$ plants are tall because the dominant allele for tall stems masks the recessive allele for short stems.

When Mendel crossed the hybrid plants in the $F_1$ generation, some of the plants inherited two dominant alleles for tall stems. These plants were tall. Other plants inherited one dominant allele for tall stems and one recessive allele for short stems. These plants were also tall. Other plants inherited two recessive alleles for short stems. These plants were short.

## Using Symbols in Genetics

Geneticists today use a standard shorthand method to write about alleles in genetic crosses. Instead of using words such as "tall stems" to represent alleles, they simply use letters, as in Figure 4. A dominant allele is represented by a capital letter. For example, the allele for tall stems is represented by $T$. A recessive allele is represented by the lowercase version of the letter. So, the allele for short stems would be represented by $t$. When a plant inherits two dominant alleles for tall stems, its alleles are written as $TT$. When a plant inherits two recessive alleles for short stems, its alleles are written as $tt$. When a plant inherits one allele for tall stems and one allele for short stems, its alleles are written as $Tt$.

## Mendel's Contribution

In 1866, Mendel presented his results to a scientific society that met regularly near the monastery. In his paper, Mendel described the principles of heredity he had discovered. Unfortunately, other scientists did not understand the importance of Mendel's research. As a result, it was forgotten for 34 years. In 1900, three different scientists rediscovered Mendel's work. They had made many of the same observations as Mendel had. The scientists quickly recognized the importance of Mendel's work. Many of the genetic principles that Mendel discovered still stand to this day. Because of his work, Mendel is often called the Father of Genetics.

---

tracing, studying the history of
geneticists, scientists who study heredity
shorthand, a fast method of writing using shorter
    forms to represent words and phrases
represent, be a sign for

---

observations, conclusions
    drawn from carefully
    watching

**BEFORE YOU GO ON**

1 What is a gene? What is an allele? Give an example.

2 Why was Mendel's work forgotten? When and how was it rediscovered?

💡 On Your Own
Many people today are interested in studying their family history, or genealogy. Why do you think this is so?

77

**Set a purpose for reading** How does Telemachus resemble his father? What does the story show about the similarities that can exist between generations?

# A Son Searches for His Father

*retold by Daniel Comstock*

*Odysseus, the hero of the battle of Troy, has been missing for nearly twenty years. Suitors have come to Odysseus's house in Ithaca, hoping to marry his wife, Penelope. Odysseus's son, Telemachus, wishes to put an end to this. Telemachus and his friend Pisistratus ride through Sparta, searching for news of Odysseus.*

Telemachus and Pisistratus arrived in Sparta, where King Menelaus was holding a great celebration, a double wedding for his son and daughter. The two young men rode to the King's house and knocked on the front door.

The King's servant, Eteoneus, approached King Menelaus and whispered in his ear: "Two well-dressed strangers are here, my lord. Should we invite them in or send them away?"

The red-haired King angrily replied, "You are being foolish, Eteoneus. How many times have you and I been invited into a stranger's house? Of course we will let them in."

▲ A mosaic depicting Telemachus with his father, Odysseus

---

**suitors**, men who want to marry a particular woman
**Ithaca**, an island in the Ionian sea, near Greece
**Sparta**, city in ancient Greece

Eteoneus let in Telemachus and Pisistratus and led them to the King. "What a beautiful house," said Telemachus, "Everything is made of ivory and gold. It is fit for the gods!"

"It is beautiful," said King Menelaus as they entered the room. "But I would trade it all for those friends who died at the battle of Troy. Surely you have heard of Troy—so many soldiers died to defend my wife, Helen. What joy can I take in these costly things, when my best friends have died on my behalf? But I feel worse still for Penelope, the wife of my friend Odysseus. And I weep for her son, Telemachus, whom he left as a newborn child."

Hearing this, Telemachus looked away and tried not to cry. The red-haired King looked on, silent, as Telemachus's tears fell on his cheek.

Helen of Troy, looking as beautiful as a goddess, came down the stairs into the room. She sat down next to her husband, the King, and asked, "Who are your guests?"

Before Menelaus could answer, Helen looked at Telemachus and said, "It is truly strange. Never before have I seen such a likeness—this boy must be Telemachus, the son of Odysseus."

The red-haired King answered, "I see it, too. He has Odysseus's hair and face. He has the same gleam in his eyes. And just now, when I spoke of Odysseus's struggle, he broke down and wept silently."

Pisistratus spoke up. "King Menelaus, my friend is too modest to boast of his heritage. You are right—this is Telemachus, the son of the hero Odysseus. We have traveled far to seek your advice. The father of Telemachus is gone, and there is no one to defend his house."

"Is it really you, Telemachus?" asked Menelaus. "Is that why you have come here?"

"Yes," said Telemachus. "I was told that you knew of my father's fate. Please tell me of him—do you know if he is still alive?"

"Were it not for Odysseus," said the King, "we would have lost the battle of Troy. But he did not return to Ithaca after the battle. Many years ago, I met Proteus, a servant of the gods. I asked him what had happened to the soldiers who didn't come home. He told me that most of them had died, but Odysseus is still alive. He is held captive, somewhere, off in the endless seas."

Telemachus smiled. "Then there is hope," he said. "I will return to Ithaca and we will await his return."

---

**on my behalf**, for me
**gleam**, an expression that appears for a moment

**BEFORE YOU GO ON**

**1** Why does Telemachus visit Menelaus?

**2** What does Menelaus tell Telemachus about Odysseus?

**On Your Own**
In what ways does Telemachus resemble his father? In what ways do you think he might want to resemble him?

# Review and Practice

## COMPREHENSION

Workbook
Page 37

### Right There

1. Why are pea plants easy to study? Give two reasons.
2. What seven traits did Mendel study in garden peas?

### Think and Search

3. In Mendel's first experiment, how was the $F_1$ generation different from the P generation? How was the $F_2$ generation different from the $F_1$ generation?
4. What is the difference between dominant and recessive alleles? What part do they play as factors in heredity?

### Author and You

5. Look at Figure 3. What do you think happened when Mendel crossed purebred plants with yellow seeds and purebred plants with green seeds? Describe the offspring in the $F_1$ and $F_2$ generations. Use symbols like the ones in Figure 4 to help you.
6. What is the author's attitude toward Gregor Mendel? Give examples from the reading to support your answer.

### On Your Own

7. Describe Mendel's character. How would you evaluate the way he did his research?
8. What have you observed in your own experience that confirms what you learned in the article?

▲ Gregor Mendel
(1822–1884)

## IN YOUR OWN WORDS

Think back over the narrative you read about Telemachus. Write down the events of the story in a sequence-of-events chart like the one below. Then go back and check any parts of the story that you are unsure of. With a partner, and using your chart as a reference, take turns retelling "A Son Searches for His Father" to each other.

🔊》 *Speaking* TIP

Use words that help your partner visualize the events in your narrative.

1. → 2. → 3. → 4.

## DISCUSSION

Discuss in pairs or small groups.

1. Why is Mendel considered the Father of Genetics?

2. Why do you think it took so long for scientists to understand the importance of Mendel's discoveries? Do you know of other instances when the work of a scientist was not understood or appreciated at first?

3. What traits do you have that are identical to traits of someone else in your family? What can you conclude about this fact? What in your family history would you like to research or investigate?

**Q** **How do generations differ from one another?** What did Mendel contribute to our knowledge of how generations may be biologically similar to and different from one another?

**Listening TIP**

Listen carefully to other people's ideas.

## READ FOR FLUENCY

Reading with feeling helps make what you read more interesting. Work with a partner. Choose two or three paragraphs from "A Son Searches for His Father." Read the paragraphs. Ask each other how you felt after reading them. Did you feel happy or sad?

Take turns reading the paragraphs aloud to each other with a tone of voice that represents how you felt when you read it the first time. Give each other feedback.

## EXTENSION    Workbook Page 37

Talk to older family members to learn about your family before you were born. Write a list of names, places, and dates in your notebook. Trace your relatives back as far as you can. The library and the Internet can help with questions to ask, information on genealogy, and the study of family lines.

# Grammar and Writing

### Infinitives of Purpose

Remember that an infinitive consists of *to* + the base form of the verb. An infinitive can be used to express a purpose. In this case, it answers the question "Why?"

> Mendel grew pea plants **to study** them.

Sometimes the infinitive is preceded by *in order*. The sentence with *in order to* + verb has the same meaning as the one with *to* + verb.

> Mendel grew pea plants **in order to study** them.

Sometimes *for* can also be used to express a purpose. It is followed by a noun. Do not use *for* with an infinitive.

> **Correct:** Mendel grew pea plants **for** study.
> **Incorrect:** Mendel grew pea plants ~~for to study them~~.

### Practice

**Workbook Page 38**

Work with a partner. Take turns matching the sentence fragments in the columns using *in order to*. Look back at the article about Mendel if necessary. Read the correct sentence aloud. Then read the same sentence again, dropping *in order* and using only an infinitive. Does the meaning remain the same?

| | | |
|---|---|---|
| 1. Mendel entered the university | | see if Mendel's observations were the same as theirs. |
| 2. He returned to the monastery | | study the inheritance of traits. |
| 3. He began experimenting with pea plants | in order to | understand the process of heredity. |
| 4. He crossed purebred tall plants with purebred short plants | | study math and science. |
| 5. He studied six other traits in peas | | compare the results. |
| 6. Other scientists studied his work | | teach at a nearby high school. |

## WRITING A NARRATIVE PARAGRAPH

### Write a Story from a Different Point of View

A narrative is a story; a narrator is the person who tells the story. Narratives can be written from different points of view. When a character in the story tells the story, that character is a first-person narrator. Readers see only what that character sees, hear only what he or she hears, and so on. A first-person narrator uses the words "I" and "me" in the narrative. When someone who is not in the story narrates, the story has a third-person narrator. A third-person narrator can tell the reader what any character thinks or feels.

| First-person point of view | Third-person point of view |
| --- | --- |
|  |  |

Here is a model of a first-person narrative. It tells "A Son Searches for His Father" from the point of view of Telemachus. Before she began writing, the writer listed her ideas in a T-chart.

*Emily Weiss*

### Searching for My Father

As I entered the palace of King Menelaus, my heart beat with excitement. Accompanied by my friend Pisistratus, I had been on a journey to seek news of my long-lost father. Now, at last, I felt close to my goal. Without telling the King my identity, I greeted him and commented on the magnificent decor of his palace. To my shock, he confessed that he would trade it all for the lives of his friends who had died in the Trojan War. He felt especially sad, he said, for the family of Odysseus, who had never returned from Troy. As I tried to hide my tears at the mention of my father's name, the King's wife realized who I was—Odysseus's son. And what joyful news the King shared with me! Menelaus has heard that my father is being held captive far away. He believes that he is alive. Alive!

**Practice**  **Workbook** Page 39

Rewrite a familiar story from a point of view that is different from that of the original story. For example, you might rewrite the story "A Son Searches for His Father" from the first-person point of view of Pisistratus, Menelaus, or Helen. Or use another story that you know well or can refer to. If you use the first-person point of view, remember to use the pronouns *I* and *me*. List your ideas in a T-chart before you start writing. Be sure to use infinitives of purpose correctly.

### Writing Checklist

**IDEAS:**
- ☑ I included ideas that are consistent with the point of view from which I am writing.

**CONVENTIONS:**
- ☑ I used infinitives of purpose correctly.

## What You Will Learn

**Reading**

- Vocabulary building:
  *Literary terms,
  word study*

- Reading strategy:
  *Read aloud for
  enjoyment*

- Text type:
  *Literature
  (poetry)*

**Grammar, Usage,
and Mechanics**
Habitual past structures

**Writing**
Write a personal
narrative

### THE BIG QUESTION

**How do generations differ from one another?** What
do older generations have to give to younger generations? What
sorts of things can be kept alive through the generations? Discuss
with a partner.

▲ Figs on a branch

### BUILD BACKGROUND

Each poem you will read in this section is like a story that tells how
a parent passes on experience or knowledge to his or her children.
**"My Father and the Figtree"** concerns a father's ties to his
culture and country of origin, in the Middle East. In **"I Ask My
Mother to Sing,"** the poet paints a picture of his mother and
grandmother and their memories of China. In **"Mother to Son,"**
a mother gives her son advice about life.

## VOCABULARY

### Learn Literary Words

**Literary** Words

rhythm
symbol
point of view

**Rhythm** is a regular repeated pattern of sounds in music or speech. When we think of rhythm, we often think of the beat of a drum. The "beat" of music is just another way of saying rhythm. When poetry is spoken, you can hear a similar type of rhythm. Read the opening lines of "The Tyger" by William Blake aloud.

> *Tyger! Tyger! burning bright*
> *In the forests of the night,*
> *What immortal hand or eye*
> *Could frame thy fearful symmetry?*

How does reading these lines aloud help you hear the rhythm?

A **symbol** is something that represents, or stands for, something else. For example, the lamb is an animal, but it is also a symbol for innocence and goodness. Literary symbols can be complex and may have several layers of meaning. In the opening lines of "The Tyger," the darkness of the night and the tiger's fiery brightness seem to portray that creature as a symbol of evil. But as the poem develops, the tiger also appears as a symbol of what the poet believes to be God's great and mysterious creative power.

> *When the stars threw down their spears,*
> *And watered heaven with their tears,*
> *Did He smile His work to see?*
> *Did He who made the Lamb, make thee?*

You have learned that **point of view** indicates the person who is telling a story. A narrative can be told from the point of view of one of the characters in it or the point of view of an outside narrator. The point of view affects what and how events are described in a narrative because every person has a different experience of events.

### Practice

Workbook
Page 40

Create your own examples of rhythm and symbol. Write a few sentences or lines of poetry in your notebook about something you find beautiful, something that is important to you, or someone you love. Then work with a partner. Read each other's examples aloud.

## Learn Academic Words

Study the red words and their meanings. You will find these words useful when talking and writing about literature. Write each word and its meaning in your notebook. After you read "My Father and the Figtree," "I Ask My Mother to Sing," and "Mother to Son," try to use these words to respond to the texts.

| | | |
|---|---|---|
| **communicate** = express thoughts or feelings | ➡ | The lecturer tried to **communicate** new ideas about family relationships to the audience. |
| **culture** = art, beliefs, or behavior of a particular group of people | ➡ | They moved from China to the United States, but they teach their children about Chinese **culture** at home. |
| **perspective** = a way of thinking about something that is influenced by the type of person you are | ➡ | From a parent's **perspective**, teenagers may seem too interested in money and friends. |
| **symbol** = a picture, person, object, etc., that represents a particular quality, idea, or organization | ➡ | A nation's flag is a **symbol** of that country's government and people. |
| **tradition** = a belief, custom, or way of doing something that has existed for a long time | ➡ | Observing Ramadan is an important religious **tradition** for Muslims in the Middle East and other parts of the world. |

**Practice**  Workbook Page 41

Work with a partner to answer these questions. Try to include the red word in your answer. Write the sentences in your notebook.

1. What do parents try to **communicate** to their children about life?
2. What is a typical example of American **culture**?
3. From your **perspective**, what is one important issue facing your generation?
4. Name a **symbol** other than a flag for a country.
5. What is an important cultural **tradition** that you have learned from your parents?

## Word Study: Word Origins

Many English words have their origin in words from other languages. This can sometimes explain why certain words are spelled the way they are. Notice that some words change their spelling, but some do not.

| English Word | Original Word | Original Language |
|---|---|---|
| okra | *nkruma* | West African language |
| arrest | *arrester* | Old French |
| accordion | *Akkordion* | German |

**Practice**  **Workbook** Page 42

Work with a partner. Find the words in the box below in the reading. Try to figure out the meaning of each word using the context of the sentence. Then look up the words in a dictionary. In your notebook, write the word, its meaning, and its language of origin. Finally, write a sentence for each word.

| | | | | |
|---|---|---|---|---|
| fruit | fig | camel | earth | branch |
| lima bean | zucchini | emblem | picnic | crystal |

## READING STRATEGY | READ ALOUD FOR ENJOYMENT

Reading aloud brings poetry to life. You can more easily discover the literary elements of poetry, such as onomatopoeia and rhythm, by reading aloud. To read a poem aloud, follow these steps:

- As you read, pay close attention to the sounds of the words.

- Think about the structure of the poem. Many poets use rhyme, but not all do. Which lines of the poem rhyme with one another?

- Notice the rhythm the poet has used within each line.

- Put as much feeling into the poem as you can while you are reading.

As you read the three poems, listen for the meaning that the sounds and rhythm of the poems suggest.

 **Workbook** Page 43

**Set a purpose for reading** Does every generation have the same voice? As you read each poem, think about who is speaking. How does the speaker's generation affect the "story" of each poem and how that story is told?

# My Father and the Figtree

For other fruits my father was indifferent.
He'd point at the cherry trees and say,
"See those? I wish they were figs."
In the evenings he sat by my bed
weaving folktales like vivid little scarves.
They always involved a figtree.
Even when it didn't fit, he'd stick it in.
Once Joha was walking down the road
and he saw a figtree.
Or, he tied his camel to a figtree
    and went to sleep.
Or, later when they caught and arrested
    him,
his pockets were full of figs.

At age six I ate a dried fig and shrugged.
"That's not what I'm talking about!" he
    said.
"I'm talking about a fig straight from the
    earth—
gift of Allah!—on a branch so heavy it
    touches the ground.
I'm talking about picking the largest,
    fattest, sweetest fig
in the world and putting it in my mouth."
(Here he'd stop and close his eyes.)

---

**indifferent**, not interested or not having
    feelings for
**Joha**, hero of popular Arab humorous tales
**shrugged**, moved my shoulders up and down
    to show I didn't care

Years passed, we lived in many houses,
    none had figtrees.
We had lima beans, zucchini, parsley,
    beets.
"Plant one!" my mother said, but my
    father never did.
He tended garden half-heartedly, forgot to
    water,
let the okra get too big.
"What a dreamer he is. Look how many
    things he starts
and doesn't finish."

The last time he moved, I had a phone
    call,
my father, in Arabic, chanting a song I'd
    never heard.
"What's that?"
"Wait till you see!"

He took me out to the new yard.
There, in the middle of Dallas, Texas,
a tree with the largest, fattest, sweetest
    figs in the world.
"It's a figtree song!" he said,
plucking his fruits like ripe tokens,
emblems, assurance
of a world that was always his own.

—*Naomi Shihab Nye*

---

**emblems**, objects that represent an idea
**assurance**, promise that makes someone
    feel less worried

**LITERARY CHECK**

*How might the poem be different if the father told his story from his own point of view?*

## ABOUT THE **POET**

**Naomi Shihab Nye** is a poet and songwriter, born in 1952 to a Palestinian father and an American mother. Her first collection of poems, *Different Ways to Pray*, examined similarities and differences between cultures, a lifelong area of focus. Nye has edited a number of poetry anthologies, for readers young and old. Her most recent collection is *Is This Forever, Or What?: Poems & Paintings from Texas*. Nye is a graduate of Trinity University, San Antonio, Texas, where she currently lives.

**BEFORE YOU GO ON**

1. When she was a child, did the poet understand why figs were important to her father? Explain.

2. What was the father's dream? How did the dream finally come true?

**On Your Own**
Do children always understand what is important to their parents? Explain.

89

# I Ask My Mother to Sing

She begins, and my grandmother joins her.
Mother and daughter sing like young girls.
If my father were alive, he would play
his accordion and sway like a boat.

I've never been in Peking, or the Summer Palace,
nor stood on the great Stone Boat to watch
the rain begin on Kuen Ming Lake, the picnickers
running away in the grass.

But I love to hear it sung;
how the waterlilies fill with rain until
they overturn, spilling water into water,
then rock back, and fill with more,

Both women have begun to cry.
But neither stops her song.

—Li-Young Lee

---

**accordion**, musical instrument that you pull in
    and out to produce sounds
**sway**, move slowly from one side to the other
**Peking**, capital city of China, now called Beijing
**picnickers**, people eating food outdoors
**spilling**, flowing over the edge
**rock**, move gently from one side to the other

✔ LITERARY CHECK
*How might the
**rhythm** of this poem
be compared to the
rhythm of a boat?*

## ABOUT THE POET

**Li-Young Lee** was born
in 1957 in Indonesia
to Chinese parents.
After fleeing the
country in the face of
anti-Chinese sentiment, the Lee family
relocated to the United States. Lee
attended the University of Pittsburgh.
Lee has won numerous awards, including
the American Book Award for his memoir
*The Winged Seed: A Remembrance.*

◀ **The Stone
Boat on Kuen
Ming Lake at the
Summer Palace in
Beijing, China**

# Mother to Son

Well, son, I'll tell you:
Life for me ain't been no crystal stair.
It's had tacks in it,
And splinters,
And boards torn up,
And places with no carpet on the floor—
Bare.
But all the time
I'se been a-climbin' on,
And reachin' landin's,
And turnin' corners,
And sometimes goin' in the dark
Where there ain't been no light.
So boy, don't you turn back.
Don't you set down on the steps
'Cause you finds it's kinder hard.
Don't you fall now—
For I'se still goin', honey,
I'se still climbin',
And life for me ain't been no crystal stair.

—Langston Hughes

✔ **LITERARY CHECK**
*How is the stair
a **symbol** of the
mother's life?
What do you
think a crystal stair
is a symbol of?*

---

**crystal**, clear glass of high quality
**tacks**, small nails with sharp points
**splinters**, small, sharp pieces of wood
**boards**, long, thin, flat pieces of wood
**landin's**, landings (a landing is the floor
   at the top of a set of stairs)

## ABOUT THE POET

**Langston Hughes** (1902–1967) is celebrated
for his insightful portrayals of African-
American life in the United States from the
1920s through the 1960s. He wrote novels,
short stories, and plays, and his works were
important contributions to the Harlem
Renaissance of the 1920s. In addition to
leaving behind a comprehensive body of poetry, his first novel,
*Not Without Laughter*, won an award for literature in 1930.

## BEFORE YOU GO ON

**1** In "I Ask My Mother
to Sing," what do
we learn about the
poet's father?

**2** In "Mother to Son,"
what advice does the
mother give her son?

💡 **On Your Own**
What does each
of the three
poems say about
the relationship
between different
generations?

# Review and Practice

## DRAMATIC READING

🔊 *Speaking* TIP

Speak clearly and slowly. You might use gestures to emphasize important ideas.

Poetry is one of the oldest forms of literature. There was poetry even before people had invented a way to write it down. Poets preserved their poems by memorizing them or reciting them aloud. People still enjoy memorizing poetry and reciting it aloud.

Working in groups of four, prepare a dramatic reading of the poem, "I Ask My Mother to Sing." The better you understand a poem, the more effective your dramatic reading of it will be. Analyzing the poetic elements of a poem will help you understand it better.

Take turns reading the stanzas, or groups of lines, of the poem aloud. Discuss the sights, sounds, and feelings that come to mind as you read or listen. Identify any similes, metaphors, or vivid sensory details. Talk about the visual images that are not specifically mentioned in the poem. Use a dictionary to check exact meanings of words.

Memorize one stanza of the poem while the other three group members memorize another stanza. As a group, recite the poem from memory. Make helpful suggestions to improve each other's readings. Then present your dramatic recitation to the rest of the class.

▲ **The Stone Boat (detail)**

## COMPREHENSION

**Workbook**
**Page 44**

### Right There

1. In "My Father and the Figtree," what did the father often do in the evenings?

2. In "Mother to Son," what has the mother been doing all her life?

### Think and Search

3. The figtree is an important symbol in "My Father and the Figtree." What does it represent?

4. An image of a boat appears in the first two stanzas of "I Ask My Mother to Sing." Compare these images. Which word in the third stanza suggests a boat?

### Author and You

5. What can we infer about the poet's father from "My Father and the Figtree"? Describe his character.

6. How would you describe the relationship between the mother and son in "Mother to Son"? Support your response.

### On Your Own

7. In your opinion, which poem is the most powerful? Why?

8. What symbol would you use to represent your life? Why?

## DISCUSSION

Discuss in pairs or small groups.

1. Why do you think the poet's father waited so long before he planted a figtree in America?

2. In "I Ask My Mother to Sing," the mother and grandmother sing a song. What do you think the song is about? Why does it make them cry?

3. Based on your experience, how do you think the son reacts to his mother's words in "Mother to Son"? How would you react?

Q **How do generations differ from one another?** Which poem best reflects your own experience with different generations? What has been passed on to you from older generations?

»)) **Listening TIP**

Do not interrupt a speaker. Save your questions until each speaker is finished.

## RESPONSE TO LITERATURE

**Workbook Page 44**

Read the poems in this section again. Write a short poem of your own about someone in your family. Use a word web to gather colors, sounds, feelings, smells, and events that tell about the person. Try to find a real thing that is a symbol for the person's life, hopes, or victory over some hardship. Decide whether you will write the poem from your point of view or the point of view of your relative. Include sensory images in your poem.

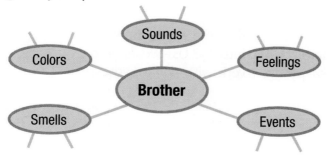

# Grammar and Writing

## Habitual Past Structures

The habitual past is used to describe actions that were repeated regularly in the past but are not going on now. To express the habitual past, use *would* + verb. The contraction of *would* is *'d*, as in *he'd*. You can also use *used to* + verb. Another way to express the habitual past is to use *was/were always* + verb with *-ing*.

| Habitual Past Structures | Example |
|---|---|
| *would* or *'d* + verb | He **would pick** figs from the tree.<br>They**'d work** in the garden. |
| *used to* + verb | He **used to pick** figs from the tree.<br>They **used to work** in the garden. |
| *was/were always* + verb with *-ing* | He **was always picking** figs from the tree.<br>They **were always working** in the garden. |

Notice that in habitual past structures, the verb does not change.

## Practice

**Workbook Page 45**

Copy the chart below into your notebook. Reread the poems on pages 88–91. Find examples of things the characters did habitually in the past. Write sentences about these actions. Use *would* or *'d* + verb, *used to* + verb, and *was/were always* + verb with *-ing*. Then work with a partner. Compare your sentences.

| Habitual Past Structures | Sentences |
|---|---|
| *would* or *'d* + verb | |
| *used to* + verb | |
| *was/were always* + verb with *-ing* | |

Talk with your partner about your memories of a time when you were younger. What did you and your family do habitually? Use *would* or *'d* + verb, *used to* + verb, and *was/were always* + verb with *-ing* to write sentences about your memories.

## WRITING A NARRATIVE PARAGRAPH

### Write a Personal Narrative

You've learned to develop point of view in your narrative writing. To write a narrative, you'll also need to learn how to tie a series of events together. In a narrative, this is called plot. A typical personal narrative might be a story about something another person did. The person's actions and the events that result constitute the story's plot. The writer organizes the events so that the story has a beginning, middle, and end. A good beginning grabs the reader's interest and introduces the characters. The main problem or conflict is presented in the middle. The problem is resolved at the end.

The model below of a personal narrative reads like a story with a clear beginning, middle, and end. Before she began writing, the writer organized the story events using a flow chart.

| Beginning |
| :---: |
| ↓ |
| Middle |
| ↓ |
| End |

Meredith Mooney

### My Grandfather Sets an Example

My grandfather was always working in the garden. He would sometimes spend the entire day there, pulling up weeds, planting new seeds, or watering the plants. When I was young, he decided to help me start my own garden. We went to the store to buy seeds and supplies. When we got home, we spent the entire day planting seeds, watering them, and fencing the area off. He left me a long list of things to do to make my garden thrive. As spring turned into summer, I was disappointed to see that the plants in my garden weren't producing any vegetables, while my grandfather's garden was flourishing. I admit I didn't work as hard in the garden as my grandfather did in his. That is why my garden failed and his didn't. My grandfather taught me an important lesson that summer: If you want to succeed at something, you have to put in the time and effort.

**Practice**

Workbook
Page 46

Write a personal narrative about someone who is important in your life. Organize your narrative so that it has a plot with an interesting beginning, a clear middle, and an end. Use a flow chart to organize your plot. Use the habitual past correctly.

**Writing Checklist**

**IDEAS:**

☑ The main idea of the story is clear.

**ORGANIZATION:**

☑ I organized the events so that the story has a clear beginning, middle, and end.

95

## What You Will Learn

**Reading**

- Vocabulary building: *Context, dictionary skills, word study*
- Reading strategy: *Monitor comprehension*
- Text type: *Informational text (social studies)*

**Grammar, Usage, and Mechanics**
Unreal conditional sentences

**Writing**
Write a friendly letter

**THE BIG QUESTION**

**How do generations differ from one another?** Do you live with or near a grandparent or other aging relative? What age is the oldest person you know? What ideas do you have about getting old? Are these ideas based on personal experience, or are they shaped by books, films, and TV?

**BUILD BACKGROUND**

In this section, you will read an informational article called **"That Older Generation"** about issues that are important in the lives of older people. The article also discusses misconceptions that people have about old age. The population of elderly Americans has been growing steadily during the last century. It is estimated that by the year 2030, one in five Americans—or 70 million people—will be age sixty-five or older.

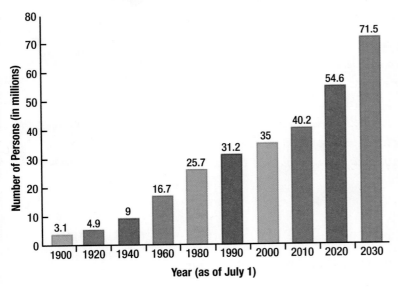

**Number of Persons 65+, 1900–2030**

Number of Persons (in millions)

| Year (as of July 1) | Persons |
|---|---|
| 1900 | 3.1 |
| 1920 | 4.9 |
| 1940 | 9 |
| 1960 | 16.7 |
| 1980 | 25.7 |
| 1990 | 31.2 |
| 2000 | 35 |
| 2010 | 40.2 |
| 2020 | 54.6 |
| 2030 | 71.5 |

▲ An elderly couple relaxes after a stroll.

96

## VOCABULARY

### Learn Key Words

Read these sentences. Use the context to figure out the meaning of the **red** words. Use a dictionary to check your answers. Then write each word and its meaning in your notebook.

**Key Words**

autonomy
longevity
maturity
respect
vitality
wisdom

1. My grandfather wants to make his own decisions about life. He insists on keeping his **autonomy**.

2. Scientific research may greatly increase **longevity**. In the year 2050, it may not be unusual for a person to live 100 years or more.

3. My grandmother gives great advice because of her **maturity**. Her character and ideas are fully formed.

4. Different generations must have **respect** for each other. Each should learn to appreciate what the other has to offer.

5. We are not worried about our grandparents' **vitality**. They exercise daily and eat healthful foods.

6. The **wisdom** of experience is earned by trial and error over the course of many years.

**Practice**  **Workbook Page 47**

Write the sentences in your notebook. Choose a key word to complete each sentence. Then take turns reading the sentences aloud with a partner.

1. The length of a person's life is called _____.

    **a.** vitality     **b.** respect     **c.** longevity

2. One measure of _____ is physical energy.

    **a.** longevity     **b.** vitality     **c.** autonomy

3. When others make our decisions for us, we have no _____.

    **a.** vitality     **b.** wisdom     **c.** autonomy

4. It takes the _____ of experience to make the right choice.

    **a.** vitality     **b.** longevity     **c.** wisdom

5. We should have _____ for the religious beliefs of others.

    **a.** autonomy     **b.** wisdom     **c.** respect

6. A fully-formed person is said to have _____.

    **a.** maturity     **b.** longevity     **c.** respect

## Learn Academic Words

Study the **red** words and their meanings. You will find these words useful when talking and writing about informational texts. Write each word and its meaning in your notebook. After you read "That Older Generation," try to use these words to respond to the text.

**Academic Words**

decline
individual
influence
vary

| | | |
|---|---|---|
| **decline** = decrease in quality, quantity, or importance | ➡ | After the accident, his general health began to **decline**. |
| **individual** = one person | ➡ | Each **individual** is responsible for his or her own actions. |
| **influence** = have an effect on the way someone develops, behaves, or thinks | ➡ | Parents try to **influence** their child's behavior by setting a positive example. |
| **vary** = be different from one another | ➡ | The level of maturity will **vary** in each individual; some individuals may be more mature than others. |

## Practice  Workbook Page 48

Work with a partner to answer these questions. Try to include the **red** word in your answer. Write the sentences in your notebook.

1. What is one reason someone's health might start to **decline**?

2. What can an **individual** do to help raise awareness of a social problem?

3. Why do parents try to **influence** their children to study?

4. Why do people **vary** in their attitudes toward different generations?

▲ A grandparent as well as a parent can influence the attitudes of a child.

98

## Word Study: Suffix -al

A suffix is a letter or group of letters added to the end of a word. When you add a suffix to a word, it changes the part of speech.

The suffix -al means *like, connected to, or having to do with*. It changes a noun to an adjective. For example, the noun *emotion* + -al becomes the adjective *emotional*. When adding -al to a word ending in *e*, drop the final *e*. When adding -al to a word ending in *y*, change *y* to *i*. Look at the chart below.

| Noun | Adjective | Meaning |
|------|-----------|---------|
| culture | cultur**al** | having to do with culture |
| tradition | tradition**al** | having to do with tradition |
| convention | | having to do with normal attitudes |
| family | | having to do with family |
| agriculture | | connected to farming |
| industry | | connected to industry |
| hexagon | | like a shape with six sides |

**Practice**  Workbook Page 49

Copy the chart above into your notebook. Then fill in the middle column with the correct spelling of the adjective ending with -al. Use a dictionary to check your answers. With a partner, find three other adjectives ending in -al. Check their meanings in a dictionary. Then write a sentence for each word.

## READING STRATEGY | MONITOR COMPREHENSION

Monitoring comprehension helps you to understand difficult texts and new ideas. To monitor comprehension, follow these steps:

- Read the text. Stop from time to time and ask yourself how much of it you have understood.
- Reread a paragraph at a time. Stop and restate what the author is saying in each paragraph.
- When you finish reading, try to restate the author's main points in your own words.

As you read "That Older Generation," stop from time to time. Monitor your comprehension by applying the steps above.

 Workbook Page 50

99

# That OLDER Generation

### Barbara Weisberg

Not too long ago, I attended a reunion with relatives I hadn't seen since I was a child. The reunion was filled with joy and unexpected discoveries. I was particularly delighted to learn that an 87-year-old uncle of mine still raises, cares for, and rides his own horses. Although rapidly losing his eyesight, he jokes that, because the horses are so large, he expects that he'll still be able to see them for a long time to come. Listening to him, I was surprised not only by his physical activity, but also by his sense of humor and acceptance as he faces the inevitable loss of his sight.

## The Process of Aging

Not everyone can continue to be as physically active in old age as my uncle has been. Some organs and functions decline as we grow older. Eventually, we may begin to walk more slowly or to hear or see less well. Some of us may become ill with diseases that strike the old more frequently than the young: arthritis or Alzheimer's, for example. The old, like the young, are individuals. They experience their old age—as they did their childhood, youth, and middle age—in distinctive ways.

Moreover, the process of aging isn't just physiological. It has emotional, social, and intellectual aspects, too. Factors ranging from personality to health care can influence the process. Some older adults are generally cheerful; others are not. Some are generally in good health; others are not. Most older people, like younger ones, have good days and bad.

The words *old*, *older*, and *elderly*, of course, are themselves relative terms. For example, a teenager may have a grandfather who is in his 50s, or one who is in his 80s. As the average life span of human beings grows longer, from about age 40 in 1900 to age 77 today, it's not unusual for four generations of a family—great-grandparents, grandparents, parents, and children—to be alive at the same time. To someone who is 80, a 60-year-old may seem youthful. Increasingly, too, some older adults are behaving more like younger people, further reshaping conventional ideas about the aging process. For a variety of economic, emotional, or other reasons, they may continue to work or travel, decide to join a gym or go back to school, or perhaps even dress in jeans and sneakers.

---

**Alzheimer's**, disease of old age that destroys parts of the brain

**physiological**, relating to the body
**intellectual**, relating to the ability to think and understand
**ranging**, varying between particular limits
**relative**, having meaning only when compared to something else

## Images and Attitudes

Whatever the differences among individuals, the experience of aging is to some extent affected by a society's attitudes towards its elders. It has been said that Americans value youth over age, individuality over community, and competition over cooperation, and this statement holds some truth about mainstream American culture. Certainly, many Americans harbor stereotypes about the process and problems of aging. For example, in this culture we tend to view old age almost exclusively as a time of diminished physical abilities, health, and mental acuity. We may believe that the elderly regret that they are no longer young. We are convinced that they must, of course, feel sad about losing physical vitality, while we ignore the benefits gained through maturity and experience. In addition, since their ideas about how to do things sometimes differ from our own, we may dismiss a lot of what our elders have to say.

These ageist attitudes have been shaped by our country's history. Beckoned onward by this continent's vast expanses, many Americans in the nineteenth century abandoned their families and communities to travel west in search of new opportunities. At the same time, the nation shifted from an agricultural to an industrial economy. Individuals who had once farmed or held jobs close to home now went off to work in crowded urban factories. Youth and vitality seemed essential in the struggle to succeed. The elderly came to be viewed as irrelevant.

---

**irrelevant**, not useful or important

---

**stereotypes**, unfair ideas that many people have about particular people or things
**acuity**, ability to think quickly and clearly
**beckoned**, attracted

> [ *The experience of aging is to some extent affected by a society's attitudes towards its elders.* ]

◀ **Many people remain physically active well into old age.**

**BEFORE YOU GO ON**

**1** What was the average life span of human beings in 1900? What is it today?

**2** How did the development of an industrial economy in the nineteenth century influence attitudes toward aging?

**On Your Own**
Do you agree that "Americans value youth over age"? Why or why not?

**101**

▲ In many cultures, older family members
make a vital contribution to family life.

Today, bias against the aged continues. Although consumers in their 60s may have income to spend, the worlds of media, fashion, and advertising prefer to court consumers in their 20s and 30s. Older workers may face job discrimination. The nation's stress on the importance of the nuclear family—parents and children—can leave older relatives such as grandparents feeling isolated. Forced to cope with health and financial issues on their own, even elders who cherish their autonomy and independence may feel vulnerable.

The United States, however, is a multicultural society, composed of and influenced by the traditions of many different cultures. And youth, individuality, and competition are by no means valued by all over age, community, and cooperation.

Traditionally, in East Asian cultures such as those of Japan, China, and Korea, individuals who reach old age are revered, honored for their experience, knowledge, and wisdom. Indeed, old age bestows on family members a privileged position in a household. Because the elders communicate the family's values, it is understood that their ideas will be heard and respected. And, if an older family member falls ill, the younger generation generally takes responsibility for that individual's care. Immigrants to the United States have tended to bring these attitudes and behaviors with them.

A tradition of caring for elders, moreover, is not unique to Asian cultures. Many cultures, among them African-American, Arab, and Hispanic, accept this responsibility. Often, relationships among generations are nurtured within close-knit extended families—families that extend beyond the nuclear family to include grandparents, aunts, and uncles; step- or adopted relatives; and friends who serve familial roles. When extended family members live within the same household or nearby, they frequently share responsibility for caring for the aged. In turn, the older generation may help out by caring for the children, relieving parents of some tasks. The older generation also serves a vital role in transmitting traditions ranging from codes of behavior to recipes and music. Bonds of affection, loyalty, and mutual responsibility tie the generations together.

---

**bias**, an unfair opinion for or against a person or thing
**vulnerable**, easily harmed
**bestows**, gives someone something important

**extend**, reach
**relieving**, replacing a person who needs a rest
**transmitting**, passing something from one person to another

## The Generation Gap

Of course, living in extended families or having a tradition of honoring elders doesn't guarantee harmony. Different generations often still struggle with what has famously been called the generation gap. A gulf in values, attitudes, and lifestyle can separate those who are older from those who are younger, parents from offspring, and immigrants to the United States from their children raised here. Older adults, for example, may feel disappointed if their grandchildren do not provide the expected consideration and respect. Young people may sometimes feel burdened with demands that seem unfair.

In most circumstances, understanding, mutual consideration, and negotiation can go a

---

**harmony**, a situation in which people are friendly and peaceful
**consideration**, caring about other people's feelings
**burdened**, heavily weighted
**mutual**, felt by two or more people toward one another
**negotiation**, discussion aimed at reaching an agreement

---

long way toward resolving problems. Remember that each generation has so much of value to offer. By sharing their wisdom and memories, older generations connect us to our family's past—and help us to live in the world today. By sharing their experiences and interests, younger generations connect us to our family's future, helping us to live in the world today.

## A Long Life

According to a study reported in the *New York Times* in 2006, there is a community of women in New Jersey who statistically—that is, estimated as a group—live longer than anyone else in the United States. Their average life span is a little more than 91 years of age. East Asian in origin, these women attribute their longevity—at least in part—to enjoying a healthy diet, having access to good health care, and feeling part of a loving and accepting community. As a society, these are gifts that we surely can attempt to provide to one and all.

---

**attribute**, give as the cause of

---

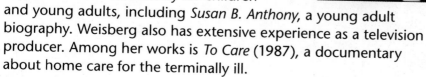

*Older generations can connect us to our family's past.*

---

### ABOUT THE **AUTHOR**

**Barbara Weisberg** is the author of *Talking to the Dead: Kate and Maggie Fox and the Rise of Spiritualism*, a nonfiction account of the lives of two young sisters considered the founders of modern Spiritualism in the nineteenth century. She has written extensively for children and young adults, including *Susan B. Anthony*, a young adult biography. Weisberg also has extensive experience as a television producer. Among her works is *To Care* (1987), a documentary about home care for the terminally ill.

---

### BEFORE YOU GO ON

**1** What examples of bias against the aged does the author mention?

**2** What are some positive attitudes toward the aged among different cultural groups in the United States?

**On Your Own**
The author states that "each generation has so much of value to offer." Think of examples that support this claim.

**103**

**COMPREHENSION**  Workbook Page 51

**Right There**

1. What are the physical problems of aging?
2. How does the author define the generation gap?

**Think and Search**

3. What does the author mean by "ageist attitudes"? Which ageist attitudes does the author mention?
4. The author discusses attitudes and behavior toward elders among different cultural groups in the United States. What similarities does she describe?

**Author and You**

5. What is the author's attitude about how Americans deal with the problems of aging? Use the text to support your answer.
6. What does the author imply about extended families? What reasons does she give?

**On Your Own**

7. What have you personally observed that confirms or contradicts what you learned in the reading?
8. What are your personal attitudes about old age and the aged? Do you think you are an ageist? Why or why not?

**IN YOUR OWN WORDS**

Work with a partner. Imagine you are describing key issues about aging to a student in another class. Take turns explaining the main ideas you remember from each section of the article. Use the subheads and a graphic organizer like the one below as a guide.

 *Speaking* TIP

For each main idea you explain, note a few significant details.

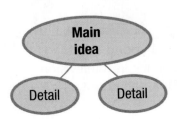

## DISCUSSION

Discuss in pairs or small groups.

1. The author suggests that the process of aging involves emotional, social, and intellectual factors. Give some specific examples of these factors. Which ones do you think are the most important in the aging process?

2. Everyone faces the prospect of old age. Can you imagine getting old, or do you "have to be there" before you can understand? What do you think your own old age will be like?

**Q How do generations differ from one another?** What do you think American society should do to solve some of the problems of an aging population?

**») Listening TIP**

Respect each speaker. Listen politely, even if you disagree with the speaker's ideas.

## READ FOR FLUENCY

When we read aloud to communicate meaning, we group words into phrases, pause or slow down to make important points, and emphasize important words. Pause for a short time when you reach a comma and for a longer time when you reach a period. Pay attention to rising and falling intonation at the end of sentences.

Work with a partner. Choose a paragraph from the reading. Discuss which words seem important for communicating meaning. Practice pronouncing difficult words. Give each other feedback.

▲ Social ties are important throughout life.

## EXTENSION

**Workbook Page 51**

What do people really think about getting old? Interview some people to find out. Prepare questions to ask a friend and a relative about aging. Do research at the library or use the Internet to help you with your questions. Ask your friend and relative the same questions. Write the answers you get in your notebook. Compare and contrast the answers. Then write a few sentences that summarize your findings. Report what you learned to the class.

# Grammar and Writing

### Unreal Conditional Sentences

Unreal conditional sentences describe unreal or contrary-to-fact conditions and their results. A conditional sentence has an *if* clause and a result clause.

| *if* clause | result clause |
|---|---|
| If grandmother fell ill, | we would take care of her. |

Present unreal conditionals are used to talk about present unreal or contrary-to-fact conditions and their results. Use the simple past in the *if* clause and *could, would,* or *might* + verb in the result clause. If the verb is *be* in the *if* clause, use *were* for all persons.

> If he **were** my grandfather, I **would visit** him more often.
> If my parents **understood**, I **would feel** better.
> If father **phoned** more often, we **might have** a closer relationship.

Past unreal conditionals are used to talk about past unreal or contrary-to-fact conditions and their results. Use the past perfect (*had* + past participle) in the *if* clause and *could have, would have,* or *might have* + past participle in the result clause.

> His mother **would have helped** him if she **had known** he was in trouble.
> If father **had listened**, he **wouldn't have been** so upset.
> If our grandparents **had moved** here, their lives **might have been** easier.

### Practice

Copy the sentences below into your notebook. Complete them using either the present or past unreal conditional. Then check your work with a partner and take turns reading the sentences aloud.

1. If my parents needed my help, I _____.
2. I _____ if an aunt or uncle moved in with us.
3. If my parents had _____, things might have been different.
4. My grandparents _____ if they hadn't had so many problems.

## WRITING a NARRATIVE PARAGRAPH

### Write a Friendly Letter

You have learned to develop point of view and create a plot—two skills you'll need to write a story at the end of this unit. Successful writers of narrative also give their writing a strong and distinctive voice. Voice is a writer's unique way of expressing thoughts or feelings in writing; it is the writer's personality, expressed through his or her choice of words, sentence structure, and other text features.

Here is a model of a friendly letter by a student named Sophie Howat. Notice how she allows her distinctive voice to come across by including her observations, ideas, and feelings. Before writing, she used a graphic organizer to put her letter into the correct format.

| | Date |
|---|---|
| Salutation or Greeting | |
| Body | |
| | Closing, Signature |

*Letter to a Friend*

March 2, 2009

Dear Casey,

Today I've been thinking about a fight I had with my great aunt. Yesterday I stopped by her house for a quick visit. I came straight from soccer practice, and I was all muddy and sweaty. As soon as she saw me, she scowled. In her mind, a lady would never be seen in such a state. She commented on my hunched posture and my dirty clothes and said such things are for boys. I tried arguing that all the kids my age, including the girls, are active and ready to get dirty! She clearly disagreed. I think when she was growing up, girls were supposed to be pretty and perfect. If she were a girl now, she'd see how hard that can be.

Love,
Sophie

### Practice

Workbook Page 53

Write a letter to a friend about an experience you had with a parent, a teacher, or another member of an older generation. Describe how you disagreed (or agreed) about an issue that was important to you. Express your personal thoughts and feelings about the experience. Use a graphic organizer to put your letter into the correct format. Be sure to use unreal conditional sentences correctly.

**Writing Checklist**

**VOICE:**
☑ I included my observations and thoughts about the experience.

**WORD CHOICE:**
☑ I chose words that express my feelings.

107

# Prepare to Read

## What You Will Learn

**Reading**
■ Vocabulary building:
   *Literary terms,
   word study*

■ Reading strategy:
   *Make inferences*

■ Text type:
   *Literature
   (short story)*

**Grammar, Usage, and Mechanics**
Possessive adjective agreement

**Writing**
Write a story with a starter

### THE BIG QUESTION

**How do generations differ from one another?** Have your parents ever had to persuade you to do the right thing? What was it? What reasons did you find to try to avoid doing what they wanted?

   The young man in the short story you are about to read listens to his grandfather tell the story of his life. Has a relative ever told you an interesting story about his or her life? How did you react?

### BUILD BACKGROUND

In this section, you will read a short story, **"An Hour with Abuelo."** The main character, Arturo, is a young Puerto Rican of sixteen and belongs to the first generation of his family to be born in the United States. Arturo dreads visiting his elderly grandfather, or *abuelo*. His *abuelo* moved to New Jersey from Puerto Rico when he was already quite old. Puerto Rico is an island territory of the United States located in the Caribbean Sea. Many Puerto Ricans have settled in the northeastern part of the United States.

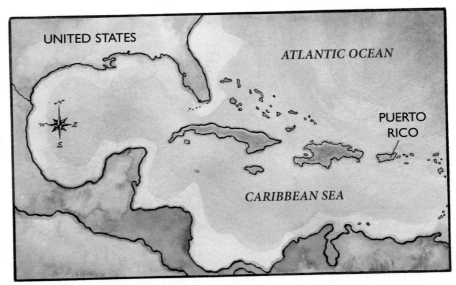

▲ Puerto Rico, an island territory of the United States

### Learn Literary Words

In fiction, writers use **characterization** to describe imaginary persons in a way that makes them believable and lifelike. Writers develop character by describing how the person looks and behaves. For example, this description enables the reader to imagine what a teacher looks like and what type of person he is: "Mr. Wilson had a stern, unsmiling expression and a military mustache. He looked down as his students walked into the room."

Writers of fiction further develop character by including **dialogue** that reveals their characters' personality and sounds the way they would really talk. For example, Mr. Wilson addresses his class as follows: "Failure to turn in your assignments on these dates will not be tolerated." The character's words and way of speaking provide more information about the type of person he is.

As you have learned, a **plot** is the sequence of events in a narrative. In a work of fiction, the plot usually involves one or more characters who experience a problem or conflict. A plot can be simple or complicated. Most plots have a clear beginning, middle, and end.

**Setting** is the time and place where the action of the story happens. The time might be the year, the season, the day, or the hour. The setting may be very specific, such as *Sunday, March 31, 1976, at 9:46 A.M. at the Golden Gate Bridge*. The setting may also be vague, such as *several years ago in a small midwestern city*. For example, a story in which Mr. Wilson is a character might begin this way: "It was the first day of classes at Midland High School. Students had not yet arrived. A single ray of morning sun brightened Mr. Wilson's classroom, which was otherwise dark and empty."

| Literary Words |
| --- |
| characterization |
| dialogue |
| plot |
| setting |

### Practice

Think of an interesting person you know well. Write one sentence describing an important detail of his or her physical appearance. Using quotes, write a sentence of dialogue that captures the way the person really talks. Finally, write one sentence describing the setting where you most often see this person. Read your sentences to a partner. Have your partner tell you about the person he or she pictured as you read your characterization.

▲ Writers develop character by describing a person's appearance.

## Learn Academic Words

Study the **red** words and their meanings. You will find these words useful when talking and writing about literature. Write each word and its meaning in your notebook. After you read "An Hour with Abuelo," try to use these words to respond to the text.

**Academic Words**

achievement
adapt
affect
impact
motivation

| | | |
|---|---|---|
| **achievement** = something important that you succeed in doing through skill and hard work | ➡ | He worked hard to finish university and become a teacher, and he was very proud of this **achievement**. |
| **adapt** = change your behavior or ideas to fit a new situation | ➡ | The old man had to **adapt** to life in the new country by learning another language. |
| **affect** = make someone feel strong emotions | ➡ | A well-told story can deeply **affect** us, making us feel joy or sadness. |
| **impact** = the effect that an event or situation has on someone or something | ➡ | The shocking ending of the story has an enormous **impact** on the reader. |
| **motivation** = the reason why a person wants to do something | ➡ | The teacher's **motivation** was to make her students enjoy learning. |

## Practice

**Workbook**
**Page 55**

Work with a partner to answer these questions. Try to include the **red** word in your answer. Write the sentences in your notebook.

1. What would be a great **achievement** for a student?

2. Have you ever had to **adapt** to a new situation? How?

3. How does the news media **affect** the way you look at the world?

4. What event in your life has had a great **impact** on you?

5. What is one **motivation** for a person to move to another country?

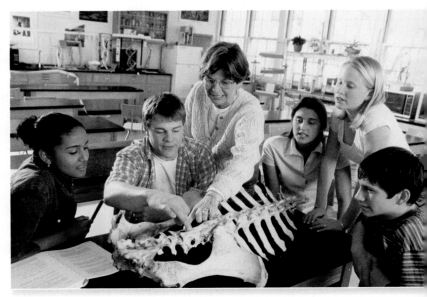

▲ Students' motivation can influence how much and how well they learn.

## Word Study: Phrasal Verbs

A phrasal verb is an expression that consists of two or more words: a verb and one or more adverbs or prepositions. Each phrasal verb has its own specific meaning that is often completely different from the verb alone. Look at the examples.

| Phrasal Verb | Meaning |
|---|---|
| **get out of** something | to avoid doing something that you have promised to do or are supposed to do |
| **catch up on** something | to do something that needs to be done that you have not had time to do |
| **drop** someone **off** | to take someone to a place in a car when you are going somewhere else |
| **use up** something | to use all of something so there is none left |
| **make** something **up** | to invent the music or words for a new song, story, poem, etc. |
| **call out** | to say something loudly |

**Practice**
Workbook
Page 56

Work with a partner. Find the phrasal verbs in the chart above in "An Hour with Abuelo." Think about the meaning of each phrasal verb and how it is used. Then write your own sentence with each new phrasal verb.

## READING STRATEGY | MAKE INFERENCES

Making inferences helps you figure out the information that authors do not always give directly. To make inferences, or infer, follow these steps:

- As you read, pay attention to the situations the author describes. What can you guess about the characters and setting?
- Think about your own experiences. Do they help you understand the situation that you are reading about?
- Now use the information in the text and your own experiences to make inferences.

As you read "An Hour with Abuelo," think about what the author means but does not say directly. What inferences can you make from what the author wrote?

Workbook
Page 57

111

**Set a purpose for reading** In what ways can the attitudes and values of one generation differ from those of another generation?

# An Hour with Abuelo

### *Judith Ortiz Cofer*

"Just one hour, *una hora*, is all I'm asking of you, son." My grandfather is in a nursing home in Brooklyn, and my mother wants me to spend some time with him, since the doctors say that he doesn't have too long to go now. *I* don't have much time left of my summer vacation, and there's a stack of books next to my bed I've got to read if I'm going to get into the AP English class I want. I'm going stupid in some of my classes, and Mr. Williams, the principal at Central, said that if I passed some reading tests, he'd let me move up.

Besides, I hate the place, the old people's home, especially the way it smells like industrial-strength ammonia and other stuff I won't mention, since it turns my stomach. And really the abuelo always has a lot of relatives visiting him, so I've gotten out of going out there except at Christmas, when a whole vanload of grandchildren are herded over there to give him gifts and a hug. We all make it quick and spend the rest of the time in the recreation area, where they play checkers and stuff with some of the old people's games, and I catch up on back issues of *Modern Maturity*. I'm not picky, I'll read almost anything.

Anyway, after my mother nags me for about a week, I let her drive me to Golden Years. She drops me off in front. She wants me to go in alone and have a "good time" talking to Abuelo. I tell her to be back in one hour or I'll take the bus back to Paterson. She squeezes my hand and says, "*Gracias, hijo*," in a choked-up voice like I'm doing her a big favor.

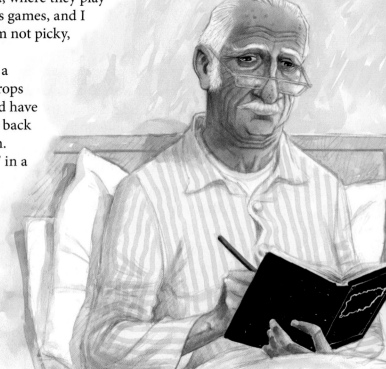

---

**nursing home**, a place where elderly people live
**I'm going stupid**, I'm very bored
**turns my stomach**, makes me sick
**herded**, made to move together as a group
**nags**, complains continuously
**choked-up**, emotional

I get depressed the minute I walk into the place. They line up the old people in wheelchairs in the hallway as if they were about to be raced to the finish line by orderlies who don't even look at them when they push them here and there. I walk fast to room 10, Abuelo's "suite." He is sitting up in his bed writing with a pencil in one of those old-fashioned black hardback notebooks. It has the outline of the island of Puerto Rico on it. I slide into the hard vinyl chair by his bed. He sort of smiles and the lines on his face get deeper, but he doesn't say anything. Since I'm supposed to talk to him, I say, "What are you doing, Abuelo, writing the story of your life?"

It's supposed to be a joke, but he answers, "Sí, how did you know, Arturo?"

His name is Arturo too. I was named after him. I don't really know my grandfather. His children, including my mother, came to New York and New Jersey (where I was born) and he stayed on the Island until my grandmother died. Then he got sick, and since nobody could leave their jobs to go take care of him, they brought him to this nursing home in Brooklyn. I see him a couple of times a year, but he's always surrounded by his sons and daughters. My mother tells me that Don Arturo had once been a teacher back in Puerto Rico, but had lost his job after the war. Then he became a farmer. She's always saying in a sad voice, "Ay, bendito! What a waste of a fine mind." Then she usually shrugs her shoulders and says, "Así es la vida." That's the way life is. It sometimes makes me mad that the adults I know just accept whatever stuff is thrown at them because "that's the way things are." Not for me. I go after what I want.

---

**depressed**, very sad
**orderlies**, workers in a hospital
**suite**, set of expensive rooms
**Ay, bendito!**, Oh, my God! (Spanish)

✔ **LITERARY CHECK**

*Where does the story take place? How does the setting affect Arturo?*

**BEFORE YOU GO ON**

**1** What is a visit to Abuelo usually like for the grandchildren?

**2** Why does Arturo sometimes get mad at adults?

**On Your Own**
Is there anything that adults do or say that makes you mad? Explain.

113

Anyway, Abuelo is looking at me like he was trying to see into my head, but he doesn't say anything. Since I like stories, I decide I may as well ask him if he'll read me what he wrote.

I look at my watch: I've already used up twenty minutes of the hour I promised my mother.

Abuelo starts talking in his slow way. He speaks what my mother calls book English. He taught himself from a dictionary, and his words sound stiff, like he's sounding them out in his head before he says them. With his children he speaks Spanish, and that funny book English with us grandchildren. I'm surprised that he's still so sharp, because his body is shrinking like a crumpled-up brown paper sack with some bones in it. But I can see from looking into his eyes that the light is still on in there.

"It is a short story, Arturo. The story of my life. It will not take very much time to read it."

"I have time, Abuelo." I'm a little embarrassed that he saw me looking at my watch.

"Yes, hijo. You have spoken the truth. La verdad. You have much time."

Abuelo reads: " 'I loved words from the beginning of my life. In the campo where I was born one of seven sons, there were few books. My mother read them to us over and over: the Bible, the stories of Spanish conquistadors and of pirates that she had read as a child and brought with her from the city of Mayagüez; that was before she married my father, a coffee bean farmer; and she taught us words from the newspaper that a boy on a horse brought every week to her. She taught each of us how to write on a slate with chalks that she ordered by mail every year. We used those chalks until they were so small that you lost them between your fingers.

---

**sharp**, able to think and understand things
**shrinking**, becoming smaller
**crumpled-up**, crushed
**campo**, countryside (Spanish)
**conquistadors**, Spanish conquerors
    of Mexico and Peru in the
    sixteenth century
**slate**, small blackboard
    that you can write
    on with chalk

" 'I always wanted to be a writer and a teacher. With my heart and my soul I knew that I wanted to be around books all of my life. And so against the wishes of my father, who wanted all his sons to help him on the land, she sent me to high school in Mayagüez. For four years I boarded with a couple she knew. I paid my rent in labor, and I ate vegetables I grew myself. I wore my clothes until they were thin as parchment. But I graduated at the top of my class! My whole family came to see me that day. My mother brought me a beautiful *guayabera*, a white shirt made of the finest cotton and embroidered by her own hands. I was a happy young man.

" 'In those days you could teach in a country school with a high school diploma. So I went back to my mountain village and got a job teaching all grades in a little classroom built by the parents of my students.

" 'I had books sent to me by the government. I felt like a rich man although the pay was very small. I had books. All the books I wanted! I taught my students how to read poetry and plays, and how to write them. We made up songs and put on shows for the parents. It was a beautiful time for me.

" 'Then the war came, and the American President said that all Puerto Rican men would be drafted. I wrote to our governor and explained that I was the only teacher in the mountain village. I told him that the children would go back to the fields and grow up ignorant if I could not teach them their letters. I said that I thought I was a better teacher than a soldier. The governor did not answer my letter. I went into the U.S. Army.

---

**boarded**, paid to stay in a room in someone's house
**drafted**, ordered to serve in the army
**ignorant**, not educated

## BEFORE YOU GO ON

**1** What is Abuelo's physical and mental condition?

**2** How did Abuelo go against the wishes of his father? How did his mother help him?

**On Your Own**
Have you ever gone against the wishes of your parents? In what situations do you think it is acceptable to do so?

**115**

" 'I told my sergeant that I could be a teacher in the army. I could teach all the farm boys their letters so that they could read the instructions on the ammunition boxes and not blow themselves up. The sergeant said I was too smart for my own good, and gave me a job cleaning latrines. He said to me there is reading material for you there, scholar. Read the writing on the walls. I spent the war mopping floors and cleaning toilets.

" 'When I came back to the Island, things had changed. You had to have a college degree to teach school, even the lower grades. My parents were sick, two of my brothers had been killed in the war, the others had stayed in Nueva York. I was the only one left to help the old people. I became a farmer. I married a good woman who gave me many good children. I taught them all how to read and write before they started school.' "

Abuelo then puts the notebook down on his lap and closes his eyes.

"*Así es la vida* is the title of my book," he says in a whisper, almost to himself. Maybe he's forgotten that I'm there.

For a long time he doesn't say anything else. I think that he's sleeping, but then I see that he's watching me through half-closed lids, maybe waiting for my opinion of his writing. I'm trying to think of something nice to say. I liked it and all, but not the title. And I think that he could've been a teacher if he had wanted to bad enough. Nobody is going to stop me from doing what I want with my life. I'm not going to let la vida get in my way. I want to discuss this with him, but the words are not coming into my head in Spanish just yet. I'm about to ask him why he didn't keep fighting to make his dream come true, when an old lady in hot-pink running shoes sort of appears at the door.

She is wearing a pink jogging outfit too. The world's oldest marathoner, I say to myself. She calls out to my grandfather in a flirty voice, "Yoo-hoo, Arturo, remember what day it is? It's poetry-reading day in the rec room! You promised us you'd read your new one today."

I see my abuelo perking up almost immediately. He points to his wheelchair, which is hanging like a huge metal bat in the open closet. He makes it obvious that he wants me to get it. I put it together, and with Mrs. Pink Running Shoes's help, we get him in it. Then he says in a strong deep voice I hardly recognize, "Arturo, get that notebook from the table, please."

✔ LITERARY CHECK

*How is Abuelo's life story central to his characterization in the larger story? What do the choices he made in his life reveal about his character?*

---

**ammunition**, things such as bullets that you can shoot from a weapon
**blow themselves up**, kill themselves in an explosion
**latrines**, toilets
**mopping**, washing the floor with a wet mop
**marathoner**, person who runs in a very long race
**flirty**, showing casual romantic interest

I hand him another map-of-the-Island notebook—this one is red. On it in big letters it says, *POEMAS DE ARTURO*.

I start to push him toward the rec room, but he shakes his finger at me.

"Arturo, look at your watch now. I believe your time is over." He gives me a wicked smile.

Then with her pushing the wheelchair—maybe a little too fast—they roll down the hall. He is already reading from his notebook, and she's making bird noises. I look at my watch and the hour *is* up, to the minute. I can't help but think that my abuelo has been timing *me*. It cracks me up. I walk slowly down the hall toward the exit sign. I want my mother to have to wait a little. I don't want her to think that I'm in a hurry or anything.

---

**wicked**, mischievous
**cracks me up**, makes me laugh a lot

✔ **LITERARY CHECK**
*What surprise turn does the **plot** take at the end of the story?*

**BEFORE YOU GO ON**

1 Why didn't Abuelo return to teaching after the war? What did he do?

2 What will Abuelo do after Arturo's visit?

💡 **On Your Own**
How are Arturo's values and attitudes toward life different from those of his grandfather?

## ABOUT THE **AUTHOR**

**Judith Ortiz Cofer** was born in 1952 in Puerto Rico, and later moved to Georgia, where she attended high school. Cofer's writing spans several genres, from poetry and short stories to young adult novels. Her style is influenced by oral storytelling, gleaned from listening to her grandmother's accounts of her family history. Cofer published her most recent book in 2005: *A Love Story Beginning in Spanish: Poems.*

**117**

# Review and Practice

**Speaking TIP**

Face the audience when you speak to the other actors. If you turn away from the audience, people may not be able to hear or understand you.

## READER'S THEATER

Act out the following scene between Arturo and his mother, which leads up to the events in "An Hour with Abuelo."

**Mother:** Arturo!

**Arturo:** *Si*, Mama?

**Mother:** Arturo, I want you to visit Abuelo this afternoon.

**Arturo:** Ay, Mama, I have too much to do. Look at all these books I have to read for school.

**Mother:** It's good that you study so hard. But I want you to get to know your grandfather.

**Arturo:** But we visit him every Christmas!

**Mother:** And what if Abuelo isn't here this Christmas? [*Arturo is quiet and thinks.*] Please, son. For me?

**Arturo:** Oh, okay.

**Mother:** Thank you! *Gracias, hijo!* You're a good boy.

**Arturo:** Yeah, I know, I know. [*His mother leaves. Arturo is silent.*]

## COMPREHENSION

Workbook
Page 58

### Right There

1. What is the name of the young man in the story? Who is he named after? Why doesn't the boy know his grandfather?

2. How did Abuelo learn to read and write? What was Abuelo's ambition as a young man? Did he achieve his ambition?

### Think and Search

3. How did the war change Abuelo's life?

4. Why do you think it meant so much to Arturo's mother that her son visit Abuelo? How are the attitudes of Arturo and his mother toward Abuelo different?

### Author and You

5. Based on what the author tells you, what can you infer about the character of Arturo and Abuelo?

6. How would you describe the author's feelings about the small mountain village where Abuelo was born? What opinion do you think she might have about the army? Support your responses.

### On Your Own

7. In your opinion, is the author fair to all of the characters or does she favor one character over another?

8. Based on your experience, why did Arturo agree to visit Abuelo? In what ways did Arturo seem real to you? Did anything about him seem unbelievable? Explain.

## DISCUSSION

Discuss in pairs or small groups.

1. What is the problem in the story? How is it resolved? What do you predict will happen in the future? Base your predictions on what you read and make inferences about what you didn't read.

2. Compare and contrast yourself with the character of Arturo. What would you do differently?

3. Imagine you are as old as Abuelo. How do you think you would feel about living in a nursing home? What did you admire or disapprove of in this character?

**Q How do generations differ from one another?** How do your attitudes and values differ from those of your parents and grandparents?

**Listening TIP**

If you don't understand what someone has said, ask the person to repeat or explain his or her comment.

## RESPONSE TO LITERATURE

**Workbook Page 58**

Characterization involves the use of description, dialogue, and narration to create vivid and believable characters. Write a short paragraph describing how you pictured Arturo and Abuelo as you read. Then reread the story and find these elements of characterization in the text. Study how the author helped you picture the characters as real people. What words did she use? What did she leave to the reader to infer? Did she control what you would infer? How?

# Grammar and Writing

## Possessive Adjective Agreement

A possessive adjective shows possession, or ownership. It is always followed by a noun. A possessive adjective agrees with the noun or pronoun that reflects who the owner is, *not* with the noun it modifies.

> She read to Abuelo and **Abuelo's** brothers.
> **Correct:** She read to Abuelo and **his** brothers.
> **Incorrect:** She read to Abuelo and ~~their~~ brothers.

| | Possessive Adjective | Modifies a Singular Noun | Modifies a Plural Noun |
|---|---|---|---|
| 1st Person Singular | **my** | **my** grandfather | **my** grandparents |
| 2nd Person Singular | **your** | **your** cousin | **your** cousins |
| 3rd Person Singular | **his** (Abuelo's)<br>**her** (mother's)<br>**its** (the book's) | **his** room<br>**her** uncle<br>**its** page | **his** rooms<br>**her** uncles<br>**its** pages |
| 1st Person Plural | **our** | **our** aunt | **our** aunts |
| 2nd Person Plural | **your** | **your** story | **your** stories |
| 3rd Person Plural | **their** (Abuelo's and Arturo's) | **their** relative | **their** relatives |

## Practice

Workbook
Page 59

Copy the biography below into your notebook. Choose the correct possessive adjective to complete the sentences. Then check your work with a partner and take turns reading the sentences aloud.

> My neighbor is an older man from Puerto Rico. He's spent most of (his / its) life there. He used to be a scientist. He told me that he loved (his / its) job. He married (her / his) wife when he was only eighteen. They lived in (its / their) house for over sixty years with (their / his) children. When he was eighty-two, (his / her) wife died. The following year, he moved to (its / my) neighborhood. Now he lives with (his / her) daughter, (his / her) husband, and (her / their) daughter.

# WRITING A NARRATIVE PARAGRAPH

## Write a Story with a Starter

Creating believable characters is an important part of narrative writing. One way to do this is by using dialogue. In the story you read, the author described the appearance and behavior of Arturo and Abuelo to make them seem real. She also brought them to life by including dialogue, or conversation, that is natural and realistic.

The writer of this model began his story with this starter: "It was my last day of community service at the nursing home." The writer used dialogue as well as physical and character traits to establish character. Before writing, he listed his ideas in a graphic organizer.

| Character's appearance |
| --- |
| ↓ |
| Character's behavior |
| ↓ |
| Character's words |

*Alan Azar*

### An Inspiring Story

It was my last day of community service at the nursing home. I had enjoyed the experience, but I certainly was looking forward to having more free time. As I was making my way to the door at the end of the day, I felt a frail hand tap my arm. Mrs. Blume, a very successful artist and a great-grandmother, asked me if I had a second. Impatiently, I sat down.

"Back when I was a lawyer," she began.

"Mrs. Blume," I interrupted, "I thought you were a painter."

"I started out as a lawyer," she answered, "but my true love was painting. So I took a great risk and changed my path in life. I have never regretted it."

I was so glad that I had taken a few minutes to talk to her. She has inspired me to follow my heart in future ventures.

**Practice**  **Workbook Page 60**

Choose one of these story starters:

- Mr. Peters walked down the street leaning on his cane.
- Every morning Helen Fogarty greeted me with a warm smile.

Then create a story by adding events and developing the character. Include dialogue that reveals something important about the character. List your ideas in a graphic organizer. Use possessive adjectives correctly.

## Writing Checklist

**IDEAS:**
- ☑ I included details that made the character seem real.

**VOICE:**
- ☑ I developed the character in a way that makes the reader want to know more about this person.

# Link the Readings

## Critical Thinking

Look back at the readings in this unit. Think about what they have in common. They all tell about generations. Yet they do not all have the same purpose. The purpose of one reading might be to inform, while the purpose of another might be to entertain or persuade. In addition, the content of each reading relates to generations differently. Now copy the chart below into your notebook and complete it.

| Title of Reading | Purpose | Big Question Link |
|---|---|---|
| "Mendel and the Laws of Heredity" "A Son Searches for His Father" | | |
| "My Father and the Figtree" "I Ask My Mother to Sing" "Mother to Son" | | |
| "That Older Generation" | | It describes attitudes toward aging. |
| "An Hour with Abuelo" | to entertain | |

## Discussion

Discuss in pairs or small groups.

- Compare and contrast the ways in which the three poems discuss relations between the generations. How are the poems similar to "An Hour with Abuelo"? How are they different?

- **Q How do generations differ from one another?** How does what you learned in "Mendel and the Laws of Heredity" help you understand how families pass on traits and behavior? How did this information influence you as you read the other texts?

## Fluency Check

Work with a partner. Choose a paragraph from one of the readings. Take turns reading it for one minute. Count the total number of words you read. Practice saying the words you had trouble reading. Take turns reading the paragraph three more times. Did you read more words each time? Copy the chart below into your notebook and record your speeds.

| | 1st Speed | 2nd Speed | 3rd Speed | 4th Speed |
|---|---|---|---|---|
| Words Per Minute | | | | |

# Projects

Work in pairs or small groups. Choose one of these projects.

**1** Vist a botanical garden or a nursery. Find out which plants are hybrids and which ones are pure breeds. Then create a chart with simple illustrations like the ones in Figure 3 on page 76. Report your findings to the class.

**2** Research the science of genetics at the library or on the Internet. What life-changing discoveries have genetic scientists made? What will the future bring? Tell your class what you learned.

**3** Interview an older man or woman in your neighborhood. Ask about the problems they face in today's world. Ask them to share their views on how to live a rewarding life. Write a report and present it to your classmates.

**4** Visit a local nursing home to find out about simple things you could do to improve the lives of the people living there. Then create a poster that will inform and persuade your class to help.

# Further Reading

To find out more about the theme of this unit, choose from these reading suggestions.

**Cinderella Man,** Marc Cerasini
In this Penguin Reader® adaptation, boxer Jim Braddock takes any job to feed his family during the Depression. When he gets the chance to box again, winning comes easily—until he meets his greatest challenge, the world champion.

**Cuba 15: A Novel,** Nancy Osa
The coming-of-age story of Chicago student Violet Paz explores family relationships and friendships.

**Sounds of the River: A Young Man's University Days in Beijing,** Da Chen
In this autobiography, the author describes the conflict of adapting to his new university life while remaining true to his family's fishing-village heritage.

# Put It All Together

## LISTENING & SPEAKING WORKSHOP

### Skit

You will write and perform a skit that illustrates the generation gap between students and their grandparents or parents.

**1  THINK ABOUT IT**  Work in small groups. Review and discuss "An Hour with Abuelo." Who are the characters? What generations do they represent? What is the setting? What are the main events?

Talk about differences between your own generation and your parents' and grandparents' generations. Think of incidents that reveal the generation gap. For example: Two grandchildren who've never learned to speak Spanish visit their grandparents, who speak little English. They communicate in spite of this.

Choose one incident that would make a good skit, or short play.

**2  GATHER AND ORGANIZE INFORMATION**  With your group, plan a skit based on your incident. Include a character for each group member.

**Order Your Notes**  Write these headings in your notebook: *Characters, Setting, Plot*. Make notes under each heading. For example, under *Characters*, list the characters you will include in your skit and one or two details about each character.

**Prepare a Script**  Decide who will play each character. Then use your notes to write a script. The dialogue should look like this:

> **Abuela:**  Can you show me a photo of your girlfriend?
> **Tony:**  Sure! I have some on my phone.
> **Abuela:**  No, not "phone." "Photo"!
> **Tony:**  I know. I understand! But I have a camera phone. It takes pictures.
> **Abuela:**  Your phone takes pictures? Is that why you never call me?

Include important details about the setting, props, and action:

> [*Tony pulls his phone out of his pocket. He sits down on the sofa next to his grandmother and shows her the screen. She looks annoyed until she sees a picture. Then she starts to laugh. Tony laughs, too.*]

**Use Visuals**  Make or find simple costumes and props for your skit. Decide how you will show the setting.

124

**3** **PRACTICE AND PRESENT** As a group, practice your skit until you can perform it without looking at the script. If possible, ask a friend or family member to serve as *prompter* while you practice. (A prompter watches the skit and follows along in the script. If someone forgets what to say or do, the prompter quietly reminds them.) Practice using your props and wearing your costumes.

**Perform Your Skit** Speak loudly enough to be heard, but use a natural voice. Face the audience as you speak, even if your body is facing another direction. If you turn away from the audience, people may not be able to hear or understand you. Relax and have fun. This will help the audience enjoy your skit.

**4** **EVALUATE THE PRESENTATION**
You will improve your skills as a speaker and a listener by evaluating each presentation you give and hear. Use this checklist to help you judge your group's skit and the skits of your classmates.

- ☑ Did the skit illustrate a generation gap?
- ☑ Could you tell who the characters were and what the setting was?
- ☑ Did the dialogue sound natural?
- ☑ Did the order of events make sense?
- ☑ What suggestions do you have for improving the skit?

## Speaking TIPS

Don't just memorize your lines—make sure you understand what they mean. Then, even if you forget a word or two, you can substitute other words to express the right meaning.

Use gestures and facial expressions to help convey your character's feelings and actions to the audience.

## Listening TIPS

Give the actors your full attention. Actors are more effective if they feel you are "with them."

Watch for actions and gestures to help you understand what the actors are saying.

# WRITING WORKSHOP
## Fictional Narrative

As you have learned, a fictional narrative is a story created from the writer's imagination. Elements of a good fictional narrative include well-developed characters, a clear setting, and an interesting plot. The events in the plot usually happen in sequence and build to a climax, or turning point. They focus on a conflict or problem that is resolved by the story's end. The narrative point of view helps shape the readers' understanding of the characters and events. Another important element of fictional narratives is dialogue, or the words characters say to one another.

Your assignment for this workshop is to write a fictional narrative about someone who experiences a problem with an older family member or with a family tradition.

**1 PREWRITE** Start with what you know. List family traditions you have strong feelings about. Remember experiences you have had with older family members. What did you enjoy about these events or people? What were the conflicts or problems? Select one event or experience to write about. Use your imagination to transform it into fiction.

**List and Organize Ideas and Details** Use a story chart to organize ideas for your fictional narrative. A student named Sophie decided to write about a conflict between a mother and daughter. Here is her story chart:

| CHARACTERS Who? | SETTING Where? |
|---|---|
| Jenny<br>Her mother | Jenny's house—<br>Living room<br>Jenny's bedroom |
| **PROBLEM**<br>What is the conflict in the plot?<br>Jenny wants to go to friends' party<br>Mother wants her to go to<br>Grandma's party. | **SOLUTION**<br>What is the resolution?<br>Jenny decides Grandma's party is<br>more important. |

**2 DRAFT** Use your story chart and the model on page 129 to help you write a first draft. Remember to tell events in chronological order. Include dialogue to help reveal what your characters are thinking and feeling.

126

**3 REVISE** Read over your draft. As you do so, ask yourself the questions in the writing checklist. Use the questions to help you revise your fictional narrative.

## SIX TRAITS OF WRITING CHECKLIST

- ☑ **IDEAS:** Are my plot and characters engaging?
- ☑ **ORGANIZATION:** Do events build to a climax?
- ☑ **VOICE:** Does my writing show energy and emotion?
- ☑ **WORD CHOICE:** Does the dialogue suit my characters?
- ☑ **SENTENCE FLUENCY:** Do my sentences vary in length and type?
- ☑ **CONVENTIONS:** Does my writing follow the rules of grammar, usage, and mechanics?

Here are the changes Sophie plans to make when she revises her first draft:

### Too Many Parties

Today, Jenny—the shy, the unnoticed—felt truly happy. She had just been invited to Paul and Pamela Harding's sixteenth birthday party. The twins were the most popular kid in school!

Jenny's campaign for to be invited had started early. Every other day, she had complimented Pamela on her clothes. Jenny had also lent Paul countless pencils and pens, none of which had ever been returned. Last week, she had helped Pamela study for a math test. But it was all worth it!

"That's wonderful," Jenny's mother exclaimed when her daughter raced in to the living room to tell her the news. "When?"

"May 18th," Jenny told her.

"Jenny! That's Grandma Sadie's eightieth birthday party! ~~You can't go.~~ *I don't think you can go, honey.*"

Jenny gasped. "But this party is so important!"

"Grandma's eightieth birthday is a very special occasion! You need to be there."

Jenny just stared at her mother. Her thoughts bounced back to the compliments, the tutoring, all those pencils.

"I hate you," she said desperately. *"I hate you!"* She barely had time to register the ~~expression~~ *shock and pain* on her mother's face before she turned and ran not stopping until she was in her room.

For a few minutes Jenny just lay on her bed. Why couldn't her mother understand? But then Jenny began to think about how disappointed Grandma Sadie would be. Were the twins really worth it. Jenny thought of her mother, and the *horrible* things she had said to her.

Slowly, Jenny walked down the stairs. She walked *past her mother* into the living room, picked up the phone, and dialed Grandma Sadie's number.

*Grandma?* "It's me, Jenny. I'm so excited about your party!"

Jenny turned and looked up. Her mother was smiling.

## 4 EDIT AND PROOFREAD

**Workbook**
**Page 61**

Copy your revised draft onto a clean sheet of paper. Read it again. Correct any errors in grammar, word usage, mechanics, and spelling. Here are the additional changes Sophie plans to make when she prepares her final draft.

Sophie Haas

## Too Many Parties

Today, Jenny—the shy, the unnoticed—felt truly happy. She had just been invited to Paul and Pamela Harding's sixteenth birthday party. The twins were the most popular kids in school!

Jenny's campaign to be invited had started early. Every other day, she had complimented Pamela on her clothes. Last week, she had helped Pamela study for a math test. Jenny had also lent Paul countless pencils and pens, none of which had ever been returned. But it was all worth it!

"That's wonderful," Jenny's mother exclaimed when her daughter raced into the living room to tell her the news. "When?"

"May 18th," Jenny told her.

"Jenny! That's Grandma Sadie's eightieth birthday party! I don't think you can go, honey."

Jenny gasped. "But this party is so important!"

"Grandma's eightieth birthday is a very special occasion! You need to be there."

Jenny just stared at her mother. Her thoughts bounced back to the compliments, the tutoring, all those pencils.

"I hate you," she said desperately. "I hate you!" She barely had time to register the shock and pain on her mother's face before she turned and ran, not stopping until she was in her room.

For a few minutes, Jenny just lay on her bed. Why couldn't her mother understand? But then Jenny began to think about how disappointed Grandma Sadie would be. Were the twins really worth it? Jenny thought of her mother, and the horrible things she had said to her.

Slowly, Jenny walked down the stairs. She walked past her mother into the living room, picked up the phone, and dialed Grandma Sadie's number.

"Grandma? It's me, Jenny. I'm so excited about your party!"

Jenny turned and looked up. Her mother was smiling.

**5** **PUBLISH** Prepare your final draft. Share your fictional narrative with your teacher and classmates.

# Family Tales

*E*ach new generation wants to carve out its own identity, creating something new and different from their parents' generation. Often the only thing that children seem to have in common with their parents is the shape of their nose or the color of their hair. Many American artists have tried to capture the subtle threads that bind generations of a family, connections that go beyond genes or fashion, to find the power in shared bloodlines and family stories.

### Charles Willson Peale, *Mrs. James Smith and Grandson* (1776)

In eighteenth-century America, portraiture was an important way to hand down family stories. In this painting by Charles Willson Peale, the grandson certainly inherited his grandmother's eyes. The artist also captures the strong affection between the two, as the boy leans toward his elderly grandmother, eager to show that he has learned his lessons. Everything in this painting—from the clothes to the book in the boy's hand—is part of a carefully staged display. We can see that the boy is reading from the famous "To be or not to be" speech in Shakespeare's play, *Hamlet*.

In 1776, when this portrait was painted, the American colonies were fighting to establish their independence from the British. The artist, who was a lieutenant in the Philadelphia city militia, was well aware of the instability of the new republic. He seems to ask whether this boy will grow up to be a leader who will safeguard the new democracy. Clearly, his grandmother hopes so!

▲ Charles Willson Peale, *Mrs. James Smith and Grandson*, 1776, oil, 36⅜ x 29¼ in., Smithsonian American Art Museum

**130**

▲ Velino Shije Herrera, *Story Teller*, about 1925–35, gouache and pencil, 10 × 15 in., Smithsonian American Art Museum

### Velino Shije Herrera, *Story Teller* (about 1925–35)

An elderly figure sits at the center of Velino Shije Herrera's painting *Story Teller*. The old man speaks to a group of ten children, who listen with respect and attentiveness. One boy places his hand on the old man's shoulder with affection; others lean in slightly as though they don't want to miss anything the old man says.

Herrera, a Native American, uses strong colors and careful placement of the figures to capture the importance of the oral tradition of his Pueblo people. Family and tribal stories were handed down among Native Americans in the same way that portraits were handed down among the colonists. In both cases, one generation is reaching out to another to continue a shared legacy.

## Apply What You Learned

**1** What role did portraits play in eighteenth-century America? What family ties does Peale's portrait show?

**2** How do the subject, colors, and figures in Herrera's painting capture the importance of the oral tradition to the Pueblo people?

### Big Question
How do you think the family tales told by the subjects of these two paintings might be different? In what ways would they be the same?

**Workbook**
Pages 63–64

# THE BIG Q QUESTION

# What makes a community?

Visit *LongmanKeystone.com*

**T**his unit is about community. You will read texts about the connections between people and between other creatures that live in groups. Reading, writing, and talking about this topic will give you practice using academic language and help you become a better student.

**READING 1: Social Studies Article**
- "The Great Migration"

**READING 2: Play Excerpt**
- From *A Raisin in the Sun* by Lorraine Hansberry

**READING 3: Science Article**
- "The Savage, Beautiful World of Army Ants," an Interview with Mark Moffett by Alex Chadwick

**READING 4: Personal Narrative and Speech**
- From *Of Beetles and Angels* by Mawi Asgedom

## Listening and Speaking

At the end of this unit, you will give a **speech** about a problem in your school, neighborhood, or city.

## Writing

In this unit you will practice **persuasive writing**. This type of writing attempts to convince people to take a specific action or to adopt a point of view. After each reading you will learn a skill to help you write a persuasive paragraph. At the end of the unit, you will use these skills to help you write a persuasive brochure.

### QuickWrite

What does the word *community* make you think of? Use a word web to list as many ideas as you can. Then share your ideas with a partner.

133

# Prepare to Read

## What You Will Learn

**Reading**

■ Vocabulary building: *Context, dictionary skills, word study*

■ Reading strategy: *Summarize*

■ Text type: *Informational text (social studies)*

**Grammar, Usage, and Mechanics**
Words that express opposition

**Writing**
Write an editorial

### THE BIG QUESTION

**What makes a community?** Have you ever moved from one community to another? How did leaving friends and relatives behind affect you? Was it hard to get used to a new place? Discuss with a partner.

### BUILD BACKGROUND

**"The Great Migration"** is a social studies article. It describes the migration of millions of African Americans from rural places in the southern United States to northern cities. At the beginning of the twentieth century, 90 percent of African Americans in the United States lived in the South. By midcentury, only 68 percent of African Americans lived there. Because so many people moved from one area of the country to another, this population movement became known as the Great Migration.

Look at the map. What routes did African Americans follow during the Great Migration? In which cities did they settle?

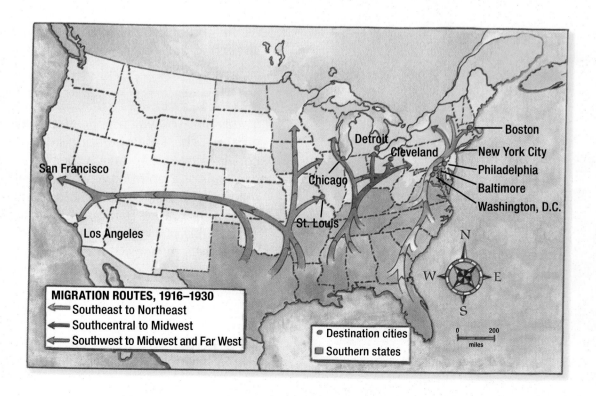

MIGRATION ROUTES, 1916–1930
⬅ Southeast to Northeast
⬅ Southcentral to Midwest
⬅ Southwest to Midwest and Far West

● Destination cities
■ Southern states

## Learn Key Words

Read these sentences. Use the context to figure out the meaning of the **red** words. Use a dictionary to check your answers. Then write each word and its meaning in your notebook.

**Key Words**

equality
livelihoods
obstacles
prejudice
riot
turmoil

1. The Civil Rights Act helped to ensure **equality**. It made certain that each citizen had the same rights under the law.

2. Poor economic conditions threaten the **livelihoods** of many people, making it difficult for them to earn a living.

3. She was able to overcome many **obstacles** because she was determined to succeed.

4. There are laws that protect people from **prejudice**, or unfair feelings of dislike because of race or religion.

5. The angry crowd started a **riot**; they became violent and behaved in an uncontrollable way.

6. The many protests and groups of angry people marching around put the city in **turmoil**.

## Practice

**Workbook**
**Page 65**

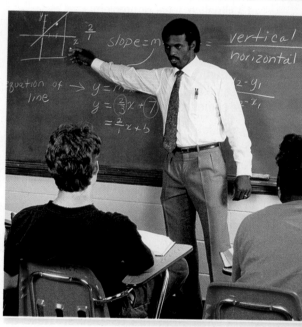

▲ Teaching is this man's livelihood.

Write the sentences in your notebook. Choose a **red** word from the box above to complete each sentence. Then take turns reading the sentences aloud with a partner.

1. During the civil rights era of the 1960s, laws were passed to combat the effects of racial _____.

2. In the United States, people of all races are guaranteed _____ under the law.

3. When the police force went on strike, it caused great _____ in the city.

4. The _____ lasted for days, and many people were hurt because of the violence.

5. Though some people are not held back by poverty or lack of education, these things are often _____ to success.

6. The _____ of many farmers were ruined because of dry weather conditions.

135

## Learn Academic Words

Study the **red** words and their meanings. You will find these words useful when talking and writing about informational texts. Write each word and its meaning in your notebook. After you read "The Great Migration," try to use these words to respond to the text.

### Academic Words

aspect
challenge
community
discrimination
participation
period

| | | |
|---|---|---|
| **aspect** = one of the parts or features of a situation, idea, or problem | → | They must address every **aspect** of the problem in order to completely solve it. |
| **challenge** = something exciting or difficult, requiring skill and effort to do | → | It is a **challenge** to move to a completely new neighborhood or city and get settled. |
| **community** = the people who live in the same area, town, or city or who have something in common | → | Many people choose to live in this **community** because it is made up of people of all different ages, races, and religions. |
| **discrimination** = the practice of treating one group of people differently from another in an unfair way | → | Female workers in that company earned less money and faced other kinds of **discrimination** just because they were women. |
| **participation** = the act of taking part in something | → | The class had a high level of **participation**; everyone contributed to class discussions. |
| **period** = a particular length of time in history | → | The Great Depression was a **period** when it was hard to find a job and make enough money to live. |

### Practice

**Workbook**
**Page 66**

Work with a partner to answer these questions. Try to include the **red** word in your answer. Write the answers in your notebook.

1. Which **aspect** of your neighborhood would a visitor find interesting?

2. What is a very difficult **challenge** that you have had to face?

3. What do you like most about the **community** you live in?

4. Give an example of **discrimination**, either past or present.

5. What can you say about student **participation** in your class?

6. What **period** of history do you find the most interesting?

▲ The community is a place where musical traditions are celebrated.

## Word Study: Suffixes -ist, -or, -er

Add the suffix -ist, -or, or -er to a word to form a noun that refers to a person who does, is connected to, or believes in something. If the base word ends with e or y, drop the e or y before adding the suffix.

| Base Word | + Suffix | Noun | Meaning |
|-----------|----------|------|---------|
| art | -ist | artist | person who creates art |
| biology | -ist | biologist | person who does research in biology |
| direct | -or | director | person who manages a company |
| operate | -or | operator | person who operates a machine |
| mine | -er | miner | person who works in a mine |
| settle | -er | settler | person who goes to live in a new place |

**Practice**  Workbook Page 67

Work with a partner. Copy the words in the box below into your notebook. For each base word, write a noun that refers to a person who does, is connected to, or believes in something. Then write a sentence using the new noun. Use a dictionary to check your work.

| inspect | labor | lead | manufacture | motor | sociology | survive |

## READING STRATEGY    SUMMARIZE

Summarizing helps you check your understanding of a text. When you summarize, you identify the main ideas in the text and rewrite them in a few short sentences. To summarize, follow these steps:

- Read the text. Then reread each paragraph or section.
- Identify the main idea in each paragraph or section. Make notes.
- Leave out details. Just focus on the most important points.
- Write a few sentences that convey the main ideas in the text. Use your own words.

As you read "The Great Migration," stop from time to time and note the main ideas. Summarize the text in two or three sentences.

 Workbook Page 68

**Set a purpose for reading** What conditions caused large numbers of African Americans to leave their communities in the South during the first part of the twentieth century? What conditions did they find when they moved north?

# The Great Migration

In the decade after the Civil War, new amendments to the United States Constitution had seemed to guarantee that civil rights could not be denied to anyone on the basis of race, creed, or color. For a time, African Americans in the South freely voted, went to school, held office, purchased land, and ran businesses.

However, life in the South became increasingly difficult for African Americans, and by the 1880s, the dream of equality for southern blacks was rapidly disappearing. In search of new opportunities, they began to leave their homes. At first, they did so in relatively small numbers. Some moved from the countryside to nearby southern towns. Others went west. Most moved to cities in the North. Then, between 1915 and 1920, the numbers of African Americans moving north swelled to a flood. In those five years, 10 percent of the South's black population resettled in cities such as Chicago, Philadelphia, Detroit, St. Louis, and Cleveland.

Called the Great Migration, this exodus became one of the largest movements of population ever to take place in the nation's history. In 1900, nine out of ten African Americans in the United States lived in the South. By the 1950s, however, only about seven out of ten African Americans in the United States lived in the South.

---

**creed**, belief
**swelled**, increased
**exodus**, large number of people that moves
   permanently from one place to another

▲ **African-American sharecroppers**

# THE EXODUS

◄ The front page of the *Chicago Defender*, September 2, 1916, shows African-American migrants in Savannah, Georgia, waiting to catch the train to go north.

## Seeking a New Start

In the late 1870s, the federal government turned the responsibility for enforcing African-American rights over to the states. Most of the former slave-holding states passed what became known as "Jim Crow" laws—laws that discriminated against African Americans. These laws segregated facilities from streetcars to schools, from drinking fountains to restaurants. Southern states also limited voting rights through requirements such as property ownership and literacy. Many former slaves did not have the money, education, or land needed to register to vote.

In fact, most land—both north and south—still belonged to white landlords. Because agriculture was the most important means of earning a living in the South, poor white and black farmers alike had no choice but to rent property. Called sharecroppers, these tenant farmers paid rent with a share of crops rather than with money. When a long period of disastrous weather, coupled with an insect invasion, destroyed crops in the late 1800s and early 1900s, sharecroppers' livelihoods were ruined. Along with losing their political rights, many African Americans saw their hopes for economic success shattered.

---

**enforcing**, making people obey the law
**literacy**, the ability to read and write
**register**, complete an official form
**share**, portion or part
**shattered**, broken

## BEFORE YOU GO ON

**1** How and why did the civil rights of African Americans improve immediately after the Civil War?

**2** Why did African Americans lose their civil rights during the late 1870s?

**On Your Own**
Do you think it's always a good idea to migrate from one place to another in search of opportunities or to escape hardship? Explain.

Worse, hate groups such as the Ku Klux Klan were growing stronger, particularly in the South. As a result, many of the millions of southern African Americans lived under the threat of racial violence, including the possibility of lynching.

In the hope that life would be better in the North, some African Americans decided to migrate. The industrial North offered far more job opportunities than the agrarian South. There were steel mills, railroads, and factories in need of workers. Laborers and farmers were not the only people, however, who chose to migrate. Doctors and ministers, teachers and artists, also decided that it was time for change.

If migration began slowly, it rapidly increased with the outbreak of World War I in 1914. For years, European immigrants had provided businesses and factories with low-paid labor. When the war temporarily ended immigration, the demand for African-American workers as a labor force skyrocketed. Long before the United States itself entered the war in 1917, businesses sent men called labor agents south to try to lure African Americans north. Labor agents promised everything from free train fare to housing. Although they seldom delivered on most of their promises, the promise of work at least was real. Black-owned newspapers spread the word, and men and women who had already moved north sent letters home urging their relatives to join them.

---

**lynching**, hanging a person without a trial
**agrarian**, mostly farming-based
**skyrocketed**, increased very quickly
**lure**, attract by making promises
**delivered on**, kept (their promises)

▼ African Americans building a steel mill

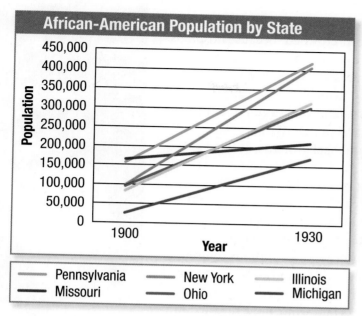

## African-American Population by State

| State | 1900 | 1930 |
|-------|------|------|
| Illinois | 85,078 | 328,972 |
| Michigan | 24,795 | 169,453 |
| Missouri | 161,234 | 223,840 |
| New York | 99,232 | 412,814 |
| Ohio | 96,901 | 309,304 |
| Pennsylvania | 156,845 | 431,257 |

▲ Between 1900 and 1930, there were huge increases in the African-American population of many northern states.

Some migrants traveled by car or boat. Most went by train. Few could afford to bring their families with them. They hoped instead to earn enough money to send for their loved ones later.

The journey itself was a terrible ordeal, with migrants packed into hot, segregated trains and barred from using white-only restrooms, drinking fountains, and food stands along the way. Often, migrants had to make the journey in stages, working for a time in one city or another to earn enough money to travel onward. But the majority of migrants did not turn back.

## Life in the North

Although the migrants faced many obstacles in their new homes, life in some ways was improved. As in the South, discrimination and segregation existed, but in general they were neither as widely written into the law nor as brutally enforced. African-American workers received lower pay than white workers but, on average, higher pay than workers of either race in the South. Nevertheless, because expenses were higher in the North, many migrants struggled in poverty.

The sheer number of migrants created problems. For example, Detroit's African-American population increased by more than 600 percent in ten years. Philadelphia's rose by 500 percent. Housing was hard to find.

---

afford, be able to pay
ordeal, a long, bad experience
barred, kept away
segregation, a set of laws that keeps different races separated
brutally, violently

### BEFORE YOU GO ON

**1** What kinds of jobs could African Americans hope to find in the North?

**2** Why was the journey to the North so difficult for African-American migrants?

**On Your Own**
Are the difficulties migrants face when moving to a new country the same as those they face when moving to a new community? Explain.

**141**

Unwelcome in white areas, most migrants were limited to cramped housing in a few neighborhoods that soon became overcrowded. Because hospitals were segregated and black doctors were rare, there was little access to health care. Death rates among African Americans remained higher than among whites.

Even some well-to-do African Americans, born and raised or long settled in the urban North, did not at first accept the migrants. The newcomers, often uneducated and from rural backgrounds, seemed as if they came from another world.

Racial violence erupted in the North as well as in the South. The fear that blacks would take away white jobs quickly became an issue. In 1917, tensions created by a labor strike, followed by rumors of a shooting, sparked a riot in East St. Louis. White mobs attacked black communities, leaving more than forty African Americans dead and hundreds injured. In 1919, riots broke out in Chicago when blacks attacked a police officer. He had arrested a black suspect, allowing the white suspect to go free. Two dozen people—among them both blacks and whites—were killed in the Chicago rioting; hundreds were wounded; a thousand, mostly African Americans, were left homeless. Other riots in other cities followed, with more lives lost and more property destroyed.

▲ King Oliver's Band in Chicago, 1923

## Community and Identity

Despite tragedy and turmoil, exciting developments and ideas also marked the growth of these new African-American communities. Dozens of black-owned newspapers and journals were published in the first decades of the twentieth century. Organizations such as the National Urban League, started in 1911 to help migrants find jobs and housing, became forces for change. Black intellectuals such as W. E. B. DuBois, one of the founders of the NAACP, demanded full social, economic, and political equality for African Americans.

In Chicago, a black city councilman, Oscar Stanton De Priest, was elected in 1915. About a decade later, he became the first African American to be elected to the United States House of Representatives in the twentieth century. Another black leader, Marcus Garvey,

---

**cramped**, having too little space
**access**, ability to get something
**rural**, of the countryside
**erupted**, happened suddenly
**tensions**, discomfort created by mistrust
**arrested**, put in prison for committing a crime
**decades**, periods of ten years

▲ Harlem Renaissance writer Zora Neale Hurston

▲ **Three fashionable young women in Harlem in the 1920s**

rejected participation in the American system altogether. He advocated instead black separatism and a return to African roots.

Black businesses, hospitals, schools, and labor unions were founded. And in African-American communities everywhere, the arts flourished. In Chicago, Cincinnati, and New Orleans, blues and jazz thrilled admirers of all races. In Harlem, a neighborhood in New York City that became predominantly black, writers such as Langston Hughes, Arna Bontemps, and Zora Neale Hurston created extraordinary poetry and novels. The flowering of art, literature, and music that took place in Harlem in the 1920s is remembered today as the Harlem Renaissance.

With the start of the Great Depression in 1929, the tide of African-American migration to the North slowed down. But by then, African Americans had formed strong new communities and developed a vital new sense of identity. Although prejudice, segregation, and discrimination would continue, African Americans had become a powerful influence on every aspect of American life.

---

**separatism**, the idea that races should stay apart
**labor unions**, organized groups of workers
**flourished**, had success
**thrilled**, excited
**flowering**, a time of great achievement

**BEFORE YOU GO ON**

1 Why did some well-to-do African Americans in the North fail to accept the migrants?

2 What was the Harlem Renaissance?

**On Your Own**
What kinds of ties should people who migrate keep with their community of origin? What kinds of ties should they develop with their new community?

**143**

**COMPREHENSION**  **Workbook** Page 69

**Right There**

1. What were "Jim Crow" laws? Where did they exist?

2. What effect did the outbreak of World War I have on the migration of African Americans to the North?

**Think and Search**

3. What were some of the problems that African Americans faced in the North?

4. What were some of the positive developments that came as a result of the Great Migration?

▲ Jacob Lawrence, *The Migration of the Negro* (panel No. 1), 1940–41

**Author and You**

5. What kinds of tensions do you think developed in the northern cities where African Americans moved?

6. In the last section of the reading, what can you infer about the author's attitude toward the value of community? Find language in the text to support your response.

**On Your Own**

7. What aspect of life in the North do you think was the most difficult for the African-American migrants? What aspect of life in the North do you think was the most satisfying for them?

8. Do you think the Great Migration was good or bad for African Americans? Was it good or bad for the northern cities in which they settled?

**IN YOUR OWN WORDS**

Work with a partner to summarize the article. Take turns summarizing each section of "The Great Migration" using a single sentence to paraphrase each paragraph. Practice delivering your summary orally.

 *Speaking* TIP

Speak slowly and clearly.

## DISCUSSION

Discuss in pairs or small groups.

1. How was the discrimination that African Americans faced in the North different from the discrimination they faced in the South? How was it similar? Was it worse in either place? Explain.

2. The article describes the progress the communities of migrants had made by 1929. How does your community compare? What do you think your community will be like in twenty years?

3. Did your own experiences help you understand the challenges faced by African Americans during the Great Migration? How were your experiences similar? How were they different?

Q **What makes a community?** What community activities have you participated in? What effect have these activities had on your community? What effect have they had on you?

**Listening TIP**

Summarize in your own mind what each speaker says. Do you agree or disagree? What new information did you learn?

## READ FOR FLUENCY

It is often easier to read a text if you understand the difficult words and phrases. Work with a partner. Choose a paragraph from the reading. Identify the words and phrases you do not know or have trouble pronouncing. Look up the difficult words in a dictionary.

Take turns pronouncing the words and phrases with your partner. If necessary, ask your teacher to model the correct pronunciation. Then take turns reading the paragraph aloud. Give each other feedback on your reading.

## EXTENSION

Workbook
Page 69

Copy the chart below into your notebook. List the people, places, and things in your community, such as teachers, neighborhoods, parks, traditions, etc. Put what you like under *Pluses*, what you dislike under *Minuses*, and what you find interesting in the last column. Then try to find out more at the library or on the Internet about your community's public services and its problems. Share what you learned with the class.

| My Community | | |
|---|---|---|
| **Pluses** | **Minuses** | **Interesting Things** |
| | | |

# Grammar and Writing

## GRAMMAR, USAGE, AND MECHANICS

### Words that Express Opposition

*However* and *nevertheless* show opposition to the first thought. Use a comma after these words when they start a sentence. Use a comma before and after these words when they appear in the middle of a sentence.

> In 1900, most African Americans lived in the South. **However,** life there had become increasingly difficult for them.
>
> Life there had, **however,** become increasingly difficult for them.
>
> After the Civil War, amendments to the Constitution seemed to guarantee the civil rights of African Americans. **Nevertheless,** by the 1880s, the dream of equality for southern blacks was rapidly disappearing.

*Although* and *despite* express an unexpected result. *Although* introduces a clause. Remember: A clause has a subject and a verb but may not be a complete thought.

> **Although** they seldom delivered on most of their promises, the promise of work was at least real.

*Despite* is a preposition and must be used with a noun.

> **Despite** tragedy and turmoil, exciting developments and ideas marked the growth of these new communities.

### Practice

Rewrite the sentences below in your notebook, using the word that expresses opposition in parentheses. Then check your work with a partner. Suggest different ways of reworking the sentences.

1. Life in Chicago was exciting. The people were poor. (although)

2. Writers in Harlem created extraordinary literature. There were difficulties. (despite)

3. They found work in Detroit. Housing was hard to find. (however)

4. They weren't accepted at first. They tried to start a new life in Philadelphia. (nevertheless)

5. The North had a lot to offer. There were problems. (although)

# WRITING A PERSUASIVE PARAGRAPH

## Write an Editorial

At the end of this unit, you will write a brochure, which is a type of persuasive writing. In persuasive writing, you offer an opinion that you would like readers to adopt or you try to convince readers to take a specific action. State your opinion clearly and include facts, examples, and other details that support your opinion or justify the action you want your readers to take. These elements of support give the reader a reason to adopt your viewpoint.

Here is a model of an editorial in a school newspaper. The writer has included specific details to support his opinion. Before writing, he used a graphic organizer to organize his ideas.

Alan Azar

Proposal for a Cultural Club at Lincoln High

Here at Lincoln High School, students come from many different ethnic, national, and cultural backgrounds. These differences can influence the clothes we wear, the languages we speak, the holidays we celebrate, and even the foods we enjoy. Sometimes these differences create social barriers and tensions. However, our differences don't have to divide us! We have a lot in common, despite our differences. I believe a cultural club would bring all the students at Lincoln together. It would enable us to celebrate and learn from one another's differences, by sharing music, food, and traditions. A cultural club would also allow individuals to see the ways in which they are similar to students of different backgrounds. For example, two students from different countries may still find the same things funny or enjoy the same movies. So let's unite by starting a cultural club at Lincoln High today!

**Practice**

Write an editorial for your school newspaper in which you urge your classmates to take a specific action to improve an aspect of school life. Include facts, examples, and other details to support your opinion. Organize your ideas before you write, using a graphic organizer. Be sure to use words that express opposition correctly.

### Writing Checklist

**IDEAS:**
☑ I included details that support my opinion.

**WORD CHOICE:**
☑ I chose words that help to persuade readers.

147

# Prepare to Read

## THE BIG QUESTION

**What makes a community?** Think about your neighborhood. When your family moved there, did your neighbors welcome you? Have other people moved to the neighborhood since you moved there? How did you behave toward them? Have people moved to your neighborhood who were different from the people already living there? How were they welcomed? Discuss with a partner.

## BUILD BACKGROUND

***A Raisin in the Sun*** is a play about an African-American family striving to realize its dream of a better life in Chicago in the 1950s. Parts of the story are autobiographical. The author, Lorraine Hansberry, grew up during a time when segregation was still common in the United States. Her family was one of the first black families to move into a white neighborhood in Chicago. Their white neighbors threatened them with violence and legal action because they wanted them to move out.

*A Raisin in the Sun* was a ground-breaking work because it presented a realistic characterization of an African-American family and its struggle in America in the 1950s. The scene you will read explores the tensions that existed between white and black people during this period.

The cast of the 2004 Broadway production of *A Raisin in the Sun* ▶

### Learn Literary Words

Plays are stories that are performed by actors who bring the characters in the story to life. You have learned that authors try to make characters believable and lifelike by describing their appearance and behavior.

Another way authors create believable and realistic characters is by describing their motivation. **Motivation** is a reason that explains why a character thinks, feels, acts, or behaves in a certain way. A character's motivation results from a combination of his or her personality and the situation he or she must deal with. Love, hatred, fear, anger, and jealousy are some common motivations. The author of a play develops a character's motivation through the use of **dialogue**.

In the last unit you learned that dialogue is used in novels and stories to develop character. In a script, or written form of a play, dialogue follows the characters' names, and no quotation marks are used. Dialogue shows what the characters say. You can learn a character's motivation by paying close attention to dialogue.

For example, in Shakespeare's *Romeo and Juliet*, two young people in love are in conflict with their families. The families have been feuding, or quarreling, for many years. The young lovers must meet in secret, for their families would oppose their relationship. The motivation of Romeo and Juliet to defy their families comes from their deep love for each other. This motivation is made clear through the dialogue in the following scene, where Juliet learns that Romeo is a Montague, her family's enemy:

> **Nurse:**  His name is Romeo, and a Montague,
> The only son of your great enemy.
> **Juliet:**  My only love sprung from my only hate!
> Too early seen unknown, and known too late!
> Prodigious birth of love it is to me
> That I must love a loathed enemy.

**Practice**  **Workbook** Page 72

In a small group, choose a movie that everyone has seen. Identify the important characters and discuss their motivation. Recall some of the dialogue that supports your answers.

## Learn Academic Words

Study the **red** words and their meanings. You will find these words useful when talking and writing about literature. Write each word and its meaning in your notebook. After you read the excerpt from *A Raisin in the Sun*, try to use these words to respond to the text.

| | | |
|---|---|---|
| **convince** = make someone feel certain that something is true | ➡ | He couldn't **convince** them he was right because he did not have good evidence. |
| **drama** = a play for the theater, television, or radio | ➡ | The **drama** had some funny moments, but the main theme was very serious. |
| **exclude** = not allow someone to enter a place or do something | ➡ | It is against the law to **exclude** anyone from living in a neighborhood because of race. |
| **organization** = a group that has been formed for a particular purpose | ➡ | This **organization** was formed to help children in need. |
| **react** = behave in a particular way because of what someone has done or said to you | ➡ | Some people **react** to rude treatment by becoming angry. |

## Practice

**Workbook** Page 73

Work with a partner to complete these sentences using the sentence starters. Include the **red** word in your sentence. Then write the sentence in your notebook.

1. Because the evidence was lost, the lawyer couldn't . . . (**convince**)
2. A comedy can make you laugh, but . . . (**drama**)
3. It isn't fair . . . (**exclude**)
4. The Red Cross is . . . (**organization**)
5. When treated unjustly, people often . . . (**react**)

▲ Soup kitchens are run by charitable organizations.

## Word Study: Shades of Meaning

To understand *A Raisin in the Sun*, you must learn to identify words
that have different shades of meaning. A euphemism is a word
that is used instead of an unpleasant or insulting word. Indirect
meanings have to be inferred from the context or previous
knowledge. Veiled meanings are used to hide the real meaning
from all but a few persons.

| Euphemisms | Plain Meanings |
|---|---|
| restroom, powder room<br>sanitation truck | toilet<br>garbage truck |
| **Indirect Meanings** | **Plain Meanings** |
| Do you have five dollars?<br>Maybe you would be happier somewhere else. | May I borrow five dollars?<br>I want you to leave. |
| **Veiled Meanings** | **Plain Meanings** |
| Operation Overlord<br>states' rights | the invasion of Normandy<br>the right to impose segregation |

**Practice**  **Workbook Page 74**

Take turns reading the words in the chart above aloud with a partner.
Then find five other words or phrases with shades of meaning. Write
them in a chart that shows both meanings of each word.

## READING STRATEGY | ANALYZE TEXT STRUCTURE

Analyzing text structure tells you what kind of text you're reading. There
are many different types of texts, including poems, plays, and stories.
Read these descriptions:

- Stories are written in paragraphs. Dialogue is enclosed within
  quotation marks.

- Poems are usually written in lines and groups of lines. The
  punctuation doesn't always follow standard rules.

- Plays are mainly written in dialogue. The dialogue has the speakers'
  names, followed by colons, and then the words the speaker says.
  Stage directions are usually in parentheses.

Review the text structure of this excerpt from *A Raisin in the Sun*.
Discuss it with a partner.

 **Workbook Page 75**

**Set a purpose for reading** Think about the community where the Younger family wants to move. Is it a community where you would like to live?

# *from* A Raisin in the Sun

## *Lorraine Hansberry*

**Lena Younger** *dreams of moving her family out of the ghetto. She uses the insurance money her late husband has left her to put a down payment on a house. The house is in an all-white neighborhood. It is moving day, and the Youngers receive a visit from one of their new neighbors.*

*The characters in this scene are Lena's daughter* **Beneatha**, *a college student who wants to go to medical school; Lena's son* **Walter**, *a chauffeur who dreams of going into business for himself; his wife* **Ruth***; and* **Karl Lindner***, the visitor from the community where the Youngers are about to move.*

## Act 2, Scene 3

[*Walter enters with a large package. His happiness is deep in him; he cannot keep still with his newfound* exuberance. *He is singing and wiggling and snapping his fingers. He puts his package in a corner and puts a phonograph record, which he has brought in with him, on the record player. As the music, soulful and sensuous, comes up he dances over to Ruth and tries to get her to dance with him. She gives in at last to his raunchiness and in a fit of giggling allows herself to be drawn into his mood. They dip and she melts into his arms in a classic, body-melding* "slow drag"]

---

**exuberance**, energetic happiness
**slow drag**, a slow dance

152

**BENEATHA:** [*Regarding them a long time as they dance, then drawing in her breath for a deeply exaggerated comment which she does not particularly mean*] Talk about—oldddddddddd-fashionedddddddd—Negroes!

**WALTER:** [*Stopping momentarily*] What kind of Negroes? [*He says this in fun. He is not angry with her today, nor with anyone. He starts to dance with his wife again*]

**BENEATHA:** Old-fashioned.

**WALTER:** [*As he dances with Ruth*] You know, when these New Negroes have their convention—[*Pointing at his sister*]—that is going to be the chairman of the Committee on Unending Agitation. [*He goes on dancing, then stops*] Race, race, race! . . . Girl, I do believe you are the first person in the history of the entire human race to successfully brainwash yourself. [*Beneatha breaks up and he goes on dancing. He stops again, enjoying his tease*] Damn, even the N double A C P takes a holiday sometimes!

[*Beneatha and Ruth laugh. He dances with Ruth some more and starts to laugh and stops and pantomimes someone over an operating table*]
I can just see that chick someday looking down at some poor cat on an operating table and before she starts to slice him, she says . . . [*Pulling his sleeves back maliciously*] "By the way, what are your views on civil rights down there? . . ."

[*He laughs at her again and starts to dance happily. The bell sounds*]

**BENEATHA:** Sticks and stones may break my bones but . . . words will never hurt me!

---

**exaggerated**, made to seem bigger than it is
**brainwash**, convince someone of something by repeating it over and over
**breaks up**, laughs
**tease**, playful joke
**pantomimes**, acts out without talking
**operating table**, bed where a patient lies during surgery
**chick**, woman (slang)
**cat**, man (slang)
**maliciously**, as if he's going to do something bad

**BEFORE YOU GO ON**

1. What kind of mood is Walter in at the beginning of this scene? How do the stage directions show this?

2. According to Walter, what is Beneatha always thinking about?

**On Your Own**
Based on the stage directions, how do you think these characters feel about one another?

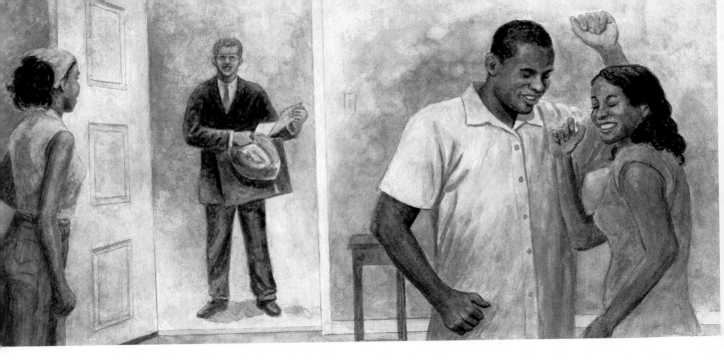

[*Beneatha goes to the door and opens it as Walter and Ruth go on with the clowning. Beneatha is somewhat surprised to see a quiet-looking middle-aged white man in a business suit holding his hat and a briefcase in his hand and consulting a small piece of paper*]

MAN:   Uh—how do you do, miss. I am looking for a Mrs.—[*He looks at the slip of paper*] Mrs. Lena Younger? [*He stops short, struck dumb at the sight of the oblivious Walter and Ruth*]

BENEATHA:   [*Smoothing her hair with slight embarrassment*] Oh—yes, that's my mother. Excuse me [*She closes the door and turns to quiet the other two*] Ruth! Brother! [*Enunciating precisely but soundlessly: "There's a white man at the door!" They stop dancing, Ruth cuts off the phonograph, Beneatha opens the door. The man casts a curious quick glance at all of them*] Uh—come in please.

MAN:   [*Coming in*] Thank you.

BENEATHA:   My mother isn't here just now. Is it business?

MAN:   Yes . . . well, of a sort.

WALTER:   [*Freely, the Man of the House*] Have a seat. I'm Mrs. Younger's son. I look after most of her business matters.

[*Ruth and Beneatha exchange amused glances*]

MAN:   [*Regarding Walter, and sitting*] Well—My name is Karl Lindner . . .

---

**clowning**, playing around
**struck dumb**, so surprised he can't talk
**oblivious**, not aware of what's happening

**WALTER:**  [*Stretching out his hand*] Walter Younger. This is my wife— [*Ruth nods politely*]—and my sister.

**LINDNER:**  How do you do.

**WALTER:**  [*Amiably, as he sits himself easily on a chair, leaning forward on his knees with interest and looking expectantly into the newcomer's face*] What can we do for you, Mr. Lindner!

**LINDNER:**  [*Some minor shuffling of the hat and briefcase on his knees*] Well—I am a representative of the Clybourne Park Improvement Association—

**WALTER:**  [*Pointing*] Why don't you sit your things on the floor?

**LINDNER:**  Oh—yes. Thank you. [*He slides the briefcase and hat under the chair*] And as I was saying—I am from the Clybourne Park Improvement Association and we have had it brought to our attention at the last meeting that you people—or at least your mother—has bought a piece of residential property at—[*He digs for the slip of paper again*]—four o six Clybourne Street . . .

**WALTER:**  That's right. Care for something to drink? Ruth, get Mr. Lindner a beer.

**LINDNER:**  [*Upset for some reason*] Oh—no, really. I mean thank you very much, but no thank you.

**RUTH:**  [*Innocently*] Some coffee?

**LINDNER:**  Thank you, nothing at all.

[*Beneatha is watching the man carefully*]

**LINDNER:**  Well, I don't know how much you folks know about our organization. [*He is a gentle man; thoughtful and somewhat labored in his manner*] It is one of these community organizations set up to look after— oh, you know, things like block upkeep and special projects and we also have what we call our New Neighbors Orientation Committee . . .

**BENEATHA:**  [*Drily*] Yes—and what do they do?

**LINDNER:**  [*Turning a little to her and then returning the main force to Walter*] Well—it's what you might call a sort of welcoming committee, I guess. I mean they, we—I'm the chairman of the committee—go around and see the new people who move into the neighborhood and sort of give them the lowdown on the way we do things out in Clybourne Park.

---

**amiably,** friendly
**a piece of residential property,** a home
**labored,** trying too hard to seem a certain way
**block upkeep,** keeping a neighborhood in good condition
**drily,** seeming serious but joking
**give them the lowdown on,** explain to them

**BEFORE YOU GO ON**

1 Who has Mr. Lindner come to see? Why?

2 What community organization does Mr. Lindner represent?

**On Your Own**
What kinds of things do community organizations usually do? Can you guess the purpose of the Clybourne Park Improvement Association?

155

**BENEATHA:** [*With appreciation of the two meanings, which escape Ruth and Walter*] Uh-huh.

**LINDNER:** And we also have the category of what the association calls— [*He looks elsewhere*]—uh—special community problems . . .

**BENEATHA:** Yes—and what are some of those?

**WALTER:** Girl, let the man talk.

**LINDNER:** [*With understated relief*] Thank you. I would sort of like to explain this thing in my own way. I mean I want to explain to you in a certain way.

**WALTER:** Go ahead.

**LINDNER:** Yes. Well. I'm going to try to get right to the point. I'm sure we'll all appreciate that in the long run.

**BENEATHA:** Yes.

**WALTER:** Be still now!

**LINDNER:** Well—

**RUTH:** [*Still innocently*] Would you like another chair—you don't look comfortable.

**LINDNER:** [*More frustrated than annoyed*] No, thank you very much. Please. Well—to get right to the point I—[*A great breath, and he is off at last*] I am sure you people must be aware of some of the incidents which have happened in various parts of the city when colored people have moved into certain areas—[*Beneatha exhales heavily and starts tossing a piece of fruit up and down in the air*] Well—because we have what I think is going to be a unique type of organization in American community life—not only do we deplore that kind of thing—but we are trying to do something about it. [*Beneatha stops tossing and turns with a new and quizzical interest to the man*] We feel— [*gaining confidence in his mission*

---

**he is off,** he begins
**exhales,** breathes out
**quizzical,** surprised
  and amused

156

*because of the interest in the faces of the people he is talking to*]—we feel that most of the trouble in this world, when you come right down to it—[*He hits his knee for emphasis*]—most of the trouble exists because people just don't sit down and talk to each other.

**Ruth:** [*Nodding as she might in church, pleased with the remark*] You can say that again, mister.

**Lindner:** [*More encouraged by such affirmation*] That we don't try hard enough in this world to understand the other fellow's problem. The other guy's point of view.

**Ruth:** Now that's right.

[*Beneatha and Walter merely watch and listen with genuine interest*]

**Lindner:** Yes—that's the way we feel out in Clybourne Park. And that's why I was elected to come here this afternoon and talk to you people. Friendly like, you know, the way people should talk to each other and see if we couldn't find some way to work this thing out. As I say, the whole business is a matter of *caring* about the other fellow. Anybody can see that you are a nice family of folks, hard-working and honest I'm sure. [*Beneatha frowns slightly, quizzically, her head tilted regarding him*] Today everybody knows what it means to be on the outside of *something*. And of course, there is always somebody who is out to take advantage of people who don't always understand.

**Walter:** What do you mean?

**Lindner:** Well—you see our community is made up of people who've worked hard as the dickens for years to build up that little community. They're not rich and fancy people; just hard-working, honest people who don't really have much but those little homes and a dream of the kind of community they want to raise their children in. Now, I don't say we are perfect and there is a lot wrong in some of the things they want. But you've got to admit that a man, right or wrong, has the right to want to have the neighborhood he lives in a certain kind of way. And at the moment the overwhelming majority of our people out there feel that people get along better, take more of a common interest in the life of the community, when they share a common background. I want you to believe me when I tell you that race prejudice simply doesn't enter into it. It is a matter of the people of Clybourne Park believing, rightly

---

**for emphasis,** showing that something is important
**nodding,** moving her head up and down to show agreement
**affirmation,** agreement
**work this thing out,** do the best for everyone
**tilted,** leaning to one side
**hard as the dickens,** very hard (slang)

✔ **LITERARY CHECK**

*What reason does Karl Lindner give for his visit to the Younger family? What is his real* **motivation?** *What does he say that reveals this?*

**BEFORE YOU GO ON**

**1** According to Mr. Lindner, what causes most of the trouble in the world? Why do you think he says this?

**2** How does Mr. Lindner describe the people of Clybourne Park?

**On Your Own**
Do you think communities should try to include people of diverse backgrounds? Why or why not?

or wrongly, as I say, that for the happiness of all concerned that our Negro families are happier when they live in their *own* communities.

**BENEATHA:** [*With a grand and bitter gesture*] This, friends, is the Welcoming Committee!

**WALTER:** [*Dumbfounded, looking at Lindner*] Is this what you came marching all the way over here to tell us?

**LINDNER:** Well, now we've been having a fine conversation. I hope you'll hear me all the way through.

**WALTER:** [*Tightly*] Go ahead, man.

**LINDNER:** You see—in the face of all the things I have said, we are prepared to make your family a very generous offer . . .

**BENEATHA:** Thirty pieces and not a coin less!

**WALTER:** Yeah?

**LINDNER:** [*Putting on his glasses and drawing a form out of the briefcase*] Our association is prepared, through the collective effort of our people, to buy the house from you at a financial gain to your family.

**RUTH:** Lord have mercy, ain't this the living gall!

**WALTER:** All right, you through?

**LINDNER:** Well, I want to give you the exact terms of the financial arrangement—

**WALTER:** We don't want to hear no exact terms of no arrangements. I want to know if you got any more to tell us 'bout getting together?

**LINDNER:** [*Taking off his glasses*] Well—I don't suppose that you feel . . .

**WALTER:** Never mind how I feel—you got any more to say 'bout how people ought to sit down and talk to each other? . . . Get out of my house, man.

[*He turns his back and walks to the door*]

**LINDNER:** [*Looking around at the hostile faces and reaching and assembling his hat and briefcase*] Well—I don't understand why you people are reacting this way. What do you think you are going to gain by moving into a neighborhood where you just aren't wanted and where some elements—well—people can get awful worked up when they feel that their whole way of life and everything they've ever worked for is threatened.

**✔ LITERARY CHECK**

*How does the* **dialogue** *reveal the Youngers' understanding of Karl Lindner's motivation? Point to specific language.*

---

**dumbfounded,** amazed
**tightly,** showing disapproval
**man,** casual word used to address someone (slang)
**ain't this the living gall!,** how rude and disrespectful!
**hostile,** angry
**assembling,** picking up
**worked up,** upset

**WALTER:** Get out.

**LINDNER:** [*At the door, holding a small card*] Well—I'm sorry it went like this.

**WALTER:** Get out.

**LINDNER:** [*Almost sadly regarding Walter*] You just can't force people to change their hearts, son.

[*He turns and puts his card on a table and exits. Walter pushes the door to with stinging hatred, and stands looking at it. Ruth just sits and Beneatha just stands. They say nothing. Mama and Travis enter*]

---

**stinging,** strong enough to be painful

## ABOUT THE **PLAYWRIGHT**

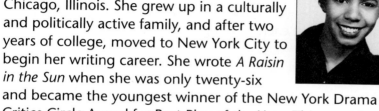

**Lorraine Hansberry** was born in 1930 in Chicago, Illinois. She grew up in a culturally and politically active family, and after two years of college, moved to New York City to begin her writing career. She wrote *A Raisin in the Sun* when she was only twenty-six and became the youngest winner of the New York Drama Critics Circle Award for Best Play of the Year. This award-winning play was eventually made into a movie. Tragically, Hansberry died in 1965, at the young age of thirty-four.

**BEFORE YOU GO ON**

**1** What does Mr. Lindner offer to do for the Younger family?

**2** How do Ruth, Beneatha, and Walter react to Mr. Lindner's offer?

**On Your Own**
How do you think each of the characters feels at the end of this scene? What do you think will happen next?

**159**

# Review and Practice

## DRAMATIC READING

 *Speaking* TIP

Speak naturally and
with feeling.

Form groups of five. Give each member a role to play in the scene
that you have just read from *A Raisin in the Sun*. One member of the
group will read the stage directions and act as the director. First, read
the scene aloud together. Next, discuss the shades of meaning in the
characters' dialogue in order to deepen your understanding of the
text. Then read the scene again, keeping in mind what you learned
from your discussion. Finally, present your dramatic reading to the
entire class. (Do not read the stage directions during this final version.)

## COMPREHENSION

Workbook
Page 76

### Right There

1. What are the family relationships of Walter, Ruth, and Beneatha?
2. According to Mr. Lindner, what does the Clybourne Park
   Improvement Association do?

### Think and Search

3. What does Lindner mean by "special community problems"? What
   does he mean by understanding "the other guy's point of view"?
4. How does Mr. Lindner explain the reason for his visit? What is
   the real reason? How do his words and behavior reveal his
   true purpose?

### Author and You

5. What can you infer about the people who belong to the
   Clybourne Park Improvement Association? What do you think
   their community probably looks like?
6. How do you think the playwright feels about each
   character? Explain.

### On Your Own

7. Imagine you are Walter, Ruth, or Beneatha. How would you have
   reacted to Mr. Lindner? What would you have done?
8. What reasons might someone have for wanting to live in a
   neighborhood where they were told they weren't wanted?

## DISCUSSION

Discuss in pairs or small groups.

»)) **Listening** TIP

Give each speaker your full attention. Make eye contact with each speaker, and don't talk to your classmates.

1. Discuss the playwright's depiction of white people in this scene. Is she realistic and fair? Does she show an understanding of the motivation of white people even though she disagrees with them? Support your opinions with lines from the script.

2. How do the stage directions help you to understand the action and the characters? Give specific examples.

3. Ruth doesn't say much in this scene, but she is a very important part of the play. What can you infer about her character from the script?

**Q** **What makes a community?** Discuss how living in a particular community affects a family's life.

## RESPONSE TO LITERATURE

Workbook
Page 76

In *A Raisin in the Sun,* a family's life is changed by the visit of a stranger. Playwrights are often inspired by imagining the dramatic effects that are caused by simple everyday events.

Work in small groups. In your notebook, make a list of strangers, such as a salesperson or a deliveryman, and the simple reasons why they might visit a family. Make another list of activities a family might be doing when they hear the knock at the door. For example, they might be watching TV or eating dinner. Combine the elements on your two lists and imagine the different scenarios that could arise. Discuss how the situations might change under different circumstances. Then write a brief scene for a play that shows what happens during one of the visits. After doing this activity, your class will have created the beginnings of several plays!

# Grammar and Writing

GRAMMAR, USAGE, AND MECHANICS

## Embedded Questions

An embedded question is a type of question that is included inside another sentence. Use an embedded question to state something you do not know or to ask a polite question.

Use *who, where, when, what, why, how,* or *how much* to introduce embedded information questions. Use *if* or *whether (or not)* to introduce embedded *yes/no* questions. Do not use *do* or *does* in an embedded question. Embedded questions usually follow regular sentence word order, not question word order.

| Information Questions |
|---|
| *Why are you reacting this way?*<br>I don't understand **why you are reacting this way**. |
| *How much do you folks know about our organization?*<br>I don't know **how much you folks know about our organization**. |
| *What do you like about the play?*<br>**What I like about the play** is the realistic portrayal of the characters. |
| **Yes/No Questions** |
| *Do you have any more to tell us?*<br>I want to know **if you have any more to tell us**. |
| *Do you want something to drink?*<br>Walter asked **whether (or not) the man wanted something to drink**. |
| *Does Lena Younger live here?* (more direct)<br>Can you tell me **if Lena Younger lives here?** (more polite) |

## Practice

**Workbook** Page 77

Copy the sentences below into your notebook. Complete each sentence with an embedded question based on the question in parentheses. With a partner, take turns reading each question and sentence aloud.

**1.** I don't know _____. (How can you explain Walter's motivation?)

**2.** He doesn't understand _____. (Why are the Youngers so angry?)

**3.** I want to know _____. (Was the play well received?)

**4.** The critic asked _____. (Are the characters believable?)

**162**

# WRITING A PERSUASIVE PARAGRAPH

## Write a Review

In a review you state an opinion of a book, play, or film and make a recommendation about it: You tell the reader either to see (or read) the work or to avoid it. To persuade the reader to follow your recommendation, your review should include supporting details that show an understanding of the work.

The writer of the review below makes a clear recommendation and includes details that support her viewpoint. Before writing, she used a graphic organizer to organize her ideas.

*Kim Kirschenbaum*

### A Raisin in the Sun

I recently read a thought-provoking scene from the play A Raisin in the Sun. What I like most about the scene is the powerful conflict it presents. The Youngers, an African-American family, are planning to move into a community whose residents are white. The Youngers know that they have the right to live wherever they want, but one family member in particular, Beneatha, worries that they will encounter racism. Ironically, the Youngers encounter prejudice first in the form of their new community's so-called "Welcoming Committee." This committee is supposed to welcome people, but instead it tries to turn the Younger family away. This scene explores important themes such as the dream of African-American equality and acceptance within the general culture. I would like to read the complete play because I want to know whether the Youngers ultimately move into their new home. I urge everyone to read this important and eloquently written play.

## Practice

**Workbook**
**Page 78**

Write a one-paragraph review of a book, play, or film. State your opinion and recommendation clearly and include supporting details that demonstrate your understanding of the work. For example, if you are reviewing a book with a specific theme, discuss how the author communicates that theme. Use a graphic organizer to organize your ideas. Use embedded questions correctly.

**Writing Checklist**

**IDEAS:**
- ☑ I stated my opinion and recommendation clearly.

**VOICE:**
- ☑ I used supporting details that show my understanding of the work.

**163**

# Prepare to Read

## What You Will Learn

**Reading**
- Vocabulary building: *Context, dictionary skills, word study*
- Reading strategy: *Distinguish fact from opinion*
- Text type: *Informational text (science)*

**Grammar, Usage, and Mechanics**
Modals: *be able to, may, might*

**Writing**
Write a formal e-mail

### THE BIG QUESTION

**What makes a community?** Have you ever watched ants at work? What were they doing? How do you think ants work together as a community? Do you think that ants and human beings have anything in common? Jot down your thoughts in a word web.

### BUILD BACKGROUND

You will read **"The Savage, Beautiful World of Army Ants,"** an interview with Mark Moffett, a scientist and award-winning photographer. He has documented ant behavior in different countries such as Ecuador and Ghana. In this interview, he talks about the behavior of army ants.

Army ants are aggressive hunters that are always on a search for insects or small animals they kill and eat. These ants work together to catch their prey. Hundreds of thousands of individual ants may cooperate in an attack. They move around a lot in order to find food. When army ants are on the move, many small animals in their path panic and try to get away. Army ants can be ferocious fighters, but they are also tireless workers in their ant colony, or community. These creatures work together to ensure the survival of all of the ants in their colony.

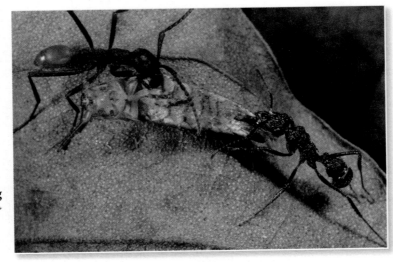

An army ant (left) stealing food from another ant ▶

164

## VOCABULARY

### Learn Key Words

Read these sentences. Use the context to figure out the meaning of the **red** words. Use a dictionary to check your answers. Then write each word and its meaning in your notebook.

1. An ant **colony** can be enormous, including hundreds of thousands of ants that live and work together.

2. A single ant is **incompetent** in its search for food. But together the ants are capable of killing animals many times larger than themselves.

3. Army ants **organize** vast groups that cooperate in the hunt for food.

4. Army ants form regular **patterns** when they search for food. They usually spread out in the shape of a fan.

5. Scientists often try to observe army ant **raids**. These sudden attacks of ants looking for food can involve 100,000 ants or more.

6. Army ants leave scents on the ground as they hunt. Other ants follow these **signals** to food that is then taken back to the colony.

**Practice**  **Workbook** Page 79

Write the sentences in your notebook. Choose a **red** word from the box above to complete each sentence. Then take turns reading the sentences aloud with a partner.

1. All army ants show the same general _____ of behavior.

2. Simple _____ by one ant can cause thousands of other ants to act.

3. Army ant _____ occur when a vast number of ants hunting for food attack a small animal or other ants.

4. Army ants are successful because they _____ huge armies in order to carry out their attacks.

5. A group of several hundred thousand ants can be a powerful army. However, one ant alone can do nothing and is _____.

6. A new queen ant will leave an overcrowded nest to start another _____.

### Key Words

colony
incompetent
organize
patterns
raids
signals

## Learn Academic Words

Study the **red** words and their meanings. You will find these words useful when talking and writing about informational texts. Write each word and its meaning in your notebook. After you read "The Savage, Beautiful World of Army Ants," try to use these words to respond to the text.

| | | |
|---|---|---|
| **attribute** = a good or useful quality that something has | ➡ | Each kind of ant has a special **attribute** that helps it play a part in the success of the colony. |
| **cooperate** = work together in order to get a job done | ➡ | Ants **cooperate** to make sure that the colony survives. |
| **emerge** = appear after being hidden | ➡ | Newly discovered facts about insects **emerge** every year. |
| **role** = the position, job, or function someone or something has in a group | ➡ | A soldier ant's **role** is to protect the colony. |

### Practice

**Workbook Page 80**

Work with a partner to answer these questions. Try to include the **red** word in your answer. Write the sentences in your notebook.

1. What would you say is your best **attribute**?

2. When have you had to **cooperate** with other people in your community?

3. What interesting things about your community or school would you like to **emerge** and become known?

4. What is your **role** in your family?

▲ Ants cooperate to form a "step."

166

## Word Study: Spelling the /ch/ Sound

Many sounds in English have more than one spelling. For example, the /ch/ sound can be spelled with *ch*, *tch*, or *t*. Look at the rules and the examples below.

| Rules | Examples |
|---|---|
| Use *ch* at the beginning of a word, after long vowels, such as /ō/ and /ē/, and after consonants. | Chadwick, cheat, chance, approach, beach, trench, belch |
| Use *tch* after short vowels, such as /a/, /e/, /i/, and /o/. Be careful! There are exceptions. | catch, match, stretch, stitch, ditch, watch |
| Use *t* before *-ure*. | capture, creature, pictures |

**Practice**

Copy the chart into your notebook. Work with a partner. Use a dictionary to find words that have the /ch/ sound and are spelled with *ch*, *tch*, and *t*. Write the words in the correct row.

▲ Chess is a challenging game.

**READING STRATEGY** | **DISTINGUISH FACT FROM OPINION**

Distinguishing facts from opinions will help you form your own ideas about what you read. A fact is something that can be proven, or is true. An opinion is what someone believes or thinks. It's not necessarily true. Texts often include both facts and opinions. To distinguish between the two, follow these steps:

- Ask yourself whether what you are reading can be proven.
- Look for phrases the author uses to give opinions, for example, *I think, I believe, I suppose, personally.*
- Make a note of the facts and opinions you are reading about. Ask yourself how you know which are facts, and which are opinions.

As you read "The Savage, Beautiful World of Army Ants," look for facts and opinions. How are they different from one another?

**Set a purpose for reading**
How is a community of ants similar to a community of humans?

# The Savage, Beautiful World of Army Ants

*An Interview with Mark Moffett by Alex Chadwick*

The ant photographs of Mark Moffett, a Harvard-trained insect scientist, are often compared to art. Moffett has a unique ability to capture the alien beauty of these deceptively simple creatures.

---

**alien**, not from Earth

Photographer Mark Moffett in the Galápagos Islands ▶

Army ants are capable of organizing vast groups. Here workers cooperate to form a living bridge. ▼

168

**Alex Chadwick:** You're going to write a series of articles for *National Geographic*—write and photograph them—about ants and the world of ants. You're beginning with army ants. Why are they called army ants?

**Mark Moffett:** Well, army ants are basically experts at the art of war. They have a couple of characteristics in that respect. Actually many, but two basic ones that are often talked about. One is their nomadism—they are migratory, moving around constantly as they run out of food. And the really critical thing is the way they actually attack, the way they work together in these massive raids that they organize.

**AC:** So you sort of imagine it like maybe trench warfare in World War I—huge numbers of guys hunkered down for a while, and then they all get up and move?

**MM:** Well, it's more like *The Lord of the Rings* movies, if you recall those. Mr. Peter Jackson did a marvelous job—maybe he was thinking of army ants, because you have these vast landscapes. You could imagine being down at the ant's level and suddenly, over the crest of the hills, would appear untold numbers of horrific warriors rushing ahead. And this is exactly what it would be like to witness the arrival of army ants if you were a frog or small creature down in the leaf litter of a rainforest. They're often called "driver ants" in parts of the world too because they

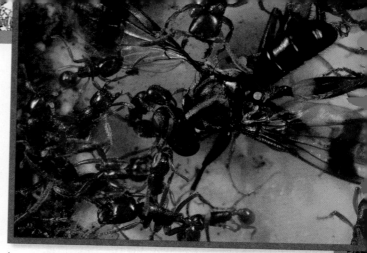

▲ The savage and alien beauty of army ants is apparent here, as they attack and kill a fly much larger than themselves.

actually drive their prey ahead of them. Because of the sheer force of numbers, the army ants are capable of killing things vastly larger than themselves.

**AC:** You write that they are blind—but in these pictures that you take of them, I see little dots on the side of their heads, which I take to be eyes.

**MM:** Well, they have no ability to form an image. Basically all they can do is tell night from day. And so the lives of army ants are lives associated with smells and vibrations. And they move amongst each other with . . . pheromones that they lay down on the ground.

**massive**, very large
**hunkered down**, staying in a safe place
**crest**, top
**leaf litter**, the leaves on the ground of a forest

**prey**, an animal being hunted
**pheromones**, chemicals that animals give off

**BEFORE YOU GO ON**

1 What two characteristics of army ants make them "experts at the art of war"?

2 How are army ants able to kill prey much larger than themselves?

**On Your Own**
Which senses are the most important to army ants?

**169**

And through very simple communication signals, they can organize vast groups—and this is a fascinating thing for scientists, and applies potentially to things like the organization of computers and other things about technology. So people are quite interested in ants, and particularly army ants.

**AC:** Because of the way they associate themselves in fairly simple patterns, but very clear patterns?

**MM:** Very clear patterns emerge from very basic behavior. A single army ant is basically incompetent—it's a soldier trained to do certain things very well. Those things seem very simple, but you add 10,000 or 100,000 or a million or more of these soldiers together, patterns emerge that are unexpected. Raids can be 15 yards across and contain 100,000 or more

---

**potentially**, possibly

ants moving in a very organized way—a swarm in front moving forward rapidly, and a fan of columns behind where the ants tear up and prepare the prey to be carried back. They're killing huge numbers of prey constantly during these attacks.

**AC:** I have to ask about one of these pictures in the [*National Geographic*] article . . . It's of one army ant confronting many other army ants. These are two different species of army ants—I didn't realize there were so many different kinds. One is very big and the others are very small. Why is that?

**MM:** There are over 130 species of army ants in the New World alone. The different species differ in many things, but one of them is polymorphism— that is, workers within one ant colony can vary quite a bit in size and shape and do different tasks or play different roles. So in that picture, you have a number of the middle-sized workers confronting a soldier of the other species. They're basically harrying it, and pulling on it as if they were trying to deal with an elephant, from this perspective. The soldiers usually function simply to deal with people like entomologists and anybody silly enough to get close to army ants. They attack vertebrates and keep the colony safe.

---

**swarm**, large group of insects
**harrying**, bullying
**entomologists**, scientists who study insects
**vertebrates**, animals with backbones

◀ Mark Moffett at work in a rainforest tree, Monteverde, Costa Rica

◀ Workers of one army ant species battle a larger soldier of another army ant species. Notice the huge jaws of the larger ant.

**AC:** You have some pictures of the jaws of these creatures that . . . look like they've got elephant tusks, for heaven's sakes.

**MM:** You can tell a lot about how cool an ant is going to be from its jaws in many cases. I'm doing this book for Harvard and I'm going around the world, often looking for the coolest jaws going. The ants with the most elaborate jaws are often the ones that do the most bizarre things. These soldiers have jaws that seem to go on forever, these vast tusks which are used to pierce vertebrates. They don't use them in killing prey—they're just after *us*. And they pierce quite deeply. They go right down, I would imagine, to the bone. . . .

---

**jaws,** biting parts of the mouth
**tusks,** a pair of very long teeth that stick out of the mouth
**elaborate,** having many parts
**bizarre,** strange
**pierce,** poke through

**AC:** When you say that you think ants are gorgeous, what is it about an ant that is gorgeous? When I look at your pictures—and they're beautiful pictures and striking images—these look like alien creatures, maybe from a bad dream.

**MM:** Well, I don't know what kind of dreams you've been having, but these are my *good* dreams right here. To me, ants are elegant creatures in what they do and how they move through the world, and the way they're built to do that. They are indeed very alien. They share a lot of the genetics with us, though, so the way they work is more like us than we might imagine sometimes.

## BEFORE YOU GO ON

**1** What patterns of behavior have scientists observed in army ant raids?

**2** What function do soldier ants serve in an ant colony?

**On Your Own**
In what ways are ants "social animals"? What other insects or animals do you know that might be considered "social"?

171

# Review and Practice

## COMPREHENSION

Workbook
Page 83

### Right There

1. Why are army ants often called driver ants?
2. About how many species of army ants are there? What are some ways that they differ?

### Think and Search

3. How do army ants use their senses? What can they see? Which other senses are important to them? Why?
4. Why does Mark Moffett say that a single ant is "incompetent"? How do you explain the success of army ant raids?

### Author and You

5. In what ways is an attack of army ants similar to an attack of human soldiers? In what ways is it different? What characteristics of army ants make them effective soldiers?
6. What is Mark Moffett's attitude toward ants?

▲ Mark Moffett on assignment in Borneo

### On Your Own

7. What kind of animal would you like to photograph and learn more about? Why?
8. Do you usually think of insects as being members of communities? Explain your answer.

## IN YOUR OWN WORDS

Work with a partner. Make a list of all the facts you can find in the interview. Then list the opinions that are expressed in the interview. Do you agree or disagree with the opinions? Can the opinions be supported by facts? Present your analysis of facts and opinions in the interview to the class.

🔊 *Speaking* TIP

Pause a few seconds after stating each fact or opinion.

## DISCUSSION

Discuss in pairs or small groups.

1. Describe an attack of army ants from the point of view of the ants. Describe the attack from the point of view of their prey. Use details from the text to create your descriptions.

2. The title of the reading calls the world of ants "savage" and "beautiful." How can something be both savage and beautiful? Explain your answer with details from the reading. Give another example from your own knowledge or experience if you can.

3. What do you find "alien" about ants? What do you find familiar? Use the text to support your answers.

**Q What makes a community?** What is the relationship of the individual ant to the colony? Could you have this attitude toward your own community? Why or why not?

**)) Listening TIP**

Listen to the verbs and adjectives each speaker uses. Try to visualize the event or thing the speaker is describing.

## READ FOR FLUENCY

When we read aloud to communicate meaning, we group words into phrases, pause or slow down to make important points, and emphasize important words. Pause for a short time when you reach a comma and for a longer time when you reach a period. Pay attention to rising and falling intonation at the end of sentences.

Work with a partner. Choose a paragraph from the reading. Discuss which words seem important for communicating meaning. Practice pronouncing difficult words. Take turns reading the paragraph aloud and give each other feedback.

## EXTENSION   Workbook Page 83

The army ant is one of the most amazing creatures on the planet. Scientists like Mark Moffett spend their lives studying them. Think about the information you learned from the interview and write three or four questions about the behavior of ants. Find the answers to your questions on the Internet and in the library and make a report to the class about what you learned.

# Grammar and Writing

### Modals: *be able to, may, might*

The expression *be able to* is similar to a modal and has the same meaning as the modals *can* or *could*. It expresses ability in the past, present, or future. Unlike real modals, *be able to* takes different forms (*am/is/are; was/were; will be*). Use *be able to* + the base form of the verb.

> **Are** ants **able to travel** very far? (present)
> The ants **were not able to find** food. (past)
> We **will be able to observe** a large colony over there. (future)

*May* and *might* have the same meaning. They express possibility in the present or future. Use *may* and *might* + the base form of the verb.

> There **may be** undiscovered species of army ants. (present)
> He **might be writing** an article about his latest research now. (present)
> Those ants **may not survive** a raid by a larger species. (future)
> We **might not find** an ant colony tomorrow. (future)

### Practice

**Workbook**
**Page 84**

Work with a partner. Copy the sentences below into your notebook. Complete each sentence using the correct form of (*not*) *be able to, may* (*not*), or *might* (*not*). More than one correct answer may be possible.

1. Ants can't really see. However, they _____ detect night from day.
2. Those two ants look exactly the same to me. I _____ tell the difference between them.
3. The scientist is going to do research in the Amazon. It's possible she _____ discover a new species of ant.
4. This colony of ants could move. We _____ see them here tomorrow.
5. There is plenty of food near the nest. The ants _____ find food.
6. Ants organize vast groups. Their behavior _____ be interesting for computer specialists to study.

174

# WRITING A PERSUASIVE PARAGRAPH

## Write a Formal E-mail

You have written persuasive paragraphs in which you support your opinion and convey your knowledge of the subject matter. In order to be effective, your persuasive writing must also reflect an awareness of your reader's interests and concerns. The points you make will be stronger if you include facts and details about things of interest to your reader. You should also think about how your reader might argue against your ideas and address those concerns in advance.

In the e-mail below, the writer argues for his choice of an author to invite to speak to the class. Notice how he used his knowledge of his classmates' interests to make his argument strong. Before writing, the writer used a graphic organizer to list his ideas.

| Class interests | Points of persuasion |
|---|---|
| | |
| | |
| | |

From: Trevor Saunders <tsaunders@coldmail.com>
Date: Tuesday, February 8, 2009 3:15 PM
To: All juniors at Central High <JRS*ALL@Central.edu>
Subject: Monthly Speaker Program

I propose that we invite Alice Walker to speak to our class. Ms. Walker has written a number of excellent books, including *The Color Purple* and *You Can't Keep a Good Woman Down*. Many of her stories deal with African-American history and civil rights. Our class has been studying these topics this year, and many students might find it interesting to explore these themes in fiction. Also, a number of students are thinking about pursuing a career in writing. Alice Walker would inspire these students to pursue their dream and keep writing. This could be a great opportunity for the young writers of our class to speak to and get advice from an accomplished author.

## Practice

Workbook Page 85

Write an e-mail in which you attempt to persuade your classmates to do something, such as invite a speaker to give a presentation at your school. State your opinion clearly and include supporting facts and details that address the interests and concerns of your audience. Before writing, list your ideas in a graphic organizer. Be sure to use the modals *be able to, may*, and *might* correctly.

**Writing Checklist**

**ORGANIZATION:**
☑ I supported my opinion with details that address the concerns of my readers.

**SENTENCE FLUENCY:**
☑ I used a variety of sentence types to make my paragraph flow.

# Prepare to Read

## What You Will Learn

**Reading**
- Vocabulary building: *Literary terms, word study*
- Reading strategy: *Identify author's purpose*
- Text type: *Literature (Personal narrative and speech)*

**Grammar, Usage, and Mechanics**
Adverb clauses of time

**Writing**
Write a letter to the editor

### THE BIG QUESTION

**What makes a community?** How does location relate to the idea of community? Can a community exist outside of a physical location? Discuss with a partner.

### BUILD BACKGROUND

In this section, you will read an excerpt and a speech from a personal narrative called ***Of Beetles and Angels.*** The writer of both is a man named Mawi Asgedom. He immigrated to the United States from a refugee camp in Sudan, in Africa, where he fled with his family from Ethiopia when he was a young boy. Refugee camps provide temporary housing for people who are forced to leave their homes and countries in time of war. In his personal narrative Asgedom writes about these experiences and the difficulties he and his family faced as immigrants.

The speech you will read is a commencement address. The word *commence* comes from Latin and means "to begin." A commencement address usually seeks to give students a sense of purpose as they begin their lives after graduation. Asgedom gave this speech to his fellow graduates at their graduation from Harvard University in 1999. In his speech Asgedom discusses the lessons his mother taught him and offers the graduates advice for the future.

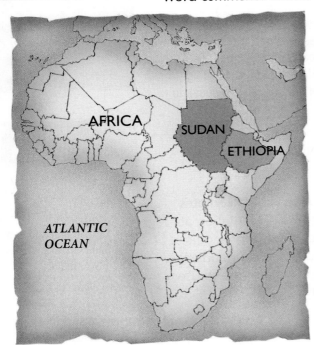

AFRICA

SUDAN

ETHIOPIA

*ATLANTIC OCEAN*

### Learn Literary Words

Mawi Asgedom uses **anecdotes** in his commencement address to show the importance of community in his life. An anecdote is a brief story, frequently taken from personal experience. Writers of persuasive speeches or essays often use anecdotes to illustrate important ideas. A story from real life can also help the reader identify with the writer. An anecdote may be funny. However, its central purpose is to illustrate and support an important point the writer wishes to make.

In an interview he once gave about his experiences, Asgedom told an anecdote about another refugee to make a point about courage and determination.

The poor woman had no shoes and had already been walking for miles. The sand and pebbles and rocks kept cutting the soles of her feet until she was bleeding and she started half-walking, half-crawling. It was a horrifying sight, impossible to forget. It was also inspiring, though, because she refused to give up. She kept going and made it to the next village.

| Literary Words |
| --- |
| anecdote |
| paradox |

A **paradox** is a statement that appears to say two conflicting things. It is a statement that seems contradictory but may actually be true. Because a paradox is surprising, it catches the reader's attention.

For example, the Greek philosopher Socrates said,

> All that I know is that I know nothing.

Socrates was one of the wisest men of all time. He used this paradox as a way of saying that despite his vast knowledge, he still felt the need to learn more.

### Practice

**Workbook Page 86**

Think about experiences you have had with people in the community you live in. Try to recall one anecdote that sums up how you feel about your community or that shows the effect your community has had on you. In small groups, take turns telling each other these anecdotes. Let your classmates respond to your anecdote to see how your story affected them.

## Learn Academic Words

Study the **red** words and their meanings. You will find these words useful when talking and writing about literature. Write each word and its meaning in your notebook. After you read the excerpt and the speech from *Of Beetles and Angels*, try to use these words to respond to the texts.

| | | |
|---|---|---|
| **benefit** = give an advantage or have a good effect | ➡ | Raising money to build a new library will **benefit** many people in the community. |
| **illustrate** = explain or make something clear by giving examples | ➡ | The author's anecdotes **illustrate** what his family life was like as he was growing up. |
| **instructions** = information or advice that tells you how to do something | ➡ | When you take a test, it is important to follow the **instructions** correctly. |
| **signify** = express a wish, feeling, or opinion by doing something | ➡ | The man frowned to **signify** his disappointment with his son's behavior. |

**Practice**  **Workbook** Page 87

Work with a partner to answer these questions. Try to include the **red** word in your answer. Write your sentences in your notebook.

1. How do good teachers **benefit** the community?
2. What examples would you give to **illustrate** what your home life was like when you were growing up?
3. When have you had to follow **instructions**?
4. What do you do to **signify** that you are unhappy about something?

Beautiful public parks benefit everyone in the community. ▼

## Word Study: Double Consonants

In English, double consonants occur in the middle and at the end of a word. Double consonants are pronounced as one sound, so spelling these words can be difficult. Look at the rules and examples below.

| Rules | Examples |
|---|---|
| Use double consonants when you add inflections (-*ed*, -*ing*, -*er*, -*est*) to one-syllable words ending with a consonant-vowel-consonant pattern. | beg, be**gg**ed<br>stop, sto**pp**ed |
| Use double consonants when you add inflections to two-syllable words when the stress is on the second syllable. | begin, begi**nn**ing<br>forget, forge**tt**ing |
| Use double consonants when a word has two or more syllables and the double consonants follow a short vowel sound, such as /e/, /i/, and /ə/. | acce**ss**, vi**ll**agers, co**mm**encement |

**Practice**  **Workbook Page 88**

Work with a partner. Copy the chart into your notebook. Find other examples of words with double consonants in *Of Beetles and Angels* and other readings in this unit. Decide which rule applies to each.

## READING STRATEGY   IDENTIFY AUTHOR'S PURPOSE

Identifying an author's purpose can help you analyze a text better. Three of the most common reasons authors write are to inform, to entertain, and to persuade. To identify an author's purpose as you read, ask yourself these questions:

- Is the text entertaining? Am I enjoying reading it?
- Am I learning new information from what I'm reading?
- Is the author trying to persuade me about something or change my opinion?
- Did the author have more than one reason for writing this? If so, what are the reasons?

As you read the excerpt from *Of Beetles and Angels*, try to identify the author's purpose or purposes for writing.

 **Workbook Page 89**

**Set a purpose for reading** What did Mawi Asgedom learn about his home and community from his mother?

*from*

# Of Beetles and Angels

## *Mawi Asgedom*

*Mawi Asgedom was only four years old when civil war broke out in Ethiopia, forcing his family to flee their home. For three years they lived in a refugee camp in Sudan. In the passage below, Asgedom explains his family's decision to immigrate to the United States in 1983.*

### *from* Chapter 1

So it was that my father started talking about a paradise called Amerikha, a distant land where everyone had a future. He told us that money grew on trees in Amerikha. Everyone was rich. Everyone had a home. Everyone had food. And everyone had peace.

Everyone lived to be one hundred years old. And had access to free education. And no wars—no wars! Yes, everyone had cars, and no one had to work more than two hours a day.

What a country! What a paradise!

But such a faraway paradise included no relatives, no friends, and no one who spoke our language. Some villagers encouraged my parents to go; others begged them to stay.

---

**paradise**, perfect place
**access to**, the ability to get

"Have you lost your mind, Haileab? Don't you care about your children? Don't you care about yourself?"

"Don't believe all the stories, Tsege. You will be lost if you go there. You and your children will be lost. You'll end up washing their mules and other livestock."

"Go, Haileab. Don't listen to them. Go, and take your family with you. Even if you remain poor, your children will become educated, and at the very least, you will have peace."

Would you go to paradise if it meant knowing no one? Would you give up everything you had ever known?

The day came when my parents had had enough. War at home. War in Sudan. My parents wanted peace, and they were ready to go. . . .

---

**livestock**, farm animals

**Refugees in Sudan** ▼

## Commencement address, delivered at Harvard in 1999

*As immigrants, Mawi Asgedom's family faced many hardships in their new home in the United States. However, Asgedom earned a full scholarship to Harvard University and gave the following commencement address when he graduated in 1999.*

When I was a child, my mother told me that I should always sleep with the covers over my head. At the time, my family was living in a Sudanese refugee camp, in Africa, and we owned nothing that we did not carry with us. On many a night, we slept out in the open, and my mother warned that if we let the covers down, snakes could slip in and slither into our mouths. We had no trouble following her advice.

Years later, in the comfort of the United States, my mother gave me another piece of advice, this one less obvious. "Always remember where you came from," she told me just before I left for Harvard. I was puzzled. The first piece of advice had been easy. Who wants a mouth full of snake! But why was it important to remember where I came from?

When I moved on to Harvard and saw new worlds open before me, I quickly forgot about trying to understand my mother. Before I knew it, I was signed up for the Tae Kwon Do Club, the Harvard African Students' Association, a Phillips Brooks House Program, the Freshman Crew Team (where I totaled a $15,000 boat against the dock), and a Freshman Bible Study (I figured I needed all the prayer that I could get). And, of course, I was taking four classes and trying to meet as many of my 1,600 classmates as wanted to meet me. As I focused my energies on myself and my immediate surroundings, remembering where I had come from seemed far less important than knowing where I was supposed to be every half hour.

During my sophomore year, however, something happened to remind me of my mother's advice. I was working as a deliveryman for the Harvard Student Agency. One day as I was waiting for my packages in the office, an elderly black woman tottered in and wearily leaned on her cane. She hoped to find someone who would type a short letter for her. Such a simple, easy thing to do. But HSA has no typing service, and the receptionist had to tell her that she had come to the wrong place. As the old woman turned to leave, frustrated and confused, one of my coworkers called her over, gently sat her down, and typed the letter. It was such a simple act. Yet never has a Harvard student seemed so great to me as in that moment of reaching out.

### BEFORE YOU GO ON

1. Did the author understand at first his mother's two pieces of advice? Explain.

2. What was life like for the author during his first year at Harvard?

**On Your Own**
What different reasons might people have for migrating from one country to another? What hardships do people face as immigrants in a new country?

---

**slither**, slide
**puzzled**, did not understand

**surroundings**, all the things around me
**tottered**, walked off-balance
**receptionist**, office worker who greets visitors

**181**

I began to reflect on what my mother might have meant. In the Sudan, we had carried with us all that we owned, but that included our devotion to one another. In that sense we carried a home, a community, a sense of mutual responsibility wherever we went. On that day in the Harvard Student Agency, my coworker carried a community with her as well: the simple community of human connection and duty.

So what have I learned from my four years at Harvard? Many facts and formulas, many new ways of thinking, a fresh understanding of the world. But what's most important to me is that after four years at Harvard I'm finally beginning to understand my mother's advice.

Remembering where you come from means holding on to the vision that you are a part of a human community that you can carry with you every day. That community has given us much. Are we not obligated to give it something back?

My mother's advice in childhood was to pull the covers over my head—that had been the easy part. But her later advice meant, I now realize, that I should know when to pull the covers down and stick my neck out. That's the hard part. Too many of us go through life with the covers over our heads. We want to reach out, but we fear to make ourselves vulnerable. And we are also busy. We have appointments to keep; we have things to do. We race through a world of demands. And then we ask ourselves almost helplessly, "What can we do as individuals?"

Some people say that a butterfly flapping its wings in Japan can cause a hurricane in Louisiana. Any one of us, however small and helpless we may feel, can spark unimagined changes. Today's small act of kindness can become tomorrow's whirlwind of human progress.

But as you all know, progress is not easy, and it will not come unsolicited. I hope that many of us will inspire positive change. There is still so much to be done both in distant lands such as the Sudan, and closer to home in our own communities. The big,

---

**devotion to**, great care for
**mutual**, shared
**duty**, what someone has to do

▲ The author's family in Sudan, from left to right: brothers Tewolde and Mehret, mother, and Mawi

---

✔ **LITERARY CHECK**

*The author realizes that his mother's advice contains a **paradox**. What is the paradox and what does it signify?*

---

**obligated**, required
**stick my neck out**, put myself in danger
**vulnerable**, easy to hurt
**unsolicited**, unless you ask for it

sweeping, revolutionary actions are always most noticeable. But quite often, it will be the small things that all of us can do that will have the most impact. Yes, we will be busy in our lives. But we can all take a little time to do a little deed of kindness. We can help write a letter; we can inscribe a little goodness on the hard surface of this world.

▲ Mawi Asgedom delivering the commencement address at Harvard in 1999

In a few minutes we shall be welcomed to the ranks of educated men and women. As we start the journey to wherever our dreams may lead, we must remember where we have come from. We must recall our membership in the human community that has nourished us; we must accept the responsibility to keep that community alive. Improving the quality of life for the entire human community is the single greatest task that faces our generation and generations to come. Of course, no worthy endeavor is without risks and pitfalls—

without snakes, if you will—but I know that you, my classmates, are ready to peek out, to see beyond yourselves, and cast off the covers. You are ready to face the snakes and drive them away. You are ready to change the world. Thank you! Good luck! And congratulations!

---

**revolutionary**, completely new and different
**impact**, effect
**inscribe**, write on something
**pitfalls**, dangers

**cast off**, throw off

---

## ABOUT THE **AUTHOR**

**Mawi Asgedom** graduated with honors from Harvard University. Afterwards, he continued to share his story with students, refugees, and community groups. In 2001, he published his autobiography, *Of Beetles and Angels*. Today, Asgedom spends his time working with teenagers and giving motivational speeches.

### BEFORE YOU GO ON

**1** What does the author feel is the most important thing he learned from his four years at Harvard?

**2** What does the author feel is the most important task facing him and his fellow graduates?

**On Your Own**
How has your own community supported you? Is there any way to give something back?

**183**

# Review and Practice

## DRAMATIC READING

In small groups of five or six, take turns reading aloud the paragraphs of Mawi Asgedom's commencement address in *Of Beetles and Angels*. Discuss the speech and decide which part of it was most effective. Assign each member of your group lines to read from that section. Then present that section of the speech to the class as a group reading.

🔊 *Speaking* TIP

Rehearse your delivery, so that you know where to pause and when to raise or lower your voice.

## COMPREHENSION

Workbook
Page 90

### Right There

1. What did the author's father say about money in America?
2. Why did the author forget about trying to understand his mother's advice when he got to Harvard?

### Think and Search

3. What different views about America did the author's father and the other villagers express? Which views do you think turned out to be accurate?
4. What two pieces of advice did the author's mother give him? What deeper understanding of the advice did the author finally gain?

### Author and You

5. What is the author's purpose in the commencement speech? Find parts of the text to support your answer.
6. What does the author feel about the importance of community? Support your answer.

### On Your Own

7. How have your own experiences shaped your feelings about the role of community in our lives? Give an example.
8. In his speech the author discusses what he considers "the single greatest task that faces our generation." What do you think is the greatest task that faces your generation?

## DISCUSSION

Discuss in pairs or small groups.

1. In your opinion, why did the anecdote about the student helping the old woman affect the author so much? How did it affect you?

2. In the author's opinion, what things prevent people from reaching out and helping others? What other reasons might explain why people sometimes fail to help each other?

**Q** **What makes a community?** Do you think that small acts of kindness can change communities? Explain your answer.

**Listening TIP**

Listen for supporting details. Ask yourself, "Did the speaker explain why these ideas are important?

## RESPONSE TO LITERATURE

Workbook Page 90

The movie *Pay It Forward* tells the story of a boy who comes up with an idea to make the world a better place: If someone does you a favor, don't pay it (the favor) *back* to that person, rather pay it *forward* by doing a good deed for three other people. Think about your community, home, neighborhood, and school. What problems do you notice? What simple things could one person do to improve the situation? Write a short talk to persuade your classmates to do some small specific thing that will improve your community.

◀ Two young women help another woman plant flowers: a small act of kindness.

185

# Grammar and Writing

## Adverb Clauses of Time

Adverb clauses of time tell when something happened. They are introduced by *when, after, before, until,* and *as soon as.* Remember: A clause has a subject and a verb but may not be a complete thought. Use a comma after an adverb clause when it appears before the main clause of the sentence.

---

**When I was a child,** my mother told me I should always sleep with the covers over my head.

**After four years at Harvard,** I'm finally beginning to understand my mother's advice.

"Always remember where you came from," she told me **before I left for Harvard**.

He had stopped thinking about his mother's advice **until he witnessed an incident during his sophomore year**.

**As soon as he moved to Harvard,** new worlds opened up for him.

---

Sentences with adverb clauses that are introduced by *while* or *as* describe two actions that occur at the same time.

---

He was working at HSA **while he was going to school**.

**As we start the journey to wherever our dreams may lead,** we must remember where we have come from.

---

## Practice

**Workbook**
Page 91

Choose the best word or phrase to complete each sentence. Compare your choices with a partner's. Then write the sentences in your notebook.

1. People were kind to me (when / while) I was finishing my studies.

2. (Before / While) I went to **college,** I didn't appreciate my community.

3. I don't want to wait (after / until) I graduate to get involved with my community.

4. (When / While) I arrived, I encountered many difficulties.

5. We started on the project (as soon as / before) we moved there.

6. (After / As) we begin our new lives as college graduates, we must remember our responsibility to the human community.

# WRITING A PERSUASIVE PARAGRAPH

## Write a Letter to the Editor

When the topic of a persuasive paragraph is very personal and important to you, you may attempt to appeal to your readers' emotions by including strong statements or adjectives. Like all persuasive writing, a paragraph that makes an emotional appeal should also include a statement of opinion and supporting facts, examples, and other details.

People who write letters to newspapers often have strong feelings about a subject. As a result, letters to the editor of a newspaper often include an emotional appeal. Notice the emotional appeal in the letter below. Before writing, the writer used a T-chart to list her ideas.

| Fact | Emotional appeal |
|------|------------------|
|      |                  |

January 7, 2009

To the editor,

I strongly believe that the voting age should be lowered to 16. Today, U.S. citizens who are 16 and 17 cannot voice their opinion on issues that dramatically affect their daily lives. This situation is shameful! After all, many 16- and 17-year-olds have a driver's license and pay for car insurance and gas. Many are employed part-time and pay taxes. But do these young people have the power to elect the representatives who pass laws about driving, working conditions, and the minimum wage? No! Teenagers under 18 have no representation in government. When an individual turns 18, the situation suddenly changes. Why not give voting rights to young Americans at an earlier age? Think about everything they contribute to our society. Their voices deserve to be heard!

Yours truly,
Olivia Kefauver, 16
Tucson, Arizona

BALLOTS

## Practice

Workbook
Page 92

Write a letter to the editor of your school or community newspaper about a topic that is important to you. In addition to a clearly stated opinion and supporting details, include an appeal to the emotions of your readers. Before you write, list your ideas in a T-chart. Be sure to use adverb clauses of time correctly.

### Writing Checklist

**VOICE:**
- ☑ I expressed strong feelings about the topic using an engaging voice.

**SENTENCE FLOW:**
- ☑ I used adverb clauses of time correctly.

187

# Link the Readings

## Critical Thinking

Look back at the readings in this unit. Think about what they have in common. They all tell about community. Yet they do not all have the same purpose. The purpose of one reading might be to inform, while the purpose of another might be to entertain or persuade. In addition, the content of each reading relates to community differently. Now copy the chart below into your notebook and complete it.

| Title of Reading | Purpose | Big Question Link |
|---|---|---|
| "The Great Migration" | | |
| From *A Raisin in the Sun* | *to entertain* | |
| "The Savage, Beautiful World of Army Ants" | | |
| From *Of Beetles and Angels* | | *discusses how people can help others in their community* |

## Discussion

Discuss in pairs or small groups.

1. How does the information you learned about army ants expand your understanding of community? How do the activities of the army ants relate to Mawi Asgedom's views on community?

2. How do "The Great Migration" and the excerpt from *A Raisin in the Sun* relate to the theme of community?

**Q** **What makes a community?** What was your favorite text in this unit? Why? Which text made you think the most? From which text did you learn the most about communities?

## Fluency Check

Work with a partner. Choose a paragraph from one of the readings. Take turns reading it for one minute. Count the total number of words you read. Practice saying the words you had trouble reading. Take turns reading the paragraph three more times. Did you read more words each time? Copy the chart below into your notebook and record your speeds.

| | 1st Speed | 2nd Speed | 3rd Speed | 4th Speed |
|---|---|---|---|---|
| Words Per Minute | | | | |

# Projects

Work in pairs or small groups. Choose one of these projects.

**1** Take a walk through your community. Take photographs or make drawings of some of the problems you see. Think about possible solutions to these problems. Make a collage of your photos or drawings and present it to the class.

**2** Reread the excerpt from *A Raisin in the Sun*. Then turn one of the anecdotes in Mawi Asgedom's personal narrative or speech into a short play. Make up dialogue to go with the events he illustrates in his speech. Perform the play for the class.

**3** Research another species besides ants that regularly migrates from one part of the world to another, like whales, birds, or monarch butterflies. Report to the class on the reasons for the migration, the routes taken, and the distances traveled.

**4** Find out about organizations in your area that benefit the community. Pick one and prepare a brief presentation about it. Tell your class what this organization does and how students can help. Include photos or other visuals found in the organization's literature or on its website.

# Further Reading

To find out more about the theme of this unit, choose from these reading suggestions.

**World Folktales**
This Penguin Reader® collection includes folktales from China, Africa, India, South America, and Europe.

**An Hour Before Daylight: Memories of a Rural Boyhood,**
Jimmy Carter
Former President Carter recalls his childhood in rural 1930s Georgia, describing the life growing up in a close-knit community.

**Chasing Monarchs: Migrating with the Butterflies of Passage,**
Robert Michael Pyle
Follow thousands of monarch butterflies as they migrate from their breeding ground in British Columbia to Mexico.

# Put It All Together

## LISTENING & SPEAKING WORKSHOP

### Speech

A good speech states a clear point of view supported by facts, examples, statistics, or personal experiences. You will give a speech that presents your point of view about an issue and urges listeners to accept your opinion or take the action you suggest.

**1 THINK ABOUT IT** Make a list of school and community problems that are important to you. Pick topics you have strong opinions about. Think about each one, and ask: "Does my audience know and care about this topic? Can I find enough facts and examples about this topic to support my point of view?" Answer these questions and choose the best topic for your speech.

**2 GATHER AND ORGANIZE INFORMATION** Find as much information as you can about your topic. Think about the needs and concerns, knowledge level, and experience of your audience. A speech has to be interesting if you want people to listen. Appropriate use of humor, anecdotes, and surprise can help. For example, you might grab the audience's attention by saying: "Our school's hallways are *boring*!" Then state your main idea: "We can add interest and beauty to our school days by creating a student art gallery on those blank, boring walls."

**Research** Use the library or Internet to collect facts about your topic. Look for interesting examples that demonstrate your point of view. Take careful notes. Write each fact or example on a separate note card.

**Order Your Notes** Arrange your note cards in a logical way and prepare an outline for your speech. Begin with an interesting example or anecdote to draw listeners in. Then clearly state your topic and point of view. Next, give good reasons for your opinion, supporting each one with facts and examples. End with a conclusion that briefly restates your thinking in a fresh, memorable way.

**Prepare a Script** Follow your outline to write a script for your speech. A strong, simple structure will help the audience understand your speech.

**Use Visuals** Visuals help keep your audience's interest. They can also demonstrate topics that are difficult to explain. Choose your visuals carefully.

**3** **PRACTICE AND PRESENT** Read your script aloud several times, until you know it well. Highlight or underline important words and phrases. Mark the beginning of each section with a different color or symbol. Practice delivering your speech without reading it, just glancing at the script from time to time. Use the marks in your script if you need to refresh your memory about key points. Keep practicing. The better you know your material, the more confident you will be.

**Deliver Your Speech** A speech is one side of a discussion with your listeners. Connect with them. Don't bury your face in your script. Take your time. Think about the points you want to make. If you get lost, don't worry. Take a moment, find your place in the script, and go on.

**4** **EVALUATE THE PRESENTATION**
You will improve your skills as a speaker and a listener by evaluating each presentation you give and hear. Use this checklist to help you judge your speech and the speeches of your classmates.

- ☑ Could you follow the logic of the speech?
- ☑ Did the speech have enough evidence to persuade you?
- ☑ Did the speech hold your attention? Why or why not?
- ☑ Could you hear and understand the speaker easily?
- ☑ What suggestions do you have for improving the speech?

### Speaking TIPS

Many people mumble the ends of their sentences, so half their words can't be heard. Work on delivering the ends of your sentences with energy and full volume.

Connect with your audience by making eye contact with as many people as possible.

### Listening TIP

Listen to the speaker's reasons for his or her opinion. Then think about the opposite point of view. What reasons could support that opinion? Which point of view is best supported by the evidence? Draw your own conclusions.

# WRITING WORKSHOP
## Persuasive Brochure

In persuasive writing, the writer tries to convince the reader to adopt a specific opinion or to take a specific action. One way to persuade others is to write a brochure. A brochure is a pamphlet that gives information in order to convince readers to do or to try something. For example, a brochure might try to persuade someone to move to a particular town, purchase a product, join an activity, or try out a service. A strong persuasive brochure begins with a paragraph that clearly states the writer's opinion. The brochure also gives reasons, facts, and examples that support the writer's position. A concluding paragraph restates the writer's opinion in a lively way.

Your assignment for this workshop is to write a five-paragraph brochure intended to persuade readers to do or to try something.

**1** **PREWRITE** Brainstorm a list of possible topics for your brochure. Choose a topic that you can write about with enthusiasm and knowledge. For example, you might write a brochure persuading others to move to your town, or to join an activity that you enjoy at school, such as a drama club or sports team.

**List and Organize Ideas and Details** After choosing a topic, think about how to persuade readers to act on your opinion. Create a flow chart stating your opinion and the most important supporting facts, details, and examples. A student named Emily decided to write a brochure persuading others to move to her community. Here is the flowchart she prepared:

> Whitemarsh Township— a great place to live! → A lot to offer families with kids! →

> good schools
> summer camps
> museums
> access to city
> beautiful nature trails

**2** **DRAFT** Use the model on page 195 and your flowchart to help you write a first draft. Remember to state your opinion clearly in your first paragraph and to end your brochure by restating your position in an interesting new way.

**3** **REVISE** Read over your draft. As you do so, ask yourself the questions in the writing checklist. Use the questions to help you revise your essay.

### SIX TRAITS OF WRITING CHECKLIST

☑ **IDEAS:** Is my opinion clear?

☑ **ORGANIZATION:** Are my reasons, facts, and examples presented in an order that makes sense?

☑ **VOICE:** Does my writing show my enthusiasm and knowledge?

☑ **WORD CHOICE:** Do I include strong persuasive words?

☑ **SENTENCE FLUENCY:** Do my sentences flow smoothly?

☑ **CONVENTIONS:** Does my writing follow the rules of grammar, usage, and mechanics?

Here are the changes Emily plans to make when she revises her first draft:

A Fabulous Community for Families

What do most people look for when they move to a new city?

Good schools, ~~various~~ a variety of leisure activities, and easy acces to both urban

areas and natural beauty are some things. that top the list for many people If these appeal to you,

Whitemarsh Township, Pennsylvania would be a great place for

you to live.

For families with children, Whitemarsh Township has much to offer.

The quality of education in this welcoming community is excellent.

There are many elementary, middle, and high schools in Whitemarsh

Township with dedicated teachers, handsome buildings, and

modern technology.

¶ ‸In addition to schools, There are nearby summer camps, both day and overnight, that are fun for kids and convenient for parents. Families can also take advantage of the many sports leagues in the area. Basketball, soccer, and softball are a few of the most active.

It's easy to get to Philadelphia to visit museums, such as the Philadelphia Museum of Art, that show the work of world-famous ~~artests~~ artists ‸ Because both the Pennsylvania Turnpike and the Route 309 Expressway go through the township, urban areas are highly accesible. However, ‸ For lovers of natural beauty, Whitemarsh Township has spacious, beautiful parks, including Miles Park and Fort Washington State Park. There are nature trails where you can run, walk the dog, or ride your bike. All of these features make Whitemarsh Township a wonderful place for families to enjoy and experience.

Next time you're looking for a place to live, think about the schools, extracurricular activities, museums, and nature trails in Whitemarsh Township, Pennsylvania. After all, what more could you want in a hometown? ‸ You need to live in Whitemarsh Township! When you make the move, ‸ it will be a decision you won't regret.

## 4 EDIT AND PROOFREAD

**Workbook**
Page 93

Copy your revised draft onto a clean sheet of paper. Read it again. Correct any errors in grammar, word usage, mechanics, and spelling. Here are the additional changes Emily plans to make when she prepares her final draft.

194

Emily Weiss

## A Fabulous Community for Families

What do most people look for when they move to a new city? Good schools, a variety of leisure activities, and easy acces$^s$ to both urban areas and natural beauty are some things that top the list for many people. If these appeal to you, Whitemarsh Township, Pennsylvania would be a great place for you to live.

For families with children, Whitemarsh Township has much to offer. The quality of education in this welcoming community is excellent. There are many elementary, middle, and high schools in Whitemarsh Township with dedicated teachers, handsome buildings, and modern technology.

In addition to schools, there are nearby summer camps, both day and overnight, that are fun for kids and convenient for parents. Families can also take advantage of the many sports leagues in the area. Basketball, soccer, and softball are a few of the most active.

Because both the Pennsylvania Turnpike and the Route 309 Expressway go through the township, urban areas are highly accesible. It's easy to get to Philadelphia to visit museums, such as the Philadelphia Museum of Art, that show the work of world-famous artists However, for lovers of natural beauty, Whitemarsh Township has spacious, beautiful parks, including Miles Park and Fort Washington State Park. There are nature trails where you can run, walk the dog, or ride your bike. All of these features make Whitemarsh Township a wonderful place for families to enjoy and experience.

Next time you're looking for a place to live, think about the schools, extracurricular activities, museums, and nature trails in Whitemarsh Township, Pennsylvania. After all, what more could you want in a hometown? You need to live in Whitemarsh Township! When you make the move, it will be a decision you won't regret.

**5 PUBLISH** Prepare your final draft. Share your brochure with your teacher and classmates. If possible, illustrate your brochure with photos or drawings.

Workbook
Page 94

# Things Communities Share

*P*eople tend to move into communities where people of the same race or ethnicity live. In big cities like Los Angeles or New York, many neighborhoods consist almost entirely of people of one particular race or ethnicity. In the nineteenth century, for example, many Chinese people came to California and settled in San Francisco, which still has a large Chinatown. These communities offer a safety net for newcomers. Relatives and neighbors can help newcomers find jobs and housing. Although different in many ways, these separate groups have a lot in common: They are all communities, and they help people survive and flourish within the community.

◄ Allan Rohan Crite, *School's Out*, 1936, oil, 30¼ x 36⅛ in., Smithsonian American Art Museum

## Allan Rohan Crite, *School's Out* (1936)

Allan Rohan Crite captured the common ground found in a community in his painting *School's Out*. In the 1930s and 1940s, he developed a series of "neighborhood paintings," as he called them, that illustrated daily life in an average African-American community. The various paintings in the series are set in Boston's South End and in nearby Roxbury, Massachusetts.

Crite said that his "intention was to show black people and to present them in an ordinary light, persons enjoying the usual pleasures of life with its mixtures of both sorrow and joy." He described himself as an "artist-reporter" who recorded what he saw. He felt a deep need to portray a realistic view of the everyday life of African Americans, because most white Americans knew little about African Americans in their society. What little they did know came from music, art, and news stories from Harlem in New York, an urban scene that Crite believed did not accurately reflect the life of the average African-American person in the United States. "Everything you see is tied into the one thing: community," Crite said.

### Detail: The Children

The school, a vital center of the neighborhood, is on the left behind a cast iron fence. The girls radiate an end-of-school-day joy that all children everywhere can relate to. Some of them stop to chat; others run, wave, argue, hold hands, or try to get their mother's attention. The universal feelings of joy, freedom, and release from tension could be taking place in any schoolyard anywhere, which is precisely Crite's point.

### Detail: The Mothers

This detail from the painting shows two mothers stopping to talk on the far sidewalk. The strong, detailed lines of the row houses serve as a backdrop.

### Apply What You Learned

**1** What conclusions can you draw about the community Allan Rohan Crite has painted? Support your conclusions with details from the painting.

**2** Why do you think Crite chose a schoolyard as his subject matter?

**Big Question**

What other subject could Crite have painted to show how and what communities share? Explain your answer.

**Workbook**
**Pages 95–96**

197

# THE BIG QUESTION

# How does the sea affect our lives?

**T**his unit is about the sea. You will read literature and informational texts that explore different aspects of the world's oceans. Reading, writing, and talking about this topic will give you practice using academic language and help you become a better student.

## READING 1: Myth
- "Poogweese," Native American myth, retold by Chief Lelooska

## READING 2: Science Article
- "Tsunamis" by Niki Walker

## READING 3: Novel Excerpt
- From *20,000 Leagues Under the Sea* by Jules Verne

## READING 4: Science Article
- "Life in the Oceans" by Miranda Macquitty

### Listening and Speaking

At the end of this unit, you will choose an aspect of the sea to investigate and you will present a **TV documentary** about it.

### Writing

In this unit you will practice **expository writing.** This type of writing explains or gives factual information about a topic. After each reading you will learn a skill to help you write an expository paragraph. At the end of the unit, you will write an expository essay.

### QuickWrite

Close your eyes and think of the sea. What images and thoughts come to mind? In what ways does the sea affect human life? Use a word web to list as many ideas as you can. Write for five minutes. Then share your ideas with a partner.

Visit *LongmanKeystone.com*

199

# Prepare to Read

**What You Will Learn**

**Reading**
- Vocabulary building: *Literary terms, context, word study, dictionary skills*
- Reading strategy: *Analyze cultural context*
- Text type: *Literature (myth)*

**Grammar, Usage, and Mechanics**
Participial adjectives

**Writing**
Write a news article

### THE BIG QUESTION

**How does the sea affect our lives?** Many cultures have myths about the sea. Why do you think this is so? Have you ever spent any time by the sea? Do you think it's mysterious in any way? Discuss with a partner.

### BUILD BACKGROUND

In this section you will read **"Poogweese,"** a retelling of a myth. The word *myth* comes from an ancient Greek word that means "story or legend." Myths are fictional stories that people told before they had scientific knowledge to explain the natural world.

The myth you will read is from the Kwakiutl people, a Native American tribe that lives in the Pacific Northwest region of North America. The Kwakiutl live between the forest and the sea, so hunting and fishing have always been important livelihoods for them. The myth tells of a time when the people needed to catch lots of fish from the sea to survive.

Poogweese is a sea spirit that the fishermen encounter one day at sea. The myth explains how the bad luck of these struggling fishermen changes and why they are suddenly able to catch many fish.

▲ A Native American dancer wearing a Poogweese mask and seagull

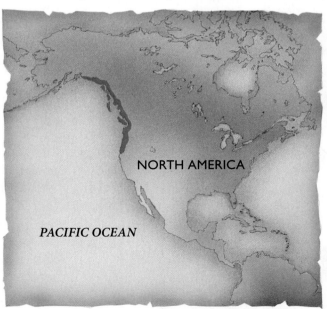

NORTH AMERICA

PACIFIC OCEAN

◄ Areas where Native Americans of the Pacific Northwest lived

## Learn Literary Words

The word **archetype** comes from a Greek word that means "original type." An archetype is an original model or pattern from which other things of the same type are copied. It is also a type of character, image, or situation that appears in literature from around the world and throughout history.

If the same kind of character appears in many different stories, that character may be based on an archetype. For example, the two main characters in Shakespeare's *Romeo and Juliet* are archetypes of tragic young lovers. This means that many other characters in literature have been modeled after them and so share many of their characteristics. Hercules, a hero from Greek myth, is the archetype of characters with superhuman strength. Many modern heroes of comic books and movies are based on the Hercules archetype.

A common archetype in many myths is a god or other character who has complete power over a vast realm, such as the sky, the sea, or the underworld. The Greek god Poseidon, who has absolute power over the sea, fits that archetype.

You have learned that **setting** is the time and place of the action in a story. In addition to a specific place or geographical location, setting may include the social, economic, or cultural situation. For example, *Girl with a Pearl Earring* on page 34 takes place in seventeenth-century Holland. The wealth of Holland helped to bring about a renewed interest in art. These economic and cultural conditions help to explain why so many people wanted their portraits painted and why artists like Vermeer were so successful.

▲ The Greek god Poseidon, who rules the sea, fits an archetype found in many myths.

## Practice  Workbook Page 97

1. Work with a partner. Think of an example of a modern character based on one of the archetypes mentioned above or another archetype with which you are familiar, such as Cinderella. Explain how your character fits the pattern.

2. Work with a partner. Choose one story or movie in which the social, economic, or cultural setting is important. Explain how the setting affects the action of the story.

## Learn Academic Words

Study the **red** words and their meanings. You will find these words useful when talking and writing about literature. Write each word and its meaning in your notebook. After you read "Poogweese," try to use these words to respond to the text.

**Academic Words**

consequence
domain
encounter
insufficient
reveal

| | | |
|---|---|---|
| **consequence** = something that happens as a result of a particular action | ➡ | One **consequence** of the shark attack was that all of the nearby beaches were closed. |
| **domain** = a particular place that is controlled by one person | ➡ | The king claimed he ruled the sea as a part of his **domain**. |
| **encounter** = unexpected meeting | ➡ | An **encounter** with a huge school of fish helped the fishermen catch enough fish for the village. |
| **insufficient** = not enough | ➡ | An **insufficient** catch of fish meant that some people might starve. |
| **reveal** = make something known that was previously secret | ➡ | He would not **reveal** where he came from, and so it remained a mystery. |

## Practice

**Workbook** Page 98

Work with a partner to answer these questions. Try to include the **red** word in your answer. Write the sentences in your notebook.

1. What is a **consequence** of not studying for an important test?

2. What is Poseidon's **domain**?

3. What is the strangest **encounter** you've ever had?

4. What would you do if you had **insufficient** information to figure out a problem?

5. When have you had to **reveal** something about yourself to strangers?

▲ An encounter with an octopus

## Word Study: Prefixes

A prefix is a group of letters added to the beginning of a word to change its meaning. Most prefixes have more than one meaning. Study the prefixes and the new words they form in the chart below. Often you will use context to figure out the meaning of a word.

| Prefix | (Meaning) | + Base Word | = New Word |
|--------|-----------|-------------|------------|
| super- | (above) | natural | supernatural |
| super- | (greater) | market | supermarket |
| dis- | (fail) | appear | disappear |
| dis- | (deprive of) | advantage | disadvantage |
| under- | (in, below) | sea | undersea |
| under- | (not enough) | educated | undereducated |
| re- | (again) | mind (pay attention) | remind |
| re- | (back) | act | react |

## Practice  Workbook Page 99

Work with a partner. Copy the chart above into your notebook. Use the prefix and the base word to try to guess the meaning of each new word. Check your work in a dictionary. Then write a sentence with each new word.

### READING STRATEGY | ANALYZE CULTURAL CONTEXT

Analyzing the cultural context of a story helps you understand it better. Cultural context includes the beliefs, art, and ideas of a particular people. It also includes the social and historical conditions in which they live. To analyze cultural context, follow these steps:

- Think about the characters' native culture. In what ways is it important to the story?

- How do the characters live? What are their houses, food, and clothing like? What do they believe?

- Think about what you already know about Native-American cultures. How does this help you understand the story?

As you read "Poogweese," try to think about the characters and events in their own cultural context.

 Workbook Page 100

**Set a purpose for reading** What kinds of experiences and beliefs do you think led people to create this myth of the sea?

# Poogweese

*A Native American myth, retold by Chief Lelooska*

Our ancestors believed there were realms in this world where supernatural beings lived. In the sky lived a great clan of thunderbirds, the birds of the winter ceremonial. In another realm far beneath the Earth, where everything was backwards, dwelled the ghosts. But the richest realm of all was beneath the sea. This is the story of how our people learned of the undersea world.

The people of the village were fearful. Fishing had been poor for a long time, and their stores of dried fish were almost gone. Winter would soon be upon them, and they might starve. Every day the village fishermen went out to sea and let down their nets. They fished and fished but caught nothing. The sea seemed without life.

One day the fishermen took their canoes off Bird Island. They let their nets sink deeper and deeper into the cold waters. Then they waited. After awhile there was a strong tugging at the lines. The fishermen knew something very large must be in the net.

> ✔ **LITERARY CHECK**
>
> *Describe the setting at the beginning of "Poogweese." How do the conditions change at the end? How is the setting central to the meaning of this myth?*

---

**realms**, lands or countries
**dwelled**, lived
**stores**, supplies
**starve**, die from not eating
**tugging at**, pulling on

It took all hands to pull the heavy net up and heave it into the canoe. Tangled in the net was a strange being like nothing the fishermen had ever seen before! It was clothed in seaweed and appeared to be something like a man. It had huge front teeth and long scraggly hair.

The creature lay there making a squeaking noise. Finally it spoke. "You do not know me, so I will tell you. I am Poogweese, the Merman. I am part man and part fish. I dwell in the world beneath the sea. I am chief messenger of Goomaquay, the lord who controls all the wealth of the ocean. I am his trusted messenger. With the help of the gulls and the loons and the sawbilled ducks, I carry the will of Goomaquay throughout his undersea domain."

The astonished fishermen listened and stared at the strange creature. They did not know what to do. They were afraid if they let Poogweese go he would tell Goomaquay about his captors. This mighty ruler of the sea might get angry and send many great storms. The fishermen would never have any luck fishing again.

---

**tangled in**, unable to get out of
**scraggly**, unwashed and uncombed
**squeaking**, high-pitched
**gulls; loons; sawbilled ducks**, birds that live on or near water
**stared**, looked at for a long time
**captors**, the men who had caught him

**BEFORE YOU GO ON**

1 Why were the people of the village fearful?

2 Who does Poogweese serve? What does he do?

**On Your Own**
What contemporary stories do you know with supernatural beings? What purpose do these stories serve?

**205**

"I know what you are thinking," said Poogweese. "You are thinking that if you let me go I will tell Lord Goomaquay. I can understand how you might well be afraid of me, and you certainly should be afraid of my master, but let us strike a bargain."

Then Poogweese explained that if the fishermen would release him to his ocean home he would talk to his master about the fishermen's kindness and about the poor fishing they had endured.

"When Lord Goomaquay realizes that you have freed me and that you know of his existence perhaps life will be better for you," said Poogweese. "And for my thanks I will give you my mask and my song as a gift."

The fishermen looked at one another. They knew they had no choice but to send this powerful creature back to the deep. So they accepted his offer. They could only hope their goodwill would please Lord Goomaquay and that he would improve the fishing and protect them from the great storms.

So the fishermen freed Poogweese from the net. He flopped over the side of the canoe and disappeared into the water. The fishermen looked at one another. One of them said, "He didn't leave us his mask or his song. Maybe he tricked us! Maybe he lied!" Another fisherman cried, "No, the supernatural ones do not lie."

✔ **LITERARY CHECK**
*Which of the characters in this myth is based on an archetype? Explain.*

---

**strike a bargain**, make a deal
**release**, let go
**endured**, experienced
**existence**, being alive
**flopped**, moved without using his hands or feet

Suddenly a shower of bubbles rose from the sea, and the mask of Poogweese floated to the surface. The fishermen pulled the mask from the water and held it. Then they heard a faint sound. It was weak at first, but they listened and listened, and soon the song of Poogweese filled their ears.

The song described the great house made of copper on the floor of the sea just off Bird Island. This was the home of Lord Goomaquay and all of his retinue of sea monsters and great creatures from the depths.

The fishermen were pleased. The weather was fair and the tides were right. They cast out their nets and caught many fish. Then the fishermen carefully wrapped the mask and took it home. They kept it hidden until the next great potlatch of their people. There they showed the mask proudly and described how it had come to them as a gift from Poogweese and Goomaquay, the Lord of the Undersea.

For all time the people would cherish the mask of Poogweese, for it reminded them of their ancestors' adventure in the beginning of time when men and supernatural spirits talked together. It reminded them why their fishermen were successful and safe upon the sea and why their village was wealthy. Through this fateful encounter with Poogweese, the Merman, the people would feel kin to all the beings within the sea forever.

---

**retinue**, those who always go with him
**cast out**, threw into the water
**potlatch**, an important ceremony among many Native American tribes
**cherish**, hold dear
**kin to**, part of the same family as

## ABOUT THE **AUTHOR**

**Chief Lelooska** was a storyteller, wood sculptor, painter, and teacher who dedicated his life to preserving the Native American culture of the Pacific Northwest Coast. His book, *Echoes of the Elders*, is a collection of oral traditions that will be passed down to future generations.

Lelooska also founded a museum and art gallery that feature artifacts and art of the Native Americans of the Northwest Coast. Through his efforts educating thousands of people, Chief Lelooska has guaranteed the survival of his people's traditions, history, and culture.

## BEFORE YOU GO ON

1. What did the fishermen see and hear after they freed Poogweese?

2. Why do the people in the village cherish the mask of Poogweese?

 **On Your Own**
What does this myth tell us about the relationship of the Kwakiutl people to the sea?

207

## READER'S THEATER

**Speaking TIP**

Exaggerate reactions with dramatic facial expressions.

Act out this modern retelling of the myth of Poogweese.

[*Three kids are in a boat. They are fishing. They aren't having any luck.*]

**Boy # 1:** [*sighs sadly*] No fish today.

**Girl:** No problem. We'll go out to eat.

**Boy # 1:** I wanted fish. Real fish.

**Boy # 2:** Uh . . . I think we've got something here. [*gives the line a tug*] Uh-oh. It's big.

**Boy # 1:** Well, pull it up! [*Poogweese flops into the boat. He has gills and is dressed in a filthy business suit and a mask.*] Who . . . What are you?

**Poogweese:** I am Poogweese, assistant to the Boss of Underwater Affairs. He said to tell you this river is way too dirty. I mean, look at my suit! What are you going to do about it?

**Girl:** It's not *our* fault. [*Poogweese stares at them, frowning.*]

**Boy # 1:** Uh . . . Once, a soda can sort of slipped out of my hand and, uh . . .

**Poogweese:** I thought so. Look, the Boss wants this river cleaned up.

**Boy # 1:** You know, he's right. This river is filthy.

**Boy # 2:** Let's organize a cleanup. We'll get everyone to join in. Maybe the fish will come back to the river.

## COMPREHENSION

**Workbook Page 101**

### Right There

1. Who is Poogweese and what does he look like?
2. What were the fishermen afraid would happen if they let Poogwese go?

### Think and Search

3. How did Poogweese convince the fishermen to let him go?
4. What are the consequences of the encounter in this story?

## Author and You

5. What can you infer about the values and beliefs of the people who created this myth?

6. What lesson do you think Chief Lelooska wants us to learn from this story?

## On Your Own

7. What natural elements and events are explained in this myth? Do you think this myth has relevance for people living in the modern world? Explain.

8. What modern myths do we have in our culture? What do they reveal about us? Give an example.

**DISCUSSION**

Discuss in pairs or small groups.

1. What clues about cultural context can you find in this myth? How do they help you understand the myth?

2. What experiences in the lives of the Kwakiutl people do you think contributed to the creation of this myth?

3. In your experience, how do people react to strange or seemingly supernatural events? Does the reaction of the fishermen make sense to you? Support your answer.

**Q How does the sea affect our lives?** What do myths explain about places like the sea that science cannot?

**》⑨ Listening TIP**

Listen carefully to other people's ideas. What facts and examples do they use to illustrate these ideas? How are their ideas similar to or different from your own?

**RESPONSE TO LITERATURE**

**Workbook**
Page 101

Understanding cultural context is very important when reading a myth. Each Native American tribe has its own customs and beliefs. Do research in the library or on the Internet to find out about tribes of the Pacific Northwest, where this myth originated. For example, organize small groups to research one aspect of the culture of the Kwakiutl, such as everyday life, customs, arts, or spiritual beliefs. Share what you find with the class.

A totem pole with a thunderbird, Vancouver Island, Canada ▶

# Grammar and Writing

## Participial Adjectives

The past and present participle forms of many verbs can be used as adjectives. A participial adjective can appear before the noun it modifies or after the verb *be*.

The present participle (*-ing* form of the verb) used as an adjective describes the cause of a feeling.

> The **astonishing** creature appeared before the fishermen. [The creature astonished the fishermen.]
> The song and mask were **pleasing** to the fishermen. [The song and mask pleased the fishermen.]

The past participle (*-ed* form of the verb) used as an adjective describes how a person feels. Sentences with past participles can usually be restated with a *by* phrase.

> The **astonished** fishermen listened and stared at the strange creature. [The fishermen were astonished by the strange creature.]
> The fishermen were **pleased**. [The fishermen were pleased by the song and mask.]

Some common participial adjectives include: *amazed/amazing, bored/boring, confused/confusing, disappointed/disappointing, excited/exciting, interested/interesting, relaxed/relaxing, shocked/shocking, surprised/surprising,* and *touched/touching.*

## Practice

**Workbook**
**Page 102**

Complete each sentence with the present or past participial adjective formed from the verb in parentheses. Check your answers with a partner.

1. Before the villagers caught Poogweese, they were _____ by the lack of fish. (disappoint)
2. At first the fishermen were _____ by the Merman. (frighten)
3. The creature's huge front teeth, scraggly hair, and seaweed clothing gave it a _____ appearance. (shock)
4. The _____ fishermen believed Poogweese's promise. (trust)
5. The people were _____ by Poogweese's gift. (touch)
6. The story has a _____ ending. (surprise)

# WRITING AN EXPOSITORY PARAGRAPH

## Write a News Article

In expository writing, you present facts, explain something, or discuss ideas. A news article is a common type of expository writing.

A news article reports the most important facts about an event. The article should answer the questions known as the 5Ws—*Who? Where? When? What?* and *Why?* In news articles, writers take care not to give their personal opinions: They remain objective by focusing on facts.

The writer of the news article below answered the 5W questions. Before writing, she listed her ideas in a graphic organizer.

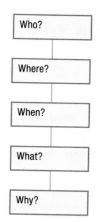

Who?

Where?

When?

What?

Why?

*Julitza Garcia*

### Strange Encounter Near Bird Island

A startling incident was reported near Bird Island yesterday, when a group of fishermen had the surprise of their lives. They allegedly caught, not a fish, but a Merman! According to the shocked fishermen, the Merman was Poogweese, messenger of Goomaquay. The possibility that Goomaquay would punish the fishermen for capturing his messenger appeared to them to be a very real threat. Interviewed after the event, the fishermen claimed to be terrified of what would happen next. They worried that Goomaquay would send life-threatening storms and dry up the fish supply. However, according to the fishermen, the Merman offered to cut a deal with them. They say that he promised to tell Goomaquay of their kindness if they released him. After he offered other gifts, the fishermen set their captive free. What will be Goomaquay's response? Will he honor his messenger's promise? This reporter will keep you informed as events unfold.

## Practice

**Workbook**
Page 103

Write a news article about a recent event in your community. You might report on an election at school or a holiday celebration in your town. List your ideas in a graphic organizer before you start writing. Be sure to use participial adjectives correctly in your article.

### Writing Checklist

**VOICE:**

☑ I used an objective tone appropriate to a news article.

**WORD CHOICE:**

☑ I chose words that describe the event in vivid detail.

**211**

## What You Will Learn

**Reading**
- Vocabulary building: *Context, dictionary skills, word study*
- Reading strategy: *Identify cause and effect*
- Text type: *Informational text (science)*

**Grammar, Usage, and Mechanics**
Subordinating conjunctions to express cause and effect

**Writing**
Write a cause-and-effect paragraph

### THE BIG QUESTION

**How does the sea affect our lives?** When we think of the sea, we usually think of vacations—relaxing on the beach or fishing. The sea can be very calming, but it also can be very frightening. Can you think of how the sea can be a dangerous place?

### BUILD BACKGROUND

As Niki Walker, the author of **"Tsunamis"** explains, "Tsunamis are the fastest, most powerful, and most destructive water waves on Earth. They can strike with little or no warning, hitting coastlines with the force of massive bombs. The waves plow across the land, flattening buildings, scattering debris for miles, and erasing whole villages."

In this science article, you will learn what a tsunami is and what causes these destructive and terrifying occurrences.

**A tsunami wave hits the island of Penang, Malaysia, on December 26, 2004.** ▼

212

## VOCABULARY

### Learn Key Words

Read these sentences. Use the context to figure out the meaning of the **red** words. Use a dictionary to check your answers. Then write each word and its meaning in your notebook.

**Key Words**

disaster
displace
disturbance
erupts
geologists
trigger
volume

1. The hurricane was a **disaster** that destroyed thousands of houses and businesses. Many people had to leave the city.

2. The rushing water was strong enough to **displace** everything in its path. We found our car miles down the road.

3. An underwater earthquake can cause a major **disturbance** in the ocean and often results in a tsunami.

4. When a volcano **erupts**, it sends smoke, fire, rocks, and lava into the sky.

5. The **geologists** were studying the Earth's crust when they discovered a kind of rock that they had never seen before.

6. A landslide can **trigger** a tsunami by sending huge rocks and other debris crashing into the ocean.

7. The **volume** of water in a bottle is measured in pints, quarts, or gallons. In the metric system, volume is measured in liters.

### Practice  Workbook Page 104

Write the sentences in your notebook. Choose a **red** word from the box above to complete each sentence. Then take turns reading the sentences aloud with a partner.

1. The _____ explained the significance of the different kinds of rock found on that mountain.

2. A natural _____ can cause terrible loss of life and billions of dollars of damage.

3. The _____ of water in a large lake is many millions of gallons.

4. When you jump into a pool, you _____ water, and this causes a splash.

5. Scientists say that if an asteroid crashed into the ocean, it might _____ a tsunami.

6. A storm is a kind of _____ that destroys the calm of the sea.

7. Mount St. Helens, a volcano in Washington, _____ a little bit every day.

## Learn Academic Words

Study the **red** words and their meanings. You will find these words useful when talking about informational texts. Write each word and its meaning in your notebook. After you read "Tsunamis," try to use these words to respond to the text.

| | | |
|---|---|---|
| **dimensions** = the measurements or size of something | → | That tsunami's **dimensions** were greater than those of any tsunami in history. The largest waves ever crashed onto shore. |
| **energy** = power that produces heat and makes things work | → | Fast-moving water in a river can be changed into **energy** to make light. |
| **occur** = happen, especially without being planned | → | Hurricanes **occur** most often between August and October. |
| **phenomena** = things that happen in nature | → | Earthquakes, volcanoes, and landslides are three **phenomena** that can trigger tsunamis. A tsunami is a terrifying phenomenon. |
| **release** = let go or let loose | → | When a volcano erupts, it will **release** ash and gases into the air. |

## Practice

**Workbook** Page 105

Work with a partner to answer these questions. Try to include the **red** word in your answer. Write the sentences in your notebook.

1. What would you use to measure the **dimensions** of a box?
2. What things in your house need **energy** to work?
3. When do thunderstorms usually **occur**?
4. What are two examples of weather **phenomena**?
5. What materials other than gases do volcanoes **release** into the air when they erupt?

The eruption of a volcano releases
a huge amount of energy. ▶

## Word Study: Roots and Origins of Words

Many English words come from or contain parts of ancient Greek or Latin words. These word parts are called roots. When words have the same root, they are part of a word family. Recognizing word families and knowing the meanings of roots will help you understand many English words. Look at the chart below.

| Root | Meaning | Origin | English Word | Meaning |
|------|---------|--------|--------------|---------|
| aster | star | Greek | disaster<br>astronomy | event that causes much harm<br>study of the sun, moon, and stars |
| geo | earth | Greek | geology<br>geography | study of rocks and how they were made<br>study of countries, oceans, rivers, etc. |
| rupt | break | Latin | abrupt<br>disrupt | sudden<br>stop a situation or event from continuing |
| struct | build | Latin | structure<br>destruction | a building, bridge, etc.<br>act of damaging something completely |
| turb | confusion | Latin | disturb<br>turbulent | interrupt or interfere with something<br>experiencing sudden changes |

**Practice**  Workbook Page 106

Work with a partner. Study the roots and their meanings in the chart. Look through the text of "Tsunamis" to find one new word for each root. Write the words in your notebook and figure out their meanings from the context. Check your definitions in a dictionary.

### READING STRATEGY | IDENTIFY CAUSE AND EFFECT

Identifying cause and effect helps you understand relationships between events. A cause is something that makes something else happen. An effect is what happens. To recognize causes and effects, follow these steps:

- As you read, look for important events. The reasons for events are causes. The events themselves may be causes or effects.

- Look for words and phrases that signal causes and effects. Examples include *because, since, so that, therefore, as a result of, triggered by,* and *caused by.*

As you read "Tsunamis," look for the causes and effects. Make sure you understand the relationship between the different events.

 Workbook Page 107

215

**Set a purpose for reading** Why are tsunami waves so much more destructive than regular ocean waves?

# Tsunamis
*Niki Walker*

## Disaster in South Asia

One of the worst natural disasters in history occurred on the morning of December 26, 2004. An earthquake in the Indian Ocean triggered the most deadly tsunami ever recorded.

The earthquake was the largest in more than 40 years. It occurred just off the coast of northern Sumatra, Indonesia, and sent waves speeding outward at more than 800 kilometers per hour (500 mph). Within 15 minutes of the earthquake, the first wave struck Sumatra. Over the next few hours, waves struck more than ten other unsuspecting countries. When the waves finally stopped seven hours later, towns, cities, fishing villages, and tourist resorts lay in ruins. More than 280,000 people had died. Many thousands more were injured or missing.

---

**unsuspecting,** not thinking that it was going to happen

▲ Countries struck by the tsunami of 2004

▼ Banda Aceh, Indonesia, after the tsunami of 2004

| | Height | Wavelength | Speed |
|---|---|---|---|
| **Normal ocean waves** | 0.3–5 meters (1–16 ft.) | 40–400 meters (130–1,300 ft.) | 56–100 kilometers per hour (35–60 mph) |
| **Tsunami waves** | 10–30 meters (30–100 ft. at shore) | 20–300 kilometers (12–180 mi.) | 800–1,000 kilometers per hour (500–600 mph) |

▲ The island of Sumatra, Indonesia, after the tsunami of 2004

## Harbor Waves

The word tsunami comes from two Japanese words, *tsu* meaning "harbor" and *nami* meaning "waves." The waves are named after harbors because that is where tsunamis are most often observed and are most destructive, especially in Japan, where there are many earthquakes. Tsunami waves are barely noticeable in the open ocean. The English term *tidal waves* is an inaccurate term to describe tsunamis, because tsunamis have nothing to do with the ocean's tides. Tides are the regular, daily rise and fall in water levels while tsunamis are rare, irregular events.

## Ocean Out of Balance

A tsunami is a series of waves that result from another ocean event, such as an underwater earthquake or the eruption of an underwater volcano. Both of these events cause a large amount of water to move, sending waves speeding out in all directions. The ocean tries to remain in a state of balance, called equilibrium. When a large volume of water suddenly moves, ripples, or waves, form on the surface of the ocean, moving away from the place where the water was disrupted. Close to shore, tsunami waves build on each other and rush over the land in a fast-moving flood of water. Tsunami waves may last up to several hours before the surface of the ocean is calm again, or regains equilibrium.

---

**disrupted**, made to be not calm

## Characteristics of Tsunami Waves

The main differences between tsunami waves and normal ocean waves are size, speed, and origin. These differences are what make tsunamis so powerful and destructive.

Waves are the movement of energy. All waves lose energy as they travel. The amount of energy that a wave loses depends on its wavelength (the distance between one crest and the next). The shorter the wavelength, the more energy a wave loses. Tsunamis have very long wavelengths, so they hardly lose any energy as they travel, and they reach shores with a great deal of force. Tsunamis travel so quickly once they reach shore that people cannot outrun them.

Regular waves have much shorter wavelengths, lose more energy as they travel, and hit shores with much less force than tsunamis.

### BEFORE YOU GO ON

1. Name ten countries that were hit by the tsunami of 2004.

2. What is the speed of normal ocean waves? What is the speed of tsunami waves?

**On Your Own**
What can people who live in coastal areas do to be prepared for tsunamis?

217

## Life of a Tsunami

A tsunami begins when an underwater disturbance suddenly displaces a column of ocean water. This abrupt movement may be caused by an underwater volcano, landslide, or earthquake. The sudden movement releases energy throughout the water, creating waves.

Tsunami waves in the open ocean are difficult to see because their long wavelengths stretch them out and keep them low. They are often less than a few feet high, but they move very quickly. People in boats might feel a tsunami wave as a sudden roll as it passes under the boat. When a tsunami wave reaches shallower water, the bottom of the wave begins to drag along the ocean floor. The wave slows down, but the water behind it continues to move quickly. The water starts to pile up, and the wave grows taller. Tsunami waves may reach heights of 10 to 30 meters (30 to 100 ft.) or more as they reach the shore.

---

**stretch them out**, make large spaces between the
  crest of each wave
**roll**, movement up and down
**shallower**, less deep
**pile up**, get higher

## Triggering Tsunamis

A few events in nature have enough power to displace massive amounts of water and create tsunamis. These events include earthquakes, volcanoes, landslides, and asteroid crashes.

### Earthquakes

Earthquakes are the cause of almost all tsunamis, but not all earthquakes trigger tsunamis. Underwater earthquakes are more likely to cause large tsunamis that travel across the entire ocean. Earthquakes near coasts can cause tsunamis, too. An underwater earthquake is likely to cause a tsunami if it is large, it happens near the ocean floor rather than far below it, and it causes part of the ocean floor to heave up or drop down.

---

**massive**, very large
**heave up**, move up forcefully

The features of a wave ▶

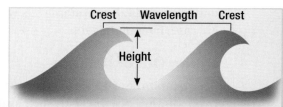

▲ The life of a tsunami

218

## Volcanoes

Volcanoes can trigger tsunamis in two ways. When a volcano located near shore erupts with a violent blast, it can blow out part of its side, sending tons of rock and lava into the nearby ocean and displacing a lot of water. Volcanoes can also trigger tsunamis by dumping a lot of lava into a nearby ocean very quickly. An underwater volcano can trigger a tsunami when it suddenly releases a lot of gas with a great deal of force. The gas blows up toward the ocean's surface, displacing a large volume of water and creating tsunami waves at the surface of the ocean.

## Landslides

Landslides occur above the water, but they also occur in the ocean, where there are underwater mountains. The falling rock and dirt from a landslide suddenly displaces a lot of water, creating a tsunami. Landslides are often triggered by underwater earthquakes. These landslides, together with the force of the quake, can cause major tsunamis.

## Asteroid Impacts

An asteroid could cause a tsunami by crashing into the ocean and displacing a large volume of water. This has never been recorded in human history, but some geologists are certain that this has happened in the past. They believe that an asteroid crashed into the ocean off present-day Mexico 65 million years ago and caused the dinosaurs to become extinct. These scientists believe that this asteroid triggered major tsunamis in several parts of the world.

---

**blast**, explosion
**blow out**, violently remove
**lava**, melted rock
**dumping**, dropping randomly
**blows up**, goes up very rapidly
**become extinct**, die out, with
   no survivors

## How to Simulate a Tsunami

**What you will need**
- A long, rectangular clear plastic container
- Sand
- Water
- A pitcher
- Toy clay

**What you will do**
1. Pack the sand against one of the short sides of the container. Shape it into a slope.
2. Using the pitcher, carefully pour water into the other end of the container, until the container is about half full. Try not to disturb the sand too much.
3. Form three clumps of clay: one small, one medium, and one large. Drop the small clump into the container, near the edge without sand. Watch how waves form and travel up the sandy slope.
4. Remove the small clump of clay, then drop in the medium clump. Next, drop in the large clump. Watch how the waves behave for each clump. What do you notice?

**What you will see**
The small clump of clay will cause the least amount of damage, demonstrating how regular ocean waves behave. The largest clump of clay will cause the most destruction on shore, because it will create the largest disturbance in the water. This is how tsunamis behave.

**BEFORE YOU GO ON**

**1** How does a tsunami begin?

**2** What is the most common cause of tsunamis? What other events can cause a tsunami?

**On Your Own**
Do you know the warning signs of a tsunami?

**219**

## COMPREHENSION

**Workbook**
**Page 108**

### Right There

**1.** What event triggered the tsunami that occurred on December 26, 2004? Where did this event begin?

**2.** Why is the term *tidal wave* an inaccurate term to describe tsunamis?

### Think and Search

**3.** How are regular ocean waves different from tsunami waves? Compare and contrast how regular ocean waves and tsunamis are formed and how they travel.

**4.** How can a volcano cause a tsunami? Describe what happens.

### Author and You

**5.** There is no record that an asteroid has ever caused a tsunami. Yet geologists have been able to infer that an asteroid could cause a tsunami. Explain how this is possible.

**6.** Do you think the author of this article would agree or disagree with the following statement: "The characteristics of tsunamis make it easy to design an early-warning system for tsunamis"? Explain.

### On Your Own

**7.** What can you remember about the 2004 tsunami? What do you know about how the tsunami affected the lives of the people in the countries where it struck?

**8.** In your opinion, is it helpful to learn about what causes tsunamis? Why or why not?

## IN YOUR OWN WORDS

Work with a partner. Imagine that you are explaining the causes of a tsunami to a younger student. First, write what you think are the most important words and facts about each of the following phenomena in your notebook: regular ocean waves, the ocean's equilibrium, tsunami waves, and events that trigger tsunamis. Then take turns telling a partner about the causes of a tsunami.

> **Speaking TIP**
>
> Use clear, simple visual aids to explain important ideas. Don't put too much information on a visual aid.

## DISCUSSION

Discuss in pairs or small groups.

1. What stories have you heard about people who have survived tsunamis? What would you do in the event of a tsunami?

2. Have you personally lived through a disaster? What disasters do you remember from television or newspapers? How can living through a disaster change people's lives?

**Q How does the sea affect our lives?** Do you think people should be allowed to build houses, hotels, and other businesses in areas where tsunamis might hit? Why or why not?

**»)) Listening TIP**

If you don't understand something a speaker says, wait until he or she has finished and then ask the speaker to explain.

## READ FOR FLUENCY

When we read aloud to communicate meaning, we group words into phrases, pause or slow down to make important points, and emphasize important words. Pause for a short time when you reach a comma and for a longer time when you reach a period. Pay attention to rising and falling intonation at the end of sentences.

Work with a partner. Choose a paragraph from the reading. Discuss which words seem important for communicating meaning. Practice pronouncing difficult words. Take turns reading the paragraph aloud and give each other feedback.

## EXTENSION

**Workbook**
**Page 108**

Research the worldwide effort to help the victims of the tsunami of 2004. What organizations did the most to help? How did they help? What do the people in the countries affected by the disaster still need? Present this information to the class with a list of organizations that need donations. Discuss the ways that you and your classmates could help.

The Red Cross relief center in Galle, Sri Lanka, in January 2005 ▶

# Grammar and Writing

## Subordinating Conjunctions to Express Cause and Effect

The subordinating conjunctions *because, when, now that, as,* and *since* express cause and effect. A subordinating conjunction always introduces a dependent clause and is always followed by a subject and a verb. A dependent clause must always be connected to an independent clause. The dependent, or subordinating, clause shows the cause. The independent, or main, clause shows the effect.

| Main Clause (Effect) | Subordinating Clause (Cause) |
|---|---|
| Tsunami waves in the open ocean are difficult to see | **because** their long wavelengths stretch them out and keep them low. |
| A tsunami begins | **when** an underwater disturbance displaces a column of ocean water. |
| Tsunamis can sometimes be predicted | **now that** scientists know what triggers them. |

A subordinating clause can also appear before the main clause. If a subordinating clause begins the sentence, use a comma.

| Subordinating Clause (Cause) | Main Clause (Effect) |
|---|---|
| **As** tsunamis are unrelated to the ocean's tides, | the term *tidal wave* is inaccurate for them. |
| **Since** harbors are where tsunamis are most often observed, | the waves are named *tsu,* meaning "harbor," and *nami,* meaning "waves." |

## Practice

**Workbook** Page 109

Write these sentence starters in your notebook. Complete each sentence with your own ideas, using either a subordinating clause or a main clause. Work with a partner. Read your sentences aloud. Then identify the clause that shows *cause* and the clause that shows *effect*.

1. Tsunamis are dangerous because . . .
2. Now that tsunamis are studied, . . .
3. As the day was clear, . . .
4. We enjoyed sailing today since . . .
5. The children get seasick when . . .

222

# WRITING AN EXPOSITORY PARAGRAPH

## Write a Cause-and-Effect Paragraph

Cause-and-effect writing explains how one event or situation causes or results in another. The writer examines the reasons something happens (causes) or the results of an event (effects). The relationship between cause and effect must be logical and stated in an order that makes sense. Some key words and phrases that express a cause-and-effect relationship are *cause, effect, result, as a result, result in, because, because of, since, therefore, for this reason, this leads to,* and *due to.*

Here is a model of a cause-and-effect paragraph about tsunamis. This writer has demonstrated how cause and effect are logically related, using key words and phrases. Before writing, she used a graphic organizer to list her ideas.

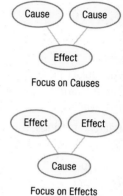

Focus on Causes

Focus on Effects

Sophie Howat

### Deadly Tsunamis

Tsunamis are some of the most powerful and destructive natural disasters ever to occur. Due to their great height and incredible speed, tsunamis can destroy towns, villages, and even entire cities. Tsunamis are caused by disturbances in the ocean such as earthquakes or landslides. These disturbances release energy throughout the water, creating the tsunami waves. Because their long wavelengths keep them low in the ocean, tsunamis are hard to spot. Even though they travel fastest in deep water, they roll by unnoticed. When the waves reach shallow waters, however, they drag on the ocean floor, building until they reach massive heights of 30 to 100 feet. The tsunami waves then destroy everything in their path with monstrous force.

## Practice

Workbook
Page 110

Write a paragraph describing the causes or effects of an event you have experienced. You could analyze causes, for example, by explaining why the school team won or lost a game. Or you could discuss effects by describing the destruction caused by a thunderstorm or other natural event. Use a graphic organizer to list your ideas. Organize your events in a logical order and use key words and phrases to explain the cause-and-effect relationship.

### Writing Checklist

**ORGANIZATION:**
☑ I stated the causes or effects in a logical order.

**WORD CHOICE:**
☑ I clearly showed the relationship of each cause and effect by using key words and phrases.

# Prepare to Read

▲ Captain Nemo on
top of the *Nautilus*, the
imaginary submarine
in *20,000 Leagues
Under the Sea*

## THE BIG QUESTION

**How does the sea affect our lives?** Although we live in an
age of air travel, we still use ships to transport goods and people
around the world. Have you ever been on a ship? Where did you
go? What did you see? Have you ever seen a movie or read a book
about the underwater world? What did you learn? Discuss with
a partner.

## BUILD BACKGROUND

**20,000 Leagues Under the Sea** is a science fiction novel written
by the French author Jules Verne in 1870. Science fiction is a kind
of fiction that takes place in imaginary fantasy worlds or describes
imaginary developments in science, such as travel in space. Aliens or
other mysterious creatures are often part of the story.

Most of *20,000 Leagues Under the Sea* takes place on a submarine,
a type of ship that travels underwater for long periods of time. At the
time that this novel was written, submarines did not exist. In almost
all of his novels, Verne, a visionary, predicted modern machines
and technological advances that would not be invented for nearly
a century after his death, including scuba-diving equipment, the
electric engine, the helicopter, the satellite, and space travel.

▼ The USS *Nautilus*, the world's first nuclear-powered submarine

## VOCABULARY

### Learn Literary Words

Authors use **suspense** to keep the reader interested in a story. Suspense is a feeling of uncertainty or tension. Writers create suspense by raising questions in the minds of their readers. Suspense makes readers ask the question, "What will happen next?" Read the example of suspense below.

> When Carmen woke up, she was lying on the beach. Her left arm was throbbing, and she felt blood dripping down her ear. The last thing she remembered was sitting on the deck of the boat. "What had happened?" she thought to herself. She looked around. The boat seemed to be far out in the ocean. But there was a large figure floating in the water nearby. She waded into the water to see what it was. When she got closer, she let out a shriek and fell backwards into the water.

What questions do you have after reading this passage? Does the use of suspense make you want to find out what happens next?

Most stories have a series of actions and a buildup of suspense that leads to a **climax**. The climax of a story is the high point of suspense. It is often the point where the events of the story turn either in favor of or against the main character. At the climax, we can predict how the story will end. Although the climax is often the most exciting part of the story, it does not have to be. Below is an example of a climax.

> As the boat neared the shore, Henry felt his eyes start to water and he couldn't stop shaking. He had been waiting for this day for more than two years. He saw people standing on the land. His heart jumped. He recognized his son and daughter. After years of worrying, his dream of reuniting with his family was finally coming true.

**Practice**  **Workbook** Page 111

Alone or in a small group, reread the examples above. Which details and words help create suspense? Which details and words help create the climax? Write your answers in your notebook.

## Learn Academic Words

Study the **red** words and their meanings. You will find these words useful when talking and writing about literature. Write each word and its meaning in your notebook. After you read the excerpt from *20,000 Leagues Under the Sea*, try to use these words to respond to the text.

| | | |
|---|---|---|
| **conduct** = the way someone behaves | → | The captain's noble **conduct** set a good example for the sailors to follow. |
| **outcome** = the final result | → | The story had a happy **outcome** because all of the ship's crew were saved. |
| **sequence** = a series of related events that have a particular result | → | People never tire of hearing about the disastrous **sequence** of events that led to the sinking of the *Titanic*. |
| **strategy** = a set of plans and skills used in order to gain success | → | The new captain's **strategy** to gain the support of the crew was to take charge of all operations. |
| **undertaking** = an important job for which a person is responsible | → | Navigating a ship in icy waters is a dangerous **undertaking** that requires considerable skill. |

## Practice  Workbook Page 112

Work with a partner to answer these questions. Try to include the **red** word in your answer. Write the sentences in your notebook.

1. What is an example of good **conduct** in an emergency?

2. When is a scientist pleased with the **outcome** of an experiment?

3. Why should you tell a story's events in the correct **sequence**?

4. What is your **strategy** for success in school?

5. Have you ever been involved in a project that you would consider a major **undertaking**? Explain.

▲ The sequence of events that led to the sinking of the *Titanic* in 1912 is well known.

## Word Study: Suffix -*ous*

The suffix -*ous* can be added to a noun to form an adjective with the meaning "full of" or "like." Here are some rules to help you remember how to spell adjectives ending in -*ous*:

- Change final *y* to *i*;
- Drop final *e* after a consonant;
- Drop *e* before final *r*;
- If the noun has the suffix -*ion*, change the suffix to -*ious*.

| Noun | Adjective | Meaning |
|------|-----------|---------|
| poison | poisonous | full of poison |
| fury | furious | full of fury |
| adventure | adventurous | full of adventure |
| monster | monstrous | like a monster |
| caution | cautious | full of caution |

**Practice**
Workbook
Page 113

Work with a partner. Copy the words in the box below into your notebook. Write an adjective ending in -*ous* for each noun. Then write a sentence using each adjective.

| disaster | fame | hazard | suspicion | victory |
|----------|------|--------|-----------|---------|

## READING STRATEGY | RECOGNIZE SEQUENCE

Recognizing sequence will help you follow the plot of a story. To recognize sequence, follow these steps as you read:

- Look for words the author uses to show sequence, such as *first, then, next, finally, last, while, during,* and *after.*

- Look for dates and time expressions such as *morning, yesterday, last week, Wednesday, in 1916.*

- You may wish to use a sequence-of-events chart to keep track of the events in the story.

As you read the excerpt from *20,000 Leagues Under the Sea,* make a note of the sequence in which events occur.

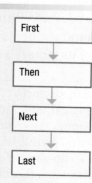

First
↓
Then
↓
Next
↓
Last

Workbook
Page 114

**Set a purpose for reading** How does the sea affect the crew of the *Nautilus*?

*from*

# 20,000 Leagues Under the Sea

**Jules Verne**, *translated by Frederick Paul Walter*

*Captain Nemo has secretly built a submarine called the* Nautilus. *No one in the world knows about it until a group sent to investigate sightings of the mysterious submarine gets captured and brought inside. The group includes the narrator, Pierre Aronnax, a marine biologist from Paris; his trusted servant, Conseil; and Ned Land, a Canadian harpooner. They travel all over the world and discover many interesting things. In this excerpt, the* Nautilus *comes across a group of giant squids.*

I stared in my turn and couldn't keep back a movement of revulsion. Before my eyes there quivered a horrible monster worthy of a place among the most farfetched teratological legends.

It was a squid of colossal dimensions, fully eight meters long. It was traveling backward with tremendous speed in the same direction as the *Nautilus*. It gazed with enormous, staring eyes that were tinted sea green. Its eight arms (or more accurately, feet) were rooted in its head, which has earned these animals the name cephalopod; its arms stretched a distance twice the length of its body and were writhing like the serpentine hair of the Furies. You could plainly see its 250 suckers, arranged over the inner sides of its tentacles and shaped like semispheric capsules.

---

**revulsion**, disgust
**teratological**, about monsters
**cephalopod**, sea-creatures with tentacles and large heads
**the Furies**, mythic winged creatures that punished people who did wrong
**suckers**, cup-shaped organs on a tentacle that stick onto things
**tentacles**, long, flexible limbs on some sea-creatures that can grab
  onto things

Sometimes these suckers fastened onto the lounge window by creating vacuums against it. The monster's mouth—a beak made of horn and shaped like that of a parrot—opened and closed vertically. Its tongue, also of horn substance and armed with several rows of sharp teeth, would flicker out from between these genuine shears. What a freak of nature! A bird's beak on a mollusk! Its body was spindle-shaped and swollen in the middle, a fleshy mass that must have weighed 20,000 to 25,000 kilograms. Its unstable color would change with tremendous speed as the animal grew irritated, passing successively from bluish gray to reddish brown.

What was irritating this mollusk? No doubt the presence of the *Nautilus*, even more fearsome than itself, and which it couldn't grip with its mandibles or the suckers on its arms. And yet what monsters these devilfish are, what vitality our Creator has given them, what vigor in their movements, thanks to their owning a triple heart!

Sheer chance had placed us in the presence of this squid, and I didn't want to lose this opportunity to meticulously study such a cephalopod specimen. I overcame the horror that its appearance inspired in me, picked up a pencil, and began to sketch it.

"Perhaps this is the same as the *Alecto*'s," Conseil said.

"Can't be," the Canadian replied, "because this one's complete while the other one lost its tail!"

---

**mandibles**, jaws
**meticulously**, very carefully

**BEFORE YOU GO ON**

**1** How does Aronnax feel as he watches the giant squid? Why?

**2** What does Aronnax start doing as he watches the squid? Why?

**On Your Own**
What other monsters, real or imagined, have you read or seen films about? What are their physical characteristics? What did they do?

**229**

"That doesn't necessarily follow," I said. "The arms and tails of these animals grow back through regeneration, and in seven years the tail on Bouguer's Squid has surely had time to sprout again."

"Anyhow," Ned shot back, "if it isn't this fellow, maybe it's one of those!"

Indeed, other devilfish had appeared at the starboard window. I counted seven of them. They provided the *Nautilus* with an escort, and I could hear their beaks gnashing on the sheetiron hull. We couldn't have asked for a more devoted following.

I continued sketching. These monsters kept pace in our waters with such precision, they seemed to be standing still, and I could have traced their outlines in miniature on the window. But we were moving at a moderate speed.

All at once the *Nautilus* stopped. A jolt made it tremble through its entire framework.

"Did we strike bottom?" I asked.

"In any event we're already clear," the Canadian replied, "because we're afloat."

The *Nautilus* was certainly afloat, but it was no longer in motion. The blades of its propeller weren't churning the waves. A minute passed. Followed by his chief officer, Captain Nemo entered the lounge.

I hadn't seen him for a good while. He looked gloomy to me. Without speaking to us, without even seeing us perhaps, he went to the panel, stared at the devilfish, and said a few words to his chief officer.

The latter went out. Soon the panels closed. The ceiling lit up.

I went over to the captain.

"An unusual assortment of devilfish," I told him, as carefree as a collector in front of an aquarium.

"Correct, Mr. Naturalist," he answered me, "and we're going to fight them at close quarters."

I gaped at the captain. I thought my hearing had gone bad.

"At close quarters?" I repeated.

"Yes, sir. Our propeller is jammed. I think the horn-covered mandibles of one of these squid are entangled in the blades. That's why we aren't moving."

---

**sprout**, start to grow
**gnashing**, biting or hitting
**jolt**, hard, sudden movement
**propeller**, a machine that spins rapidly to make a ship move
**churning**, moving violently
**gaped**, stared with an open mouth
**jammed**, stuck

"And what are you going to do?"

"Rise to the surface and slaughter the vermin."

"A difficult undertaking."

"Correct. Our electric bullets are ineffective against such soft flesh, where they don't meet enough resistance to go off. But we'll attack the beasts with axes."

"And harpoons, sir," the Canadian said, "if you don't turn down my help."

"I accept it, Mr. Land."

"We'll go with you," I said. And we followed Captain Nemo, heading to the central companionway.

There some ten men were standing by for the assault, armed with boarding axes. Conseil and I picked up two more axes. Ned Land seized a harpoon.

By then the *Nautilus* had returned to the surface of the waves. Stationed on the top steps, one of the seamen undid the bolts of the hatch. But he had scarcely unscrewed the nuts when the hatch flew up with tremendous violence, obviously pulled open by the suckers on a devilfish's arm.

Instantly one of those long arms glided like a snake into the opening, and twenty others were quivering above. With a sweep of the ax, Captain Nemo chopped off this fearsome tentacle, which slid writhing down the steps.

Just as we were crowding each other to reach the platform, two more arms lashed the air, swooped on the seaman stationed in front of Captain Nemo, and carried the fellow away with irresistible violence.

✔ **LITERARY CHECK**
*Which details and words create **suspense** during this scene?*

---

**slaughter the vermin**, kill all squids
**hatch**, door
**quivering**, shaking
**writhing**, moving from side to side uncontrollably
**platform**, a flat raised space to stand on
**swooped**, moved down suddenly and quickly through the air

**BEFORE YOU GO ON**

1. Why does the Nautilus come to a sudden stop?

2. What does Captain Nemo want to do? How?

☀ **On Your Own**
How would you evaluate Captain Nemo's leadership? If you were the captain of the *Nautilus*, how would you handle this situation?

**231**

Captain Nemo gave a shout and leaped outside. We rushed after him.

What a scene! Seized by the tentacle and glued to its suckers, the unfortunate man was swinging in the air at the mercy of this enormous appendage. He gasped, he choked, he yelled: "Help! Help!" These words, *pronounced in French*, left me deeply stunned! So I had a fellow countryman on board, perhaps several! I'll hear his harrowing plea the rest of my life!

The poor fellow was done for. Who could tear him from such a powerful grip? Even so, Captain Nemo rushed at the devilfish and with a sweep of the ax hewed one more of its arms. His chief officer struggled furiously with other monsters crawling up the *Nautilus*'s sides. The crew battled with flailing axes. The Canadian, Conseil, and I sank our weapons into these fleshy masses. An intense, musky odor filled the air. It was horrible.

For an instant I thought the poor man entwined by the devilfish might be torn loose from its powerful suction. Seven arms out of eight had been chopped off. Brandishing its victim like a feather, one lone tentacle was writhing in the air. But just as Captain Nemo and his chief officer rushed at it, the animal shot off a spout of blackish liquid, secreted by a pouch located in its abdomen. It blinded us. When this cloud had dispersed, the squid was gone, and so was my poor fellow countryman!

---

**appendage**, limb
**done for**, going to die
**entwined**, wrapped up
**brandishing**, waving around
**secreted**, produced

What rage then drove us against these monsters! We lost all self-control. Ten or twelve devilfish had overrun the *Nautilus*'s platform and sides. We piled helter-skelter into the thick of these sawed-off snakes, which darted over the platform amid waves of blood and sepia ink. It seemed as if these viscous tentacles grew back like the many heads of Hydra. At every thrust Ned Land's harpoon would plunge into a squid's sea-green eye and burst it. But my daring companion was suddenly toppled by the tentacles of a monster he could not avoid.

Oh, my heart nearly exploded with excitement and horror! The squid's fearsome beak was wide open over Ned Land. The poor man was about to be cut in half. I ran to his rescue. But Captain Nemo got there first. His ax disappeared between the two enormous mandibles, and the Canadian, miraculously saved, stood and plunged his harpoon all the way into the devilfish's triple heart.

"Tit for tat," Captain Nemo told the Canadian. "I owed it to myself!" Ned bowed without answering him.

This struggle had lasted a quarter of an hour. Defeated, mutilated, battered to death, the monsters finally yielded to us and disappeared beneath the waves.

Red with blood, motionless by the beacon, Captain Nemo stared at the sea that had swallowed one of his companions, and large tears streamed from his eyes.

✔ **LITERARY CHECK**
*Identify the **climax** of the scene. Which details lead up to it?*

---

**helter-skelter**, wildly
**tit for tat**, something bad you do to someone because that person did something bad to you
**mutilated**, very badly cut up

## ABOUT THE **AUTHOR**

**Jules Verne** (1828–1905) is considered by many to be the founder of science fiction. His books have been translated into countless languages and are known throughout the world. His best-known works include *Journey to the Center of the Earth, 20,000 Leagues Under the Sea,* and *Around the World in 80 Days.* Verne's classic science fiction tales have also inspired many film and TV versions.

**BEFORE YOU GO ON**

1 What happens to the sailor who is captured by the giant squid?

2 How does the battle end?

💡 **On Your Own**
What aspects of the sea does this scene show? How do you think Captain Nemo would describe the sea?

233

## READER'S THEATER

Act out this interview with Ned Land and a TV reporter.

**Reporter:** I'm here with Ned Land, who's spent the last few months on the *Nautilus*. Ned, tell the TV viewers about some of your adventures at sea.

**Ned Land:** Well, the most incredible experience I've ever had was our encounter with a group of giant squids.

**Reporter:** That sounds scary! What does a giant squid look like?

**Ned Land:** They're huge—more than twenty feet long. They have big green eyes and eight arms covered with suckers. They also have beaks, sort of like birds.

**Reporter:** Incredible! There are reports the crew had to fight one.

**Ned Land:** Not just one—we battled at least ten of them!

**Reporter:** How did that happen?

**Ned Land:** First, we saw them outside the submarine.

**Reporter:** And then what happened?

**Ned Land:** Then one got caught in the submarine's propellers.

**Reporter:** How did you get moving again?

**Ned Land:** We floated to the surface of the water, but the giant squids followed us. We had to battle them to get free.

**Reporter:** What did you use to fight them?

**Ned Land:** I used a harpoon. The other crew members used axes.

**Reporter:** What happened next?

**Ned Land:** I was almost bitten in half by one of the squid! But luckily, Captain Nemo saved me.

**Reporter:** Wow—you're lucky to be alive!

**Speaking TIP**

Imagine you are the character as you say your lines. Try to project the thoughts and the feelings that your character would have.

## COMPREHENSION

**Workbook**
**Page 115**

**Right There**

1. How long is the giant squid? How much does it weigh?

2. What other name do the sailors call the giant squids?

### Think and Search

**3.** What is Captain Nemo's plan of attack? Why?

**4.** What does Captain Nemo mean when he says, "tit for tat"?

### Author and You

**5.** What can you infer about Captain Nemo's character from the author's description? Give details to support your answer.

**6.** How do you think the crew members feel about Captain Nemo?

### On Your Own

**7.** After reading this selection, would you be more or less likely to read more science fiction? Why or why not?

**8.** When this novel was written in 1870, readers thought the science predictions were amazing. In your opinion, why is this novel still interesting to readers?

## DISCUSSION

**Listening TIP**

Think about what your classmates are saying. Try to relate what you hear to what you already know.

Discuss in pairs or small groups.

**1.** How can you tell what is fact and what is fiction in the excerpt? Give examples from the reading.

**2.** Why is suspense an important part of stories and novels? Do you think novels need suspense to tell a good story? Why or why not?

**Q** **How does the sea affect our lives?** Why do you think Jules Verne chose the sea as the setting for his story? Can you think of other stories that have the sea as the setting? Is the way in which the sea is represented similar to or different from this story? Explain.

## RESPONSE TO LITERATURE

**Workbook Page 115**

Science fiction writers often use their knowledge of real science to make their stories seem possible. They try to predict where science and technology will lead us in the future.

Think about the technology we use every day, for example, cars, airplanes, the cell phone, the computer, and television to name a few. In a small group, brainstorm predictions about how these things will change in the future. The wilder your ideas, the better. Use a word web to connect your ideas. Then discuss how these changes will affect the way people live. How could you make stories from the ideas you have listed? Share your favorite ideas with the class.

# Grammar and Writing

## Expressions That Indicate Sequence

Certain words help us understand sequence, or the order in which actions or events happen. Common sequence words include *first, second, third, then, next, afterwards, last,* and *finally.* There are also expressions that indicate sequence. A writer can use these to add interest to his or her writing. Look at the sentences describing how to kill a devilfish, or a giant squid in *20,000 Leagues Under the Sea.*

| Sequence Expressions | Imperatives |
|---|---|
| First of all,<br>To start with, | get a harpoon. |
| After that,<br>Following that, | open the hatch. |
| At this point,<br>Once you have [done that], | shoot the devilfish in the heart. |
| Last of all,<br>To finish, | close the hatch. |

*Note:* Use a comma after these words and expressions but NOT after the word *then.*

## Practice

**Workbook**
**Page 116**

Read the instructions on how to set up an aquarium and copy them into your notebook. Work with a partner to put the instructions in the correct order. Choose a sequence word or expression to complete each sentence. Then take turns reading each sentence aloud.

_____ pour sand or gravel into the tank.

_____ add the fish to your tank.

_____ slowly fill the tank with water, trying not to disturb the plants and rocks.

_____ plant some aquatic plants in the sand.

_____ let the filter run for one day.

_____ clean the aquarium tank with clean water and a cloth.

_____ put some large rocks between the plants.

_____ attach a filter to the tank, so it is at least half-way under water.

# WRITING AN EXPOSITORY PARAGRAPH

## Write Instructions

Instructions tell you how to do something. Written instructions usually include a sequence of steps.

When writing instructions, make your sentences short and easy to understand. You may wish to begin by giving a list of the materials that will be needed. Then state each step clearly, in the correct order. Be careful not to leave out a step.

Here is a model of instructions that explain how to use a boogie board. Notice how the writer used sequence words and expressions to make the order of the steps clear. Before writing, she used a sequence-of-events chart to list the steps in order.

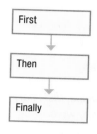

First

Then

Finally

*Sophie Haas*

### How to Use a Boogie Board

Boogie boards are relatively cheap and can be purchased at any surfing goods store. The only necessary feature is a strap that can be attached to your wrist. The strap prevents the board from being carried out to sea. To begin, attach the strap and wade into the ocean until the water reaches your thighs. Then turn around so that you're facing the beach. Next, hold the board against yourself, with one hand on each side. Bend your knees slightly. Finally, as a wave breaks behind you, jump forward and fall against the board, allowing the wave to carry you to shore. Be sure to jump just as the wave breaks. If you jump too soon, you'll miss the force of the wave. If you jump too late, you'll be sucked under the wave. Keep these tips in mind, and you should be all set to try boogie boarding for yourself!

**Practice**  **Workbook** Page 117

Write instructions that show how to do something, such as baking cookies, using a computer, or demonstrating a sports skill (for example, hitting a tennis ball). Be sure to use sequence words and expressions to make the order of your steps clear. Before you write, use a sequence-of-events chart to list the steps in order.

## Writing Checklist

**ORGANIZATION:**
☑ I explained the steps in the correct order.

**SENTENCE FLUENCY:**
☑ My instructions are clear and easy to follow.

237

# Prepare to Read

## What You Will Learn

**Reading**

■ Vocabulary building: *Context, dictionary skills, word study*

■ Reading strategy: *Compare and contrast*

■ Text type: *Informational text (science)*

**Grammar, Usage, and Mechanics**
Adjective clauses: review

**Writing**
Write a paragraph that classifies something

 **THE BIG QUESTION**

**How does the sea affect our lives?** You've probably seen the ocean in books or on TV, or perhaps you live near one. Have you ever visited the ocean? How many different kinds of ocean animals do you know? Discuss with a partner.

**BUILD BACKGROUND**

The science article **"Life in the Oceans"** will show you another way to think about the sea and the creatures that live in it. Because they are so vast and deep, oceans contain most of the living space on our planet, occupying almost three-quarters of Earth's surface. Humans have explored only a very small part of this immense underwater world. Scientists believe that as many as 80 percent—or more—of all the creatures on Earth live in the oceans.

▲ Oceans cover most of Earth's surface.

## VOCABULARY

### Learn Key Words

Read these sentences. Use the context to figure out the meaning of the red words. Use a dictionary to check your answers. Then write each word and its meaning in your notebook.

**Key Words**

camouflage
currents
decrease
depth
plentiful
recycle
surface

1. Fish camouflage themselves with color. In this way, they blend in with the background and hide from danger.

2. A river's currents show the direction that the river is moving. Currents can also show the part of a river that is moving fastest.

3. Some fish are getting harder to find. Their numbers decrease every year because too many people catch them for food.

4. The depth of the ocean is only a few inches when you enter it. The water gets deeper and deeper as you go out farther.

5. Blue whales migrate from the south to the north every year. In the north, the food is plentiful; in the south, it is harder to find anything to eat.

6. We can reuse most metals. That is why we recycle aluminum cans.

7. Most ships sail on the surface of the ocean. Submarines travel underwater.

### Practice

**Workbook Page 118**

Write the sentences in your notebook. Choose a red word from the box above to complete each sentence. Then take turns reading the sentences aloud with a partner.

1. Water temperatures in the ocean _____ as you go deeper and deeper.

2. Never dive into a pool until you know the _____ of the water.

3. Seaweed floats near the _____ of the water.

4. Dark green colors _____ this fish and make it hard to see.

5. All river _____ flow to the ocean.

6. Many seagulls and other birds can be seen in coastal areas because fish are _____ there.

7. A five-cent deposit on cans persuades many people to _____ them.

## Learn Academic Words

Study the red words and their meanings. You will find these words useful when talking and writing about informational texts. Write each word and its meaning in your notebook. After you read "Life in the Oceans," try to use these words to respond to the text.

**Academic Words**

category
constitute
environment
extract
maximum
significant
survival

| | | |
|---|---|---|
| **category** = a group of people or things that have the same qualities | ➡ | Science fiction is a **category** of fiction. |
| **constitute** = if several parts constitute something, they form it together | ➡ | Hydrogen and oxygen are the elements that **constitute** a molecule of water. |
| **environment** = the land, water, and air in which people, animals, and plants live | ➡ | Clean water and air make a healthy **environment** for living creatures. |
| **extract** = remove an object or substance from the place where it comes from | ➡ | Plants need to **extract** water and minerals from the soil in order to grow. |
| **maximum** = the largest that is possible, allowed, or needed | ➡ | The **maximum** number of fish that you are allowed to catch is called a fishing limit. |
| **significant** = noticeable or important | ➡ | A **significant** change in the wind may mean a storm is coming. |
| **survival** = the state of continuing to live or exist, especially after a difficult or dangerous situation | ➡ | The **survival** of many human beings depends on a large supply of fish to eat. |

## Practice

Workbook Page 119

Work with a partner to answer these questions. Try to include the red word in your answer. Write the sentences in your notebook.

1. What do books in the biography **category** tell about?
2. What are two foods that might **constitute** a good breakfast?
3. What constitutes a good **environment** for plants to grow?
4. What important mineral do we **extract** from ocean water? *Hint:* We put it on food to give it flavor.
5. What is the **maximum** speed on a highway called?
6. In your opinion, what is the most **significant** reason to recycle?
7. Why are healthy oceans important for our **survival**?

240

## Word Study: Compound Words

A compound word consists of two or more words that make a single word. In an open compound, the two words are separate, as in *whale shark* or *blue whale*. In a closed compound, the two words are together, as in *seabed*. A hyphenated compound is a compound word with a hyphen, as in *pitch-black* or *half-light*.

**Practice**  Workbook Page 120

With a partner, combine words from column A with words from column B to form compound words. Write the words in your notebook. Use a dictionary to find out whether the words are written as one word, as two words, or with a hyphen.

| A | B |
|---|---|
| **1.** awe | minded |
| **2.** spring | in-law |
| **3.** father | struck |
| **4.** kind | profit |
| **5.** well | care |
| **6.** not-for | year |
| **7.** health | time |
| **8.** school | keeper |
| **9.** narrow | being |
| **10.** book | hearted |

▲ A whale shark

## READING STRATEGY | COMPARE AND CONTRAST

Comparing and contrasting helps you to understand what you read more clearly. When you compare, you see how things are similar. When you contrast, you see how things are different. To compare and contrast, ask yourself these questions:

- What things or ideas are being compared?
- How are the things or ideas similar?
- How are the things or ideas different?

As you read "Life in the Oceans," compare and contrast the different ocean zones.

Zone 1
Zone 2   Zone 3

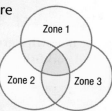 Workbook Page 121

**Set a purpose for reading** What different challenges do the creatures that inhabit different areas of the ocean face? How are their struggles similar?

# Life in the Oceans

*Miranda Macquitty*

From the seashore to the deepest depths, oceans are home to some of the most diverse life on earth. Plants are found only in the sunlit surface waters, where there is enough light for growth. Animals are found at all depths of the oceans, though are most abundant in the surface waters, where food is plentiful. Not all free-swimming animals stay in one zone. The sperm whale dives to over 500 meters (1,640 ft.) to feed on squid, returning to the surface to breathe air. Some animals that live in cold, deep waters, such as the Greenland shark in the Atlantic, are also found in the cold surface waters of polar regions.

**depths**, distances below the surface
**abundant**, frequently found

**zone**, an area that has a special quality
**dives**, swims downward sharply
**polar**, close to the North Pole
    or the South Pole

▲ **Bluestripe grunts and porkfish**

▲ **Green turtles**

▲ **Crown-of-thorns starfish**

Oceanographers divide the ocean up into broad zones, according to how far down sunlight penetrates. In the sunlit zone, there is plenty of light, much water movement, and seasonal changes in temperature. Beneath this is the twilight zone, the maximum depth to which light penetrates. Temperatures here decrease rapidly with depth to about 5° Centigrade (41°F). Deeper yet is the dark zone, where there is no light and temperatures drop to about 1–2° Centigrade (34–36°F). Still in darkness and even deeper is the abyss. The deepest part of the ocean occurs in the trenches.

**oceanographers**, scientists who study the ocean
**penetrates**, gets through
**twilight**, with little light
**abyss**, an extremely deep place
**trenches**, long and narrow, yet very deep parts of the ocean

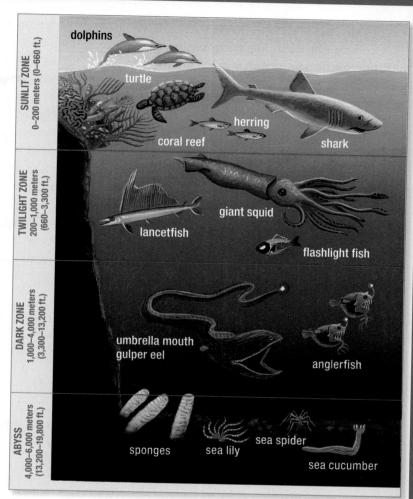

▲ The zones of the ocean

A great white shark ▼

**BEFORE YOU GO ON**

1 In which ocean zone are plants found? Why?

2 What is the depth of the twilight zone? How was that depth determined?

**On Your Own**
Have you ever seen any of the animals mentioned here in real life or on TV? Describe what you saw.

243

## The Sunlit Zone

Plant plankton are minute plants that float along the ocean's surface, carried about by waves and currents. Too small to be seen with the naked eye, they are the most abundant plants in the ocean. Like all plants, they need sunlight to grow, so are found only in the ocean's upper zones. In addition to sunlight, they need nutrients from the seawater. The most light occurs in the tropics, but nutrients there are often in short supply. Vast "meadows" of plant plankton are found in cooler waters where nutrients are brought up from the bottom during storms.

Plant plankton are eaten by swarms of tiny, drifting animal plankton, forming the second link in many food chains. The animal plankton provide a feast for small fish, such as herring. Those in turn are eaten by larger fish, such as tuna, which are eaten by still larger fish or other predators, such as dolphins. Some larger ocean animals (whale sharks and blue whales) feed directly on animal plankton. Thus all animals feed on plankton, either directly or indirectly, making it the basic food supply of the ocean.

Many types of fish and other animals, including mammals (such as whales and sea lions) and reptiles (such as sea turtles) inhabit the sunlit zone or visit it to feed.

---

**nutrients**, chemicals or foods needed to live
**in short supply**, hard to get
**drifting**, moving with the water

---

**predators**, animals that eat other animals
**inhabit**, live in

▼ Pacific spotted dolphins

▲ Copepods (animal plankton)

▲ Diatoms (plant plankton)

# Coral Reefs

Coral reefs are a fascinating form of animal life found in the sunlit zone. They cover vast areas of the warm, crystal-clear waters of the tropics. Most stony corals are colonies of many tiny individual animals called polyps. Each polyp makes its own hard limestone skeleton, which protects its soft body. To make their skeletons, the coral polyps need the help of microscopic, single-celled algae that live inside them. The algae need sunlight to grow, which is why coral reefs are found only in sunny, surface waters. Corals get some food from the algae. They also capture plankton with their tentacles. Only the upper layer of a reef is made of living corals, which build upon skeletons of dead polyps. Corals grow in an exquisite variety of shapes and colors.

Coral reefs are the most diverse habitats in the ocean. They support an extraordinary variety of marine life, from multitudes of brightly colored fish to giant clams wedged into rocks. Every bit of space on the reef provides a hiding place or shelter for some animal or plant. At night, swarms of amazing creatures emerge from coral caves and crevices to feed. All the living organisms on the reef depend for their survival on the stony corals, which recycle the scarce nutrients from the clear, blue, tropical waters.

---

**limestone**, a kind of rock made of calcium
**skeleton**, the bony structure of an animal
**microscopic**, too small to be seen
**algae**, tiny plants that live in water

---

**wedged**, placed firmly in a narrow space
**emerge**, come out
**crevices**, narrow cracks in rock

▲ Staghorn corals

▲ An orange-fin anemonefish and sea anemone

## BEFORE YOU GO ON

1. What are plankton? What are the two types of plankton?

2. What are stony corals? Why do they need algae?

**On Your Own**
How does the concept of zones help us understand life in the ocean? Can you think of other ways to classify life in the ocean?

## The Twilight Zone

Between the bright sunlit waters of the upper ocean and the pitch-black depths is the half-light of the twilight zone. It ranges from 200 to 1,000 meters (660 to 3,300 ft.) below the surface. Fish living in the twilight zone often have rows of light organs on their undersides to camouflage them against the soft light filtering down from above. These glowing lights can be produced by chemical reactions or by colonies of bacteria living in the light organs. Many animals, including some lanternfish and a variety of squid, spend only their days in the twilight zone. At night they journey upward to feed in the food-rich surface water. By doing this, they are less at risk from daytime hunters such as sea birds. Others, such as the lancetfish, spend their lives in the twilight zone eating any available food. The skinny lancetfish has a stretchy stomach so it can take in a large meal if it finds one.

## The Dark Zone

There is no light in the oceans below 1,000 meters (3,300 ft.), just inky blackness. Many fish in the dark zone are black too, making them almost invisible. Light organs are used to lure prey or communicate with a mate. Food is scarce in the cold, dark depths. All animals have to rely on what little drifts down from above. Deep-sea fish make the most of any available food by having huge mouths and stretchy stomachs. Often they are small or weigh little. Being lightweight helps fish in the dark zone maintain neutral buoyancy. This allows them to keep at one level without having to swim.

---

**organs**, parts of a living thing that have a unique purpose
**filtering down**, coming down dimly
**glowing**, shining steadily

**stretchy**, able to expand
**lure**, attract in order to catch
**scarce**, hard to find
**buoyancy**, the ability to float

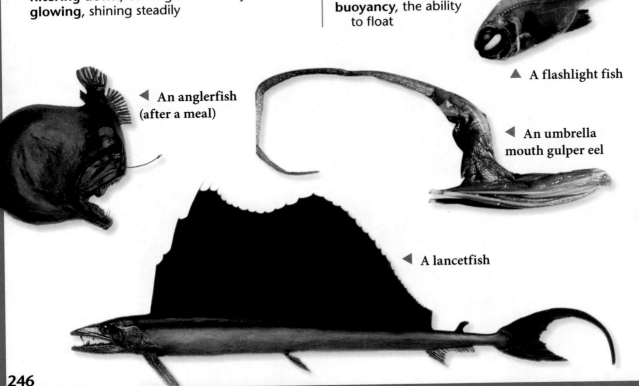

◀ An anglerfish (after a meal)

▲ A flashlight fish

◀ An umbrella mouth gulper eel

◀ A lancetfish

## On the Bottom

The bottom of the deep ocean is not an easy place to live. It is pitch-black, the water is almost freezing, and there is little food. Much of the seabed is covered with soft clays or mudlike oozes made of skeletons of tiny sea animals and plants. The ooze on the vast open plains of the abyss can reach several hundred yards thick. Animals walking along the bottom have long legs to avoid stirring it up. Some grow anchored to the seabed and have long stems to keep their feeding structures clear of the ooze. Food particles can be filtered out of the water, for example, by the feathery arms of sea lilies or through the many pores in sponges. Some animals, such as sea cucumbers, feed on the seabed by extracting food particles from the ooze. Food particles are the remains of dead animals (and their droppings) and plants that have sunk down from above. Occasionally a larger carcass reaches the bottom uneaten, prompting an immediate frenzy of feeding activity.

---

**oozes**, slimy mud
**stirring it up**, making it move and rise
**anchored**, fixed

**filtered out of**, removed from
**pores**, small openings on a living thing
**carcass**, dead body

Yellow sponges ▶

▲ A sea lily

### BEFORE YOU GO ON

**1** What are light organs? Why do many fish living in the twilight and dark zones have them?

**2** What food can be found on the bottom of the ocean? How do animals living there get food?

**On Your Own**
In what ways is life in the oceans similar to life on land? In what ways is it different?

247

## COMPREHENSION

**Workbook**
**Page 122**

### Right There

1. How do oceanographers divide the ocean up? Why? Which ocean zones does the article describe?

2. Why are more plant plankton found in cooler waters than in tropical waters?

### Think and Search

3. Why is plant life so important in the ocean? Describe a typical ocean food chain.

4. What constitutes a coral reef? Where are coral reefs found?

### Author and You

5. Why don't fish in the sunlit zone need large mouths and stomachs for survival? Why does the amount of food decrease below the sunlit zone?

6. Coral reefs recycle nutrients. Based on facts presented in the reading, infer ideas about how this is done. Why do so many different kinds of animals live near coral reefs?

### On Your Own

7. What do you think are the most significant challenges that the animals in each zone face?

8. Think of the ocean zones as "neighborhoods." Compare and contrast the ocean "communities" to human communities.

## IN YOUR OWN WORDS

Make a fact chart for "Life in the Oceans." Include each of the five headings from the reading. List the facts you remember from each section below each heading. Go back to the reading if you need to check a fact. Then form groups and explain the zones of the ocean using your chart. Listen to your classmates' explanations and add facts you forgot to your chart.

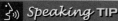 *Speaking* TIP

Make eye contact with your classmates. Talk to your audience, not to your chart.

## DISCUSSION

Discuss in pairs or small groups.

1. How are the zones of the ocean connected? Why are there so many different kinds of plants and animals in the ocean?

2. How are the animals in each zone able to survive? What physical structures enable them to find food and protect themselves from predators? Give an example for each zone.

3. How do you think pollution might affect the environment of each of the ocean zones? What effect could global warming have?

**Q How does the sea affect our lives?** Does life in the ocean seem harder to you than life on land? If you could choose to be any creature in the ocean, which would you choose? Why?

»)) **Listening** TIP

Take notes as you listen so that you'll remember the main points.

## READ FOR FLUENCY

It is often easier to read a text if you understand the difficult words and phrases. Work with a partner. Choose a paragraph from the reading. Identify the words and phrases you do not know or have trouble pronouncing. Look up the difficult words in a dictionary.

Take turns pronouncing the words and phrases with your partner. If necessary, ask your teacher to model the correct pronunciation. Then take turns reading the paragraph aloud. Give each other feedback on your reading.

## EXTENSION  **Workbook** Page 122

Pick the zone of the ocean that you are most interested in. Go to the library or research on the Internet to find out more about the animals that live in that zone. Write a short report describing the animals in an ocean food chain in that zone. Show the relationships of the animals to each other. Explain the dangers the animals in that zone face. Share your report with the class.

An orange squid ▶

249

# Grammar and Writing

## Adjective Clauses: Review

Remember that an adjective clause can modify a noun or a pronoun. Adjective clauses begin with relative pronouns: *which* and *that* refer to a thing; *who* (for a subject) / *whom* (for an object) and *that* refer to a person; *when* and *that* refer to a time; and *where* refers to a place.

An adjective clause can modify the subject of the sentence.

> The **polyp's skeleton** is hard limestone. **The skeleton** protects its body. →
> The polyp's skeleton, **which** protects its body, is hard limestone.
>
> Plankton are minute **plants**. **The plants** float along the ocean's surface. →
> Plankton are minute plants **that** float along the ocean's surface.

An adjective clause can also modify the object of a verb or the object of a preposition. Notice that the relative pronoun comes at the beginning of the adjective clause. When the adjective clause modifies an object, the relative pronoun may be omitted, except with *where*.

> We read **the article**. Miranda Macquitty wrote it. →
> We read the article (**that**) Miranda Macquitty wrote.
>
> He is the **sailor**. I read about him. →
> He is the sailor (**whom**) I read about.
>
> I remember **the week**. We studied the sea then. →
> I remember the week (**when**) we studied the sea.
>
> Most animals are found **in the surface waters**. Food is plentiful **there**. →
> Most animals are found in the surface waters **where** food is plentiful.

## Practice

Workbook
Page 123

Read the pairs of sentences. Rewrite them as one sentence with an adjective clause. Compare your sentences with a partner's.

1. Algae are tiny plants. Corals use algae to make their skeletons.
2. *Moby Dick* is a novel about the sea. It was written by Melville.
3. That is the oceanographer. I saw him on television.
4. We sailed on a ship. It was called the *Queen Elizabeth II*.
5. That is the coral reef. I went scuba diving there.
6. I remember the day. We went fishing.

# WRITING AN EXPOSITORY PARAGRAPH

## Write a Paragraph That Classifies Something

Classification puts different things with similar qualities into larger classes, or categories. Classifying things makes them easier to study. For example, scientists have classified all living creatures. Three of those classes are mammals, reptiles, and birds. Each class is based on the physical traits that animals in that class share.

| Plankton | Nekton | Benthos |
|----------|--------|---------|
|          |        |         |

The writer of the paragraph below explains a way of classifying ocean life that is different from the one in the article you read. Before writing, he used a graphic organizer to list his ideas.

*Trevor Saunders*

### Forms of Ocean Life

The ocean is home to many plants and animals, but survival is more difficult for some forms of life than for others. Many of the smaller ocean animals eat the plants, while most of the larger animals eat the smaller animals. The tiniest forms of ocean life, called plankton, include all the plants and animals that drift. The ocean animals probably most familiar to humans, called nekton, are the ones that can swim wherever they want. These include fish. Although some nektonic animals are relatively small, others—for example, sharks, which are fish, and whales, which are mammals— are huge. Finally, if ocean animals haven't been eaten first, they sink to the bottom of the ocean when they die. Then their decomposing bodies are eaten by animals that live on the ocean floor. Animals that live on the ocean bottom, including crabs and lobsters, are called benthos.

**Practice**
**Workbook**
**Page 124**

Write a paragraph explaining how something is classified. For example, you might write about bicycles, classifying them into three categories: city bikes, mountain bikes, and racing bikes. Describe the physical traits or other details that constitute your categories. Organize your paragraph in a way that makes these categories clear. Before writing, list your ideas in a graphic organizer. Be sure to use adjective clauses correctly.

### Writing Checklist

**ORGANIZATION:**
☑ I organized my writing in a way that makes my categories clear.

**CONVENTIONS:**
☑ I checked for correct spelling and punctuation and proofread for grammatical errors.

# Link the Readings

## Critical Thinking

Look back at the readings in this unit. Think about what they have in common. They all tell about the sea. Yet they do not all have the same purpose. The purpose of one reading might be to inform, while the purpose of another might be to entertain or persuade. In addition, the content of each reading relates to the sea differently. Now copy the chart below into your notebook and complete it.

| Title of Reading | Purpose | Big Question Link |
|---|---|---|
| "Poogweese" | | |
| "Tsunamis" | | |
| From *20,000 Leagues Under the Sea* | *to entertain* | |
| "Life in the Oceans" | | *describes categories of ocean life* |

## Discussion

Discuss in pairs or small groups.

- Compare and contrast the ways each of the readings in this unit describes different aspects of the sea.

- **Q How does the sea affect our lives?** Would you say that in general the sea is a calm place or a frightening place? Why do you think this is so?

## Fluency Check

Work with a partner. Choose a paragraph from one of the readings. Take turns reading it for one minute. Count the total number of words you read. Practice saying the words you had trouble reading. Take turns reading the paragraph three more times. Did you read more words each time? Copy the chart below into your notebook and record your speeds.

| | 1st Speed | 2nd Speed | 3rd Speed | 4th Speed |
|---|---|---|---|---|
| Words Per Minute | | | | |

# Projects

Work in pairs or small groups. Choose one of these projects.

**1** Do research on the Internet on how to make a freshwater or saltwater home aquarium. Find out about cost, materials, caring for the fish, and keeping the aquarium clean. Give a report to the class using materials and illustrations to demonstrate the instructions.

**2** Create your own modern-day myth about the sea or other geographical feature such as a river or mountains. Brainstorm ideas about how this feature affects your life.

**3** Research the effect fishing has on the ocean food chains. Focus on two overfished species: the codfish, a major predator, and the Atlantic menhaden, a small fish that supports many larger creatures, including whales. Present a report and two colorful food chain charts to the class.

**4** Go to your local fish market and interview the manager about where the fish in the store come from and how they get to your community. Organize the information from your interview in an illustrated sequence-of-events chart.

# Further Reading

To find out more about the theme of this unit, choose from these reading suggestions.

**Snow Falling on Cedars,** David Guterson
In this Penguin Reader® adaptation, a Japanese-American man, living in the Pacific Northwest, is on trial for murder in a community still struggling with the aftermath of World War II.

**The Old Man and the Sea,** Ernest Hemingway
An old Cuban fisherman faces his supreme ordeal—a relentless battle with a giant marlin far out in the Gulf Stream.

**Coral Reefs,** Charles Sheppard
The ecology of coral reefs is brought to life through the personal experiences of top researchers, naturalists, and scientists.

# Put It All Together

### TV Documentary

A TV documentary is a show about real events, places, or people. It is longer and more detailed than a TV news report. Documentaries usually include narration, interviews, film clips, photos, and other visuals. With a group, you will present a documentary about the relationship between people and the ocean or another important geographical feature.

**1 THINK ABOUT IT** Work in small groups. Think about what you have learned about the ocean and how it affects communities. Then with your group, discuss a geographical feature (the ocean, a river, mountains, etc.) that affects your community. How does it affect your community? Do people have jobs that depend on this feature? How does the community pollute and/or protect it? Next, based on your discussion, list possible topics for a documentary. For example, if you were discussing the ocean, you might list these topics:

- Livelihoods that depend on the ocean
- Large corporations that dump waste into the ocean
- New kinds of fish for your dinner table
- Environmental groups that clean up oil spills

Together, pick one idea for your documentary.

**2 GATHER AND ORGANIZE INFORMATION** As a group, write down what you know about your topic and what you would like to find out about it. Remember to ask *Who, Where, When, What,* and *Why* questions. You may wish to use a word web to organize your thoughts.

**Research** Use the library and the Internet to research your topic. Give each member of the group a research assignment. Take notes on the information you find, and watch for useful pictures, props, or other visuals.

**Order Your Notes** Share your notes with the group. Together, decide what information to include in your documentary, and choose an order that makes sense for your topic. Make an outline for your presentation and assign part of it to each group member. Prepare questions to ask in real or role-played interviews. Make note cards to use during your part of the documentary.

**Use Visuals** List the visuals you'll need. Decide who will find or make each visual. Use a variety of images, including photos and maps. If a video recorder is available, you may film important images and interviews with people. Or you can role-play an interview during your presentation, letting one group member play an expert by answering questions with real quotes from that person.

**3** **PRACTICE AND PRESENT** Practice your part until you know it well. Use your note cards only as a memory aid. Then practice your documentary as a group. Listen carefully to each other, and give suggestions to help make the presentation clearer and more interesting. If you plan to show video clips, make sure you have the necessary equipment and know how to use it. Practice as a group until the whole presentation runs smoothly.

**Deliver Your TV Documentary** Present your documentary to the class. When it's your turn to speak, face the audience (or imaginary TV camera) and speak loudly and clearly. Hold up your visuals and/or pass them around the class at appropriate times.

**4** **EVALUATE THE PRESENTATION**
You will improve your skills as a speaker and a listener by evaluating each presentation you give and hear. Use this checklist to help you judge your documentary and the documentaries of your classmates.

- ☑ Was the subject of the documentary clear and appropriate?
- ☑ Did the group use visuals to illustrate important points?
- ☑ Did the documentary answer the 5Ws—*who, where, when, what,* and *why*?
- ☑ Was the group well prepared?
- ☑ What suggestions do you have for improving the documentary?

**Speaking TIPS**

Write just a few words on each note card, in big letters, to remind you of your main ideas.

Focus on presenting facts, not your own opinions. Identify the sources of your information and visuals.

**Listening TIPS**

Listen for answers to the 5Ws: *who, where, when, what,* and *why*.

Write down anything you find especially interesting or surprising, so you can ask questions or do more research later.

# WRITING WORKSHOP
## Expository Essay

You've learned that an expository essay informs the reader about a topic or explains an issue, using facts and examples to support the main idea. A good expository essay begins with an introductory paragraph that presents the main focus of the essay. The essay includes facts and examples that support the main idea in each paragraph. A clear and logical form of organization, such as cause and effect or classification, is used to present the information. A conclusion that restates the main idea ends the essay.

You will write a five-paragraph expository essay on a topic related to the sea.

**1** **PREWRITE** You can expand one of the paragraphs you wrote about by exploring it further for your essay, or you can think of another idea. Make a list of topics related to the sea. Then read your list and choose one topic to write about.

**List and Organize Ideas and Details** Earlier in the unit, you used a 5Ws chart to help you plan a paragraph for a news article. A 5Ws chart can also be used to organize an expository essay. A student named Emily decided to write an essay about Jacques Cousteau after visiting an exhibit about the oceanographer at an aquarium. Here is the 5Ws chart she prepared:

| Who? | Oceanographer Jacques Cousteau |
| --- | --- |
| Where? | Expeditions of his ship around the world |
| When? | Invented the Aqua-Lung in 1943 (assisted by Emile Gagnan) |
| What? | Invention of the Aqua-Lung and creation of underwater films |
| Why? | So that individual divers could stay underwater |

**2** **DRAFT** Use the model on page 259 and your graphic organizer to help you write a first draft. Write an introductory paragraph that clearly states your topic and purpose. Include three body paragraphs that give the facts you found in your research. Finally, write a concluding paragraph that sums up how the information you found fulfills the purpose of your essay.

**3 REVISE** Read over your draft. As you do so, ask yourself the questions in the writing checklist. Use the questions to help you revise your essay.

## SIX TRAITS OF WRITING CHECKLIST

☑ **IDEAS:** Are my topic and purpose stated clearly?

☑ **ORGANIZATION:** Are my facts presented in a logical order?

☑ **VOICE:** Is my tone serious and free of opinions and attitude?

☑ **WORD CHOICE:** Did I use the formal, correct names for things?

☑ **SENTENCE FLUENCY:** Did I use transition words to connect my facts and ideas?

☑ **CONVENTIONS:** Does my writing follow the rules of grammar, usage, and mechanics?

Here are the changes Emily plans to make when she revises her first draft:

Jacques Cousteau: Inventor and Filmmaker

Although he died in 1997, French oceanographer Jacques Cousteau

is remembered as one of the worlds most revolutionary marine

scientists. Not only did his popular television series make it possible

for viewers to see the depths of the ocean, his development of

innovative equipment for deep-sea diving also made it possible for

~~adventureous~~ individuals to *experience* the ocean. [adventurous]

Have you ever been scuba diving? Were you able to see firsthand

stunning fish or coral reefs? If so, you have Jacques Cousteau

to thank. The word *scuba* stands for Self-Contained Underwater

Breathing Apparatus, also known as the Aqua-Lung. Cousteau

developed the Aqua-Lung in 1943 with the assistance of his colleague,

Emile Gagnan. Without this amazing invention, no one would be able to explore under the sea as easily as divers do now.

Cousteau was prompted to invent the Aqua-Lung when the only other alternative was a clumsy diving suit. It had to be connected ^that to the surface with an air tube. Moreover, the Aqua-Lung wasn't Cousteau's only contribution to undersea exploration. He also helped to develop a mini-submarine that carried a crew of two. It was sometimes called "the diving saucer." It resembled a flying saucer. ^because

Many people know Cousteau's name. He created the television series ^because ^fascinating "The Undersea World of Jacques Cousteau". In it, Cousteau narrated the worldwide expeditions that he and his crew made aboard his ship, the *calypso*. He introduced viewers to deep-sea species they might not have known existed. ~~In a variety of ways,~~ Jacques Cousteau made his mark in the history of marine science. Whether he was making under water movies, inventing important scuba gear, or discovering ^gear the sea for himself, Jacques Cousteau was one of the most important oceanographers in history.

**4** **EDIT AND PROOFREAD**  **Workbook** Page 125

Copy your revised draft onto a clean sheet of paper. Read it again. Correct any errors in grammar, word usage, mechanics, and spelling. Here are the additional changes Emily plans to make when she prepares her final draft.

Emily Weiss

### Jacques Cousteau: Inventor and Filmmaker

Although he died in 1997, French oceanographer Jacques Cousteau is remembered as one of the world's most revolutionary marine scientists. Not only did his popular television series make it possible for viewers to see the depths of the ocean, his development of innovative equipment for deep-sea diving also made it possible for adventurous individuals to *experience* the ocean.

Have you ever been scuba diving? Were you able to see firsthand stunning fish or coral reefs? If so, you have Jacques Cousteau to thank. The word *scuba* stands for Self-Contained Underwater Breathing Apparatus, also known as the Aqua-Lung. Cousteau developed the Aqua-Lung in 1943 with the assistance of his colleague, Emile Gagnan. Without this amazing invention, no one would be able to explore under the sea as easily as divers do now.

Cousteau was prompted to invent the Aqua-Lung when the only other alternative was a clumsy diving suit that had to be connected to the surface with an air tube. Moreover, the Aqua-Lung wasn't Cousteau's only contribution to undersea exploration. He also helped to develop a mini-submarine that carried a crew of two. It was sometimes called "the diving saucer" because it resembled a flying saucer.

Many people know Cousteau's name because he created the fascinating television series "The Undersea World of Jacques Cousteau." In it, Cousteau narrated the worldwide expeditions that he and his crew made aboard his ship, the *calypso*. He introduced viewers to deep-sea species they might not have known existed.

Jacques Cousteau made his mark in the history of marine science in a variety of ways. Whether he was making under water movies, inventing important scuba gear, or discovering the sea for himself, Jacques Cousteau was one of the most important oceanographers in history.

**5 PUBLISH** Prepare your final draft. Share your essay with your teacher and classmates.

Workbook
Page 126

# The Power of the Sea

*F*or early explorers, the sea was unknown territory, full of mystery and adventure. For fishermen, the sea is a place of work. For vacationers, the sea is a peaceful and relaxing escape from city life. American artists have for centuries depicted people's relationship with the sea. Some artists painted tranquil beach scenes. Other artists explored the darker side, where humans are reduced to a speck against nature's watery expanse.

## Albert Pinkham Ryder, *Flying Dutchman* (completed by 1887)

Albert Pinkham Ryder grew up in the nineteenth-century whaling town of New Bedford, Massachusetts. In *Flying Dutchman*, he painted a scene based on a seafarer's tale involving a Dutch captain, who boasted that he could sail around one of the most treacherous stretches of water in the world—the Cape of Good Hope off the coast of South Africa—and is cursed to sail the seas forever. The legend tells that the ship, the *Flying Dutchman*, can never again reach land until the captain asks for forgiveness for his pride and the curse is lifted.

▲ Albert Pinkham Ryder, *Flying Dutchman*, completed by 1887, oil, 14¼ x 17¼ in., Smithsonian American Art Museum

In the center of the painting a man, barely distinguishable from the overwhelming sea, reaches out his hand toward a ship in the distance. It's the Dutch captain's son, who has grown old looking for the object that could break the curse. He has failed in his quest and can only look on as his father's ship, the *Flying Dutchman*, continues its endless voyage.

Ryder fought a heroic battle of his own with his painting process. Eager to enrich his work with a unique glow and power, Ryder experimented with different paint mixtures, many of which contained a lot of oil. The layers of color often never dried, so over time the paintings shriveled and cracked. Ryder loved to rework his paintings again and again. In a way, he, too, was on a never-ending journey as an artist who was never quite finished with a piece, in search of the perfect paint for his canvases.

### Joseph Cornell, *Untitled* (about 1940–60)

Joseph Cornell saw these compasses in a window in New York City. He then saw some boxes in another window. He was curious about how these objects might work together as a unit. He found that when he put an ordinary object into one of the finely crafted boxes, the object suddenly came alive and gained a special quality that it lacked when alone. Cornell roamed the streets looking for objects and thinking of magical ways to create relationships between one found item and another. He wished to celebrate the "beauty of the commonplace," as he called it. Of course, for a sailor lost at sea, a compass is hardly commonplace—it is a lifesaving device of great power.

▲ Joseph Cornell, *Untitled*, about 1940–60, mixed media, 2½ × 20⅝ × 9½ in., Smithsonian American Art Museum

## Apply What You Learned

**1** How do both artworks relate to the power of the sea?

**2** Which of the two artworks do you think best shows the power of the sea? Why?

 **Big Question**
How would you illustrate the power of the sea?

 **Workbook**
Pages 127–128

# THE BIG QUESTION

# How do struggles build character?

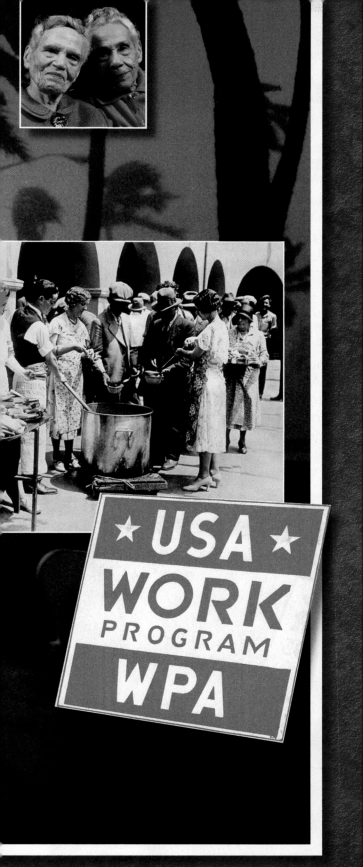

**T**his unit is about struggles. You will read about economic hardships, social conflicts, and struggles with nature. Reading, writing, and talking about these topics will give you practice using academic language and will help you become a better student.

**READING 1: Social Studies Article and Song**
- "Hard Times and Happy Days" by Barbara Weisberg
- "Happy Days Are Here Again" by Milton Ager and Jack Yellen

**READING 2: Novel Excerpt**
- From *The Grapes of Wrath* by John Steinbeck

**READING 3: Science Article**
- "Extreme Weather"

**READING 4: Novel Excerpt and Poem**
- From *Things Fall Apart* by Chinua Achebe
- "A Bedtime Story" by Mitsuye Yamada

### Listening and Speaking

At the end of this unit, you will prepare and deliver a **TV news show** about your school.

### Writing

In this unit you will continue to practice **expository writing**. At the end of the unit, you will write an expository essay.

### QuickWrite

What struggles do people face in their lives? How does struggle affect people? List as many ideas as you can. Then share your ideas with a partner.

# Prepare to Read

## What You Will Learn

**Reading**

- Vocabulary building: *Context, dictionary skills, word study*

- Reading strategy: *Identify problems and solutions*

- Text type: *Informational text (social studies) and song*

**Grammar, Usage, and Mechanics**
Past perfect and past perfect progressive

**Writing**
Write a problem-and-solution paragraph

### THE BIG QUESTION

**How do struggles build character?** Money is something everyone needs. Everyone makes choices about how to earn it and how to spend it. How do you earn and spend your money? How do you manage when you don't have enough money? Do you think having to struggle financially can build character? How? Discuss with a partner.

### BUILD BACKGROUND

The year 1929 was the beginning of a hard time for the American people. On October 29, the New York Stock Exchange, a place where people buy and sell stocks, or shares in businesses, crashed. Stocks suddenly became worth less money than before, and as a result, people lost a great deal of money. A period called the Great Depression began. In a depression, business is bad. Jobs are extremely difficult to find. A severe depression is a time of great suffering for ordinary people. The Great Depression lasted until the United States entered World War II. **"Hard Times and Happy Days"** is an informational article about events and conditions during the Great Depression.

People gather outside the New York Stock Exchange in New York City on the day the market crashed. ▶

**Learn Key Words**

Read these sentences. Use the context to figure out the meaning of the red words. Use a dictionary to check your answers. Then write each word and its meaning in your notebook.

1. When everyone wants a new car, there is a strong demand for cars.

2. The retired worker used his monthly pension to pay bills and buy food.

3. Automobile production increases when many people have money to buy automobiles.

4. After we bought the company's stock, we owned a small part of that company.

5. Farmers supply the nation with food. When bad weather destroys crops, they may be unable to provide enough food.

6. Farmers sometimes grow too much wheat. This crop surplus can cause the price of wheat to fall.

7. Unemployment can have terrible consequences. People need jobs in order to live.

| Key Words |
| --- |
| demand |
| pension |
| production |
| stock |
| supply |
| surplus |
| unemployment |

**Practice**
Workbook
Page 129

Write the sentences in your notebook. Choose a red word from the box above to complete each sentence. Then take turns reading the sentences aloud with a partner.

1. The _____ of cars requires large amounts of steel and various other materials.

2. Successful stores _____ their customers with things they need.

3. A _____ of heating oil that year caused the price of heating oil to fall.

4. When there is high _____, many people cannot find jobs.

5. There is a great _____ today for cell phones.

6. Social Security is a type of _____ you begin to collect when you retire.

7. People buy a company's _____ hoping it will increase in value.

## Learn Academic Words

Study the **red** words and their meanings. You will find these words useful when talking and writing about informational texts. Write each word and its meaning in your notebook. After you read "Hard Times and Happy Days," try to use these words to respond to the text.

### Academic Words

assistance
economy
invest
recovery
regulate

| | |
|---|---|
| **assistance** = help or support | Victims of a natural disaster need the government's **assistance** to return to normal. |
| **economy** = the way that money and products are produced and used in a particular country, area, etc. | Low unemployment is one sign of a healthy **economy**. High productivity is another. |
| **invest** = give money to a company, bank, etc., in order to get a profit later | When people think a company will be successful, they are willing to **invest** money in it. |
| **recovery** = the process of returning to a normal condition after a period of trouble or difficulty | The city is still in the process of **recovery** from the hurricane. Homes are being rebuilt and the streets are being cleaned up. |
| **regulate** = control an activity or process, usually by having rules | During emergencies states **regulate** prices to keep them from going up. |

## Practice

**Workbook** Page 130

Work with a partner to complete these sentences using the sentence starters. Include the **red** word in your sentence. Then write the sentence in your notebook.

1. Food, money, or housing for flood victims are . . . (**assistance**)
2. Creating new jobs is one way to . . . (**economy**)
3. The stock market is . . . (**invest**)
4. Government aid after a disaster like a tsunami helps . . . (**recovery**)
5. Many people believe governments should . . . (**regulate**)

Students build houses to aid in the recovery process following Hurricane Katrina. ▶

## Word Study: Frequently Misspelled Words

Spelling can be difficult in English. Some words are particularly tricky. Learning how to spell these words correctly can save you time looking up words in a dictionary. Look at the examples below.

| Frequently Misspelled Words | Spelling Errors |
|---|---|
| guarantee, budgeted | Missing silent letters: *garantee, bugeted* |
| recommended, generally | Missing double letters: *recomended, generaly* |
| desperate | Missing unstressed letters, such as *desprate* |
| tragedy, ambitious | Confusing vowel or consonant sounds: *tragidy, ambisious* |
| profitable | Confusing endings: *profitible* |
| believed, receive | Mixing up letters: *beleived, recieve* |
| until | Adding double letters: *untill* |

**Practice**  **Workbook Page 131**

Work with a partner. Correct the spelling errors in the following words. Find the words in the reading to check your work. Then write your own sentence using each word.

| | | | | |
|---|---|---|---|---|
| acters | busness | charitible | niether | prosprous |
| briges | candidite | goverment | presidencial | sucessful |

---

### READING STRATEGY | IDENTIFY PROBLEMS AND SOLUTIONS

Identifying problems and solutions helps you understand a text better. Many informational texts describe a problem or problems and explain how they were solved. To identify problems and solutions, follow these steps:

- Ask yourself: What problem or problems are described?
- Think about your own experience and knowledge of similar situations. What would you have done to solve the problem?
- Now read on and find out how the problem was actually solved. Was the solution a good one? Can you think of other solutions that would have been equally—or more—effective?

As you read "Hard Times and Happy Days," ask yourself what problems are presented. How were these problems resolved?

 **Workbook Page 132**

**Set a purpose for reading** What hardships did Americans face during the Great Depression? How did the country's leaders attempt to deal with the situation? How might these hardships have built the character of American citizens?

# HARD TIMES AND HAPPY DAYS

*Barbara Weisberg*

In the spring of 1929, the economy of the United States seemed to be flourishing. The stock market had been rising steadily for almost a decade. Business was booming, and unemployment was low. Factories were producing exciting new products such as radios. Middle- and upper-class Americans felt more prosperous than ever. Few people recognized that the nation was about to fall into an economic slump so deep and terrible that it would be called the Great Depression.

## Trouble Ahead

In fact, trouble had been building throughout the 1920s. Much of the nation's wealth was owned by only a small percentage of the population. Poorer people such as low-paid factory workers and struggling farmers had difficulty supporting their families. In an effort to earn a decent living, some farmers had planted so much that they had created a surplus of crops. As a result, the price of wheat and other crops had fallen. Many farmers had to borrow money from banks just to continue farming.

As for those who seemed to get richer every day, the fortunes created in the 1920s were far from secure. Many investors were buying stocks on margin. This meant that they were borrowing money from banks and other financial institutions to invest. If the price of a stock dropped, the investor lost money. In addition, there were no guarantees that businesses would remain as profitable as they had been. For example, demand was already slowing down for some products, such as cars. Americans who could afford to buy cars had already bought them.

## The Stock Market Crash

In the fall of 1929, confidence in business and the stock market began to waver. On October 24, a day that came to be called Black Thursday, investors panicked and rushed to sell their stocks. Anxious crowds jammed the streets around the New York Stock Exchange shouting "Sell, sell." Many investors were financially ruined when stock prices collapsed.

---

**flourishing**, growing well
**prosperous**, rich and successful
**slump**, sudden fall in the value of something

**profitable**, producing money from selling things
**waver**, be uncertain
**collapsed**, fell suddenly

Five days later, on October 29—a date now known as Black Tuesday—the stock market crashed, falling even lower. Within a month, stocks had lost more than a third of their value. Although the stock market crash alone did not cause the Great Depression, it signaled that the catastrophe had begun.

## The Great Depression

The downturn in the economy affected almost everyone, rich and poor alike. Men and women raced to the bank to try to remove their savings, only to find that the banks had locked their doors. Over the next three years, thousands of banks failed. Since most Americans had little or no money to make purchases, production slowed almost to a stop. Owners shut down their businesses, corporations, and factories. Workers were laid off. By 1933, more than a quarter of America's work force was unemployed.

In cities around the country, unemployed workers, hoping for a little food, stood for hours in long breadlines run by charities. Former business executives sold pencils and apples on the street to earn a few pennies. Many people were left not only hungry but homeless. The homeless created whole villages of flimsy tents and cardboard shelters, called "Hoovervilles" after President Hoover, whom many blamed for the country's woes. Some of the homeless hid in the boxcars of trains and rode from town to town, becoming known as tramps or hoboes.

---

**value**, amount of money something is worth
**catastrophe**, terrible event that causes a lot of suffering
**failed**, went out of business due to lack of money

---

**were laid off**, lost their jobs
**charities**, organizations that give help
**shelters**, places that protect you from bad weather

▲ Hoovervilles like this one sprung up around the country.

▲ Breadlines were a common sight.

**BEFORE YOU GO ON**

1. What happened when the stock market crashed in 1929?

2. How did the downturn in the economy affect businesses? How did it affect banks?

**On Your Own**
Imagine that you are a businessperson or a worker during the Depression. Describe the problems that you face.

★ USA ★ WORK PROGRAM WPA

## The Dust Bowl

During the Great Depression, the problems in rural areas also deepened. Since many farmers had over-planted their fields, the soil in these regions was no longer fertile. Across the middle of the nation—a wide area that included parts of Texas, Oklahoma, New Mexico, Kansas, and Colorado—nature added to the tragedy. There was a terrible drought, a period when no rain fell. Dry from drought and overuse, the soil began to blow away in great clouds of dust. Dust covered cars, blew through windows, settled on food, burned eyes, and sometimes grew so thick that it blocked sunlight.

The area struck by drought became known as the Dust Bowl. Unable to farm, many Dust Bowl residents could not pay back their mortgages, the money they had borrowed on their homes and land. When banks foreclosed, farmers lost everything they owned. Tenant farmers, who rented land from a bank or landlord, could not pay their rent. Farmers by the thousands were forced from their homes in the early 1930s and traveled west in search of a new way of life. Many reached California but found little work there except migrant labor.

**rural**, related to the countryside
**deepened**, got worse
**fertile**, able to produce a lot of plants

**foreclosed**, took away their property
**migrant labor**, work done by people who move from place to place

## THE DUST BOWL STATES

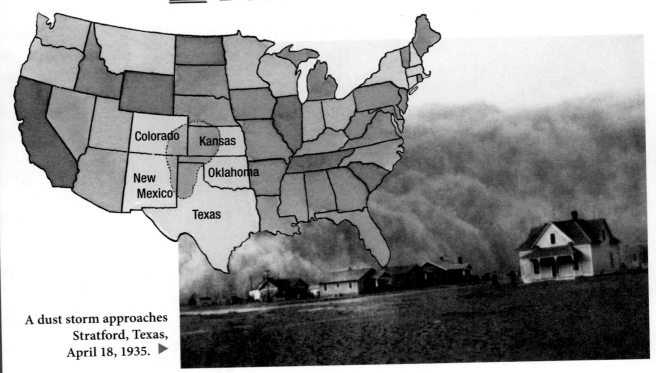

A dust storm approaches Stratford, Texas, April 18, 1935. ▶

▲ President Herbert Hoover

▲ Franklin D. Roosevelt shaking hands with a coal miner in West Virginia during a campaign trip

## Presidents Take Action

When the Great Depression struck in 1929, the federal government had no programs, such as those that exist today, to help Americans through difficult times. There was neither unemployment insurance, nor Social Security, nor protection for individuals' personal savings if banks failed.

The president of the United States, Herbert Hoover, was a Republican who had only recently been elected in 1928—a year in which America still seemed prosperous. Hoover, a successful mining engineer, had previously served as Secretary of Commerce. Like many other business and government leaders—both then and now—he believed that the nation's economy worked best when government did not interfere in business and industry. Hoover also felt that

people grew stronger by solving their own problems rather than by relying on government assistance. He had faith that charitable and voluntary efforts would cure the Depression.

President Hoover, however, soon recognized that more unusual and drastic measures were needed. He asked Congress for money to begin ambitious public works projects such as bridges, roads, and dams—projects intended to put the unemployed back to work.

His efforts seemed to a mostly despairing public to be too little and to come too late.

---

**unemployment insurance**, money paid by the government to people who have no job
**Social Security**, money paid by the government to people who are old
**interfere**, get involved

**drastic**, extreme
**public works**, projects built by the government for public use
**despairing**, feeling there is no hope

**BEFORE YOU GO ON**

1 Why were many tenant farmers in the Dust Bowl forced to leave their homes in the early 1930s?

2 According to President Hoover, how did the nation's economy work best?

**On Your Own**
What do you think everyday life would be like during a drought or a dust storm? What problems would you face?

★ USA ★ WORK PROGRAM WPA

In 1932, Hoover lost the presidential election to a Democratic candidate who promised the nation a fresh start. The new president's name was Franklin Delano Roosevelt, and he offered Americans what he called "A New Deal." The theme song of his campaign began with the words, "Happy Days Are Here Again."

Although wealthy himself, Roosevelt had great sympathy for suffering Americans, in part because he had overcome great obstacles in his own life. In 1921, at the age of 39, he had contracted polio. The disease had left him unable to walk without assistance, and he generally used a wheelchair.

A man who believed in action, Roosevelt recommended an astonishing number of new programs to Congress. These were aimed at using the government's power to improve the lives of Americans. During his administration, the Federal Deposit Insurance Corporation (FDIC) was created. This organization still insures bank customers' savings. Congress also passed laws to regulate the stock market.

In addition, money was budgeted to put people back to work. Congress approved money for New Deal programs such as the Civilian Conservation Corps (CCC). The CCC hired jobless young people to work outdoors, planting trees, fighting forest fires, and building roads and bridges. The Tennessee Valley Authority created dams and public power plants to supply a vast area of rural America with electricity for the first time. The Works Progress Administration (WPA), employed writers, artists, actors, and musicians on projects such as painting colorful murals and performing free concerts.

Roosevelt also ensured that funds were allocated to provide food and shelter for the hungry and homeless. The Social Security Act, passed during the New Deal, guaranteed that the elderly, who could no longer work, would receive a pension. Many New Deal programs, including Social Security, remain in force today.

Roosevelt's policies were controversial. Some leaders argued that his policies would not end the Depression but instead would delay recovery. They worried that New Deal programs would burden both businesses and the public with high taxes and encourage individuals to depend too much on federal aid.

In fact, only America's entry into World War II in 1941 actually brought the Great Depression to an end. Still, the majority of Americans felt thankful to Franklin Delano Roosevelt for his achievements on their behalf. As president, he not only gave the country hope during desperate times. He also used the federal government's powers in bold and lasting new ways to offer needy Americans a helping hand.

contracted, became ill with
insures, protects
budgeted, set aside

" . . . the only thing we have to fear is fear itself—nameless, unreasoning, unjustified terror which paralyzes needed efforts to convert retreat into advance."
—President Franklin D. Roosevelt

allocated, set aside
controversial, causing a lot of disagreement
delay, make late
burden, cause trouble for

# Happy Days Are Here Again

## Music and Lyrics by Milton Ager and Jack Yellen

★ ★ ★ ★ ★ ★ ★ ★ ★

So long sad times
Go long bad times
We are rid of you at last

Howdy gay times
Cloudy gray times
You are now a thing of the past

Happy days are here again
The skies above are clear again
So let's sing a song of cheer again
Happy days are here again

---

**are rid of you**, made you go away
**howdy**, hello (informal)
**gay**, bright and happy

Altogether shout it now
There's no one
Who can doubt it now
So let's tell the world about it now

Happy days are here again
Your cares and troubles are gone
There'll be no more from now on
From now on . . .

Happy days are here again
The skies above are clear again
So let's sing a song of cheer again

Happy times
Happy nights
Happy days
Are here again!

◄ A WPA
mural depicting
factory workers,
Coit Tower,
San Francisco

## BEFORE YOU GO ON

**1** What role did President Roosevelt think the government should play in fighting the Depression? Did everyone agree with him? Explain.

**2** What was the Social Security Act and why was it important?

💡 **On Your Own**
Why do you think programs like the CCC and the WPA were successful?

★ USA ★ WORK PROGRAM WPA

# Review and Practice

## COMPREHENSION

**Workbook** Page 133

### Right There

1. When did the downturn in the U.S. economy begin? Who was affected by it?
2. What name was given to the region hit by drought during the Great Depression? What states did this region include?

### Think and Search

3. Describe the problems faced by farmers during the Depression.
4. How did Presidents Hoover and Roosevelt try to end the Depression?

### Author and You

5. What were some signs of economic trouble during the 1920s? Why do you think people didn't pay attention to these signs? What does this suggest about attitudes during this period?
6. Which solution to the problem of the Great Depression does the author favor? Support your answer. Point to parts of the text that show the author's attitude about the presidents.

### On Your Own

7. What do you think you would have done to survive during the Depression?
8. In your opinion, what can people and their leaders do to prevent problems in the economy?

▲ A man in a dust storm in the Dust Bowl region during the 1930s

## IN YOUR OWN WORDS

Work with a partner. Take turns describing the problems the country faced during the Great Depression. Explain the causes and effects of these problems and what the country's leaders did to solve them.

> **Speaking TIP**
>
> Use examples and visual aids that support your main points.

## DISCUSSION

Discuss in pairs or small groups.

1. In his First Inaugural Address in 1933, President Roosevelt told the American people, "The only thing we have to fear is fear itself." What did he mean? How can fear contribute to a problem?

2. The song "Happy Days Are Here Again" was written after the stock market crash. Read the song aloud. Why do you think it was so popular during the Great Depression?

3. What experiences have you had that help you understand that you are part of a community economy?

**Q How do struggles build character?** Hoover believed that in hard times people should help themselves. Roosevelt believed they should have government assistance. Who do you agree with and why?

**Listening TIP**

When listening to your classmates' responses, listen for examples they use to illustrate their ideas. Think about how these ideas are similar to or different from your own.

## READ FOR FLUENCY

When we read aloud to communicate meaning, we group words into phrases, pause or slow down to make important points, and emphasize important words. Pause for a short time when you reach a comma and for a longer time when you reach a period. Pay attention to rising and falling intonation at the end of sentences.

Work with a partner. Choose a paragraph from the reading. Discuss which words seem important for communicating meaning. Practice pronouncing difficult words. Give each other feedback.

## EXTENSION  Workbook Page 133

The hardship and struggles that people experienced during the Great Depression were recorded in many different art forms, including photos, paintings, songs, personal narratives, and oral histories. Use the Internet and the library to find examples and information about one of these forms of expression during the Depression years. Write a brief report and present the results of your research to the class. Include examples and explain how they deepen our understanding of the Depression.

# Grammar and Writing

## Past Perfect and Past Perfect Progressive

Use the past perfect to describe an event or action that was completed before a certain time in the past. The past perfect is formed with *had* + the past participle.

> Within a month, stocks **had lost** more than a third of their value.
> In 1921, at the age of 39, Roosevelt **had contracted** polio.

Use the past perfect progressive to describe an event or action that was in progress before another event or action in the past. The past perfect progressive is formed with *had* + the past participle + verb + *-ing*.

> By early 1929, the stock market **had been rising** steadily for almost a decade.
> In fact, trouble **had been building** throughout the 1920s.

Use both of these forms with the simple past to show the order in which two past events happened.

> simple past         past perfect
> The crash **occurred** in 1929. Stock prices **had been** high for months.
>
> [1st event: Stock prices were high. 2nd event: The crash occurred.]
>
> past perfect progressive        simple past
> He **had been working** in the factory for a year when the stock market **crashed**.
>
> [1st event: He was working in the factory. 2nd event: The stock market crashed.]

## Practice

**Workbook** Page 134

Copy the sentences below into your notebook. Underline all the verbs. With a partner, identify the order of the events in each sentence.

1. When Hoover left office, the economy had been in a slump for three years.
2. They had already lost their jobs when the company closed.
3. When stock prices fell, he had been selling his stocks for two weeks.
4. The workers had organized a union before they went on strike.

276

# WRITING AN EXPOSITORY PARAGRAPH

## Write a Problem-and-Solution Paragraph

In a problem-and-solution paragraph, the writer describes a problem and explains how the problem was solved. The writer might also discuss why the solution was effective.

| Problem | Solutions |
|---------|-----------|
|         |           |

For example, imagine that you wanted to buy a car but didn't have the money. Your paragraph would describe the problem (lack of money) and explain how you solved it (you got a job after school and saved for a year). You might also discuss how working and saving are effective strategies for getting a large sum of money.

Notice how the writer of the model below clearly describes both the problem and the solution and also explains why the solution worked. Before writing, the writer used a T-chart to list her ideas.

Casey Baginski

### Making Our School Green

Last year, I noticed that students were throwing away a huge number of empty juice and water bottles at school. Since these bottles could easily be recycled, my friends and I decided to dedicate ourselves to acquiring recycling bins for the classrooms and cafeteria. We proposed the idea to the administration, and, within a short time, recycling bins were placed in many convenient spots. At first, we thought the problem had been solved, but, in fact, it had been getting worse. After discussing the situation, we realized that many students had been tossing bottles in the trash their whole lives and found it difficult to break the habit. We made a plan to create signs near the bins to draw attention to them. We also organized a school assembly to explain the importance of recycling. Our new attempts worked! Our efforts also inspired us to form a club dedicated to the preservation of Earth.

**Practice**  Workbook Page 135

Write a paragraph in which you describe a problem in your school or community. Explain how the problem was solved and why the solution was effective. Use a T-chart to list your ideas. Be sure to use the past perfect and past perfect progressive in your paragraph.

## Writing Checklist

**IDEAS:**
☑ I stated the problem clearly.

**ORGANIZATION:**
☑ I organized the paragraph so that the solution follows my statement of the problem.

## What You Will Learn

**Reading**

■ Vocabulary building:
*Literary terms,
dictionary skills,
word study*

■ Reading strategy:
*Draw conclusions*

■ Text type:
*Literature
(novel excerpt)*

**Grammar, Usage, and Mechanics**
Adjective clauses reduced to adjective phrases

**Writing**
Write a summary

### THE BIG QUESTION

**How do struggles build character?** Major events like wars, natural disasters, or economic downturns can change the course of ordinary lives. Has a large event ever affected your life or the life of someone you know? What was the event? How did it change your life?

### BUILD BACKGROUND

In the preceding article you read about the great drought that spread across large areas of the central United States beginning in 1931. By 1934, the lack of rain had turned much of the farmland in Oklahoma, Texas, New Mexico, Colorado, and Kansas to dust. Unable to grow crops in this desert, tenant farmers could not pay their rent. Families who had lived on the land for generations had to leave their homes. Without money or a way to grow their own food, people had to find work. Many made the long journey to California to look for jobs.

*The Grapes of Wrath* is a novel about one of these families and its struggle to survive. The novel put a human face on the terrible suffering that so many people endured during this period.

▲ An impoverished family on the New Mexico Highway during the Depression, 1936

## VOCABULARY

### Learn Literary Words

A **conflict** is a struggle between opposing forces. Conflict can occur between individuals or groups. Some conflicts are internal or psychological. For example, a character may struggle to decide to do the right thing. Other conflicts are external, such as when a character or group struggles against another character or group or against the forces of nature, the economy, or society. Conflict is the main problem in a story. It is central to storytelling because it sets the story's plot in motion. Without conflict, there is usually no story.

In this scene from *Moby Dick,* by Herman Melville, Captain Ahab and a sailor named Starbuck talk about the conflict between Ahab and the great white whale that wounded him. Ahab's conflict is an external one, against a force of nature.

> **Literary Words**
>
> conflict
> mood

> "Vengeance on a dumb brute!" cried Starbuck, "that simply struck thee from blindest instinct! Madness! To be enraged with a dumb thing, Captain Ahab. . . ."
> "I'd strike the sun if it insulted me . . ."

**Mood** is the general feeling created in a reader by a literary text. A writer creates mood by using imagery to describe settings, objects, or the emotions of characters. This imagery makes the reader feel fear, horror, delight, or other emotions, depending on the writer's purpose.

The following description of a once great, but now decaying, old house sets the uneasy, fearful mood of "The Fall of the House of Usher," a famous horror story by Edgar Allen Poe.

> "I looked . . . upon the bleak walls—upon the vacant eye-like windows . . . a few white trunks of decayed trees . . . There was an iciness, a sinking, a sickening of the heart—an unredeemed dreariness of thought . . . What was it that so unnerved me in the contemplation of the House of Usher?"

**Practice**

**Workbook** Page 136

Work in small groups. Explain the nature of the conflict in a film you have seen or book you have read. Pick another film or book and describe its mood.

## Learn Academic Words

Study the **red** words and their meanings. You will find these words useful when talking and writing about literature. Write each word and its meaning in your notebook. After you read the excerpt from *The Grapes of Wrath*, try to use these words to respond to the text.

| | | |
|---|---|---|
| **assess** = make a judgment about a person or situation after thinking carefully about it | ➡ | After the storm, my father tried to **assess** the situation to see how much damage had been done. |
| **finance** = provide money for something | ➡ | Banks **finance** a new business if they think it will be successful. |
| **institution** = a large organization that has a particular purpose, such as scientific, educational, or medical work | ➡ | Public education is an important **institution** in this country; everyone must go to school until the age of sixteen. |
| **method** = planned way of doing something | ➡ | The scientist used a very careful **method** to set up the experiment. |
| **region** = a fairly large area of a state, country, etc., usually without exact limits | ➡ | This year, the northeast **region** of the country has had very little snow; the northwest has had several feet of snow. |

## Practice

**Workbook**
Page 137

Work with a partner to answer these questions. Try to include the **red** word in your answer. Write the sentences in your notebook.

1. What do you do to **assess** a problem?
2. Where can a person find money to **finance** the purchase of a house?
3. Which community **institution** is most important to you?
4. What **method** do you find most effective for studying for an important test?
5. In which **region** of the country do you live?

Farming methods can affect the quality of the soil. ▼

## Word Study: Related Words

Related words are words in the same word family. They are formed from the same base word and have related meanings. Look at the similarities and differences between the related words below.

| Verb | Noun | Adjective(s) |
|------|------|--------------|
| measure | measurement | measurable |
| inform | information | informative |
| help | help | helpful/helpless |

Once you know the meaning of one word in a word family, you can infer the meanings of other words in that family. Try to memorize the meanings of as many suffixes as possible. This will help you when you are trying to understand the meanings of related words.

**Practice**

Work with a partner. Copy the following words into your notebook: *inventive, hope, manage, prevention, enjoy, care.* Use a dictionary to find related words. List the related words in a chart like the one above. Then use each related word in a sentence.

## READING STRATEGY    DRAW CONCLUSIONS

Drawing conclusions helps you figure out the meanings of clues and events in a text. Good readers are like detectives. They put together the clues they find, using them to draw a conclusion. To draw a conclusion, follow these steps:

- Look for clues in the text. Does the information make sense?
- Think about what you already know from similar situations that you have read about or experienced.
- Use a graphic organizer to list the clues you find.
- Add the clues and what you know together to draw a conclusion about what is happening in the text.

As you read the excerpt from *The Grapes of Wrath*, look for clues that will enable you to draw conclusions about what is happening in this episode.

**Set a purpose for reading** How do people react when they learn that they will lose their home and their livelihood? Read the excerpt to find out.

# *from* The Grapes of Wrath

### *John Steinbeck*

*A terrible drought has ravaged farmlands in Oklahoma, blowing away the soil in enormous black clouds of dust. Having lost their crops, the tenant farmers are unable to pay the rent on their farms. The banks, which own the land, send agents to tell the farmers they must leave.*

The owners of the land came onto the land, or more often a spokesman for the owners came. They came in closed cars, and they felt the dry earth with their fingers, and sometimes they drove big earth augers into the ground for soil tests. The tenants, from their sun-beaten dooryards, watched uneasily when the closed cars drove along the fields. And at last the owner men drove into the dooryards and sat in their cars to talk out of the windows. The tenant men stood beside the cars for a while, and then squatted on their hams and found sticks with which to mark the dust.

In the open doors the women stood looking out, and behind them the children—corn-headed children, with wide eyes, one bare foot on top of the other bare foot, and the toes working. The women and the children watched their men talking to the owner men. They were silent.

Some of the owner men were kind because they hated what they had to do, and some of them were angry because they hated to be cruel, and some of them were cold because they had long ago found that one could not be an owner unless one were cold. And all of them were caught in something larger than themselves.

---

**augers**, tools used to make holes
**soil tests**, tests to see if the soil is still fertile
**squatted on their hams**, sat with knees bent, balanced
   on their feet
**corn-headed**, blond

Some of them hated the mathematics that drove them, and some were afraid, and some worshiped the mathematics because it provided a refuge from thought and from feeling. If a bank or a finance company owned the land, the owner man said, The Bank—or the Company—needs—wants—insists—must have—as though the Bank or the Company were a monster, with thought and feeling, which had ensnared them. These last would take no responsibility for the banks or the companies because they were men and slaves, while the banks were machines and masters all at the same time. Some of the owner men were a little proud to be slaves to such cold and powerful masters. The owner men sat in the cars and explained. You know the land is poor. You've scrabbled at it long enough, God knows.

The squatting tenant men nodded and wondered and drew figures in the dust, and yes, they knew, God knows. If the dust only wouldn't fly. If the top would only stay on the soil, it might not be so bad.

*How would you describe the general mood of this scene? What details of the setting and characterization help to create the mood?*

---

**worshiped**, showed respect and admiration for
**refuge**, safe place
**ensnared**, caught in a dangerous situation
**masters**, men in control
**scrabbled**, felt around with your fingers

## BEFORE YOU GO ON

1 Why do the owners and their agents come to talk to the tenants?

2 Why are some owners kind? Why are some cold? Why are some proud?

**On Your Own**
Have you ever been, like the people in this novel, "caught in something larger than" yourself? Explain.

283

The owner men went on leading to their point: You know the land's getting poorer. You know what cotton does to the land; robs it, sucks all the blood out of it.

The squatters nodded—they knew, God knew. If they could only rotate the crops they might pump blood back into the land.

Well, it's too late. And the owner men explained the workings and the thinkings of the monster that was stronger than they were. A man can hold land if he can just eat and pay taxes; he can do that.

Yes, he can do that until his crops fail one day and he has to borrow money from the bank.

But—you see, a bank or a company can't do that, because those creatures don't breathe air, don't eat side-meat. They breathe profits; they eat the interest on money. If they don't get it, they die the way you die without air, without side-meat. It is a sad thing, but it is so. It is just so.

The squatting men raised their eyes to understand. Can't we just hang on? Maybe the next year will be a good year. God knows how much cotton next year. And with all the wars—God knows what price cotton will bring. Don't they make explosives out of cotton? And uniforms? Get enough wars and cotton'll hit the ceiling. Next year, maybe. They looked up questioningly.

✔ **LITERARY CHECK**
*What kind of* **conflict** *is at the center of this scene? How does the author present each side?*

---

**sucks all the blood out of it**, destroys it
**rotate**, change
**pump blood back into the land**, make the land productive again
**hang on**, stay
**explosives**, bombs
**hit the ceiling**, bring a very high price

We can't depend on it. The bank—the monster has to have profits all the time. It can't wait. It'll die. No, taxes go on. When the monster stops growing, it dies. It can't stay one size.

Soft fingers began to tap the sill of the car window, and hard fingers tightened on the restless drawing sticks. In the doorway of the sun-beaten tenant houses, women sighed and then shifted feet so that the one that had been down was now on top, and the toes working. Dogs came sniffing near the owner cars and wetted on all four tires one after another. And chickens lay in the sunny dust and fluffed their feathers to get the cleansing dust down to the skin. In the little sties the pigs grunted inquiringly over the muddy remnants of the slops.

The squatting men looked down again. What do you want us to do? We can't take less share of the crop—we're half starved now. The kids are hungry all the time. We got no clothes, torn an' ragged. If all the neighbors weren't the same, we'd be ashamed to go to meeting.

And at last the owner men came to the point. The tenant system won't work any more. One man on a tractor can take the place of twelve or fourteen families. Pay him a wage and take all the crop. We have to do it. We don't like to do it. But the monster's sick. Something's happened to the monster.

But you'll kill the land with cotton.

We know. We've got to take cotton quick before the land dies. Then we'll sell the land. Lots of families in the East would like to own a piece of land.

---

**go to meeting,** go to church

**BEFORE YOU GO ON**

**1** Why is the land getting poorer? How do the farmers think the land can be saved?

**2** With what do the owners want to replace the tenant system?

**On Your Own**
Do you think the farmers give the owners good reasons for allowing them to stay on the land? Why or why not?

The tenant men looked up alarmed. But what'll happen to us? How'll we eat?

You'll have to get off the land. The plows'll go through the dooryard.

And now the squatting men stood up angrily. Grampa took up the land, and he had to kill the Indians and drive them away. And Pa was born here, and he killed weeds and snakes. Then a bad year came and he had to borrow a little money. An' we was born here. There in the door—our children born here. And Pa had to borrow money. The bank owned the land then, but we stayed and we got a little bit of what we raised.

We know that—all that. It's not us, it's the bank. A bank isn't like a man. Or an owner with fifty thousand acres, he isn't like a man either. That's the monster.

Sure, cried the tenant men, but it's our land. We measured it and broke it up. We were born on it, and we got killed on it, died on it. Even if it's no good, it's still ours. That's what makes it ours—being born on it, working it, dying on it. That makes ownership, not a paper with numbers on it.

We're sorry. It's not us. It's the monster. The bank isn't like a man.

Yes, but the bank is only made of men.

No, you're wrong there—quite wrong there. The bank is something else than men. It happens that every man in a bank hates what the bank does, and yet the bank does it. The bank is something more than men, I tell you. It's the monster. Men made it, but they can't control it.

The tenants cried, Grampa killed Indians, Pa killed snakes for the land. Maybe we can kill banks—they're worse than Indians and snakes. Maybe we got to fight to keep our land, like Pa and Grampa did.

And now the owner men grew angry. You'll have to go.

But it's ours, the tenant men cried. We—

✔ **LITERARY CHECK**
*How is the conflict developed?*

---

**alarmed,** worried
**plows,** large farming machines that cut the soil
**acres,** units of area used to measure land

286

No. The bank, the monster owns it. You'll have to go.

We'll get our guns, like Grampa when the Indians came. What then?

Well—first the sheriff, and then the troops. You'll be stealing if you try to stay, you'll be murderers if you kill to stay. The monster isn't men, but it can make men do what it wants.

But if we go, where'll we go? How'll we go? We got no money.

We're sorry, said the owner men. The bank, the fifty-thousand-acre owner can't be responsible. You're on land that isn't yours. Once over the line maybe you can pick cotton in the fall. Maybe you can go on relief. Why don't you go on west to California? There's work there, and it never gets cold. Why, you can reach out anywhere and pick an orange. Why, there's always some kind of crop to work in. Why don't you go there? And the owner men started their cars and rolled away.

*Editor's note: All over the Dust Bowl, agricultural conditions worsen, and along with them, the economy. The banks take over the land, forcing the tenant farmers to leave. Many of them pack up all their belongings and set out for California, drawn by the promise of work and good weather.*

---

**go on relief**, take money for food from the government

## ABOUT THE **AUTHOR**

**John Steinbeck** (1902–1968) is one of the best-known American authors of the twentieth century. Raised in rural California, he wrote about the working class and migrant workers whose lives he observed firsthand. His first few novels didn't receive much attention, but his later works, such as *Tortilla Flat, Of Mice and Men*, and *The Grapes of Wrath*, are considered classics. In 1962, Steinbeck won the Nobel Prize for Literature.

**BEFORE YOU GO ON**

1. Why do the farmers feel like they own the land?

2. What will happen to the land when the farmers leave? What do the owners suggest that the farmers do?

**On Your Own**
How would you react if you were forced to leave your home? What might you do?

287

## READER'S THEATER

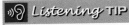 **Listening TIP**

Listen carefully to the other actor so that you know when to say your lines. Listen for cues—words or actions that signal it is your turn to speak.

Act out this conversation between a tenant farmer and his wife.

**Wife:** What did the owner want? What did you talk about?

**Husband:** We had a long conversation. I have some bad news.

**Wife:** [*alarmed*] What is it?

**Husband:** The soil is going bad. The bank's making us move away.

**Wife:** Oh, no!

**Husband:** The owner says that one tractor can do the work of twelve or fourteen families. They don't need us.

**Wife:** [*with emphasis*] But we've always been here! Before us, it was your father's land. Before him, it was your grandfather's land. This is our land!

**Husband:** [*with resignation*] Well, we may live on this farm, but the bank owns it. And now the bank is taking it away.

**Wife:** Can't we beg the owner to let us stay? Maybe he'll be kind.

**Husband:** The owner isn't making us leave, the bank is. And the bank isn't like a person. It isn't kind or mean. It's just trying to make money. And it doesn't care about us.

**Wife:** Where'll we go? We have no money.

**Husband:** I don't know. Out west, maybe, to California.

## COMPREHENSION

 **Workbook Page 140**

### Right There

1. Who are the "owner men"? What plans do they have for the land?

2. What will happen if the farmers fight?

### Think and Search

3. Why do the owners' spokesmen use the word *monster*? What is the monster? What does it eat? How could it die?

4. Why are the tenant farmers angry? What do they try to persuade the owners' spokesmen to do? What arguments do they use?

## Author and You

5. What can you infer about the thoughts and feelings of the wives and children of the tenant farmers as they watch this scene? What evidence can you find to support your answer?

6. Do you think the author shows both sides of this conflict fairly? Is he more sympathetic to one side or the other? Support your answer.

## On Your Own

7. What do you think will happen next? Where will the tenant farmers go? What will they do? What challenges will they face?

8 How did this excerpt add to your understanding of the conditions in the Dust Bowl? Why do you think *The Grapes of Wrath* had such a huge impact when it was published in 1939?

## DISCUSSION

Discuss in pairs or small groups.

1. How does the tenant farm system work? Who owns the land? Who works the land? What happens to the crops? In your opinion, is the system fair?

2. Why is there often conflict over money, land, or employment? What are some ways these conflicts could be resolved?

Q **How do struggles build character?** What was life like for ordinary people during the Great Depression? Do you think that kind of experience builds character? If so, how? Compare and contrast life during the 1930s with life now.

🔊 *Speaking* **TIP**

Make positive comments about the ideas of others. Respect everyone's ideas and feelings.

## RESPONSE TO LITERATURE

**Workbook**
**Page 140**

In small groups, discuss stories of real-life struggles that involve money or property. They can be stories about people you know in your community or stories you read or heard about in the news. Pick the most interesting story and analyze it. What is the conflict? Has it been settled? Was everyone involved in the conflict happy with the solution? Why or why not? Prepare a documentary-style presentation about your story for the class. Assign members of the group to present the facts of the situation, explain the reasons for the conflict, and describe the resolution of the conflict. Include interviews with each of the two parties involved in the conflict.

# Grammar and Writing

## GRAMMAR, USAGE, AND MECHANICS

### Adjective Clauses Reduced to Adjective Phrases

A clause is a group of words that has a subject and a verb. A phrase is a group of words that does not have a subject and a verb. Both adjective clauses and adjective phrases describe nouns. An adjective clause can sometimes be reduced to an adjective phrase to say the same thing with fewer words. To reduce an adjective clause that contains the *be* form of the verb, omit the relative pronoun and the *be* verb.

| Adjective Clause | | Adjective Phrase |
|---|---|---|
| They sell explosives **that are made out of cotton**. | ➡ | They sell explosives **made out of cotton**. |
| The meeting, **which was held on July 18, 2008**, was the struggle's defining moment. | ➡ | The meeting, **held on July 18, 2008**, was the struggle's defining moment. |

An adjective clause that does not contain the *be* form of the verb can sometimes be reduced to an adjective phrase. Omit the relative pronoun and change the verb to its *-ing* form.

| Adjective Clause | | Adjective Phrase |
|---|---|---|
| Lots of families **that live in the East** would like to own a piece of land. | ➡ | Lots of families **living in the East** would like to own a piece of land. |

**Practice**

Rewrite the sentences below in your notebook, reducing the adjective clauses to adjective phrases. Then work with a partner. Check your work by reading your sentences aloud.

1. The companies that were located in that state closed their factories.
2. The people who worked in those factories all lost their jobs.
3. The farmers who were forced off the land had nowhere to go.
4. The family that lived in their neighborhood was very poor.
5. The man, who was an employee of the bank, was very cold.
6. The soil that was in the Dust Bowl was no longer fertile.

# WRITING AN EXPOSITORY PARAGRAPH

## Write a Summary

A common type of expository writing involves preparing a summary. A summary is a restatement in your own words of the main ideas and supporting details of a text. A summary of a story, novel, or play would include the title and author and information about the setting, the main characters, and the main plot events. A summary includes only the most important events in the plot and essential details about the setting and characters.

| Setting | |
|---|---|
| Characters | |
| Plot | |

The paragraph below provides a summary of the excerpt you read from *The Grapes of Wrath*. The writer included only the most important details about the setting, characters, and plot. Before writing, the writer used a graphic organizer to list the important details.

> Trevor Saunders
>
> *The Grapes of Wrath: Excerpt Summary*
>
> In this passage from John Steinbeck's novel <u>The Grapes of Wrath</u>, the land, reduced to dust by drought, is the scene of a great drama: the tenant farmers living on the land for generations are forced to leave and let the banks take over. The greedy banks know that using the land to grow only cotton will eventually ruin the soil, making it unfit to grow other crops, but they care only about making a large, quick profit. The farmers owe the banks money because their crops have failed, and they have no other way to earn money to pay off their debts. The landowners, driven by banks and finance companies, have come to tell the farmers they cannot stay. Some owners feel bad about telling the farmers to leave, but others do not seem to care. A few owners suggest that the farmers move to California where they might find new work.

**Practice**

Write a summary of a story or scene from a novel or play. Remember to include only the most important events and details. Use a graphic organizer to help organize your ideas. Include adjective phrases reduced from adjective clauses.

### Writing Checklist

**IDEAS:**

☑ I included only the most important events and details.

**ORGANIZATION:**

☑ I presented the main story elements in a way that is clear and easy to follow.

# Prepare to Read

## What You Will Learn

**Reading**
- Vocabulary building: *Context, dictionary skills, word study*
- Reading strategy: *Use prior knowledge*
- Text type: *Informational text (science)*

**Grammar, Usage, and Mechanics**
Count and noncount nouns

**Writing**
Write a compare-and-contrast paragraph

### THE BIG QUESTION

**How do struggles build character?** You have probably seen the effects of hurricanes, tornadoes, and blizzards on TV. Perhaps you have experienced some of these and other weather events. How do you think such an experience helps to build character in a person?

### BUILD BACKGROUND

Extreme weather includes weather that is hotter, colder, wetter, or drier than normal. Every year extreme weather events cause terrible loss of life and destruction. In the following article, **"Extreme Weather,"** you will read about what constitutes extreme weather and how it differs from ordinary weather patterns.

A pick-up truck nearly swept away in a hurricane ▶

◀ Two people walking in a snowstorm

### Learn Key Words

Read these sentences. Use the context to figure out the meaning of the **red** words. Use a dictionary to check your answers. Then write each word and its meaning in your notebook.

**Key Words**

circulates
humidity
moisture
pressure
reservoirs
torrents
turbulence

1. The heart pushes blood through our arteries and veins. In this way blood **circulates** to every part of our bodies.

2. The air in the desert is very dry; there is very little **humidity**.

3. A small amount of liquid was on the glass. The **moisture** on the glass made it slippery.

4. The **pressure** in my bicycle's tires was very high. This kept my tires from going flat.

5. The city's drinking water comes from the mountains and is stored in **reservoirs** until we are ready to use it.

6. **Torrents** of water rushed down the mountain. The little stream moved more slowly and the water was much calmer.

7. Flying through air **turbulence**, the airplane bumped around as it was pounded by sudden winds.

**Practice**  Workbook Page 143

Write the sentences in your notebook. Choose a **red** word from the box above to complete each sentence. Then take turns reading the sentences aloud with a partner.

1. On a spring morning, _____ collects on the grass in tiny drops of water called dew.

2. Air _____ decreases as you climb a mountain. This is because fewer molecules of air are pressing down on you.

3. Air _____ made my flight a very rough trip.

4. There might be a water shortage this summer, because the _____ are only half full due to lack of rain.

5. The worst part of summer weather on the Gulf Coast is not the heat, but the _____, the warm stickiness of the air.

6. _____ of rain fell during the storm, flooding the valley.

7. Steam heating is very effective. Heat _____ through a series of pipes to the whole building.

## Learn Academic Words

Study the red words and their meanings. You will find these words useful when talking and writing about informational texts. Write each word and its meaning in your notebook. After you read "Extreme Weather," try to use these words to respond to the text.

| | | |
|---|---|---|
| **cycle** = a number of related events that happen again and again in the same order | ➡ | An animal's life **cycle** includes birth, death, and other stages of development that it goes through during its life. |
| **exceed** = be more than a particular number or amount | ➡ | Weather forecasters expect the number of hurricanes this year to **exceed** the number last year by several storms. |
| **generate** = produce or make something | ➡ | Blizzards can **generate** a tremendous amount of snow. |
| **process** = a series of actions, developments, or changes that happen naturally | ➡ | The aging **process** involves both physical and mental changes that occur gradually over time. |

**Practice**
**Workbook Page 144**

Work with a partner to answer these questions. Try to include the red word in your answer. Write the sentences in your notebook.

1. What is an example of a cycle in nature?

2. What happens when you exceed the baggage limit at the airport?

3. What kinds of storms generate large amounts of rain?

4. What is an example of a biological process?

▲ Hurricanes can generate extremely high winds and waves.

294

## Word Study: Irregular Plurals

Regular plurals are formed by adding *-s* or *-es* to the end of a noun. Nouns from Latin and Greek that end in *-is* or *-us* and nouns from Greek that end in *-on* have irregular plurals. Irregular plurals do not follow general spelling rules and must be memorized.

| Noun ending | -is | -us | -on |
|---|---|---|---|
| **Singular** | cris**is** | cact**us** | phenomen**on** |
| **Plural** | cris**es** | cact**i** | phenomen**a** |

**Practice**
Workbook
Page 145

Work with a partner. Copy the following nouns into your notebook: *analysis, basis, criterion, nucleus, synopsis*. Write the plural form of each noun. Write a sentence using the plural or singular form. Use a dictionary to find the meanings of words you don't know.

## READING STRATEGY | USE PRIOR KNOWLEDGE

Using prior knowledge as you read connects your personal experience with the author's point of view and experience. It also helps you to understand the topic. To use prior knowledge, follow these steps:

- Before you read, ask yourself what you know about the subject.
- After you read, compare the new information to what you already know. Is it similar or different from what you know? Use a K-W-L-H chart to help you.
- Ask yourself if the new information helps you understand the subject better.

Before you read "Extreme Weather," think about what you know. After you read the article, ask yourself how your prior knowledge helped you understand the article.

Workbook
Page 146

**Set a purpose for reading** What sorts of struggles do you think a person might go through because of extreme weather?

# Extreme Weather

▲ This satellite photo of Hurricane Katrina shows its huge size.

One of the worst hurricanes in American history, Hurricane Katrina, slammed into the Gulf Coast of the United States in August 2005. Katrina devastated the entire region, including the famous and beautiful city of New Orleans, Louisiana. About 1,800 residents of that city died as a result of the hurricane and the flooding that followed it. A year afterward, more than half of the 450,000 people who lived in New Orleans before Katrina still had not returned to their homes. Damage to the city amounted to billions of dollars. Hurricane

devastated, destroyed completely

Katrina offered tragic proof that extreme weather events such as blizzards, tornadoes, hurricanes, and droughts can have a shocking and destructive effect on places and people.

To understand extreme weather such as Katrina, it helps to understand ordinary weather. We may talk about a hot or cold day, sun or rain, but weather is actually made by changes in Earth's atmosphere, the blanket of air around this planet. These changes involve the air's temperature, pressure, and humidity; the formation of clouds; the speed and direction of winds; and precipitation, or rain, hail, and snow.

## Sun, Earth, and Air

Perhaps the most important force creating weather is the sun's energy in the form of heat. Because of Earth's position and movement in relation to the sun, the sun's heat makes our world warmer in certain places, such as near the equator; at certain times, such as mid-day; and during certain seasons, such as summer. As the sun's heat warms the earth, the earth in turn warms the air. Warm air, which is light, rises. Then, colder, heavier air circulates around and underneath it. In a continuing process of circulation, warm air rises, is cooled, and falls.

When a large body of air has the same basic temperature and moisture throughout, it is called an air mass. Because an air mass is similar to the surface over which it forms, an air mass that forms over a warm, wet swamp will basically be warm and humid. And so, too, will be the weather in that region. An air mass that forms over a cold, dry plain, on the other hand, will basically be cold and dry, as will the weather in that region. The average weather in a place over a long period of time is called climate.

The weather, however, is not always average. Weather events occur in every climate, mostly because air masses travel. They are moved around the globe by winds, another product of the sun's energy. Surprisingly, even when air masses travel, however, they keep the same general characteristics. When masses of warm, humid air collide with masses of cooler or cold air, dramatic weather events such as storms often take place.

average, usual
collide, hit together with a lot of force

## The Water Cycle

Of course, storms involve precipitation. Another important influence on the weather is a process called the water cycle. As the sun warms the earth, water from lakes, streams, and oceans evaporates into the air as water vapor. The warm, moist air then rises and cools. The water vapor within it condenses into droplets that, in turn, form clouds. Eventually, under certain conditions, the clouds release the moisture, which falls to the ground in the form of rain, hail, or snow, depending on the temperature.

The water that returns to the earth as precipitation is essential. Without it, everything would die. Sometimes, however, weather events are extreme, causing destruction rather than supporting life.

evaporates, changes from liquid to gaseous form
vapor, gaseous form of water
condenses, changes from gas to liquid form
release, let go

◀ A thunderstorm with bolts of lightning

### BEFORE YOU GO ON

1 What happens to the air as the sun warms the earth?

2 What is climate?

**On Your Own**
What kind of climate do you prefer? Why?

297

▲ A tornado with a huge black funnel

▲ A blizzard with whiteout conditions

## Storms

Thunderstorms occur when a mass of warm, humid air meets and rises up violently through a mass of cooler air, releasing tremendous energy and creating turbulence and drenching rains. Thunderclouds produce electrical charges called lightning, and lightning is dangerous. In the state of Florida alone, about fifty people are injured by lightning every year.

Thunderstorms can also generate tornadoes, known as twisters. Tornadoes are spinning, funnel-shaped windstorms that can travel up to 40 miles per hour and can tear houses from the ground. Tornadoes occur most often in an area of the American Midwest sometimes called "Tornado Alley." A series of 147 tornadoes ripped through thirteen states in less than twenty-four hours in 1974.

Blizzards are another type of storm. In cold regions or seasons, a cold air mass can collide with an even colder air mass. Circulating air currents and the processes of evaporation, condensation, and precipitation take place. Instead of rain, the precipitation that falls is snow or ice. Unlike ordinary snowstorms, though, blizzards have high winds that exceed 35 miles per hour. Wind-blown snow can make it impossible for someone caught in a blizzard to see beyond a few inches and can create drifts more than 20 feet deep.

The most furious storms on earth are known as hurricanes in the United States and as cyclones or typhoons elsewhere in the world. A hurricane begins as a storm over warm, tropical waters such as the Caribbean Sea. As the storm is blown by wind, it gathers up heat and energy from the warm water. Releasing this heat and energy in precipitation, wind, and air turbulence, the storm begins to rotate and whips up the water. The energy of the water adds to the energy of the storm and vice versa, until the storm grows into a hurricane.

---

**spinning,** turning around very fast
**ripped,** moved quickly and violently

**rotate,** turn around like a wheel
**whips up,** beats very hard, making waves

298

Some hurricanes are as huge as 600 miles across, and all hurricanes have raging winds between 75 and 200 miles per hour. The winds spin in a circle around a calm center called the hurricane's eye. Within the eye, the weather seems clear and sunny. After the eye crosses an area, however, the hurricane's fury returns full-force. Hurricanes slowly lose power once they reach land. However, they usually cause great damage as they come to shore. Together, high winds, torrents of rain, giant waves, and flooding destroy property and lives.

## Drought

Dangerous droughts occur when there is less rainfall in an area than usual over a long period of time. Without rain, the water in lakes, streams, rivers, and even reservoirs dries up. People have less water to drink. Soil, which needs water for crops to grow, becomes less fertile. Finally, as in the Dust Bowl in the 1930s, the soil can become so dry that it simply blows away.

People can have an influence on drought through how they farm. Surprisingly, the ground itself holds water from underground rivers and precipitation. Plants and trees also hold water in their leaves and roots. Water in the ground, plants, and trees goes through the water cycle.

Sometimes, however, farmers will plow up the natural growth of plants and trees in order to produce more crops. For example, in the Dust Bowl, farmers had destroyed all the grass to make room for more wheat fields. If the ground becomes dry from over-planting, the process of evaporation, condensation, and precipitation is interrupted. Then, if a drought occurs, it may be even harsher and longer.

## Forecasting the Weather

Human beings have attempted to forecast, or predict, the weather for as long as they have occupied Earth, with varying degrees of success. In recent years, technological advances have brought considerable improvements to the science of weather forecasting. Nonetheless, we remain subject to the forces of nature, as extreme weather events like Hurricane Katrina demonstrate all too clearly.

---

**raging**, very strong and violent
**shore**, land at the edge of a large area of water
**fertile**, able to grow a lot of plants

**plow up**, break the ground with heavy equipment

Drought in parts of Africa has left the soil parched and cracked. ▼

**BEFORE YOU GO ON**

**1** What is a blizzard? What causes it?

**2** What happens during a drought?

**On Your Own**
What would you do if a very powerful hurricane were coming to your area?

299

## COMPREHENSION

Workbook
Page 147

### Right There

1. What is an air mass? What is the temperature and humidity of an air mass that forms over a cold, dry plain?

2. Which storm can generate tornadoes? What is a tornado?

### Think and Search

3. What three basic processes occur during the water cycle? How are they related to each other?

4. Explain the process by which a hurricane is formed. How do hurricanes become so large and powerful?

### Author and You

5. The author implies that certain methods of farming can fight the effects of drought. Infer from the reading and your prior knowledge what those methods might be.

6. Do you think the author would agree with the following statement: "The processes that generate destructive weather are the same processes that support life on Earth"? Explain.

### On Your Own

7. How would you describe the climate in your region of the country?

8. How does the weather shape the community you live in? How does weather affect the livelihood of people in your area? Do you know people whose jobs are directly affected by weather?

## IN YOUR OWN WORDS

Work in small groups. Take turns telling one another about one topic you remember from the article. Use the headings to make sure you cover the main topics. Listen and take notes on facts you forgot and details your classmates help you remember. Keep adding facts until together you have covered all the important facts in the article. Then, as a group, give a short summary of the article.

### Speaking TIP

Organize your information. You might use a graphic organizer to show your main idea and details.

## DISCUSSION

Discuss in pairs or small groups.

**Listening** TIP

As you listen, write questions to ask each speaker at the end of the discussion.

1. What part do human beings play in the water cycle? How do we help water circulate? How do we get in the way?

2. What knowledge do you have about global warming? Why is global warming a controversial issue?

3. What things do people do to protect themselves from hurricanes, tornadoes, and blizzards? Could they do more?

**Q** **How do struggles build character?** Have you experienced extreme weather personally, or have you seen people struggling with serious storms on television? How did the experience change lives? In what ways did those storms cause damage or put lives in danger?

## READ FOR FLUENCY

It is often easier to read a text if you understand the difficult words and phrases. Work with a partner. Choose a paragraph from the reading. Identify the words and phrases you do not know or have trouble pronouncing. Look up the difficult words in a dictionary.

Take turns pronouncing the words and phrases with your partner. If necessary, ask your teacher to model the correct pronunciation. Then take turns reading the paragraph aloud. Give each other feedback on your reading.

## EXTENSION

**Workbook Page 147**

Research the latest scientific information on El Niño. What is El Niño? What causes it? How does this phenomenon affect world weather patterns? Are there other weather phenomena similar to El Niño? Share your research with the class.

Farming methods can cause or prevent drought. ▶

# Grammar and Writing

### Count and Noncount Nouns

A count noun can be counted in units with numbers. Regular plural count nouns end in *-s* or *-es*. However, there are irregular plural count nouns, such as *children*, *people*, and *women*. Singular count nouns are often preceded by *a* or *an*.

| Count Nouns | |
|---|---|
| **Singular** | **Plural** |
| a hurricane | several hurricanes |
| one tornado | two tornadoes |

Noncount nouns cannot be counted and are not used with *a* or *an*. Noncount nouns are measured by volume or size, and they usually have no plural form. Many noncount nouns fall into these categories.

| |
|---|
| **Natural phenomena:** weather, hail, thunder, lightning, rain, snow, wind, fog |
| **Fluids:** water, milk, juice, gravy, oil, tea, syrup, gasoline |
| **Solids (food, objects, etc.):** bread, meat, butter, cheese, paper, wood, plastic |
| **Gases:** air, hydrogen, oxygen, carbon dioxide, pollution |
| **Particles:** dust, dirt, sand, salt, wheat, rice, flour |
| **Abstractions:** courage, experience, fun, generosity, happiness, knowledge, patience, wisdom |

Some nouns can be count or noncount nouns.

| Count | Noncount |
|---|---|
| I would like **a glass** of water. **A light** shone in the window. | Windowpanes are made of **glass**. The sun let **light** into the room. |

**Practice**  **Workbook** Page 148

Work with a partner. Take turns identifying the following nouns as count or noncount nouns: *cats, juice, fun, drought, sand, thunder, clouds, knowledge, plastic, students.* Write a sentence in your notebook for each noun.

# WRITING AN EXPOSITORY PARAGRAPH

## Write a Compare-and-Contrast Paragraph

Another type of expository writing compares and contrasts. In a compare-and-contrast paragraph, the writer analyzes what is similar and different about two or more people, places, or things. A compare-and-contrast paragraph can be organized in two ways. The writer might present similarities first and then differences. Or the writer might present points of comparison one at a time, telling what is similar and different about each.

The writer of this paragraph discusses similarities first and then differences. Before writing, she listed her ideas in a Venn diagram.

*Emily Weiss*

**The Climates of San Francisco and Philadelphia**

The climates of San Francisco and Philadelphia are similar in some ways and different in others. For example, the average yearly high and low temperatures for the cities are similar: San Francisco's average high is 63 degrees (Fahrenheit); its average low is 51. Philadelphia's average high is 64; its average low is 46. Both cities also enjoy mild temperatures in the spring and fall.

However, the summers and winters in San Francisco and Philadelphia are very different. San Francisco's summers are cool and dry, whereas Philadelphia's summers are hot and humid. San Francisco has mild, rainy winters, while winters in Philadelphia are cold, usually with a couple of snowstorms a year. Though the climates of these two cities are similar in terms of average yearly high and low temperatures and the mildness of spring and fall, their climates during summer and winter are not at all alike.

**Practice**
**Workbook** Page 149

Write a compare-and-contrast paragraph. Examples of topics include two traveling experiences, two sports, or two fictional characters. Introduce what you are comparing and contrasting, and then present specific similarities and differences. Use a Venn diagram to help organize your ideas. Be sure to use count and noncount nouns correctly.

**Writing Checklist**

**ORGANIZATION:**
☑ The organization of my paragraph allows the reader to see both similarities and differences clearly.

**WORD CHOICE:**
☑ I used words that paint a vivid picture of similarities and differences.

## What You Will Learn

**Reading**

- Vocabulary building: *Literary terms, context, word study*

- Reading strategy: *Identify with a character*

- Text type: *Literature (novel excerpt and poetry)*

**Grammar, Usage, and Mechanics**
Noun clauses with *that*

**Writing**
Write an interpretation

A child being sent to an internment camp in California during World War II ▼

### THE BIG QUESTION

**How do struggles build character?** Think about a time in your life when things were difficult and you had to struggle. What did you struggle against? What lessons did you learn? Discuss your experiences and thoughts on this topic with a partner.

### BUILD BACKGROUND

You will read two very different texts in this section. One is an excerpt from the novel *Things Fall Apart*, written by an African, Chinua Achebe. The other, **"A Bedtime Story,"** is a poem written by Mitsuye Yamada, whose parents were Japanese immigrants to America.

Both writers witnessed and personally experienced great struggle in their lives. Achebe's nation, Nigeria, was torn by civil war. Yamada and her family were interned, or imprisoned, during World War II in a camp for Japanese Americans. The struggles of these authors define their work. Achebe writes about the ways traditional African culture has been destroyed by Western customs. Yamada's experiences of war and injustice during her imprisonment also shaped her as a writer. She is a supporter of human rights and peace in her life and her work.

Both writers believe people can find the things they truly value in hardship and struggle and grow stronger in the process.

A dried-up riverbed: one of the ravages of drought in Africa ▶

### Learn Literary Words

Some stories teach a **moral**. A moral is a lesson about right and wrong ways to act. The moral of a story can be stated directly or it can be implied.

A fable is a brief story, usually with animal characters, that has a moral. "The Grasshopper and the Toad," a Nigerian fable, teaches a practical lesson that appears in a moral at the end.

**Literary** Word

moral

Grasshopper arrived at his friend Toad's house for dinner. Before they sat down to eat, both washed their legs. As Grasshopper washed, he made a loud chirping noise.

Toad said, "Friend Grasshopper, would you please stop chirping? I can't eat with that noise."

Grasshopper tried to eat quietly, without rubbing his legs together, but it was impossible. Grasshopper grew more and more frustrated, and could no longer eat. Finally, he gave up and asked Toad to come to his home for dinner.

The next night, at Grasshopper's house, both washed their legs before eating. When Toad finished, he hopped toward the food. Grasshopper told him to go back and wash again, as his legs had gotten dirty when he hopped to the table. Toad did so and returned to the table. As he reached for some food with his front legs, Grasshopper stopped him again, telling him that his legs were still dirty. Now Toad was very angry.

"You just don't want me to eat with you!" he cried. "You know very well that I must use my legs to hop about. I can't help it if they get a bit dirty between the water jar and the table."

Grasshopper answered, "You're the one who started the fight yesterday. You know I can't rub my legs together without making a noise."

From that moment on, Grasshopper and Toad were no longer friends.

*Moral: If you wish to have true friendship with someone, learn to accept each other's faults, as well as each other's good qualities.*

**Practice**   **Workbook Page 150**

In a small group, think of other fables and stories that teach a moral. Write a story of one paragraph that has a moral. Read your stories aloud. Try to guess the moral of each story.

## Learn Academic Words

Study the **red** words and their meanings. You will find these words useful when talking and writing about literature. Write each word and its meaning in your notebook. After you read the excerpt from *Things Fall Apart* and "A Bedtime Story," try to use these words to respond to the texts.

**Academic Words**

appreciation
attitude
compensation
unpredictable

| | | |
|---|---|---|
| **appreciation** = something you say or do to thank someone or show you are grateful | ➡ | We showed our **appreciation** for the meal by sending our host a thank-you note and flowers. |
| **attitude** = the opinions and feelings that you usually have about a particular thing, idea, or person | ➡ | The writer's **attitude** is hopeful, but he is also realistic about how difficult it will be to end the conflict and bring peace to the area. |
| **compensation** = money paid to someone who has suffered injury, loss, or damage | ➡ | The workers were paid unemployment **compensation** when they lost their jobs. |
| **unpredictable** = changing so much that you do not know what to expect | ➡ | Life can be very **unpredictable**. No matter how carefully you plan, you never really know what is going to happen. |

## Practice

Work with a partner to answer these questions. Try to include the **red** word in your answer. Write the sentences in your notebook.

1. How does an **appreciation** of the struggles of other people affect your life?

2. How does a person's **attitude** affect his or her success in life?

3. What should you give in **compensation** if you damage someone's property?

4. In your life, what one thing is most **unpredictable**?

▲ The facial expressions of the Delany sisters, who lived to be more than a hundred, reveal their positive attitude toward life.

## Word Study: The Silent Letters *gh*

In English, there are certain letter combinations that are silent, or not pronounced. Silent letters create problems for students, as they make it more difficult to guess the spelling of spoken words. A common silent letter combination is *gh*. The silent letters *gh* often follow certain vowel sounds. Look at the examples below.

| | |
|---|---|
| /ô/ [as in *ball*] + silent *gh* | daughter, ought, taught, brought |
| /ī/ [as in *bike*] + silent *gh* | night, foresight, high, height |
| /ā/ [as in *cake*] + silent *gh* | neighbors, eight, weigh, straight |
| /ō/ [as in *boat*] + silent *gh* | although, thorough |
| /o͞o/ [as in *moon*] + silent *gh* | throughout |
| /ou/ [as in *house*] + silent *gh* | drought |

**Practice**  Workbook Page 152

Find other words in the readings in this unit that have the silent letters *gh*. Write these words in your notebook. Work with a partner. Take turns reading words from your list as your partner writes them down.

## READING STRATEGY  |  IDENTIFY WITH A CHARACTER

Identifying with a character helps you enjoy and understand a story better. When you identify with a character, you understand his or her actions and feelings. To identify with a character, follow these steps:

- Think about the character's actions. What does he or she do?
- Identify how the character feels.
- Think about your own experiences. Would you do the same thing as the character? How would you feel?

As you read the excerpt from *Things Fall Apart* and the poem "A Bedtime Story," imagine how it would feel to be the main character in each. Think about the things you would do differently from each character. How would you feel if you were in the same situation?

 Workbook Page 153

**Set a purpose for reading** What lessons do the characters in the novel excerpt and the poem learn from the struggles that they face?

*from*

# Things Fall Apart

## *Chinua Achebe*

*The story takes place in the part of Africa that became Nigeria, in the 1890s, just before the arrival of English missionaries. Okonkwo, the main character, is a wealthy farmer and brave warrior, widely respected in the Igbo tribe. His success was hard won, however. He inherited nothing from his father, who was a lazy failure. In this passage, Okonkwo's struggles as a young man starting out are recalled.*

The year that Okonkwo took eight hundred seed-yams from Nwakibie was the worst year in living memory. Nothing happened at its proper time; it was either too early or too late. It seemed as if the world had gone mad. The first rains were late, and, when they came, lasted only a brief moment. The blazing sun returned, more fierce than it had ever been known, and scorched all the green that had appeared with the rains. The earth burned like hot coals and roasted all the yams that had been sown. Like all good farmers, Okonkwo had begun to sow with the first rains. He had sown four hundred seeds when the rains dried up and the heat returned. He watched the sky all day for signs of rain clouds and lay awake all night. In the morning he went back to his farm and saw the withering tendrils. He had tried to protect them from the smoldering earth by making rings of thick sisal leaves around them. But by the end of the day the sisal rings were burned dry and gray. He changed them every day, and prayed that the rain might fall in the night. But the drought continued for eight market weeks and the yams were killed.

Some farmers had not planted their yams yet. They were the lazy easy-going ones who always put off clearing their farms as long as they could.

---

**mad**, crazy
**scorched**, burned the surface of
**yams**, sweet potatoes
**sown**, planted
**withering tendrils**, dying stems of plants
**smoldering**, burning slowly without a flame

This year they were the wise ones. They sympathized with their neighbors with much shaking of the head, but inwardly they were happy for what they took to be their own foresight.

Okonkwo planted what was left of his seed-yams when the rains finally returned. He had one consolation. The yams he had sown before the drought were his own, the harvest of the previous year. He still had the eight hundred from Nwakibie and the four hundred from his father's friend. So he would make a fresh start.

But the year had gone mad. Rain fell as it had never fallen before. For days and nights together it poured down in violent torrents, and washed away the yam heaps. Trees were uprooted and deep gorges appeared everywhere. Then the rain became less violent. But it went from day to day without a pause. The spell of sunshine which always came in the middle of the wet season did not appear. The yams put on luxuriant green leaves, but every farmer knew that without sunshine the tubers would not grow.

That year the harvest was sad, like a funeral, and many farmers wept as they dug up the miserable and rotting yams. One man tied his cloth to a tree branch and hanged himself.

Okonkwo remembered that tragic year with a cold shiver throughout the rest of his life. It always surprised him when he thought of it later that he did not sink under the load of despair. He knew that he was a fierce fighter, but that year had been enough to break the heart of a lion.

"Since I survived that year," he always said, "I shall survive anything." He put it down to his inflexible will.

---

**foresight,** ability to imagine what will happen in the future
**heaps,** large piles
**gorges,** narrow valleys with steep sides
**luxuriant,** healthy and growing thickly
**tubers,** potato roots
**rotting,** going bad
**inflexible,** firm and unbendable

## ABOUT THE **AUTHOR**

**Chinua Achebe** was born in 1930 in Nigeria and is considered one of his country's finest authors. He has written short stories, poems, and novels, including *Things Fall Apart* and *No Longer at Ease*. Achebe, now a college professor in the United States, is still very active within his home country and helped lead a literacy movement there. He has been an inspiration and mentor to many other African writers.

## BEFORE YOU GO ON

**1** What happened to the rains when Okonkwo planted his first seed-yams?

**2** When did Okonkwo plant what was left of his seed-yams? What happened to those plants?

**On Your Own**
Have you ever had to face a very difficult situation? Did it make you stronger? Explain.

# A Bedtime Story

Once upon a time,
an old Japanese legend
goes as told
by Papa,
an old woman traveled through
many small villages
seeking refuge
for the night.
Each door opened
a sliver
in answer to her knock
then closed.
Unable to walk
any further
she wearily climbed a hill
found a clearing
and there lay down to rest
a few moments to catch
her breath.

The village town below
lay asleep except
for a few starlike lights.
Suddenly the clouds opened
and a full moon came into view
over the town.

The old woman sat up
turned toward
the village town
and in supplication
called out
Thank you people
of the village,
If it had not been for your
kindness
in refusing me a bed
for the night
these humble eyes would never
have seen this
memorable sight.

Papa paused, I waited.
In the comfort of our
hilltop home in Seattle
overlooking the valley,
I shouted
"That's the *end?*"
                    —Mitsuye Yamada

---

**refuge**, a safe place
**sliver**, thin crack
**clearing**, small area in a forest where no trees grow
**in supplication**, asking for help from someone in power
**humble**, not proud, insignificant

✔ **LITERARY CHECK**
*Choose the **moral**
that works best with
this poem. Justify
your choice.*
1. *It is foolish to ask
   strangers for help.*
2. *Hardship has
   unexpected
   rewards.*
3. *Wisdom can
   be gained
   only through
   experience.*

## ABOUT THE **POET**

**Mitsuye Yamada** was born in Japan and grew
up in Seattle, Washington. An accomplished
poet, she has written about many subjects.
Some of her most popular works deal with the
time her family spent in an internment camp
for Japanese Americans during World War II.
She has published collections of her poetry, including
*Camp Notes and Other Poems* and *Desert Run: Poems and Stories.*
Yamada is also the founder of Multicultural Women Writers
of Orange County.

**BEFORE YOU GO ON**

**1** Who is the speaker
of the poem? How
old do you think
she is? How do
you know?

**2** Why does the
old woman thank
the villagers?

**On Your Own**
Have you ever had
a bad experience
that had a happy
ending? Explain.

**311**

# Review and Practice

## DRAMATIC READING

**Speaking TIP**

Use a strong, clear tone of voice. Change your tone to communicate changes in the poem.

Work in small groups. Assign each group member lines to read aloud from "A Bedtime Story." Read the poem aloud as a group. Then discuss the images the words create in your mind. Find ways to give expression to the poem's mood in your dramatic reading. For example, a student who sounds older can read expressively the lines spoken by the old woman, and one who sounds younger can read the words of the young person listening to the story. Read the poem again. How was the reading different? How could it be improved? Practice and present your dramatic reading to the class.

## COMPREHENSION

Workbook
Page 154

### Right There

1. How did Okonkwo try to protect his plants from the sun and heat? What was the result?

2. What does the old woman seek from the villagers? How do they respond to her?

### Think and Search

3. In *Things Fall Apart*, why did the world seem to go mad? What was the pattern of the rainfall, and how did it affect the crops?

4. Why were the lazy, easygoing farmers the "wise ones"? Why was a little rain as bad as none at all?

### Author and You

5. What can you infer about Okonkwo's character from this episode? What do his attitude and behavior reveal about him as a farmer and as a man?

6. What is the mood in this excerpt from *Things Fall Apart*? What language does the writer use to create that mood? Give examples.

On Your Own

**7.** What can you predict about the novel from the title *Things Fall Apart*? What did you guess about the poem from the title "A Bedtime Story"?

**8.** Do you know people who have struggled? What helped them get through their hard times?

## DISCUSSION

Discuss in pairs or small groups.

**1.** What is the moral of the episode from *Things Fall Apart*? Support your answer with language from the text.

**2.** What is the mood of "A Bedtime Story"? What imagery does the poet use to create that mood?

**3.** Compare and contrast Okonkwo and the other farmers. In your opinion, did Okonkwo's struggle form his character or reveal it?

**Q How do struggles build character?** Think of people you know who have struggled through hard times. Do you think that hardship makes someone a better person? Why or why not?

**Listening TIP**

Pay attention to each speaker's tone of voice, gestures, and facial expressions. What do they tell you about how each speaker feels about the topic?

## RESPONSE TO LITERATURE

Workbook
Page 154

Imagine you are Okonkwo and many years have passed. Your grandchildren are struggling with problems in their lives, and you decide to write them a letter. Describe how you struggled during the year of drought and rain, and explain the lessons that you learned. Use the wisdom you gained from your own experiences to give your grandchildren advice and encouragement.

# Grammar and Writing

## Noun Clauses with *that*

Noun clauses with *that* are often used as objects of verbs. Look at the sentence below. The noun clause is the object of the verb *knew*.

> Every farmer <u>knew</u> **that without sunshine the tubers would not grow**.

Noun clauses with *that* are often the objects of verbs that communicate thinking or feeling. *That* is often omitted, especially in speaking.

> He <u>prayed</u> **(that) the rain might fall in the night**.
> He <u>knew</u> **(that) he was a fierce fighter**.
> She <u>discovered</u> **(that) the plants were growing**.
> She <u>hoped</u> **(that) they would survive the drought**.

When a noun clause with *that* is used as a subject, the word *that* may not be omitted. However, this type of sentence is not very common. A clause beginning with the pronoun *it* or a phrase such as *the fact*, *the idea*, etc., is used before the subject noun clause.

> **That the rains would come** was unlikely.
> <u>It was unlikely</u> **that the rains would come**.
> <u>The idea</u> **that the rains would come** was unlikely.

**Practice**  **Workbook Page 155**

Work with a partner. Complete each sentence starter with a noun clause. Take turns reading each sentence aloud. First, read the sentence with the word *that*. Then read the sentence without *that*, if it is possible to do so. Write the sentences in your notebook.

1. I believe . . .
2. The fact . . .
3. Have you considered . . . ?
4. I hope . . .
5. It was surprising . . .
6. I forgot . . .

**314**

# WRITING AN EXPOSITORY PARAGRAPH

## Write an Interpretation

An interpretation is a type of expository writing in which the writer discusses the meaning of a literary work. An interpretation states the meaning of the work and uses examples and other details from the text to support the statement. For example, an interpretation of the excerpt from *Things Fall Apart* might begin like this: "Although *Things Fall Apart* might appear to be a story of defeat, it is really about the victory of Okonkwo's spirit over the forces of nature." The paragraph would then present examples from the excerpt to demonstrate this idea.

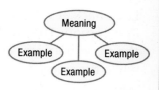

Here is an interpretation of "A Bedtime Story." Before writing, the writer listed his ideas in a main-idea-and-details web.

> *Alan Azar*
>
> ### Half-Empty or Half-Full?
>
> In "A Bedtime Story" by Mitsuye Yamada, the father tells a story to his daughter in order to teach her that the simple pleasures are accessible to anyone willing to look for them. The poor old woman in the tale chooses to see the glass as half-full instead of half-empty. When she is refused refuge by the villagers, she is able to find the good even in her downtrodden situation in life. This theme is emphasized by the father's choice of words as he tells the story. His language conveys the old woman's swift turn from weariness to enthusiasm and thankfulness at the sight of the beautiful moon. However, the fact that the daughter shouts, "That's the end?" is ironic. Her response reveals that she has yet to learn the valuable lesson that the story teaches—that it is possible to find the beauty within every situation.

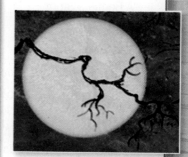

## Practice

**Workbook Page 156**

Write an interpretation of a poem, story, or literary work, such as any of the literature readings in this book or a poem or story you have read on your own. Remember, you will need to refer to the text, so you must have a copy of it. Before writing, list your ideas in a main-idea-and-details web. Use noun clauses with *that* correctly.

### Writing Checklist

**IDEAS:**

☑ The main idea of my interpretation is stated clearly.

**VOICE:**

☑ I demonstrated my knowledge of the text by supporting my interpretation with details from the text.

# Link the Readings

## Critical Thinking

Look back at the readings in this unit. Think about what they have in common. They all tell about struggles. Yet they do not all have the same purpose. The purpose of one reading might be to inform, while the purpose of another might be to entertain or persuade. In addition, the content of each reading relates to the theme of struggles differently. Copy the chart below into your notebook and complete it.

| Title of Reading | Purpose | Big Question Link |
|---|---|---|
| "Hard Times and Happy Days" "Happy Days Are Here Again" | | |
| From *The Grapes of Wrath* | | *illustrates the struggles of farmers during the Depression* |
| "Extreme Weather" | *to inform* | |
| From *Things Fall Apart* "A Bedtime Story" | | |

## Discussion

Discuss in pairs or small groups.

- How does the information in "Hard Times and Happy Days" help you understand *The Grapes of Wrath*? How does the information in "Extreme Weather" help you understand *Things Fall Apart*?
- **Q How do struggles build character?** Compare and contrast the different types of struggle each reading in this unit describes. Do you think that certain types of struggle tend to build character more than others? Explain.

## Fluency Check

Work with a partner. Choose a paragraph from one of the readings. Take turns reading it for one minute. Count the total number of words you read. Practice saying the words you had trouble reading. Take turns reading the paragraph three more times. Did you read more words each time? Copy the chart below into your notebook and record your speeds.

| | 1st Speed | 2nd Speed | 3rd Speed | 4th Speed |
|---|---|---|---|---|
| Words Per Minute | | | | |

# Projects

Work in pairs or small groups. Choose one of these projects.

**1** The Federal Theater Project's "Living Newspaper" took problems of the Great Depression from the daily newspaper and performed them to inform, entertain, and call for action. Work in a group and make your own living newspaper with stories in the news and perform them for the class.

**2** Watch the film version of *The Grapes of Wrath*. After you watch the movie, write a review of it and share it with your class.

**3** Research the most serious extreme weather threats in your region. Find out what the dangers are, if your community is prepared, and what you can do to be prepared in an extreme weather emergency. Draw a chart to show how weather patterns move through your community. Share your research with the class.

**4** Find out ways a community can save water, and check your home, neighborhood, and school to make sure that not a drop is wasted. Draw up a list of water conservation tips and share them with the class.

# Further Reading

To find out more about the theme of this unit, choose from these reading suggestions.

**Oliver Twist,** Charles Dickens
This Penguin Reader® is an adaptation of the classic Dickens story. Oliver escapes from a workhouse and runs away to the teeming streets of Victorian London. There he meets the Artful Dodger, Fagin, kind-hearted Nancy, and the evil Bill Sikes.

**Dust Bowl Diary,** Anne Marie Low
Ann Marie Low's diary captures the "gritty nightmare" of the Dust Bowl as it was lived by one rural family in the 1920s and 30s.

**The Piano Lesson,** August Wilson
In this Pulitzer Prize-winning drama, conflict arises when two siblings argue about selling the family's heirloom piano to purchase a piece of land.

# Put It All Together

## LISTENING & SPEAKING WORKSHOP

### TV News Show

With a group, you will present a TV news show about your school.

**1** **THINK ABOUT IT** Work in small groups to develop story ideas for your show. Write down your ideas. For example:

- The day's top news story: an important event, accomplishment, or situation involving your school
- The weather report for this week, with comments about how the weather will affect students and school activities
- A human interest story: a teacher or student who met an important challenge or overcame a difficult situation

**2** **GATHER AND ORGANIZE INFORMATION** Discuss and plan the overall structure of your show. If possible, watch a TV news show to get ideas. Have each group member choose a story from the list. Choose one person to be the "anchor," who will introduce each story and its reporter. The anchor will report on a story, too.

**Research** Interview students and staff, look at bulletin boards and the school website, and check school and community newspapers to find information for your story. Take notes and get the answers to *Who*, *Where*, *When*, *What*, and *Why* questions. If you have access to an audio or video recorder, tape your interviews so you can play quotations from them during your show.

**Order Your Notes** Make a list of the main points in your story. Think about the best order for telling it, and make an outline showing your main points in order.

**Use Visuals** Look for pictures, props, and other visuals that will help viewers understand your news story. Think about how and when you will show each visual, and mark those places in your outline. Also, plan for any audio or video clips you want to use.

**Prepare a Script** Use your outline and notes to write a script for your news story. Remember to focus on the 5Ws. With the rest of your group, write a short opening and closing for your newscast to be presented by the anchor.

**3 PRACTICE AND PRESENT** Read your script several times until you know it well. As a group, practice presenting your TV news show until all members can deliver their stories confidently, glancing at their scripts only occasionally. Help one another with visuals and sound equipment as needed. Work on making smooth transitions between stories.

**Deliver Your TV News Show** Follow your planned order and scripts. Listen to one another so you know when it's your turn to speak. Emphasize key ideas by pausing, slowing down, speaking more loudly, or restating them at the end of your story.

**4 EVALUATE THE PRESENTATION**
You will improve your skills as a speaker and a listener by evaluating each presentation you give and hear. Use this checklist to help you judge your group's TV news show and the news shows of your classmates.

- ☑ Was the news show presented in a professional way? Was the reporting accurate?
- ☑ Was each story interesting, brief, and clear?
- ☑ Did each story answer the 5Ws?
- ☑ Could you hear and understand each speaker easily?
- ☑ What suggestions do you have for improving the show?

### Speaking TIPS

Always face the audience (or imaginary TV camera) when you speak. Don't hide behind your script or visuals!

Don't interrupt the anchor or other reporters by coming in too soon. Don't leave an awkward pause by coming in too late.

### Listening TIP

Summarize each story in your own mind. How does it fit with what you already know? What new information did you learn?

# WRITING WORKSHOP
## Expository Essay

In this unit you have been learning the skills of expository writing. Now you will use these skills to write a five-paragraph essay that expands one of the paragraphs you wrote earlier in this unit. Expanding upon a topic means investigating and presenting the topic in greater depth. Using the writing elements and structure of your original paragraph, your essay will go into more detail in order to fully develop your topic.

**1 PREWRITE** Reread each of the paragraphs you wrote in this unit. Which topic did you find most interesting? Which topic was too big to be covered effectively in a single paragraph? Decide on your topic. Then think about your readers. What do they already know about your topic? What questions do you think they will have? Brainstorm interesting details you want to add when you expand your paragraph into an essay.

**List and Organize Ideas and Details** Use the same graphic organizer you created for your paragraph, or another one you have learned about in this book, to organize ideas for your essay. A student named Sophie decided to expand the paragraph she wrote interpreting a work of literature. Here is the word web she prepared:

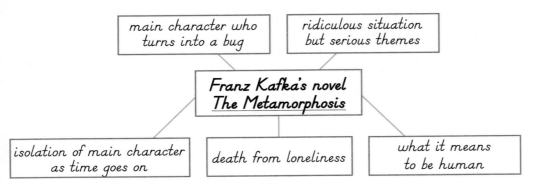

**2 DRAFT** Use the model on page 323 and your graphic organizer to help you write a draft of your essay. Write an introductory paragraph that clearly states your topic and purpose. Include three body paragraphs that extend and deepen your ideas and are structured in a logical way. Finally, write a concluding paragraph that sums up your main points.

**3 REVISE** Read over your draft. As you do so, ask yourself the questions in the writing checklist. Use the questions to help you revise your essay.

### SIX TRAITS OF WRITING CHECKLIST

☑ **IDEAS:** Do I state my topic and purpose clearly?

☑ **ORGANIZATION:** Do I present facts, details, and examples in a logical order?

☑ **VOICE:** Is my tone appropriate for the type of essay I am writing?

☑ **WORD CHOICE:** Do I use words accurately?

☑ **SENTENCE FLUENCY:** Do my sentences begin in different ways?

☑ **CONVENTIONS:** Does my writing follow the rules of grammar, usage, and mechanics?

Here are the changes Sophie plans to make when she revises her first draft:

---

A Strange and Interesting Story

The novel *The Metamorphosis*, by Austrian writer Franz Kafka, tells ^the bizarre story of a man who turns into a bug. Although it has some comical and even ridiculous aspects the novel explores serious themes. Kafka makes readers think about what it means to be human and what it means to lose the things that are necessary for human survival.

The main character, Gregor samsa, awakes one morning to find that he has ^been transformed into a beetle-like creature. In the beginning he perceives his new physical form as an inconvenience. (No explanation is given to the reader or to Gregor, and he is forced to accept his situation.) he worries about being late for work and tries to continue with his daily routine.

---

Gradually, however, Gregor realizes he cannot even open his

bedroom door When family members ^miss him and come to check on him, he

responds in an unfamiliar raspy voice. They soon discover that their

son and brother is now an insect.

^As the story progresses, Gregor becomes increasingly isolated and behaves more and more

like ~~the~~ ^an insect. He stands on the ceiling, crawls across furniture,

and performs tumbling routines. Those who once care about him are

disgusted by him and avoid him as much as possible. They bring him

food on a tray but do not engage in conversation or act^s of kindness.

After a few years, this rejection becomes too much for him. He finally

dies from loneliness ^and despair.

By relating Gregor's outrageous experiences in a matter-of-fact

and straightforward manner, Kafka created a completely new kind

of novel. Clearly, it was a work without ordinary hero^es or villains.

Audiences realized ~~that~~ he had ~~wrote~~ ^written a story that was different from

any other. Gregor's confusion and alienation represented a situation

larger then his own—that of all man^e and woman^e in modern society.

No one who reads *The Metamorphosis* will easily forget it.

## 4 EDIT AND PROOFREAD

**Workbook Page 157**

Copy your revised draft onto a clean sheet of paper. Read it again. Correct
any errors in grammar, word usage, mechanics, and spelling. Here are the
additional changes Sophie plans to make when she prepares her final draft.

Sophie Howat

A Strange and Interesting Story

The novel *The Metamorphosis*, by Austrian writer Franz Kafka, tells the bizarre story of a man who turns into a bug. Although it has some comical and even ridiculous aspects the novel explores serious themes. Kafka makes readers think about what it means to be human and what it means to lose the things that are necessary for human survival.

The main character, Gregor Samsa, awakes one morning to find that he has been transformed into a beetle-like creature. No explanation is given to the reader or to Gregor, and he is forced to accept his situation. In the beginning he perceives his new physical form as an inconvenience. he worries about being late for work and tries to continue with his daily routine.

Gradually, however, Gregor realizes he cannot even open his bedroom door When family members miss him and come to check on him, he responds in an unfamiliar raspy voice. They soon discover that their son and brother is now an insect.

As the story progresses, Gregor becomes increasingly isolated and behaves more and more like an insect. He stands on the ceiling, crawls across furniture, and performs tumbling routines. Those who once cared about him are disgusted by him and avoid him as much as possible. They bring him food on a tray but do not engage in conversation or acts of kindness. After a few years, this rejection becomes too much for him. He finally dies from loneliness and despair.

By relating Gregor's outrageous experiences in a matter-of-fact and straightforward manner, Kafka created a completely new kind of novel. Audiences realized he had written a story that was different from any other. Clearly, it was a work without ordinary heroes or villains. Gregor's confusion and alienation represented a situation larger than his own—that of all men and women in modern society. No one who reads *The Metamorphosis* will easily forget it.

**5 PUBLISH** Prepare your final draft. Share your essay with your teacher and classmates.

Workbook
Page 158

323

# Showing the Strain

*E*veryone at some stage in life experiences pain or hardship. This explains why we often feel empathy when we see others facing difficulty, even if we have never dealt with their problem ourselves. During the Great Depression in the 1930s, one-quarter of American adults were unemployed and millions were homeless. Nearly every family in the country felt the pinch of the hard economic times. Artists are drawn to stories of struggle because these stories are often dramatic and inspirational.

### James E. Allen, *Prayer for Rain* (1938)

In this lithograph, Allen shows a family brought to their knees in prayer by the calamity of the ruined fields. The cattle's skeleton in the far left, the obscured farm in the distance, and the buried plow reflect a lifestyle that has died for this family. Even though this black and white print has a glow, the artist uses light and shadow to create an ominous mood. The V-shaped dip in the land in front of the father seems to be pulling the family down.

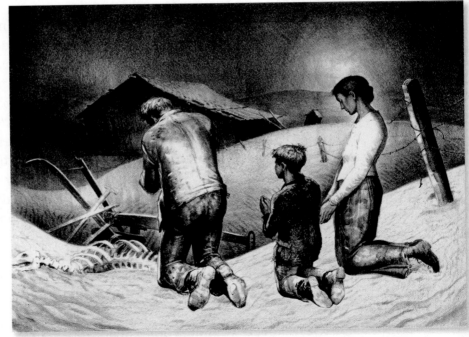

▲ James E. Allen, *Prayer for Rain*, 1938, lithograph, 10½ × 14⅛ in., Smithsonian American Art Museum

324

◀ Alexandre Hogue, *Dust Bowl*, 1933, oil, 24 x 32⅝ in., Smithsonian American Art Museum

## Alexandre Hogue, *Dust Bowl* (1933)

Alexandre Hogue's *Dust Bowl* explores the farmers' struggle during the Great Depression. Farmers in the Midwest watched the rich topsoil blow off their land as record heat and drought hit year after year. The dust clouds took away any chance they had of making a living on their farms. Hundreds of thousands of them had to leave. Most headed west to California, hoping to find work picking fruit in the orchards.

Hogue uses a repeated V shape in the wind-brushed sand, the fence posts, and wire to draw the viewer into his painting. A set of footprints marks the sand, perhaps belonging to a farmer who left. The broken wire and fence overshadow the farm in the distant background. The deep red sky has a blood-like quality, which in turn gives the dust a pinkish tint. Despite the warm colors used, the overall effect is dark and conveys a sense of hopelessness.

Both artists captured the despair of many families who lost everything in the Great Depression. Allen includes the physical figures in his piece, but the faint footsteps in Hogue's painting are enough to tell the viewer that someone was here, and something vital was lost.

### Apply What You Learned

**1** How do these artists use light and shadow in their artworks to create a mood?

**2** Do you think people who first saw these artworks when they were finished reacted differently than people who see them today? Why or why not?

 **Big Question**
Which of these two artworks do you think best captures the struggle people experienced during the Great Depression?

**Workbook**
**Pages 159–160**

THE BIG Q QUESTION

# Why are ideals important?

In this unit you will read about the ideals of people, groups, and countries. Reading, writing, and talking about these topics will give you practice using academic language and will help you become a better student.

**READING 1: Social Studies Article**
- "The Civil Rights Movement" by Eric Waldemar

**READING 2: Speech**
- "I Have a Dream" by Dr. Martin Luther King Jr.

**READING 3: Website**
- "The Peace Corps: An American Ideal"

**READING 4: Essay and Biography**
- "We Are Each Other's Business" by Dr. Eboo Patel
- "Raoul Wallenberg and the Rescue of Hungary's Jews"

## Listening and Speaking

At the end of this unit, you will prepare and present an **oral report** on a topic related to the theme of ideals.

## Writing

In this unit you will practice writing a **research report**. This type of writing presents and analyzes information based on an in-depth study of a subject. After each reading you will learn a skill to help you write a research report. At the end of this unit, you will write a research report about an important idea, issue, or event.

## QuickWrite

What does it mean to have ideals? What are some of your ideals? Use a word web to explore your ideas about these topics. Then share your ideas with a partner.

# Prepare to Read

## What You Will Learn

**Reading**

■ Vocabulary building: *Context, dictionary skills, word study*

■ Reading strategy: *Take notes*

■ Text type: *Informational text (social studies)*

**Grammar, Usage, and Mechanics**
Parallel structure with coordinating conjunctions

**Writing**
Write an introductory paragraph

## THE BIG QUESTION

**Why are ideals important?** Are individual rights an ideal worth fighting for? What would you do if you were denied your rights, for example, the right to go to school, to the movies, or to the shopping mall? Discuss with a partner.

## BUILD BACKGROUND

**"The Civil Rights Movement"** is a social studies article. After slavery was abolished in the United States, African Americans in all parts of the nation were free citizens. They were not, however, free from racial discrimination. Many Americans still held the racist belief that blacks were inferior. As you saw in Unit 3, Jim Crow laws in many parts of the country denied employment, housing, and other opportunities to African Americans.

Obtaining equal political rights and social freedoms and equal protection under the law became a central goal of African Americans during the middle of the last century. The events from 1955 to 1968 that led to the creation and enforcement of federal antidiscrimination laws are known as the American civil rights movement.

Protesters marching to demand civil rights legislation ▶

## VOCABULARY

### Learn Key Words

Read these sentences. Use the context to figure out the meaning of the **red** words. Use a dictionary to check your answers. Then write each word and its meaning in your notebook.

**Key Words**

boycott
enforced
integrate
intervene
oppression
reform

1. We asked everyone to join our **boycott** of the company. Many people agreed and refused to buy the company's products.

2. The police in that city **enforced** the traffic laws consistently. Drivers knew that speeding would result in heavy fines.

3. It took many years to **integrate** the public schools. Many people did not want black students and white students to attend school together.

4. The argument became so loud that friends had to **intervene**; they separated the two men and calmed them down.

5. The leader's **oppression** of his people was a brutal means of gaining control of the country.

6. Conditions in the city's schools were terrible. Both educators and parents called for **reform** of the educational system.

### Practice

**Workbook Page 161**

Write the sentences in your notebook. Choose a **red** word from the box above to complete each sentence. Then take turns reading the sentences aloud with a partner.

1. The teacher had to _____ , or else the two girls would have started to fight.

2. The editorial said that _____ of city government was needed to correct the mistakes of the last mayor.

3. Our _____ of goods from that country was a way of demonstrating that we did not agree with the policies of its government.

4. The government's _____ of the people led to much suffering. The people eventually rebelled and overthrew the government.

5. Before the civil rights movement in the 1960s, laws meant to protect the rights of African Americans were not always _____ .

6. For many years, black students and white students in this country attended separate schools. That changed, however, following a long battle fought to _____ the public schools.

## Learn Academic Words

Study the **red** words and their meanings. You will find these words useful when talking and writing about informational texts. Write each word and its meaning in your notebook. After you read "The Civil Rights Movement," try to use these words to respond to the text.

| | | |
|---|---|---|
| **access** = a way of being able to use or do something | → | Students have **access** to the school's computers during school hours only. |
| **deny** = refuse to allow someone to have or do something | → | The Civil Rights Act of 1964 made it illegal to **deny** people access to restaurants and other public places on the basis of their race, color, religion, or national origin. |
| **issue** = a subject or problem that people think is important | → | Voters were very concerned about the **issue** of education and listened carefully to what each candidate had to say on this subject. |
| **objective** = something that you are working hard to achieve | → | During the 1960s many people participated in protest marches with the **objective** of changing the laws. |
| **status** = a person's social position in relation to other people | → | The **status** of women improved when they began to enter the workforce in large numbers. |

## Practice  Workbook Page 162

Work with a partner to answer these questions.
Try to include the **red** word in your answer.
Write the sentences in your notebook.

1. What people, places, and things do students need to have **access** to?
2. Do authorities ever have the right to **deny** people access to public places? Explain.
3. What is the most significant **issue** facing your generation?
4. What is your most important **objective** at school?
5. How would you describe the **status** of teenagers in American society?

▲ It is important to build public facilities that allow everyone to have access.

330

# Word Study: Suffixes *-ment*, *-ness*, and *-ship*

You have learned that a suffix is a group of letters added to the end of a word to form a new word. Adding a suffix often changes the word's meaning and its part of speech. The suffixes *–ment*, *-ness*, and *-ship* are used to form nouns. Look at the changes in meaning and part of speech of the base words below.

| Base Word | Suffix and Meaning | New Word |
|---|---|---|
| treat (*verb*) | -ment: result of an action | treat**ment** |
| willing (*adjective*) | -ness: having a particular quality | willing**ness** |
| leader (*noun*) | -ship: condition, position, or state | leader**ship** |

**Practice**  **Workbook** Page 163

Work with a partner. Add the suffix *-ment*, *-ness*, or *-ship* to the words below. Then write a sentence using each new word in your notebook. Use a dictionary to check your work.

| scholar | move | advance | happy | friend | nervous | establish |
|---|---|---|---|---|---|---|

## READING STRATEGY  |  TAKE NOTES

Taking notes keeps you focused on what you are reading. It also helps you understand and remember new information. To take notes, follow these steps:

- Think about your purpose for reading the text.
- Scan the text for the key information you need.
- Look for dates, names, places, and events.
- Write notes about the most important facts you need, not the details.
- Don't write in complete sentences. Use short notes, for example: *arrested 4/16/63*

As you read "The Civil Rights Movement," think about the information you want to remember. Take notes while you read. Review your notes and check that they're correct.

**Workbook** Page 164

**Set a purpose for reading** The article focuses on three events in the civil rights movement. How did each event advance the cause of civil rights? How did the people who participated in the events hold to their ideals?

# THE CIVIL RIGHTS MOVEMENT

*Eric Waldemar*

Among the most important events in the American civil rights movement are the Montgomery Bus Boycott; the sit-ins; and the Birmingham campaign.

## The Montgomery Bus Boycott

By 1955, members of the Montgomery, Alabama, chapter of the National Association for the Advancement of Colored People (NAACP) had been working intensively on a plan to protest the segregation of public transportation that occurred in most parts of the South. At the time, the law required African Americans to sit in the back of the bus. If all seats were occupied, the driver could make black passengers give up their seats for whites. Refusing to do so might lead to arrest and time in jail.

Every movement for change benefits from having a "face" that ordinary people can relate to. Rosa Parks, a forty-three-

year-old seamstress who took the bus to and from her job in downtown Montgomery every day, became that face.

On December 1, 1955, Parks boarded a bus for home as usual. She found a seat in the section marked for black people. When no more seats were available and a white man boarded, the driver ordered Parks to stand and give up her seat. Rosa Parks refused. The police were called and Parks was arrested and charged with breaking the law.

**Rosa Parks sitting in the front of a city bus in Montgomery, Alabama** ▼

---

**intensively**, hard
**segregation**, separation of people by race
**occupied**, taken

▲ African Americans walking to work during the Montgomery Bus Boycott

The next day, tens of thousands of fliers were distributed to the African Americans of Montgomery, alerting them to the arrest of Rosa Parks. An active member of the NAACP, Parks was a small, soft-spoken woman well liked by members of the community. Other African Americans could easily relate to her and were angered by her arrest. The leaflets urged them to show solidarity by not riding the public buses for one day. However, civil rights leaders in the community wanted more. They called for an extended boycott, in which no African-American man, woman, or child would ride the buses until their demands for fair and just treatment were met.

Leading the boycott was a passionate young minister, Dr. Martin Luther King Jr. Only twenty-six at the time, King quickly rose to a position of leadership. He saw the boycott as an ideal way to enact social reform through nonviolent protest. A gifted speaker, King delivered church sermons that inspired and united the African-American community.

---

**distributed**, given out
**solidarity**, loyalty and support
**extended**, lengthy
**enact**, bring about

"We are tired," he said, "tired of being segregated and humiliated; tired of being kicked about by the brutal feet of oppression. . . . One of the great glories of democracy is the right to protest for right."

The African Americans of Montgomery agreed with King and responded to his call. They boycotted the buses, not just for one day or even several days. Showing their determination and willingness to make sacrifices, they continued the boycott for over a year. People carpooled, hitchhiked, and walked, rather than set foot on the buses.

The economic impact on the city was significant. Buses that were once full were suddenly half-empty. Some segregationists reacted by bombing the houses of civil rights leaders. However, King urged Montgomery's African Americans to remain nonviolent. "Hate cannot drive out hate," he said. "Only love can do that."

The boycott ended on December 21, 1956, when the Supreme Court ruled that Alabama's bus segregation law was unconstitutional. The Montgomery Bus Boycott drew national attention to the civil rights movement, and it established nonviolence as one of its key tactics. It also thrust Dr. Martin Luther King Jr. into the spotlight as the movement's primary leader.

---

**humiliated**, made to feel ashamed or embarrassed
**make sacrifices**, not have or do some things in order to get something more important
**hitchhiked**, traveled by asking for free rides in other people's cars
**tactics**, skillfully planned actions to achieve something

## BEFORE YOU GO ON

1 What was the original plan for the bus boycott? How did the plan change?

2 How did the boycott affect the city's economy? How did it affect the laws of Alabama?

**On Your Own**
Why do you think the Montgomery Bus Boycott was so successful?

▲ A sit-in at a lunch counter in Greensboro, North Carolina

## YALE STUDENTS PICKET WOOLWORTH STORE

*NEW HAVEN, Conn., Feb. 19 (AP)*—Eight Yale students today picketed a Woolworth store in what they call a demonstration against racial segregation in the South.

Police first interfered with the demonstration but then, after some of the students talked with Mayor Richard C. Lee, let them go ahead.

Leaflets passed out by the students said:

"We are attempting to communicate to others that Woolworth's branches in Greensboro, Raleigh, Fayetteville and Durham, N.C., like many other Southern stores, treat their Negro customers undemocratically and deny to them the same seated meal service provided to white people."

---

**interfered with**, prevented from happening the way it was planned

## The Sit-Ins

On February 1, 1960, four African-American students from the North Carolina Agricultural and Technical College in Greensboro sat down at the F.W. Woolworth Company lunch counter. The section that they sat in was reserved for white customers only. The men were fully aware of this fact but attempted to order lunch anyway. When they were refused service, they did not leave the counter. Instead, they remained in their seats until the store closed. Through this single nonviolent act the protesters drew attention to their cause and showed once again the effectiveness of civil disobedience, which involves breaking a law one considers unjust in order to change it.

---

**lunch counter**, place in a store where quick, simple meals are served

334

| 1957 | 1960 | 1961 | 1963 |

**Black students stage sit-ins to desegregate lunch counters.** (1960)

**African Americans stage sit-ins and marches during Birmingham campaign.** (1963)

↑ Public school integration begins when Little Rock Nine enroll at Central High School. (1957)

↑ Freedom Riders travel the South to integrate white-only facilities. (1961)

↑ Dr. Martin Luther King Jr. gives "I Have a Dream" speech at March on Washington. (1963)

The first sit-in was viewed merely as an annoyance by the store manager and attracted little attention from outsiders. However, when the four men returned the next day with more students, newspapers took notice. Word quickly spread and African-American college students in other cities throughout the country began to enact similar sit-ins at segregated lunch counters, with many targeting the Woolworth Company in particular.

Sometimes these students were waited on, but usually they were not served. Often they were physically and verbally abused by angry whites. By refusing to move, however, the students forced others to take action. Frequently, police were called in, and the students were arrested for disobeying the law. Whenever this occurred, a new group of students quickly took their places at the counter.

By 1961, over 70,000 African Americans across the country had participated in sit-ins, and more than 3,000 had been arrested. Over time, the demonstrations spread to include other public places, such as libraries, museums, theaters, parks, and beaches where discriminatory laws were in effect.

These well-organized, nonviolent sit-ins proved to be an effective and popular method for protesting segregation in public facilities. They also helped train young African Americans for positions of power. Many campus organizers of sit-ins would take on adult leadership roles within the civil rights movement in the years to come.

---

**demonstrations**, events at which people meet to protest or support something
**facilities**, buildings or places

## GROUP ASKS PROTEST SUPPORT

*By The Associated Press*

A North Carolina church group Friday called for support of Negroes in their demand for equal service at lunch counters in stores.

The Human Relations Committee of the North Carolina Council of Churches, meeting in Raleigh, said it recognized "the democratic and moral right of Negroes to equality of service at the lunch counters of stores serving the public."

The statement issued by the committee urged "our fellow citizens, and especially our Christian brethren, to unite with us in openly and firmly defending this basic human right."

The statement was signed by the co-chairman of the committee, Dr. H. Shelton Smith, professor of American religious thought at Duke University in Durham; and the Rev. W.R. Grigg, secretary of the North Carolina Baptist State Convention's Department of Interracial Cooperation.

Meanwhile, there was relative quiet on the wide front sketched out in the last two weeks by Negro demonstrators, many of them college students, protesting segregated eating facilities.

Students continued to picket several Raleigh variety and drug stores in protest against being excluded from lunch counters which traditionally serve only whites.

---

**picket**, march in front of a building to protest something

### BEFORE YOU GO ON

1 Where did the first sit-in take place? Who were the participants? What did they do?

2 What was the goal of the sit-ins?

**On Your Own**
In what situations do you think a sit-in would be effective? In what situations might it not be effective?

335

College students register black voters during Freedom Summer.

Civil Rights Act of 1968 is signed into law.

1964          1965                    1968

↑ Civil Rights Act of 1964 is signed into law.

↑ Voting Rights Act of 1965 is signed into law.

## The Birmingham Campaign

While African Americans suffered discrimination throughout the country, it was far worse in the Deep South. Blacks and whites in these states lived segregated lives. Public accommodations, such as hotels and restaurants, were often segregated, and black and white children attended different schools, even if they lived near each other. The facilities for blacks, though, were frequently far from equal to those of whites. Schools in black neighborhoods, for example, were usually in worse condition and had fewer supplies and other resources.

In 1963, Birmingham, Alabama, was one of the most segregated cities in the South, yet it was also experiencing a change in political power. Voters had elected a mayor who was more moderate in his attitude toward segregation. They hoped that this would force police chief Eugene "Bull" Connor, to step down. Bull Connor enforced segregation laws and did not want to see public facilities integrated. He prevented civil rights organizers from holding rallies, and during peaceful protests he had many African-American demonstrators arrested.

Dr. Martin Luther King Jr. and fellow members of the Southern Christian Leadership Conference (SCLC) organized a campaign to integrate the public facilities in Birmingham. They proposed using nonviolent methods, such as sit-ins and marches, to achieve this goal.

By the time King and the SCLC members arrived in Birmingham, the city government

---

**moderate**, not extreme
**rallies**, large public meetings

336

had issued an injunction banning any further demonstrations. King disobeyed the order and took to the streets with other marchers. Mass arrests followed and King was sent to jail on April 12, 1963.

Placed in solitary confinement, King wrote the now famous "Letter from Birmingham Jail." In this open letter to the public, he explained why civil disobedience was needed in order to advance the cause of civil rights for African Americans.

"For years now I have heard the word 'Wait!' It rings in the ear of every Negro with piercing familiarity. This 'Wait' has almost always meant 'Never.'" He went on to write that, "One who breaks an unjust law must do so openly, lovingly, and with a willingness to accept the penalty. I submit that an individual who breaks a law that conscience tells him is

---

**injunction**, court order to stop something
**banning**, saying that something must not be done
**placed in solitary confinement**, kept alone
**penalty**, punishment for not obeying a law
**conscience**, inner sense of right and wrong

**Dr. Martin Luther King Jr. in a jail cell at the Jefferson County Courthouse in Birmingham** ▼

▲ Young demonstrators facing fire-hoses in Birmingham, Alabama

▲ A police dog attacking a young African-American man during a demonstration in Birmingham

unjust, and who willingly accepts the penalty of imprisonment in order to arouse the conscience of the community over its injustice, is in reality expressing the highest respect for law."

Upon his release from jail on April 20, 1963, King and his supporters began to realize that their campaign was slipping. Many African Americans risked losing their jobs if they marched, and few demonstrators were willing to go to jail. SCLC decided to turn to high school students.

On May 2, over a thousand African-American teenagers left school to join the demonstrations. The police avoided using force when arresting more than 600 of these young students. The next day, when another thousand showed up, Bull Connor ordered his police force to unleash dogs and turn high-pressure fire-hoses on them. Television cameras captured these horrific acts, and they were seen by millions of Americans.

Public outrage led President Kennedy's administration to intervene and serve as mediators between Birmingham's city officials and SCLC. Fearing more unrest and further demonstrations, business leaders within the community agreed to integrate many of their establishments and do away with discriminatory hiring practices.

The events in Birmingham had symbolic as well as practical value. The television images made it clear that segregation was morally unacceptable. Later that year the March on Washington would bring several hundred thousands of Americans together in a powerfully symbolic event.

---

arouse, awaken

---

unleash, let loose
high-pressure, powerful
fire-hoses, long water tubes used to put water onto fires
outrage, great anger
unrest, situation in which people express anger or dissatisfaction
establishments, businesses

## ABOUT THE AUTHOR

**Eric Waldemar** is a playwright, actor, and educator. He has received many awards for his plays, including Columbia University's John Golden Award for Playwriting, and the prestigious Lorraine Hansberry Playwriting Award. He teaches elementary school in New York City and is helping to establish a drama program for the Ellen Lurrie School.

## BEFORE YOU GO ON

**1** Who was Bull Connor? Why did civil rights leaders oppose him?

**2** What was the goal of the Birmingham campaign? Why was it successful?

💡**On Your Own**
In what situations do you think it's worthwhile to have a protest? What other options can you think of for bringing about change?

337

**Right There**

1. What event started the Montgomery Bus Boycott? When and why did the boycott end?

2. What is a "sit-in"?

**Think and Search**

3. How did the sit-ins advance the goals of the civil rights movement? What effects did the sit-ins have on the civil rights movement itself?

4. What is civil disobedience? Why did Dr. Martin Luther King Jr. feel it was a necessary tactic of the civil rights movement?

**Author and You**

5. What is the author's opinion of Rosa Parks? How do you think he would describe her character?

6. What does the author suggest about the effects of the events in Birmingham on the American public? Find language in the text to support your answer.

**On Your Own**

7. What do you think Dr. Martin Luther King Jr. meant when he said, "One of the great glories of democracy is the right to protest for right"? Do you agree?

8. How was the civil rights movement able to achieve its objectives? What tactics and attitudes led to its success?

## IN YOUR OWN WORDS

Work in small groups. Using the notes you took on "The Civil Rights Movement," tell the story of each event described in the article in your own words. Listen to each group member and take notes on facts you forgot.

 *Speaking* TIP

Use active, colorful verbs and adjectives to describe the events.

## DISCUSSION

Discuss in pairs or small groups.

1. What does "separate but equal" mean? Can separate facilities or services ever be equal? Explain.

2. Discuss the tactics of nonviolent civil disobedience. What do the protesters do? How does it actually work? What does it demand of a person?

3. What dangers did civil rights protesters face? What would you have done if you had been a teenager in Birmingham in 1963?

**Q** **Why are ideals important?** How does promoting the ideal of individual rights for one group affect society as a whole? How has life changed since the events described in the article? To what extent do you think the ideal of individual rights has been fulfilled in the United States?

»🎧 *Listening* TIP

Listen for key words and important details. Take notes to help you remember the ideas your classmates express.

## READ FOR FLUENCY

When we read aloud to communicate meaning, we group words into phrases, pause or slow down to make important points, and emphasize important words. Pause for a short time when you reach a comma and for a longer time when you reach a period. Pay attention to rising and falling intonation at the end of sentences.

Work with a partner. Choose a paragraph from the reading. Discuss which words seem important for communicating meaning. Practice pronouncing difficult words. Take turns reading the paragraph aloud and give each other feedback.

## EXTENSION  Workbook Page 165

Dr. Martin Luther King Jr. learned about the tactics of nonviolence from the Indian leader Mohandas Gandhi. During the first half of the twentieth century, Gandhi led a movement that forced the British Empire to give India its independence. He did it without an army and without weapons. Go to the library or use the Internet to read about one of the most important figures in twentieth-century history. Take notes on what you learn about Gandhi and his philosophy of nonviolence. Use your notes to report to the class on what you have learned, or write a short narrative about how Gandhi won India's independence.

▲ Mohandas Gandhi (1869–1948)

# Grammar and Writing

## Parallel Structure with Coordinating Conjunctions

When using the coordinating conjunctions *and, but*, and *or* with a pair or a series, you must use parallel structure. Parallel structure means that all words, phrases, and clauses are in the same form. Look at the examples below.

---

past verbs
People carpooled, hitchhiked, and walked.

singular nouns
No African-American man, woman, or child would ride the buses until their demands for fair and just treatment were met.

The demonstrations spread to include other public places, such as
plural nouns
libraries, museums, theaters, parks, and beaches.

adjectives
We are tired of being segregated and humiliated.

adverbs
Unite with us in openly and firmly defending this basic human right.

clauses in passive voice
Sometimes these students were waited on, but usually they were not served.

---

## Practice

**Workbook**
Page 166

Work with a partner. Copy the sentences below into your notebook. Find and correct the mistakes in parallel structure.

1. Dr. Martin Luther King Jr. gave sermons that united, motivated, and were inspiring to the African-American community.

2. African Americans showed their determination, willingness, and that they were able to make sacrifices.

3. Policemen tried to stop the demonstration, but they can't.

4. Rosa Parks was a well-liked community member and spoke softly.

# WRITING A RESEARCH REPORT

## Write an Introductory Paragraph

At the end of this unit, you will write a research report. On this page you will learn how to introduce the topic of your report. But first you must choose a topic that is clear and focused. Ask yourself a question to direct your research. This will help you define the specific area you will investigate and will give your report a thesis, or controlling idea.

Research question
Specific area
Controlling idea

Once you have completed your research and organized your ideas, you can write an introductory paragraph. In this paragraph, you present, in an interesting way, the question that guided your research and you tell what you learned. The writer of the introductory paragraph below has asked a question about Jim Crow laws and, in her research, has found an answer. Before writing, she used an inverted pyramid to narrow her topic and establish her thesis.

Casey Baginski

### Jim Crow Laws

The Jim Crow laws were a set of regulations that defined the rights of black citizens in the United States from 1877 until the mid-1960s. Although prejudice existed throughout the nation, discrimination and segregation were legislated in most southern states. The Jim Crow laws furthered the belief held by many whites that blacks were of an inferior race and of a lower intellectual and cultural caliber. These laws affected almost every aspect of life. They determined the schools that blacks were allowed to attend, the places where they were allowed to eat, the individuals whom they were allowed to marry, and even the votes that they were allowed to cast. Particularly in the South, blacks were surrounded by constant reminders of the unequal status imposed on them by whites.

WAITING ROOM
FOR WHITE ONLY
BY ORDER
POLICE DEPT.

## Practice

**Workbook**
Page 167

Think of a topic for a brief research report on an issue related to the civil rights movement, and write a question to direct your research. Use an inverted pyramid to narrow your topic. Then do some research to find the answer to your question. Write an introductory paragraph that presents your research question and the answer you learned. Include some coordinating conjunctions with parallel structure.

**Writing Checklist**

**VOICE:**
☑ I presented the question that directed my research in an interesting way.

**SENTENCE FLUENCY:**
☑ I used parallel structure in my sentences.

341

## What You Will Learn

**Reading**
- Vocabulary building: *Literary terms, word study*
- Reading strategy: *Analyze historical context*
- Text type: *Literature (speech)*

**Grammar, Usage, and Mechanics**
Identifying and nonidentifying adjective clauses

**Writing**
Support ideas with facts and details

## THE BIG QUESTION

**Why are ideals important?** Have you ever been in a situation where you had to stand up for your ideals? Have you ever had to stick up for someone else who was being treated unfairly? What did you do? How did the situation turn out? Do you still feel that the ideal you defended was worthwhile? Discuss with a partner.

## BUILD BACKGROUND

By 1963, the civil rights movement had achieved a number of key objectives, such as the integration of transportation and other public facilities in many parts of the country. However, segregation and unfair practices in schools, the workplace, and housing were still widespread. Continuing racial prejudice made this a time of turmoil and violence.

In August 1963 civil rights leaders organized the March on Washington for Jobs and Freedom. Attended by 250,000 people, this massive demonstration called for the passage of federal civil rights legislation, the elimination of segregation in public schools, and the creation of a public works program to provide jobs. There Dr. Martin Luther King Jr. delivered his **"I Have a Dream"** speech, one of the most important speeches in American history.

### Learn Literary Words

A **metaphor** is a figure of speech that compares two different things without using *like* or *as*. An **extended metaphor** deepens the comparison by continuing it for several lines or more in a longer text. The extended metaphor, "I Have a Dream," in Dr. Martin Luther King Jr.'s famous speech continues for eight paragraphs. The lengthy development of this metaphor expresses the speaker's hopes and aspirations for his people.

**Tone** is the attitude of the writer or speaker toward his or her subject and audience. For example, the tone of a text can be formal or informal, serious or light, joyful or sad. The tone of this passage from the "I Have a Dream" speech is strongly optimistic.

### Literary Words

extended metaphor
tone
repetition

> **Let freedom ring** from the snow-capped Rockies of Colorado. **Let freedom ring** from the curvaceous slopes of California.
> But not only that; **let freedom ring** from Stone Mountain of Georgia.
> **Let freedom ring** from Lookout Mountain of Tennessee.

**Repetition** is the use of a sound, word, phrase, or other element of language more than once to emphasize an idea and create rhythm. In the above passage, the repetition of the phrase "Let freedom ring" creates a powerful rhythm and vivid, inspiring images of the country.

### Practice
**Workbook Page 168**

Below is the first stanza of a poem written in 1865 after the assassination of President Abraham Lincoln. In small groups, take turns reading the lines aloud. Identify extended metaphor, repetition, and tone in the poem. Discuss how each device helps create sensory images and deep, emotional meanings in the poem.

> O Captain! my Captain! our fearful trip is done;
> The ship has weather'd every rack, the prize we sought is won;
> The port is near, the bells I hear, the people all exulting,
> While follow eyes the steady keel, the vessel grim and daring:
>       But O heart! heart! heart!
>       O the bleeding drops of red,
>       Where on the deck my Captain lies,
>       Fallen cold and dead.
>
>       — *Walt Whitman, "O Captain! My Captain!"*

## Learn Academic Words

Study the **red** words and their meanings. You will find these words useful when talking and writing about literature. Write each word and its meaning in your notebook. After you read "I Have a Dream," try to use these words to respond to the text.

**Academic Words**

demonstration
legislation
policy
principle

| | | |
|---|---|---|
| **demonstration** = an event at which many people meet to protest or support something in public | ➡ | Over 15,000 people marched in a **demonstration** in support of workers' rights. |
| **legislation** = a law or set of laws | ➡ | During the 1960s civil rights leaders worked to pass **legislation** that guarantees all citizens equal rights under the law. |
| **policy** = a plan that has been agreed to by a political party, government, or other organization | ➡ | The school has a strict **policy** on attendance. Students must have a doctor's note for absences of more than one day. |
| **principle** = a moral rule or set of ideas that makes you behave in a particular way | ➡ | Equality of all people is an important **principle** of American political life. |

**Practice**  **Workbook** Page 169

Work with a partner to answer these questions. Try to include the **red** word in your answer. Write the sentences in your notebook.

1. How does a protest **demonstration** achieve its objectives?

2. What body of American government makes **legislation**?

3. What is your school's **policy** on student dress?

4. What is one **principle** that guides your daily conduct?

President Lyndon B. Johnson signs historic civil rights legislation: the Civil Rights Act of 1964. ▶

## Word Study: Related Words

You have learned that related words are words in the same word family. They are formed from the same base word and have related meanings. Notice the related words in the chart below:

| Verb | Noun | Adjective |
|------|------|-----------|
| tranquilize | tranquility | tranquil |
| dramatize | drama | dramatic |
| prosper | prosperity | prosperous |

**Practice**  **Workbook** Page 170

Work with a partner. Copy the following words into your notebook: *satisfy, demonstrate, oppress, symbolize, nationalize, discriminate*. Use a dictionary to find related words. List the related words in a chart like the one above. Then use each related word in a sentence.

## READING STRATEGY  ANALYZE HISTORICAL CONTEXT

Analyzing the historical context of a story or text can make it more meaningful and easier to understand. Historical context includes the political and cultural changes that were happening at a particular time. To analyze historical context, follow these steps:

- As you read, pay attention to the events in the text. What was happening?

- Think about where the text takes place. How does that affect the events and people involved?

- Think about what you already know about the place or time of the text. How does that help you understand it better?

- Notice how the people are reacting to the events that happen.

As you read "I Have a Dream," think about the time and place that the speech was given. What events happened in America in 1963? What do you know about that time? Discuss it with a partner.

 **Workbook** Page 171

**Set a purpose for reading** Why do you think this speech caused so many people to begin to share the ideal it expresses?

# I Have a Dream

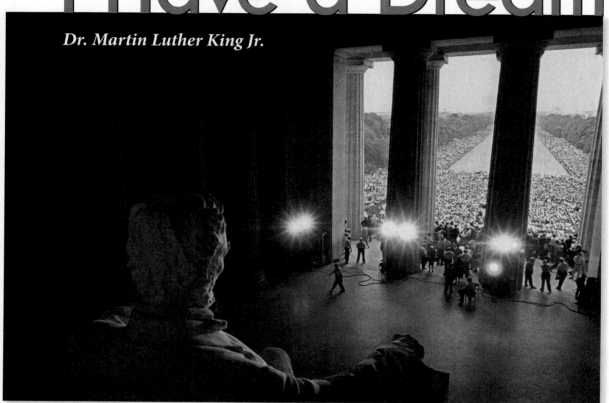

*Dr. Martin Luther King Jr.*

¹ I am happy to join with you today in what will go down in history as the greatest demonstration for freedom in the history of our nation.

² Five score years ago, a great American, in whose symbolic shadow we stand today, signed the Emancipation Proclamation. This momentous decree came as a great beacon light of hope to millions of Negro slaves who had been seared in the flames of withering injustice. It came as a joyous daybreak to end the long night of their captivity.

---

**five score years ago,** one hundred years ago

**the Emancipation Proclamation,** official act that freed the slaves in the Confederate states

**beacon light of hope,** something that guides and encourages people

**long night of their captivity,** long period of slavery

**346**

³ But one hundred years later, the Negro still is not free. One hundred years later, the life of the Negro is still sadly crippled by the manacles of segregation and the chains of discrimination. One hundred years later, the Negro lives on a lonely island of poverty in the midst of a vast ocean of material prosperity. One hundred years later, the Negro is still languished in the corners of American society and finds himself an exile in his own land. And so we've come here today to dramatize a shameful condition.

⁴ In a sense we've come to our nation's capital to cash a check. When the architects of our republic wrote the magnificent words of the Constitution and the Declaration of Independence, they were signing a promissory note to which every American was to fall heir. This note was a promise that all men—yes, black men as well as white men—would be guaranteed the unalienable rights of life, liberty, and the pursuit of happiness.

⁵ It is obvious today that America has defaulted on this promissory note insofar as her citizens of color are concerned. Instead of honoring this sacred obligation, America has given the Negro people a bad check, a check that has come back marked "insufficient funds."

⁶ But we refuse to believe that the bank of justice is bankrupt. We refuse to believe that there are insufficient funds in the great vaults of opportunity of this nation. And so we've come to cash this check, a check that will give us upon demand the riches of freedom and security of justice. We have also come to this hallowed spot to remind America of the fierce urgency of now. This is no time to engage in the luxury of cooling off or to take the tranquilizing drug of gradualism. Now is the time to make real the promises of democracy. Now is the time to rise from the dark and desolate valley of segregation to the sunlit path of racial justice. Now is the time to lift our nation from the quicksands of racial injustice to the solid rock of brotherhood. Now is the time to make justice a reality for all of God's children.

⁷ It would be fatal for the nation to overlook the urgency of the moment. This sweltering summer of the Negro's legitimate discontent will not pass until there is an invigorating autumn of freedom and equality.

---

**crippled by the manacles of segregation,** prevented from living freely because of racial discrimination
**promissory note,** document promising to pay money before a particular date
**to which every American was to fall heir,** that every U.S. citizen would receive
**unalienable,** cannot be taken away
**citizens of color,** nonwhite U.S. citizens
**bankrupt,** unable to pay its debts
**take the tranquilizing drug of gradualism,** accept the idea that equality should be achieved slowly over a long period of time

✔ LITERARY CHECK
*What **extended metaphor** does Dr. King use in paragraphs 4-6 to illustrate the situation of African Americans? Explain the metaphor and trace its development.*

**BEFORE YOU GO ON**

**1** In paragraph 2, what came as a "great beacon light of hope"? When? Why?

**2** What is the "shameful condition" that King refers to in paragraph 3?

**On Your Own**
What are your feelings as you read the speech?

Nineteen sixty-three is not an end but a beginning. Those who hoped that the Negro needed to blow off steam and will now be content will have a rude awakening if the nation returns to business as usual. There will be neither rest nor tranquility in America until the Negro is granted his citizenship rights. The whirlwinds of revolt will continue to shake the foundations of our nation until the bright day of justice emerges.

8 But there is something that I must say to my people who stand on the warm threshold which leads into the palace of justice. In the process of gaining our rightful place we must not be guilty of wrongful deeds. Let us not seek to satisfy our thirst for freedom by drinking from the cup of bitterness and hatred. We must forever conduct our struggle on the high plane of dignity and discipline. We must not allow our creative protest to degenerate into physical violence. Again and again we must rise to the majestic heights of meeting physical force with soul force. The marvelous new militancy which has engulfed the Negro community must not lead us to a distrust of all white people, for many of our white brothers, as evidenced by their presence here today, have come to realize that their destiny is tied up with our destiny. And they have come to realize that their freedom is inextricably bound to our freedom. We cannot walk alone.

9 And as we walk, we must make the pledge that we shall always march ahead. We cannot turn back. There are those who are asking the devotees of civil rights, "When will you be satisfied?" We can never be satisfied as long as the Negro is the victim of the unspeakable horrors of police brutality. We can never be satisfied

▲ **Dr. Martin Luther King Jr. waves to the crowd gathered to hear him speak.**

---

**blow off steam,** let out anger
**bitterness,** anger
**degenerate,** collapse; disintegrate
**engulfed,** overwhelmed; taken over
**brutality,** cruelty; viciousness

**348**

as long as our bodies, heavy with the fatigue of travel, cannot gain lodging in the motels of the highways and the hotels of the cities. We cannot be satisfied as long as the Negro's basic mobility is from a smaller ghetto to a larger one. We can never be satisfied as long as our children are stripped of their selfhood and robbed of their dignity by signs stating "for whites only." We cannot be satisfied as long as a Negro in Mississippi cannot vote and a Negro in New York believes he has nothing for which to vote. No, no we are not satisfied and we will not be satisfied until justice rolls down like waters and righteousness like a mighty stream.

¹⁰ I am not unmindful that some of you have come here out of great trials and tribulations. Some of you have come fresh from narrow jail cells. Some of you have come from areas where your quest for freedom left you battered by storms of persecution and staggered by the winds of police brutality. You have been the veterans of creative suffering. Continue to work with the faith that unearned suffering is redemptive.

¹¹ Go back to Mississippi, go back to Alabama, go back to South Carolina, go back to Georgia, go back to Louisiana, go back to the slums and ghettos of our northern cities, knowing that somehow this situation can and will be changed.

¹² Let us not wallow in the valley of despair. I say to you today my friends—so even though we face the difficulties of today and tomorrow, I still have a dream. It is a dream deeply rooted in the American dream.

¹³ I have a dream that one day this nation will rise up and live out the true meaning of its creed: "We hold these truths to be self-evident, that all men are created equal."

¹⁴ I have a dream that one day on the red hills of Georgia the sons of former slaves and the sons of former slave owners will be able to sit down together at the table of brotherhood.

¹⁵ I have a dream that one day even the state of Mississippi, a state sweltering with the heat of injustice, sweltering with the heat of oppression, will be transformed into an oasis of freedom and justice.

¹⁶ I have a dream that my four little children will one day live in a nation where they will not be judged by the color of their skin but by the content of their character.

¹⁷ I have a dream today.

---

mobility, ability to move easily from one place to another
unmindful, unaware
trials and tribulations, difficulties; suffering
persecution, cruel or unfair treatment; discrimination
unearned suffering is redemptive, you will be rewarded for having suffered undeserved pain
wallow, allow ourselves to be sad and upset for too long a time
creed, belief

✔ LITERARY CHECK

*What adjectives would you use to describe the overall tone of the speech? Find language on these pages to support your description.*

**BEFORE YOU GO ON**

**1** What does King say about the role of white people in the struggle for racial equality?

**2** When can those fighting for racial equality be satisfied?

**On Your Own**
Do you think this speech is effective? Why or why not?

349

**18** I have a dream that one day down in Alabama, with its vicious racists, with its governor having his lips dripping with the words of interposition and nullification—one day right there in Alabama little black boys and black girls will be able to join hands with little white boys and white girls as sisters and brothers.

**19** I have a dream today.

**20** I have a dream that one day every valley shall be exalted, and every hill and mountain shall be made low, the rough places will be made plain, and the crooked places will be made straight, and the glory of the Lord shall be revealed and all flesh shall see it together.

**21** This is our hope. This is the faith that I go back to the South with. With this faith we will be able to hew out of the mountain of despair a stone of hope. With this faith we will be able to transform the jangling discords of our nation into a beautiful symphony of brotherhood. With this faith we will be able to work together, to pray together, to struggle together, to go to jail together, to stand up for freedom together, knowing that we will be free one day.

**22** This will be the day, this will be the day when all of God's children will be able to sing with new meaning "My country 'tis of thee, sweet land of liberty, of thee I sing. Land where my fathers died, land of the Pilgrims' pride, from every mountainside, let freedom ring!"

**23** And if America is to be a great nation, this must become true. And so let freedom ring from the prodigious hilltops of New Hampshire. Let freedom ring from the mighty mountains of New York. Let freedom ring from the heightening Alleghenies of Pennsylvania.

**24** Let freedom ring from the snow-capped Rockies of Colorado. Let freedom ring from the curvaceous slopes of California.

**25** But not only that; let freedom ring from Stone Mountain of Georgia.

**26** Let freedom ring from Lookout Mountain of Tennessee.

▲ A young civil rights demonstrator at the March on Washington

---

**words of interposition and nullification,**
   attempts to prevent and reverse progress
**exalted,** filled with great happiness
**despair,** sadness; hopelessness
**discords,** conflicts; fights
**prodigious,** huge
**curvaceous,** having curves; rounded

◀ Young men at the March on Washington

<sup>27</sup> Let freedom ring from every hill and molehill of Mississippi—from every mountainside.

<sup>28</sup> Let freedom ring. And when this happens, and when we allow freedom to ring—when we let it ring from every village and every hamlet, from every state and every city, we will be able to speed up that day when all of God's children—black men and white men, Jews and Gentiles, Protestants and Catholics—will be able to join hands and sing in the words of the old Negro spiritual: "Free at last! Free at last! Thank God Almighty, we are free at last!"

---

**Gentiles**, Christians
**Negro spiritual**, a type of religious song created by slaves in the United States

**✔ LITERARY CHECK**

*What aspect of Dr. King's overall message does the **repetition** in paragraphs 22–28 express? What is its effect?*

## ABOUT THE **AUTHOR**

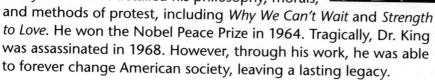

**Dr. Martin Luther King Jr.** (1929–1968) was the premier civil rights leader in the United States during the 1950s and 60s. Through nonviolent protest, King helped African Americans achieve equal rights and end segregation. He wrote many books that detailed his philosophy, morals, and methods of protest, including *Why We Can't Wait* and *Strength to Love*. He won the Nobel Peace Prize in 1964. Tragically, Dr. King was assassinated in 1968. However, through his work, he was able to forever change American society, leaving a lasting legacy.

**BEFORE YOU GO ON**

**1** In your own words, describe one of Dr. King's dreams.

**2** Describe the closing images of the speech. How do these images evoke the song "My Country 'Tis of Thee"?

💡 **On Your Own**
Do you think any of King's dreams have come true? If so, which ones?

# Review and Practice

## DRAMATIC READING

🔊 *Speaking* TIP

Project your voice.

In small groups, discuss the speech and decide which part of it was most effective. Choose a section of the speech to read aloud. Assign each member of your group lines to read from that section. Then present that section of the speech to the class as a dramatic reading.

## COMPREHENSION

Workbook
Page 172

### Right There

1. According to Dr. Martin Luther King Jr., what promise did the Constitution and the Declaration of Independence make to all U.S. citizens?

2. What warning is given to those who seek to satisfy their "thirst for freedom"?

### Think and Search

3. How does King view the relationship between black people and white people? What does he mean when he says, "We cannot walk alone"?

4. What injustices does Dr. King outline? Why were the people involved in the civil rights movement unsatisfied?

### Author and You

5. According to Dr. King, what principles are central to American democracy? How do you think King would have described the state of American democracy in 1963?

6. What feelings do you think Dr. King was trying to stir in his audience? What was he trying to accomplish with this speech?

### On Your Own

7. In what ways does Dr. King appeal to logic and reason? In what ways does he appeal to emotion? Do you find one appeal more effective than the other? Explain.

8. Many civil rights leaders rose to prominence during the 1960s. What do you think was Dr. Martin Luther King Jr.'s unique contribution to the civil rights movement?

## DISCUSSION

Discuss in pairs or small groups.

1. Who was Dr. Martin Luther King Jr.'s audience? How did he bring the different groups together?

2. How do the metaphors and repetition in this speech help communicate its message? Give specific examples.

3. How would you characterize Dr. King's "dream"? If King were alive today, how do you think he would evaluate progress toward his dream?

**Q** **Why are ideals important?** Did you already know about this speech? Why do you think this speech and the March on Washington were so important at the time? What is their importance now? Do people still believe in the ideal they express?

»)⟩ *Listening* TIP

Summarize what each speaker says in your own mind. Do you agree or disagree?

## RESPONSE TO LITERATURE

**Workbook**
Page 172

In 1963, John Lewis was the president of the Student Non-Violent Coordinating Committee. He also spoke to the 250,000 people at the Lincoln Memorial the day Dr. Martin Luther King Jr. delivered his "I Have a Dream" speech. Forty years later, John Lewis was elected to the U.S. Congress. He said that King, through his speech, "educated, he inspired, he informed [not just] the people there, but people throughout America and unborn generations." What is your reaction to Dr. King's words? Use a word web to write down feelings, ideas, and images that came to you as you first heard or read this speech. Write a short poem or paragraph that captures your feelings.

# Grammar and Writing

### Identifying and Nonidentifying Adjective Clauses

An adjective clause modifies a noun or noun phrase. Here's an example:

> This momentous decree came as a great beacon light of hope to millions of Negro slaves **who had been seared in the flames of withering injustice**.

An adjective clause can be identifying or nonidentifying. An **identifying clause** tells which person, place, or thing the sentence refers to. An identifying clause is necessary to the meaning of the sentence. Do not use commas before and after an identifying clause. A **nonidentifying clause** gives *extra* information, but the meaning of the sentence is clear without it. Use commas with nonidentifying clauses.

> The speech **that inspired hundreds of thousands of Americans during the March on Washington** was called "I Have a Dream." [identifying clause]
> Dr. Martin Luther King Jr., **who delivered the famous speech "I Have a Dream,"** was a powerful African-American leader. [nonidentifying clause]

## Practice
Workbook Page 173

Copy the sentences below into your notebook. With a partner, determine whether the adjective clause in each sentence is identifying or nonidentifying. Add commas to the nonidentifying clauses.

1. The Lincoln Memorial which is near the Potomac River was the site of Dr. Martin Luther King Jr.'s "I Have a Dream" speech.

2. The speech that was delivered at the historic March on Washington in 1963 has become world famous.

3. Marian Anderson who sang the National Anthem was one of many singers who performed for the people gathered that day.

4. The people who participated in the March on Washington will never forget the events of that day.

5. Birmingham, Alabama which is sometimes called the Pittsburgh of the South was a key target of the civil rights movement in 1963.

# WRITING A RESEARCH REPORT

## Support Ideas with Facts and Details

After you write the introduction to your research report, you'll need to develop your thesis with ideas supported by facts and details. Suppose you write that the March on Washington was an important event. To support this idea, you would include the fact that many people took part in this protest. Details might include the widespread media coverage of the event. Writers gather information from sources such as books, articles, encyclopedias, or reliable websites.

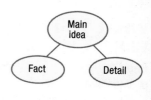

Here is a paragraph from a research report about the March on Washington. Before writing, the writer used a main-idea-and-details web to organize her ideas.

Meredith Mooney

### The March on Washington

On August 28, 1963, 250,000 people participated in a historic demonstration for the cause of "jobs and freedom." The crowd marched from the Washington Monument to the Lincoln Memorial to support the passage of meaningful civil rights legislation. The protesters wanted the elimination of racial barriers that prevented many blacks from voting; the end of racial segregation in public schools; the prohibition of racial discrimination in hiring; protection for demonstrators against police brutality; a public works program to provide jobs; and a raise in the minimum wage. The march, which was the largest ever in the nation's capital, was one of the first demonstrations to receive extensive media coverage. Many important speakers addressed the demonstrators, and Dr. Martin Luther King Jr. delivered his famous "I Have a Dream" speech. The march had a great and lasting impact on the nation.

## Practice

**Workbook**
**Page 174**

Write a paragraph for a research report about an aspect of the "I Have a Dream" speech, such as important themes in the speech or how people reacted to it. Before writing, list your main idea and supporting facts and details in a main-idea-and-details web. Include identifying and nonidentifying adjective clauses.

### Writing Checklist

**IDEAS:**
☑ I included facts and details that support my main idea.

**WORD CHOICE:**
☑ I chose words that make my facts and details clear.

## What You Will Learn

**Reading**
- Vocabulary building: *Context, dictionary skills, word study*
- Reading strategy: *Scan*
- Text type: *Informational text (social studies)*

**Grammar, Usage, and Mechanics**
Expressions that introduce examples

**Writing**
Support ideas with examples

## THE BIG QUESTION

**Why are ideals important?** Do you think it is possible to prevent wars? Can peaceful solutions to disagreements be found? Do you think that people who believe in the ideal of peace can really make a difference? Discuss with a partner or in small groups.

## BUILD BACKGROUND

The early 1960s were the peak years of the Cold War, a state of high tension between the Soviet Union and the United States. This shared mistrust made the world a very dangerous place. During the presidential campaign of 1960, John F. Kennedy spoke to a large group of students—perhaps as many as 10,000 students—at the University of Michigan. Kennedy asked the students if they would be willing to serve their country and the cause of world peace by helping the people of other nations. Students across the country responded with 30,000 letters in favor of the idea.

In 1961, President Kennedy signed an order that created a new kind of Cold War weapon, the Peace Corps. At first, people laughed at the Peace Corps, calling it "Kennedy's Kiddie Korps." But it has outlived its critics and even the Cold War it was created to fight.

You will read a selection called **"The Peace Corps: An American Ideal"** from the Peace Corps website. It is about the organization and one of the volunteers who served in it.

▲ A Peace Corps volunteer teaching English in the Philippines

## VOCABULARY

### Learn Key Words

Read these sentences. Use the context to figure out the meaning of the **red** words. Use a dictionary to check your answers. Then write each word and its meaning in your notebook.

**Key Words**

association
entrepreneurs
humanitarian
innovative
malnutrition
support
volunteers

1. We belonged to the chess club, an **association** where we could meet other players, talk about chess, and improve our skills.

2. **Entrepreneurs** are skilled at starting and running businesses.

3. Clara Barton was an important American **humanitarian**. She brought medical aid to wounded soldiers during the American Civil War, working tirelessly to save lives and end suffering.

4. The farmers in that region took an **innovative** approach to growing crops. Their planting methods had never been tried before.

5. Thousands of people suffer from **malnutrition** because of shortages of food and clean water.

6. Parents **support** their children financially and also emotionally, by giving them love and understanding.

7. After the earthquake, many **volunteers** worked long hours without pay to provide relief and help rebuild.

**Practice**  **Workbook Page 175**

▲ Volunteers rescue a woman after an earthquake in Turkey.

Write the sentences in your notebook. Choose a **red** word from the box above to complete each sentence. Then take turns reading the sentences aloud with a partner.

1. Often both parents must work to _____ the family.

2. There are many cases of _____ in regions affected by war, because people are unable to secure a healthy, balanced diet.

3. The people in that community formed an _____ whose purpose was to maintain the local parks and playgrounds.

4. The rescue team consisted entirely of unpaid _____ who worked selflessly to help people stranded after the hurricane.

5. That teacher's _____ methods were highly successful and were eventually adopted by all the teachers in his school.

6. A group of _____ assisted people in starting small businesses.

7. The doctor was known as a _____ because she worked long hours in the free clinic.

## Learn Academic Words

Study the red words and their meanings. You will find these words useful when talking and writing about informational texts. Write each word and its meaning in your notebook. After you read "The Peace Corps: An American Ideal," try to use these words to respond to the text.

**Academic Words**

awareness
establish
implement
promote
resources

| | | |
|---|---|---|
| **awareness** = knowledge or understanding of a particular subject or situation | ➡ | The TV ads raised the public's **awareness** of community issues. |
| **establish** = start something such as a company, system, situation, etc., especially one that will exist for a long time | ➡ | After considerable planning and much hard work, he was able to **establish** his own business last year. |
| **implement** = if you implement a plan, process, etc., you begin to make it happen | ➡ | The first step is to create a business plan. The second step is to **implement** the plan. |
| **promote** = help something develop and be successful | ➡ | Organizations like the Peace Corps help to **promote** understanding between cultures. |
| **resources** = all the money, property, skills, etc., that you have available to use | ➡ | She was determined to find the financial **resources** to pay for college. |

### Practice  Workbook Page 176

Work with a partner to answer these questions. Try to include the red word in your answer. Write the sentences in your notebook.

1. What is one result of a greater public awareness of the effect of human beings on the environment?

2. What should teachers do to establish a good atmosphere for learning in their classes?

3. What plans for the future do you want to implement now?

4. In your opinion, what is the best way to promote world peace?

5. What community resources can be used during an emergency?

▲ Doctors Without Borders is an organization that provides medical care and resources to people in times of war and natural disaster.

## Word Study: Homophones

Homophones are words that sound alike but have different meanings. For example, a *core* is the center of something, as in *apple core*. A *corps* is a group of people, usually in the military, as in the *Marine Corps*. Homophones may or may not have different spellings. The meaning of a homophone can usually be inferred from the context. This chart contains some common homophones.

| | | | | |
|---|---|---|---|---|
| air / heir | bored / board | fined / find | raise / raze | tail / tale |
| allowed / aloud | break / brake | flea / flee | scene / seen | war / wore |
| alter / altar | capitol / capital | morning / mourning | seem / seam | week / weak |
| beat / beet | fair / fare | rain / reign / rein | sent / cent | whole / hole |

**Practice**  Workbook Page 177

In small groups take turns reading the pairs of homophones in the chart. Then write sentences for five pairs of homophones. Look up the definitions of words that you do not know.

## READING STRATEGY    SCAN

Scanning helps you find the key information you need quickly. When you scan, you look for particular things that you want to know, for example, dates, numbers, ideas, names, and other types of information. To scan, follow these steps:

- Look at the title, headings, visuals, captions, and labels to see if they contain the information you need.
- Start reading the beginning of the text. Move your eyes quickly over the lines.
- Don't stop if you see a word you don't know.
- Look for key words related to the information you want to find. When you find a key word, stop scanning and begin reading.

As you read "The Peace Corps: An American Ideal," use the scanning strategy to find some information you want to know. Begin by looking at the side banners, the headings, and the visuals.

 Workbook Page 178

**Set a purpose for reading** How did the experience of the Peace Corps volunteer influence her future work? How did the ideal she believed in affect her work?

**Life is calling. How far will you go ?**

## About the Peace Corps

# The Peace Corps: An American Ideal

### › What Is the Peace Corps?

**Mission:**

In 1961, President John F. Kennedy established the Peace Corps to promote world peace and friendship.

The Peace Corps' mission has three simple goals:

1. Helping the people of interested countries in meeting their need for trained men and women.

2. Helping promote a better understanding of Americans on the part of the peoples served.

3. Helping promote a better understanding of other peoples on the part of Americans.

### › What Do Volunteers Do?

Think of the Peace Corps and you might imagine teaching in a one-room schoolhouse or farming in a remote area of the world. But while education and agriculture are still an important part of what the Peace Corps does, today's volunteers are just as likely to be working on HIV/AIDS awareness, helping to establish computer learning centers, or working on small business development.

### › Education, Youth Outreach, and Community Development

Volunteers introduce innovative teaching methodologies, encourage critical thinking in the classroom, and integrate issues like health education and environmental awareness into English, math, science, and other subjects.

---

**remote,** far away
**methodologies,** set of methods used when doing a particular type of work

> **Business Development**

Volunteers work in education, private businesses, public organizations, government offices, cooperatives, women's and youth groups, and more.

> **Environment**

Volunteers work on a wide variety of activities, from teaching environmental awareness to planting trees within a community.

> **Agriculture**

Volunteers work with small farmers to increase food production while promoting environmental conservation practices.

> **Health and HIV/AIDS**

Volunteers educate and promote awareness of HIV/AIDS, as well as other issues, such as malnutrition and safe drinking water.

> **Information Technology**

Volunteers help communities capitalize on technology by teaching computer skills, developing regional databases, and implementing networks for businesses and government offices.

---

**cooperatives,** farms or companies owned and operated by people working together
**capitalize on,** use something in order to gain an advantage
**databases,** large amounts of information stored in a computer system
**networks,** groups of people or organizations that work together

## BEFORE YOU GO ON

**1** Who started the Peace Corps? When? Why?

**2** What do Peace Corps volunteers in the field of education do?

**On Your Own**
Do you think the Peace Corps is a good idea? Why or why not?

**361**

# Peace Corps

## About the Peace Corps

Life is calling.
How far
will you go **?**

> **Where Do Volunteers Go?**

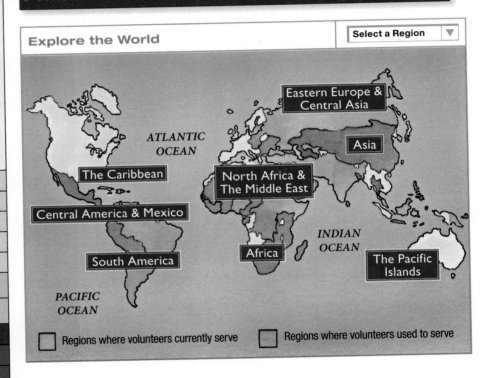

Explore the World

Select a Region ▼

ATLANTIC OCEAN

PACIFIC OCEAN

INDIAN OCEAN

Eastern Europe & Central Asia

Asia

The Caribbean

North Africa & The Middle East

Central America & Mexico

South America

Africa

The Pacific Islands

☐ Regions where volunteers currently serve     ☐ Regions where volunteers used to serve

The Peace Corps works in countries from Asia to Central America, and from Europe to Africa. In each of these countries, volunteers work with governments, schools, and entrepreneurs to address changing and complex needs in education, health and HIV/AIDS, business, information technology, agriculture, and the environment.

Click on a region above, use the menu to the left, or choose a region in the pull-down menu to learn more about the countries in which Peace Corps volunteers are currently serving.

---

**information technology,** use of computers to gather and store information
**pull-down menu,** list of options that appears on a computer screen

Volunteers work and live within communities both large and small, and rural and urban. They speak the local language, whether that is French, Spanish, Romanian, or Hausa. Most importantly, Peace Corps volunteers discover the richness of another culture the best way possible: by living it.

## › What's It Like to Volunteer?

> › In Their Own Words
> **Profile: Carmenza Cespedes, and her mother, Isabel Cespedes**

▲ Carmenza Cespedes
and a Panamanian artisan

**CARMENZA'S STORY:** My name is Carmenza Cespedes. I am 28 years old, and I was born in New York City. I went to Baruch College, City University of New York, and then served as a Peace Corps volunteer in Panama. . . .

I had participated in a career fair where there were lots of big corporations taking resumes from students, and there was a table for the Peace Corps. I spoke to some returned Peace Corps volunteers, and I was very interested in the programs. As I was going through the brochures, I realized they had a small business development program, which took me by surprise, but also interested me.

I applied a year and a half after I graduated, and within six months I got my acceptance and left for Panama. I was sent to Panama as a small business development volunteer to work with a nonprofit association that helps to organize small businesses to find strength in numbers, and get resources from the government or banks. I also had the opportunity to branch out and work with individual businesses and with indigenous

---

**rural**, related to the country
**urban**, related to the city
**nonprofit**, organization that uses the money it earns to help people instead of making a profit
**branch out**, do something new
**indigenous**, native

## BEFORE YOU GO ON

**1** In what parts of the world do Peace Corps volunteers serve? What languages do they learn to speak?

**2** Where did Carmenza Cespedes serve in the Peace Corps? What kind of work did she do?

**On Your Own**
Would you like to join an organization like the Peace Corps? Why or why not?

**363**

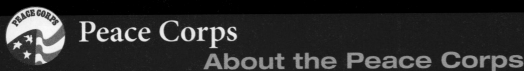

female artisan groups. The work I did with indigenous women was a very important project to me. I helped them organize and taught them the importance of leadership and communication skills so that they could work better together. We covered a lot, and it was definitely a learning experience on both sides.

When I returned from the Peace Corps I wanted to work with small business owners who needed help in the United States. Currently I work for a nonprofit microlending organization that provides small business loans to New York City business owners. I find this job 100 percent fulfilling. Prior to the Peace Corps I worked in the private sector in the heart of New York City, the financial capital of the world. I was doing interesting work but I always felt a bit small. I couldn't necessarily work one-on-one with people and really develop that side of myself, which is so important to me. I had a business degree, but the term "business humanitarian" doesn't exist. Now I am doing what I like.

As the daughter of immigrants, there is always pressure. We come to this land to take advantage of all the opportunities, which means education, so that you can support your family. When I graduated with my business degree, I was making good money. The idea of the Peace Corps was not such a great thing to my mother. . . .

I tried to educate my mom about the Peace Corps and encouraged her to speak to other people, and she eventually turned around. In her heart she knew I was leaving, and she made the decision as a really good mom to say, "She's going to do what she wants to do, because that's the way I raised her, and I can either stand by her or fight her." She stood by me.

My mother came to understand why what I am doing is so important to me. She sees the great advantages that the Peace Corps provided for me.

---

**artisan**, someone who does skilled work with his or her hands
**microlending**, very small loans to people too poor to get a loan from a bank
**private sector**, private businesses (not run by the government)

**ISABEL'S STORY:** I grew up in Colombia. We were poor, really poor. It was a hard time for us, but we were very happy. I met my husband, and we decided to get married and move to the United States. We came to New York in 1968 because my husband had some relatives here.

I saw all of my children, not only Carmenza, as important people. I had big hopes for them, and every day at the table, or whenever I had the opportunity to speak to them, I would let them know that I had big hopes for them. This is a hard country, and if you want to succeed, you have to work hard.

When Carmenza told me she wanted to join the Peace Corps—ouch!—she almost killed me. At the time, she was the one helping me to pay the bills for the house, because my husband was retired. I worked full time, and she helped me with the bills. I was surprised when she told me she was going to join the Peace Corps. But then I started thinking that she would be helping my people, and she would see, with her own eyes, the scenes that I told my children about when I raised them. I thought, "What can I do?" She wanted to do it, and I had to support her. It was her life, and I knew she was going to learn very good things.

I went to visit her and we had a very good time. Carmenza is a leader, so she got along very well with the people. I saw that she could live by herself and all that she was able to achieve. I now see that the decision she made was right. Her experience in the Peace Corps has been very good for her.

**UPDATE ABOUT CARMENZA:** Since writing the personal narrative above, Carmenza completed her M.B.A. and moved to London, where she works in consumer banking for a large British bank. She feels that her Peace Corps experience has had a profound influence on her both professionally and personally.

▲ **Isabel Cespedes and two Panamanian artisans**

---

**ouch!,** exclamation that expresses sudden pain
**retired,** no longer working because of old age
**M.B.A.,** an advanced college degree in business

**BEFORE YOU GO ON**

**1** According to Carmenza, what pressures do the children of immigrants experience?

**2** Describe Isabel's background. What hopes did she have for her children?

**On Your Own**
How would you describe the pressures that immigrants and their children experience?

**365**

# Review and Practice

**COMPREHENSION**  **Workbook** Page 179

## Right There

1. What are the three goals of the Peace Corps's mission?
2. What do Peace Corps volunteers do to promote agriculture? What do they do to promote health?

## Think and Search

3. What effect did the experience Carmenza Cespedes had as a Peace Corps volunteer have on her life and work when she returned home?
4. How did Isabel Cespedes react when her daughter told her she wanted to join the Peace Corps? How does Isabel explain her reaction? Why did she change her mind?

## Author and You

5. What do the stories of Carmenza and Isabel suggest about the value of the Peace Corps experience?
6. Why do you think the profile of Carmenza's mother was included on the website? What do Isabel's thoughts about her daughter's Peace Corps service add to the stories about what it's like to volunteer?

## On Your Own

7. Compare and contrast the way you imagined life in the Peace Corps with the description in the reading.
8. In your experience, does working with other people always promote understanding? Why or why not?

▲ A journalist returns to the village in Panama where she once lived as a Peace Corps volunteer.

## IN YOUR OWN WORDS

Work with a partner. What information on the website leads you to think that you would or would not like the life of a Peace Corps volunteer? List your reasons in a T-chart with the headings *Would like* and *Would not like*. Then explain how the information you learned influenced your feelings about joining the Peace Corps.

> **Speaking TIP**
> Refer to your chart when you need to, but keep your eyes on your partner as much as possible.

## DISCUSSION

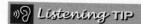
Listening TIP

Write questions to ask each speaker at the end of the discussion.

Discuss in pairs or small groups.

1. Discuss the purpose of the reading. Did it give you a clear picture of life as a Peace Corps volunteer? What else would you like to know about the experience of serving in the Peace Corps?

2. What did you feel as you read the story of Carmenza Cespedes? Do you know anyone like her?

3. Imagine that other countries sent their citizens to work as Peace Corps volunteers in America. How would the people in your community react? What knowledge, insights, and experience might a foreign Peace Corps volunteer bring to the United States?

**Q Why are ideals important?** How do you feel about helping others or accepting their help? In what ways can both the helper and the person helped benefit from the experience? Is helping others an important ideal? Explain.

## READ FOR FLUENCY

It is often easier to read a text if you understand the difficult words and phrases. Work with a partner. Choose a paragraph from the reading. Identify the words and phrases you do not know or have trouble pronouncing. Look up the difficult words in a dictionary.

Take turns pronouncing the words and phrases with your partner. If necessary, ask your teacher to model the correct pronunciation. Then take turns reading the paragraph aloud. Give each other feedback on your reading.

## EXTENSION

Workbook
Page 179

Carmenza Cespedes joined the Peace Corps because she wanted to find a way to help humanity. What does being a humanitarian actually involve? Research the volunteer organizations in your community. Then call and ask questions about one organization and what it does. Present a report about the organization to the class.

# Grammar and Writing

## GRAMMAR, USAGE, AND MECHANICS

### Expressions That Introduce Examples

Expressions that introduce examples let the reader know that what follows is an example of an idea that you have just presented or explained. Look at the expressions below.

> We studied many topics. **For example**, we studied sociology and history.
> Many volunteers spoke a second language. **For instance**, Julie spoke Spanish.
> The roads were very rugged. **To illustrate**, there were potholes everywhere.
> We learned many new techniques, **specifically**, how to relate to the native people.
> We were part of the team that worked in West Africa, **to be specific**, in Ghana.
> Volunteers educate and promote awareness of HIV/AIDS, as well as other issues,
>     **such as** malnutrition and safe drinking water.
> She was interested in learning **such** skills **as** purifying water and growing crops.

Notice that some expressions appear at the beginning of a sentence, while others appear in the middle. Use a comma after an expression when it comes at the beginning of a sentence. Commas are often used both before and after these expressions when they appear in the middle of a sentence.

### Practice  Workbook Page 180

Work with a partner. Take turns reading the sentences below aloud. Then read each sentence again, using a different expression from the box above. Be sure that the expression is appropriate.

1. Peace Corps volunteers have served in many countries. For example, many have gone to Panama, Brazil, and Sudan.

2. Power tools, such as saws and drills, are dangerous, so only skilled volunteers can use them.

3. This organization has helped the community in many ways. For instance, it raised money to help the school buy new computers.

4. One skill matters more than any other, specifically, the ability to learn new languages.

▲ Peace Corps volunteers work in many countries. These men, for instance, are in New Guinea.

368

# WRITING A RESEARCH REPORT

## Support Ideas with Examples

Another skill you'll need to know in order to write your research report is how to support your ideas with examples. An effective example gives the reader a clear illustration of a paragraph's main idea. For instance, to demonstrate the results of not taking proper care of a car, you could use a personal anecdote as an example: *As a result of failing to check the engine's oil for months, my car broke down on a lonely stretch of highway. I faced a long walk to find help.*

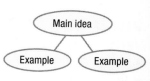

The writer of the paragraph below supports his main idea with examples. He used a graphic organizer to list his ideas.

Alan Azar

### The Red Cross

The mission of the Red Cross is to protect human rights and prevent human suffering. One way it is able to accomplish this goal is by taking an active role in conflicts all around the world. The organization provides invaluable services to the citizens of countries at war. For example, the Red Cross supplies food and water to civilian populations in need. The Red Cross also ensures the relative well-being of prisoners of war and gives medical attention to soldiers injured in battle. For instance, during World War II, the Red Cross sent 27 million aid packages to Allied prisoners of war and 300,000 tons of supplies overseas. Since it was established in 1881, the Red Cross has been able to positively affect the lives of millions of people around the world in their time of need.

## Practice

**Workbook**
Page 181

Write a paragraph for a research report about a humanitarian organization, such as UNESCO or Doctors Without Borders. Include examples that support your main idea. Before writing, use a graphic organizer to list your ideas. Introduce your examples with appropriate expressions.

**Writing Checklist**

**IDEAS:**
☑ I chose examples that support my main idea.

**SENTENCE FLUENCY:**
☑ I used appropriate expressions to introduce my examples.

# Prepare to Read

## What You Will Learn

**Reading**
- Vocabulary building: *Literary terms, word study*
- Reading strategy: *Connect ideas*
- Text type: *Literature (essay and biography)*

**Grammar, Usage, and Mechanics**
Punctuation of quoted speech

**Writing**
Include quotations and citations

 **THE BIG QUESTION**

**Why are ideals important?** What is responsibility? What responsibility do we have toward others? Do we have the same obligation to help a stranger as we do a friend or family member? How do we express this ideal of responsibility toward people? Discuss with your classmates.

**BUILD BACKGROUND**

You will read two selections about our responsibility to other people. In 2005 Dr. Eboo Patel read his essay, "**We Are Each Other's Business**," on National Public Radio. The essay calls for each of us to accept the responsibility for what happens to other people.

Many years earlier, Raoul Wallenberg took on this responsibility and, as a result, saved many lives. Before and during World War II, the Nazis tried to kill all the Jewish people in Europe, an event known as the Holocaust. Jews were sent to concentration camps, or huge prisons, where they were enslaved and killed; one of the largest was Auschwitz, in Poland. In 1944, Wallenberg, a young Swedish businessman, arrived in Hungary on a mission to rescue its Jewish citizens. "**Raoul Wallenberg and the Rescue of Hungary's Jews**" is from the PBS website that describes the program "America and the Holocaust: Deceit and Indifference," by Martin Ostrow.

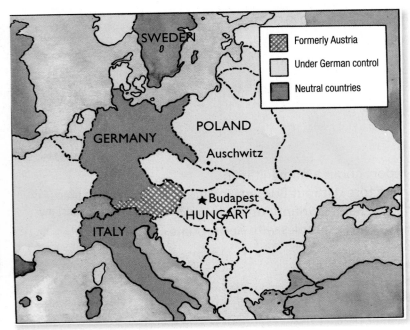

◀ Wallenberg's Europe

### Learn Literary Words

**Voice** is a writer's unique "sound," or way of "speaking" on the page. Writers use voice to express their personality and their attitude toward the subject. Voice is determined by such things as the writer's choice of words, style of composing sentences, and use of literary devices.

The writer of the following passage paints a stark picture of her first night as a prisoner in a concentration camp. She describes the sights, sounds, and other sensations in a precise, controlled manner, using short, clipped sentences. Her emotion is not directly expressed. Her voice is that of a detached observer and contrasts sharply with the terror of the experience.

> It was night when we drove through a gate and saw the guard towers and the barbed wire. I knew at once we had been delivered to a concentration camp. Inmates stood lined up in the quadrangle surrounded by barracks. They seemed to have been lined up just to greet the new transport. . . . Searchlights blinded my eyes, and the sound of the Nazi voices shouting echoed between the barracks. We stood waiting. Contained and still. Our breathing poured smoke into the icy air.
> —*Anita Lobel*, No Pretty Pictures

**Practice**

**Workbook** Page 182

Work with a partner. Read the following passage in which the writer Elie Wiesel reflects on his first night in Auschwitz. How would you characterize Wiesel's voice? Discuss how he uses words, sentence structure, and poetic devices to establish his voice.

> Never shall I forget that night, the first night in camp, which has turned my life into one long night, seven times cursed and seven times sealed. Never shall I forget that smoke. Never shall I forget the little faces of the children, whose bodies I saw turned into wreaths of smoke beneath a silent blue sky.
>    Never shall I forget those flames which consumed my faith forever.
> —*Elie Wiesel*, Night

**inmates,** prisoners
**barracks,** groups of buildings in which the prisoners lived
**transport,** train full of new prisoners

## Learn Academic Words

Study the **red** words and their meanings. You will find these words useful when talking and writing about literature. Write each word and its meaning in your notebook. After you read "We Are Each Other's Business" and "Raoul Wallenberg and the Rescue of Hungary's Jews," try to use these words to respond to the texts.

**Academic Words**

conform
diversity
prohibit
resolve
transform
ultimately

| | | |
|---|---|---|
| **conform** = act or think in a way similar to what is expected by the community | ➡ | To **conform** to the expectations of his friends, he began to talk and act like everyone else. |
| **diversity** = variety; a state of being made up of different things or people | ➡ | There is great ethnic **diversity** in our city. People of many different ethnic groups live here. |
| **prohibit** = refuse to allow; forbid | ➡ | The school's policy is to **prohibit** cell phone use. Students may not bring cell phones to class. |
| **resolve** = firm purpose | ➡ | His mother had made up her mind, and nothing could change her **resolve**. |
| **transform** = change the nature, appearance, or character of something | ➡ | He had been a prisoner of war for several years. Such an intense experience can **transform** a person, and he was now a different man. |
| **ultimately** = at last; finally | ➡ | After much thought, she **ultimately** decided to finish school and get her diploma. |

## Practice

**Workbook Page 183**

Write the sentences in your notebook. Choose a **red** word from the box above to complete each sentence. Then take turns reading the sentences aloud with a partner.

1. Ben was determined to get a better job, and no one could change his _____ in this matter.

2. Teenagers want to _____ to their friends' ideas and behavior.

3. The school's plan was intended to _____ junk-food-loving students into consumers of a healthful diet.

4. Most states _____ smoking in public places.

5. After many hours of discussion, the planning committee _____ reached a decision.

6. When people from many different ethnic and national groups live side by side peacefully, there is cultural _____ in a community.

372

## Word Study: Spelling the /k/ Sound

The /k/ sound can be spelled with the letters *c*, *k*, *ck*, and *cc*. Study the rules for the spelling of /k/. The best way to learn difficult spellings is to look at the words, read them aloud, and write them down.

| Letters | Rules and Examples |
|---------|--------------------|
| c | begins a word and precedes *a*, *o*, *u*, or a consonant: *cat, clap, cloth, come, common, crane, cup, cut*<br>ends a multisyllable word: *frolic, mimic, panic, topic* |
| k | begins a word and is followed by *e* or *i*: *keynote, kick, kiss, kitten*<br>ends a one-syllable word and follows a long vowel or consonant: *bank, bike, cake, desk, honk, mask, milk, peek, soak* |
| ck | ends a one-syllable word and follows a short vowel: *back, clock, deck, duck, kick, luck, neck, pack, sick* |
| cc | appears in a multisyllable word after a short vowel: *account, accrue, accurate, occupy, occur* |

**Practice**
Workbook
Page 184

Work with a partner. Look through the readings in this unit and other units. Find a word with the /k/ sound for each spelling rule above.

## READING STRATEGY | CONNECT IDEAS

Connecting ideas in a text or in different texts helps you understand what the author or authors want you to know. When you connect ideas, you look for the most important idea and see how it fits with all the other ideas. To connect ideas, follow these steps:

- Read the first paragraph or selection. What is the main idea?
- Now read the entire text or texts. Make a list of the main ideas.
- Review the list you made. How are they similar?

As you read the two selections, look for ideas that are similar. Think about the main idea of "We Are Each Other's Business" and "Raoul Wallenberg." How are they similar? Do the two selections share other ideas and details? Discuss them with a partner.

Workbook
Page 185

**Set a purpose for reading** Do you think Dr. Eboo Patel lives up to his ideals? Explain. What were Raoul Wallenberg's ideals? How did he live up to them?

# WE Are Each Other's Business

### Dr. Eboo Patel

I am an American Muslim. I believe in pluralism. In the Holy Quran, God tells us, "I created you into diverse nations and tribes that you may come to know one another." I believe America is humanity's best opportunity to make God's wish that we come to know one another a reality.

In my office hangs Norman Rockwell's illustration *Freedom of Worship.* A Muslim holding a Quran in his hands stands near a Catholic woman fingering her rosary. Other figures have their hands folded in prayer and their eyes filled with piety. They stand shoulder-to-shoulder facing the same direction, comfortable with the presence of one another and yet apart. It is a vivid depiction of a group living in peace with its diversity, yet not exploring it.

We live in a world where the forces that seek to divide us are strong. To overcome them, we must do more than simply stand next to one another in silence.

I attended high school in the western suburbs of Chicago. The group I ate lunch with included a Jew, a Mormon, a Hindu, a Catholic and a Lutheran. We were all devout to a degree, but we almost never talked about

▲ *Freedom to Worship*, by Norman Rockwell

✔ LITERARY CHECK

*What adjective(s) would you use to describe the author's* **voice?** *Look for language that supports your description.*

---

**pluralism**, principle that people of different races, religions, and political beliefs can live together peacefully

**Quran**, holy book of the Muslim religion

**rosary**, string of beads used by Roman Catholics for counting prayers

**piety**, respect for God and religion

**devout**, having very strong religious beliefs

religion. Somebody would announce at the table that they couldn't eat a certain kind of food, or any food at all, for a period of time. We all knew religion hovered behind this, but nobody ever offered any explanation deeper than "my mom said," and nobody ever asked for one.

A few years after we graduated, my Jewish friend from the lunchroom reminded me of an experience we both wish had never happened. A group of thugs in our high school had taken to scrawling anti-Semitic slurs on classroom desks and shouting them in the hallway.

I did not confront them. I did not comfort my Jewish friend. Instead I averted my eyes from their bigotry, and I avoided my friend because I couldn't stand to face him.

My friend told me he feared coming to school those days, and he felt abandoned as he watched his close friends do nothing. Hearing him tell me of his suffering and my complicity is the single most humiliating experience of my life.

My friend needed more than my silent presence at the lunch table. I realize now that to believe in pluralism means I need the courage to act on it. Action is what separates a belief from an opinion. Beliefs are imprinted through actions.

In the words of the great American poet Gwendolyn Brooks: "We are each other's business; we are each other's harvest; we are each other's magnitude and bond."

I cannot go back in time and take away the suffering of my Jewish friend, but through action I can prevent it from happening to others.

---

**anti-Semitic,** showing feelings of hatred toward Jewish people
**averted my eyes,** looked away
**bigotry,** intolerance toward people whose race, religion, or politics is different from yours
**humiliating,** making someone feel ashamed or embarrassed
**imprinted,** fixed permanently in memory

## ABOUT THE **AUTHOR**

**Dr. Eboo Patel** has written for such major publications as the *Chicago Tribune* and has been featured on TV news stations such as the BBC and CNN. He is co-editor of *Building the Interfaith Youth Movement* and *Acts of Faith: The Story of an American Muslim.* Dr. Patel is perhaps best known as the founder and executive director of the Interfaith Youth Core in Chicago. He gave the keynote speech at the Nobel Peace Prize Forum with President Jimmy Carter.

## BEFORE YOU GO ON

**1** Describe Rockwell's illustration, *Freedom to Worship.* Why does Patel have it hanging in his office?

**2** What incident does Dr. Patel relate about his high school years? What does he regret about his behavior?

**On Your Own**
Have you ever regretted something you did or did not do? Explain. How did the experience affect you?

▲ Raoul Wallenberg (left); Jews being deported (right)

# Raoul Wallenberg
## and the Rescue of Hungary's Jews

In June of 1944, 32-year-old Raoul Wallenberg, a businessman and a member of one of the wealthiest and most illustrious families in Sweden, volunteered to go to Budapest to help save Hungarian Jews. Although Wallenberg was sent as an attaché to the Swedish legation in Budapest, he became in effect the representative of the recently established U.S. War Refugee Board. Its mission was to rescue as many of the remaining European Jews as possible. And the largest community of surviving Jews was in Hungary. Until March of 1944, Hungary had been a relatively safe haven for Jews, but on March 19, Hitler, frustrated by the Hungarian government's refusal to deport Jews, sent in occupying forces. Adolf Eichmann soon began rounding up Jews in the provinces and by May 15, he began sending Jews to Auschwitz-Birkenau.

Wallenberg arrived in Budapest in July. By then the city had already been turned into a living hell for Jews. Their homes had been seized, and as many as 125 were crammed into small apartments. The Nazis had confiscated all Jewish businesses and bank accounts. Jews could not use the city's parks, entertain visitors, or use air raid shelters, and uniformed members of the Hungarian fascist party regularly attacked Jews on the street. In August, the Budapest Jews, who had survived earlier rounds of deportations, were now in grave danger of being sent to Auschwitz.

---

**deport**, send to a concentration camp
**occupying forces**, army that takes control of an area
**Adolf Eichmann**, Nazi official responsible for mass killings
**confiscated**, officially took property away from its owner
**fascist**, state-controlled

Within a month of his arrival, Wallenberg had come up with a plan to save Jewish lives. He persuaded the Swedish government to issue protective Swedish passports to Hungarian Jews. By January of 1945, Wallenberg had distributed Swedish papers to at least 20,000 Budapest Jews, 13,000 of whom he had sheltered in buildings above which he flew the Swedish flag. Writing home to his mother, he noted, "Everywhere you see tragedies of the greatest proportions. But the days and nights are so full of work that one seldom has time to react."

In carrying out his mission, Wallenberg frequently put himself in danger. On one occasion, armed Hungarian fascists began seizing Jews in one of the Swedish-protected buildings. Wallenberg arrived on the scene and shouted: "This is Swedish territory. . . . If you want to take them, you'll have to shoot me first." At other times he would board deportation trains, handing out passes and then demanding that the people holding them be let off the train.

Life for the Jews in Budapest got even worse in mid-October of 1944. With the Soviet Red Army just 100 miles away from Budapest, Hungarian head of state Miklós Horthy considered signing an armistice with the Allies. The Nazis acted swiftly, forcing him to resign and replacing him with the head of Hungary's anti-Semitic Arrow Cross party. Throughout the fall and winter, the Arrow Cross party unleashed a reign of terror. More than 10,000 Jews were killed, and their dead bodies were left in the streets or thrown in the Danube River.

In November, the Nazis, in dire need of slave labor, began marching Jews from Budapest to Austria. Thousands of them died on route. Wallenberg carried food and medical supplies to the Jews on the marches and frequently succeeded in removing Jews from the columns under the pretext that they were protected Swedish citizens. In the last few days before Budapest fell to the Russians, the Hungarian fascists were planning the swift killing of the 115,000 inhabitants of the Budapest Jewish ghetto. Wallenberg warned that if the action were carried out, the perpetrators would be tried as war criminals. The ghetto was left alone. Wallenberg is frequently credited with saving its inhabitants.

In the last few weeks of the war, Wallenberg knew that he was a target for the Nazis, and he successfully evaded them by hiding in different houses. But on January 17, 1945, he vanished. He was last seen leaving Budapest by car to meet Soviet military officials in Eastern Hungary. Authorities in the West have never been able to find out for certain what ultimately happened to the Swedish hero.

---

**armistice**, agreement to stop fighting
**unleashed**, let loose
**pretext**, false reason given for doing something
**perpetrators**, people who commit crimes
**vanished**, disappeared suddenly

## BEFORE YOU GO ON

**1** What steps did Wallenberg take to save Jewish lives?

**2** What were the Hungarian fascists planning to do to the Jews in Budapest in the last days of the war? What actually happened to the Jews when the city fell to the Russians?

**On Your Own**
Can you think of other people who risked their lives to save others? Why do you think some people behave in this way?

# Review and Practice

## DRAMATIC READING

In small groups, take turns reading aloud the biography of Raoul Wallenberg. Decide which paragraphs you would like to prepare as a dramatic reading. Assign each member of your group lines to read from one of the paragraphs you've chosen. Imagine that you are presenting the reading as part of a radio documentary about the Holocaust. Then present that section of the biography to the class as a dramatic reading.

> **Speaking TIP**
>
> Read with expression. Try to visualize the events described as you read aloud, so that your dramatic reading brings them to life.

## COMPREHENSION

**Workbook** Page 186

### Right There

1. What were some of the religious beliefs of the students at the high school Dr. Eboo Patel attended? How were the students aware of one another's religion?

2. What was the mission of the U.S. War Refugee Board?

### Think and Search

3. Why did Hungary still have a large Jewish community in 1944? When and why did that change?

4. Why was life a "living hell" for Jews in Budapest? Why did it get worse in mid-October 1944?

### Author and You

5. What does Patel mean when he writes, "action is what separates a belief from an opinion"? What belief do you think his anecdote refers to? What actions should he have taken to support that belief?

6. Infer the reason Wallenberg was able to survive as long as he did. Does the author imply what finally happened to him?

### On Your Own

7. Do you think it's important to stand up for other people? Why or why not? Are we really "each other's business"? Explain.

8. Do you know people who would do the right thing, even if they had to stand alone? How are these people different from the average person?

## DISCUSSION

Discuss in pairs or small groups.

 **Listening TIP**

Listen for examples your classmates use to illustrate their ideas. Think about how their ideas are similar to or different from your own.

1. A mission is a strongly felt aim, ambition, or calling. Discuss the mission that Dr. Eboo Patel felt and what inspired it. What part of the essay did you find most persuasive? Why?

2. How do the two readings connect? How does each one specifically affect your understanding of the other?

3. Do you always know what to do when you need to take action? If you miss the moment to do the right thing for someone else, what can you do to make up for it?

**Q Why are ideals important?** Do you think that the ideal expressed in these readings is a realistic one? What can happen when you stand up for another person? What are the risks you take?

## RESPONSE TO LITERATURE

**Workbook Page 186**

At some point, everyone faces a test of his or her beliefs and ideals. Think about the tests you have read about in this section. Have *you* ever been tested? Think about a time when you wish you had acted differently. Write a brief journal entry in your notebook describing the event. If you don't feel that you've been tested, write about the character and courage of someone you know or read about who faced such a test.

▲ Paul Rusesabagina was a hotel manager in Rwanda who saved over 1,000 people from being killed during the Rwandan genocide of 1994.

379

# Grammar and Writing

## GRAMMAR, USAGE, AND MECHANICS

### Punctuation of Quoted Speech

Use quotation marks and a comma to separate quoted speech from the phrase identifying the speaker. If the quoted speech follows the phrase identifying the speaker, use a comma after the phrase. Capitalize the first word of the quoted speech.

> **"Everywhere you see tragedies of the greatest proportions,"** said Wallenberg.
> Wallenberg said, **"Everywhere you see tragedies of the greatest proportions."**

If the phrase identifying the speaker interrupts the quoted speech, use a comma after the first part of the quoted speech and after the phrase. If each part of the quote is a complete sentence, put a period after the phrase identifying the speaker.

> **"But the days and nights are so full of work,"** he said, **"that one seldom has time to react."**
> **"This is Swedish territory,"** shouted Wallenberg. **"If you want to take them, you'll have to shoot me first."**

If the quoted speech is a question or an exclamation, use a question mark or an exclamation mark instead of a comma at the end of the quoted speech.

> **"Why didn't you tell me?"** he asked.     **"You scared me!"** she cried.

## Practice

Workbook Page 187

Work with a partner. Write the sentences below in your notebook. Add the correct punctuation and capitalization to the quoted speech.

1. Wallenberg said I will go to Sweden
2. I have a plan said Wallenberg
3. What happened in 1944 asked the interviewer
4. In mid-October the narrator said life for the Jews got even worse
5. The interviewer asked what happened to Raoul Wallenberg

## WRITING A RESEARCH REPORT

### Include Quotations and Citations

Including quotations in your research report can add authority and depth to your writing. Whenever you quote text from a source, you must show that the words are not your own by placing them within quotation marks. You must also include an "in-text citation" (the author or title of the piece and the page number, if known). The citation should be keyed to an alphabetized "Works Consulted List." There, the reader can get more information about your source. There are many ways to cite sources. See pages 449–450 for some common methods.

This model paragraph from a research report includes a quotation, an in-text citation, and the source. The writer used a main-idea-and-details web to organize her ideas.

Main idea

Detail          Detail

Quotation

---

Olivia Kefauver

#### Oskar Schindler

By the end of World War II, a factory owner named Oskar Schindler had saved the lives of more than a thousand Jews. After witnessing a Nazi raid in which many of his Jewish factory laborers were murdered, Schindler began negotiating with Nazi officers to protect the other Jews who worked for him. He risked being labeled a dangerous dissident for his efforts. Schindler also provided food and shelter for the Jews he was protecting. When asked why he had risked his own life, Schindler replied, "I knew the people who worked for me . . . when you know people, you have to behave toward them like human beings" (Roberts 91). Schindler's acts of compassion are honored to this day.

#### Works Consulted List

Roberts, Jack L. _The Importance of Oskar Schindler._ San Diego: Lucent Books, 1996.

---

### Practice

**Workbook**
Page 188

Write a paragraph about an individual who took risks or made sacrifices to help other people. Include a quotation and a citation. Use a main-idea-and-details web to organize your ideas. Be sure to punctuate quotations properly.

**Writing Checklist**

**IDEAS:**
☑ I supported my main idea with a quotation and included a correct citation for the quotation.

**CONVENTIONS:**
☑ My quotation is punctuated correctly.

**381**

# Link the Readings

## Critical Thinking

Look back at the readings in this unit. Think about what they have in common. They all tell about ideals. Yet they do not all have the same purpose. The purpose of one reading might be to inform, while the purpose of another might be to entertain or persuade. In addition, the content of each reading relates to ideals differently. Now copy the chart below into your notebook and complete it.

| Title of Reading | Purpose | Big Question Link |
|---|---|---|
| "The Civil Rights Movement" | | |
| "I Have a Dream" | | *expresses a national and universal ideal* |
| "The Peace Corps: An American Ideal" | *to inform* | |
| "We Are Each Other's Business" "Raoul Wallenberg and the Rescue of Hungary's Jews" | | |

## Discussion

Discuss in pairs or small groups.

● How does the information in "Raoul Wallenberg" help you understand "The Civil Rights Movement"?

Q Compare and contrast the ways each reading in this unit describes different aspects of the theme of ideals. Is there one ideal that is harder to uphold than others? Explain. What are some other ideals that you think are important?

## Fluency Check

Work with a partner. Choose a paragraph from one of the readings. Take turns reading it for one minute. Count the total number of words you read. Practice saying the words you had trouble reading. Take turns reading the paragraph three more times. Did you read more words each time? Copy the chart below into your notebook and record your speeds.

| | 1st Speed | 2nd Speed | 3rd Speed | 4th Speed |
|---|---|---|---|---|
| Words Per Minute | | | | |

# Projects

Work in pairs or small groups. Choose one of these projects.

**1** Do research in the library or on the Internet to find photographs about the civil rights movement. Choose a few photos and learn the stories behind them. Arrange them in a photo essay. Show the photos to the class as you tell their stories.

**2** Do research in the library or on the Internet to find out about the life and work of another civil rights leader, for example, Thurgood Marshall, John Lewis, James Farmer, or another prominent figure. Present a report to your class about the activities of this person and the contribution he or she made to the cause of civil rights.

**3** Create a poster that gives visual expression to one of your ideals. First, write a statement that expresses your ideal. Then design graphics to go with your statement. Present your poster to the class. Explain your design.

**4** Anne Frank was a young girl caught in the horror of World War II. Read *The Diary of Anne Frank*, the diary she kept as her family tried to evade Nazi oppression. Then give an oral book report to your class and describe your personal reaction to it.

# Further Reading

To find out more about the theme of this unit, choose from these reading suggestions.

**Les Miserables,** Victor Hugo
This Penguin Reader® adaptation tells the story of Jean Valjean, who was sentenced to hard labor for stealing a loaf of bread.

**The Horsecatcher,** Mari Sandoz
Young Elk is expected to be a warrior, but he would rather catch and tame the mustangs that run in herds than hunt and kill. He must earn the right to live as he wishes and find a place in his community.

**I Was Dreaming to Come to America: Memories from the Ellis Island Oral History Project,** Veronica Lawlor
Fifteen immigrants from various ethnic backgrounds—most of them under twenty—recount their reasons for coming to America.

# Put It All Together

### Oral Report

You will present a ten-minute oral report about a global issue that is of special interest to you. Your presentation should include well-researched facts, examples, explanations, and/or quotations that support your main idea.

**1** **THINK ABOUT IT** With a partner, brainstorm a list of global issues. For example:

- Health care
- Natural resources
- Changing lifestyles
- Education
- Population growth

Pick two issues from your list to discuss in more detail. How do these issues affect people all over the world? What do you already know about these issues? What would you like to learn? Write down your ideas.

**2** **GATHER AND ORGANIZE INFORMATION** Choose one issue from your list. Read some general information about it on a reliable website or at the library. Then narrow your topic down to a specific main idea; for example: *Cities create environmental problems, but they can also create solutions*. Use an upside-down pyramid to narrow your topic.

**Research** Review the skills you learned in the writing sections of this unit. Then use reference books, newspapers, magazines, the Internet, and other sources to gather information about your topic. Look for evidence and examples that support your main idea. Take clear, concise, and accurate notes. Be sure to identify your sources.

**Order Your Notes** When you have collected information from several sources, arrange it in a logical order. Use a graphic organizer, such as a main-idea-and-details web, to organize your information. Then make an outline that lists your main idea, along with the facts, examples, and details that support it. Copy the parts of your outline onto numbered note cards.

**Use Visuals** Decide if your report needs visuals, such as photos, charts, or models. Will visuals increase audience interest? Do you need a visual to explain a key point? Give each visual careful thought, and mark your outline or note cards to show where you will use it.

**3 PRACTICE AND PRESENT** Practice giving your oral report, referring to your outline or note cards to make sure you include all the important ideas and facts. Practice in front of other people. Ask questions to see if your ideas are coming across. Are you saying what you want to say? If not, rework your outline and note cards as needed. Time yourself with a clock or stopwatch to make sure your oral report is not too long or too short. Keep practicing until you can speak smoothly and confidently.

Review the tips in the other Listening & Speaking Workshop sections of this book. Think about the other presentations you have made. Which ones were the most successful? How can you improve your skills? Choose one speaking tip to work on as you practice your oral report.

**Deliver Your Oral Report** Make sure your note cards are in the proper order before you deliver your report. Check that your visual aids are ready. Focus on the ideas in your report, explaining them as if you were talking to a friend. Remember to face the audience and make eye contact with your listeners.

**4 EVALUATE THE PRESENTATION**
You will improve your skills as a speaker and a listener by evaluating each presentation you give and hear. Use this checklist to help you judge your oral report and the reports of your classmates.

- ☑ Did the oral report hold your attention? Why or why not?
- ☑ Was the speaker's main idea clear?
- ☑ Did the speaker support his or her main idea with facts, examples, and details?
- ☑ Was the speaker well prepared?
- ☑ What suggestions do you have for improving the oral report?

*Speaking* TIP

Speak in a loud but natural voice. Ask your listeners if they can hear you and understand your words.

*Listening* TIPS

Take notes on the most important points. Can you identify the speaker's main idea?

Think about what you hear. Do all the facts, examples, and details support the main idea? Does the speaker's information come from reliable sources?

# WRITING WORKSHOP
## Research Report

In this unit you have been learning the skills you need to write a research report. In a research report, writers explain a topic they have studied in detail. They draw information from more than one source and include a bibliography of sources at the end of the report. The first paragraph introduces the topic and states a controlling idea or thesis. Each body paragraph focuses on a main idea that develops the thesis. Main ideas are supported with facts, examples, explanations, and quotations. A concluding paragraph sums up what the writer has explained.

Your assignment for this workshop is to write a five-paragraph research report about an important idea, issue, or event.

**1 PREWRITE** Review the four paragraphs you wrote for this unit. Select the one that interests you the most to expand into a report. You may also write your report about an event in the timeline on pages 334–336 or about a human rights struggle in another country. After choosing your topic, identify reliable sources and do research. Use your own words to take complete and accurate notes on note cards. On the back of each note card, record information about your source, such as the author's name and the title of the book or website.

### List and Organize Ideas and Details

Use an outline to organize your ideas. One student, Kim, decided to write her research report about the desegregation of a high school in Little Rock, Arkansas. Here is the outline she prepared:

I. 1957 desegregation of Little Rock Central High School
    A. Event shows how dangerous fighting for civil rights could be
    B. It involved nine African-American students
II. Background of event
    A. 1954 Supreme Court ruling prepared the way
    B. Arkansas governor tried to bar black students
III. Confrontation
    A. U.S. President Eisenhower called out Army
    B. Army protected black students
IV. An amazing year
    A. First black student graduated Little Rock Central
    B. Most white students at school upheld the law
V. Heroism of "Little Rock Nine"
    A. They went on to productive and successful lives
    B. They left an important legacy to the nation

**2 DRAFT** Use the model on pages 390–391 and your outline to help you write a draft of your research report. Structure your report logically to connect the information from your research to your thesis, main ideas, and purpose. Remember to add a bibliography listing your sources at the end of your report.

**Citing Sources** Look at the style, punctuation, and order of information in the following sources. Use these examples as a model.

---

**Book**

Stanchak, John. <u>Civil War</u>. New York: Dorling Kindersley, 2000.

**Magazine article**

Kirn, Walter. "Lewis and Clark: The Journey That Changed America Forever." <u>Time</u> 8 July 2002: 36–41.

**Internet website**

Smith, Gene. "The Structure of the Milky Way." <u>Gene Smith's Astronomy Tutorial</u>. 28 April 1999. Center for Astrophysics & Space Sciences, University of California, San Diego. 20 July 2009 <http://casswww.ucsd.edu/public/tutorial/MW.html>.

**Encyclopedia article**

Siple, Paul A. "Antarctica." <u>World Book Encyclopedia</u>. 1991 ed.

---

**3 REVISE** Read over your draft. As you do so, ask yourself the questions in the writing checklist. Use the questions to help you revise your research report.

## SIX TRAITS OF WRITING CHECKLIST

- ☑ **IDEAS:** Have I stated my thesis and main ideas clearly?
- ☑ **ORGANIZATION:** Do I present information in a logical order?
- ☑ **VOICE:** Is my tone serious and suitable for a research report?
- ☑ **WORD CHOICE:** Except for quotations in quotation marks, is my research report in my own words?
- ☑ **SENTENCE FLUENCY:** Do I use transition words to connect ideas?
- ☑ **CONVENTIONS:** Does my writing follow the rules of grammar, usage, and mechanics?

Here are the changes Kim plans to make when she revises her first draft:

### The Desegregation of Little Rock Central High School

Especially during the 1950s and 1960s, the civil rights movement was by no means as "civil" as its name may imply. <sup>For example,</sup> The 1957 desegregation of Little Rock Central High School in Little Rock, Arkansas demonstrated how dangerous the struggle for racial equality could be. This event involved nine African-American students, known as "the Little Rock Nine."

Changes in the law prepared the way for the confrontation in Little Rock. In 1896, the supreme court had upheld the doctrine of "separate but equal," in effect legalizing segregation. For the next half century, in some parts of the country, black people had to attend different schools, eat at different restaurants, and even use different water fountains (McWhorter 19–21) from those open to white people. Finally, in 1954, the supreme court reversed itself, ruling that "separate educational facilities are inherently unequal." (Brown v. Board of Education). Three years later, Little Rock was prepared to desegregate its school system. <sup>However,</sup> On September 2, 1957, which was the night before the first day of school, Arkansas Governor Orval Faubus called out the National Guard to surround Little Rock Central High School and prevent any black students from entering (Fitzgerald 29).

The Army patrolled the school for the remainder of the year to protect the black students. **Outraged,** President Dwight D. Eisenhower had ordered a division of the U.S. Army to escort the nine black students into the school. Melba Pattillo Beals, one of the nine, later remembered realizing, "After three full days inside Central, I knew that integration is a much bigger word than I thought." ("What happened in 1957?")

During that year, the eyes of America were focused on Little Rock Central High School. Inside the school, the majority of the two thousand students, as well as most of the faculties and ~~the people who were hired~~ in administration, worked to put the law of the land into effect.

**Today, the Little Rock Nine are remembered as heroes.** For all their suffering, the nine students went on to lead productive and successful lives. **In addition,** They left an important legacy paving the way for an America that would never allow such segregation to occur again.

**Works Consulted List**

"Brown v. Board of Education." <u>We Shall Overcome—Historic Places of the Civil Rights Movement</u>. 26 July 2007. National Park Service. 27 July 2007 <http://www.nps.gov/history/nr/travel/civilrights>.

Fitzgerald, Stephanie. <u>Little Rock Nine: Struggle for Integration</u>. Minneapolis: Compass Point Books, 2007.

McWhorter, Diane. <u>A Dream of Freedom</u>. New York: Scholastic Inc, 2004.

Miller, Jake. <u>The Little Rock Nine: Young Champions for School Integration</u>. 1st ed. New York: PowerKids Press, 2004.

"What happened in 1957?" <u>Little Rock Central High 50th</u>. 7 May 2009 <http://www.rsd.org/centralhigh50th/1957.htm>.

Copy your revised draft onto a clean sheet of paper. Read it again. Correct any errors in grammar, word usage, mechanics, and spelling. Here are the additional changes Kim plans to make when she prepares her final draft.

Kim Kirschenbaum

### The Desegregation of Little Rock Central High School

Especially during the 1950s and 1960s, the civil rights movement was by no means as "civil" as its name may imply. For example, the 1957 desegregation of Little Rock Central High School in Little Rock, Arkansas demonstrated how dangerous the struggle for racial equality could be. This event involved nine African-American students, known as "the Little Rock Nine."

Changes in the law prepared the way for the confrontation in Little Rock. In 1896, the supreme court had upheld the doctrine of "separate but equal," in effect legalizing segregation. For the next half century, in some parts of the country, black people had to attend different schools, eat at different restaurants, and even use different water fountains (McWhorter 19–21) from those open to white people. Finally, in 1954, the supreme court reversed itself, ruling that "separate educational facilities are inherently unequal." (Brown v. Board of Education). Three years later, Little Rock was prepared to desegregate its school system. However, on September 2, 1957, the night before the first day of school, Arkansas Governor Orval Faubus called out the National Guard to surround Little Rock Central High School and prevent any black students from entering (Fitzgerald 29).

Outraged, President Dwight D. Eisenhower ordered a division of the U.S. Army to escort the nine black students into the school. The Army patrolled the school for the remainder of the year to protect the black students. Melba Pattillo Beals, one of the nine, later remembered realizing, "After three full days inside Central, I knew that integration is a much bigger word than I thought" ("What happened in 1957?").

During that year, the eyes of America were focused on Little Rock Central High School. Inside the school, the majority of the two thousand students, as well as most of the faculties and administration, worked to put the law of the land into effect.

Today, the Little Rock Nine are remembered as heroes. For all their suffering, the nine students went on to lead productive and successful lives. In addition, they left an important legacy paving the way for an America that would never allow such segregation to occur again.

**Works Consulted List**

"Brown v. Board of Education." <u>We Shall Overcome—Historic Places of the Civil Rights Movement</u>. 26 July 2007. National Park Service. 27 July 2007 <http://www.nps.gov/history/nr/travel/civilrights>.

Fitzgerald, Stephanie. <u>Little Rock Nine: Struggle for Integration</u>. Minneapolis: Compass Point Books, 2007.

McWhorter, Diane. <u>A Dream of Freedom</u>. New York: Scholastic Inc, 2004.

Miller, Jake. <u>The Little Rock Nine: Young Champions for School Integration</u>. 1st ed. New York: PowerKids Press, 2004.

"What happened in 1957?" <u>Little Rock Central High 50th</u>. 7 May 2009 <http://www.rsd.org/centralhigh50th/1957.htm>.

**5** **PUBLISH** Prepare your final draft. Share your work with your teacher and classmates.

Workbook
Page 190

*Learn about Art with the*

# Smithsonian American Art Museum

# The Pursuit of Equality

*When artists aspire to depict an emotional or political ideal, they face a unique set of challenges. How does a painter capture "hope" or "equality" on a canvas? Many artists can answer this question only after they have looked inward at their own beliefs and arrived at some conclusions about how they think and feel. They often play with the boundaries of their particular medium to express what they want to say. The end results can surprise us with their power and depth. In these three images—a quilt, a photograph, and a painted canvas—each artist uses the life of Martin Luther King Jr. to celebrate his call for equality among all peoples.*

### L'Merchie Frazier, *From a Birmingham Jail: MLK* (1996)

In her quilt, L'Merchie Frazier transferred photographs of Martin Luther King Jr. and portions of his inspirational essay "Letter from Birmingham Jail" (which King wrote while in a jail cell) onto silk. She then used her skill with beadwork and dyes to pull the piece together. She celebrates the work of the civil rights leader and what he accomplished for African Americans like herself. Her art also falls within a long and rich tradition of quilt making in the African-American community that stretches back to the eighteenth and nineteenth centuries.

**L'Merchie Frazier, *From a Birmingham Jail: MLK*, 1996, silk, photo transfer, 40 x 42 in., Smithsonian American Art Museum** ▶

## Sam Gilliam, *April 4* (1969)

In *April 4*, Sam Gilliam pays tribute to Martin Luther King Jr. on the first anniversary of his assassination. King was shot to death on April 4, 1968, in Memphis, Tennessee. Many cities experienced rioting in the weeks following the assassination, including Washington, D.C., where Gilliam lived at the time. He saw angry crowds damage stores in his own neighborhood. To create *April 4*, Gilliam dripped and splattered paint across a wet canvas, folded it up, and let it dry overnight. The next day, when he unwrapped it, the wet colors had blended to give the appearance of tears, blood, and anguish.

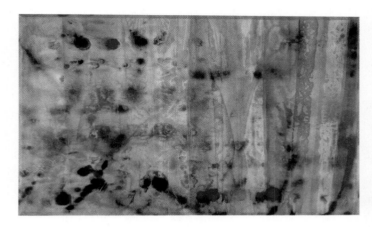

▲ Sam Gilliam, *April 4*, 1969, acrylic, 110 x 179¾ in., Smithsonian American Art Museum

## Roy DeCarava, *Mississippi Freedom Marcher, Washington, D.C.* (1963/printed 1982)

In this photograph, Roy DeCarava zoomed in on the inspired face of a young woman attending the Civil Rights March in Washington, D.C., in 1963, where King gave his famous "I Have a Dream" speech. In this speech, King imagined a "time when blacks and whites could work, play, and pray together." Instead of taking a panoramic shot of the enormous crowds at the march, the photographer chose to record the magnitude of the event with the power of one face. The woman's intense gaze projects resolve, hope, and awe. Clearly, King's words are bringing her to an emotional place deep within herself.

These three artworks use different media to capture the power of memory and hope, and the agony of failure as Americans pursue the ideals of equality and freedom.

▲ Roy DeCarava, *Mississippi Freedom Marcher, Washington, D.C.*, 1963/printed 1982, gelatin silver print, 10⅞ x 13⅞ in., Smithsonian American Art Museum

### Apply What You Learned

**1** In what way does each of these artworks reflect a different aspect of the struggle for civil rights?

**2** Which of these artworks do you feel is the most powerful? Explain your answer.

**Q Big Question**
Which artistic medium do you think best captures the ideal of equality? Explain your answer.

**Workbook**
**Pages 191–192**

# Contents
## Handbooks and Resources

# Study Skills and Language Learning

## HOW TO LEARN LANGUAGE

Learning a language takes time, but, just like learning to swim, it can be fun. Whether you're learning English for the first time or adding to your knowledge of English by learning academic or content-area words, you're giving yourself a better chance of success in your studies and in your everyday life.

Learning any language is a skill that requires you to be active. You listen, speak, read, and write when you learn a language. Here are some tips that will help you learn English more actively and efficiently.

### Listening

1. Set a purpose for listening. Think about what you hope to learn from today's class. Listen for these things as your teacher and classmates speak.

2. Listen actively. You can think faster than others can speak. This is useful because it allows you to anticipate what will be said next. Take notes as you listen. Write down only what is most important, and keep your notes short.

3. If you find something difficult to understand, listen more carefully. Do not give up and stop listening. Write down questions to ask afterward.

4. The more you listen, the faster you will learn. Use the radio, television, and Internet to practice your listening skills.

### Speaking

1. Pay attention to sentence structure as you speak. Are you saying the words in the correct order?

2. Think about what you are saying. Don't worry about speaking fast. It's more important to communicate what you mean.

3. Practice speaking as much as you can, both in class and in your free time. Consider reading aloud to improve your pronunciation. If possible, record yourself speaking.

4. Do not be afraid of making mistakes. Everyone makes mistakes!

## Reading

1. Read every day. Read as many different things as possible: Books, magazines, newspapers, and websites will all help you improve your comprehension and increase your vocabulary.

2. Try to understand what you are reading as a whole, rather than focusing on individual words. If you find a word you do not know, see if you can figure out its meaning from the context of the sentence before you look it up in a dictionary. Make a list of new vocabulary words and review it regularly.

3. Read texts more than once. Often your comprehension of a passage will improve if you read it twice or three times.

4. Try reading literature, poems, and plays aloud. This will help you understand them. It will also give you practice pronouncing new words.

## Writing

1. Write something every day to improve your writing fluency. You can write about anything that interests you. Consider keeping a diary or a journal so that you can monitor your progress as time passes.

2. Plan your writing before you begin. Use graphic organizers to help you organize your ideas.

3. Be aware of sentence structure and grammar. Always write a first draft. Then go back and check for errors before you write your final version.

## HOW TO BUILD VOCABULARY

### 1. Improving Your Vocabulary
### Listening and Speaking

The most common ways to increase your vocabulary are listening, reading, and taking part in conversations. One of the most important skills in language learning is listening. Listen for new words when talking with others, joining in discussions, listening to the radio or audio books, or watching television.

You can find out the meanings of the words by asking, listening for clues, and looking up the words in a dictionary. Don't be embarrassed about asking what a word means. It shows that you are listening and that you want to learn. Whenever you can, use the new words you learn in conversation.

### Reading Aloud

Listening to texts read aloud is another good way to build your vocabulary. There are many audio books available, and most libraries have a collection of them. When you listen to an audio book, you hear how new words are pronounced and how they are used. If you have a printed copy of the book, read along as you listen so that you can both see and hear new words.

### Reading Often

Usually, people use a larger variety of words when they write than when they speak. The more you read, the more new words you'll find. When you see new words over and over again, they will become familiar to you and you'll begin to use them. Read from different sources—books, newspapers, magazines, Internet websites—in order to find a wide variety of words.

### 2. Figuring Out What a Word Means
### Using Context Clues

When you come across a new word, you may not always need to use a dictionary. You might be able to figure out its meaning using the context, or the words in the sentence or paragraph in which you found it. Sometimes the surrounding words contain clues to tell you what the new word means.

Here are some tips for using context clues:

- Read the sentence, leaving out the word you don't know.
- Find clues in the sentence to figure out the new word's meaning.
- Read the sentence again, but replace the word you don't know with another possible meaning.
- Check your possible meaning by looking up the word in the dictionary. Write the word and its definition in your vocabulary notebook.

## 3. Practicing Your New Words

To make a word part of your vocabulary, study its definition, use it in your writing and speaking, and review it to make sure that you really understand its meaning.

Use one or more of these ways to remember the meanings of new words.

### Keep a Vocabulary Notebook

Keep a notebook for vocabulary words. Divide your pages into three columns: the new words; hint words that help you remember their meanings; and their definitions. Test yourself by covering either the second or third column.

| Word | Hint | Definition |
|------|------|------------|
| zoology | zoo | study of animals |
| fortunate | fortune | lucky |
| quizzical | quiz | questioning |

### Make Flashcards

On the front of an index card, write a word you want to remember. On the back, write the meaning. You can also write a sentence that uses the word in context. Test yourself by flipping through the cards. Enter any hard words in your vocabulary notebook. As you learn the meanings, remove these cards and add new ones.

### Say the Word Aloud

A useful strategy for building vocabulary is to say the new word aloud. Do not worry that there is no one to say the word to. Just say the word loud and clear several times. This will make you feel more confident and help you to use the word in conversation.

### Record Yourself

Record your vocabulary words. Leave a ten-second space after each word, and then say the meaning and a sentence using the word. Play the recording. Fill in the blank space with the meaning and a sentence. Replay the recording until you memorize the word.

# HOW TO USE REFERENCE BOOKS

## The Dictionary

When you look up a word in the dictionary, you find the word and information about it. The word and the information about it are called a dictionary entry. Each entry tells you the word's spelling, pronunciation, part of speech, and meaning. Many English words have more than one meaning. Some words, such as *handle*, can be both a noun and a verb. For such words, the meanings, or definitions, are numbered. Sometimes example sentences are given in italics to help you understand how the word is used.

Here is part of a dictionary page with its important features labeled.

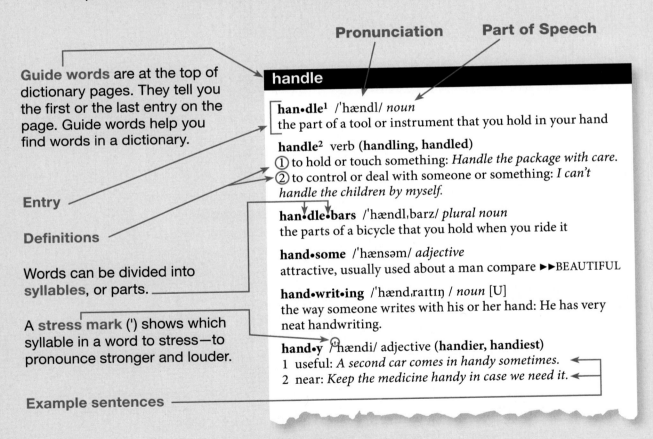

**Pronunciation**

**Part of Speech**

**Guide words** are at the top of dictionary pages. They tell you the first or the last entry on the page. Guide words help you find words in a dictionary.

**Entry**

**Definitions**

Words can be divided into **syllables**, or parts.

A **stress mark** (') shows which syllable in a word to stress—to pronounce stronger and louder.

**Example sentences**

**handle**

**han•dle¹** /'hændl/ *noun*
the part of a tool or instrument that you hold in your hand

**handle²** verb (**handling, handled**)
① to hold or touch something: *Handle the package with care.*
② to control or deal with someone or something: *I can't handle the children by myself.*

**han•dle•bars** /'hændl,barz/ *plural noun*
the parts of a bicycle that you hold when you ride it

**hand•some** /'hænsəm/ *adjective*
attractive, usually used about a man compare ▶▶BEAUTIFUL

**hand•writ•ing** /'hænd,raɪtɪŋ / *noun* [U]
the way someone writes with his or her hand: He has very neat handwriting.

**hand•y** /'hændi/ adjective (**handier, handiest**)
1 useful: *A second car comes in handy sometimes.*
2 near: *Keep the medicine handy in case we need it.*

## The Thesaurus

A thesaurus is a kind of dictionary. It is a specialized dictionary that lists synonyms, or words with similar meanings, for words. You can use a print thesaurus (a book) or an online thesaurus on the Internet.

A thesaurus is a useful writing tool because it can help you avoid repeating the same word. It can also help you choose more precise words. Using a thesaurus regularly can help build your vocabulary by increasing the number of words you know that are related by an idea or concept.

In a thesaurus, words may either be arranged alphabetically or be grouped by theme. When the arrangement is by theme, you first have to look up the word in the index to find out in which grouping its synonyms will appear. When the thesaurus is arranged alphabetically, you simply look up the word as you would in a dictionary.

The entry below is from a thesaurus that is arranged alphabetically.

**sad** *adjective* Tending to cause sadness or low spirits : blue, cheerless, depressed, depressing, dismal, dispiriting, downcast, gloomy, heartbreaking, joyless, melancholy, miserable, poignant, sorrowful, unhappy. See **happy** (antonym) in index.
—See also **depressed, sorrowful**.

Choose synonyms carefully. You can see from the thesaurus entry above that there are many synonyms for the word *sad*. However, not all of these words may be the ones you want to use. For example, *depressed* can mean that you have an illness called depression, but it can also mean that you feel sad. If you are not sure what a word means, look it up in a dictionary to check that it is, in fact, the word you want to use.

## HOW TO TAKE TESTS

In this section, you will learn some ways to improve your test-taking skills.

### 1. Taking Tests

Objective tests are tests in which each question has only one correct answer. To prepare for these tests, you should study the material that the test covers.

### Preview the Test

1. Write your name on each sheet of paper you will hand in.
2. Look over the test to get an idea of the kinds of questions being asked.
3. Find out whether you lose points for incorrect answers. If you do, do not guess at answers.
4. Decide how much time you need to spend on each section of the test.
5. Use the time well. Give the most time to questions that are hardest or worth the most points.

### Answer the Questions

1. Answer the easy questions first. Put a check next to harder questions and come back to them later.
2. If permitted, use scratch paper to write down your ideas.
3. Read each question at least twice before answering.
4. Answer all questions on the test (unless guessing can cost you points).
5. Do not change your first answer without a good reason.

### Proofread Your Answers

1. Check that you followed the directions completely.
2. Reread questions and answers. Make sure you answered all the questions.

### 2. Answering Different Kinds of Questions

This section tells you about different kinds of test questions and gives you specific strategies for answering them.

### True-or-False Questions

True-or-false questions ask you to decide whether or not a statement is true.

1. If a statement seems true, make sure that it is *all* true.
2. Pay special attention to the word *not*. It often changes the meaning of a statement entirely.
3. Pay attention to words that have a general meaning, such as *all, always, never, no, none,* and *only.* They often make a statement false.
4. Pay attention to words that qualify, such as *generally, much, many, most, often, sometimes,* and *usually.* They often make a statement true.

## Multiple-Choice Questions

This kind of question asks you to choose from four or five possible answers.

1. Try to answer the question before reading the choices. If your answer is one of the choices, choose that answer.
2. Eliminate answers you know are wrong. Cross them out if you are allowed to write on the test paper.

## Matching Questions

Matching questions ask you to match items in one group with items in another group.

1. Count each group to see whether any items will be left over.
2. Read all the items before you start matching.
3. Match the items you know first, and then match the others. If you can write on the paper, cross out items as you use them.

## Fill-In Questions

A fill-in question asks you to give an answer in your own words.

1. Read the question or exercise carefully.
2. If you are completing a sentence, look for clues in the sentence that might help you figure out the answer. If the word *an* is right before the missing word, this means that the missing word begins with a vowel sound.

## Short-Answer Questions

Short-answer questions ask you to write one or more sentences in which you give certain information.

1. Scan the question for key words, such as *explain*, *compare*, and *identify*.
2. When you answer the question, give only the information asked for.
3. Answer the question as clearly as possible.

## Essay Questions

On many tests, you will have to write one or more essays. Sometimes you are given a choice of questions that you can answer.

1. Look for key words in the question or questions to find out exactly what information you should give.
2. Take a few minutes to think about facts, examples, and other types of information you can put in your essay.
3. Spend most of your time writing your essay so that it is well planned.
4. Leave time at the end of the test to proofread and correct your work.

## STUDY SKILLS AND LEARNING STRATEGIES

### 1. Understanding the Parts of a Book
### The Title Page
Every book has a **title page** that states the title, author, and publisher.

### The Table of Contents and Headings
Many books have a **table of contents**. The table of contents can be found in the front of the book. It lists the chapters or units in the book. Beside each chapter or unit is the number of the page on which it begins. A **heading** at the top of the first page of each section tells you what that section is about.

### The Glossary
While you read, you can look up unfamiliar words in the **glossary** at the back of the book. It lists words alphabetically and gives definitions.

### The Index
To find out whether a book includes particular information, use the **index** at the back of the book. It is an alphabetical listing of names, places, and subjects in the book. Page numbers are listed beside each item.

### The Bibliography
The **bibliography** is at the end of a nonfiction book or article. It tells you the other books or sources where an author got information to write the book. The sources are listed alphabetically by author. The bibliography is also a good way to find more articles or information about the same subject.

### 2. Using the Library
### The Card Catalog
To find a book in a library, use the **card catalog**—an alphabetical list of authors, subjects, and titles. Each book has a **call number**, which tells you where to find a book on the shelf. Author cards, title cards, and subject cards all give information about a book. Use the **author card** when you want to find a book by an author but do not know the title. The **title card** is useful if you know the title of a book but not the author. When you want to find a book about a particular subject, use the **subject card**.

### The Online Library Catalog
The **online library catalog** is a fast way to find a book using a computer. Books can be looked up by author, subject, or title. The online catalog will give you information on the book, as well as its call number.

**404**

## 3. Learning Strategies

| Strategy | Description and Examples |
|---|---|
| Organizational Planning | Setting a learning goal; planning how to carry out a project, write a story, or solve a problem |
| Predicting | Using parts of a text (such as illustrations or titles) or a real-life situation and your own knowledge to anticipate what will occur next |
| Self-Management | Seeking or arranging the conditions that help you learn |
| Using Your Knowledge and Experience | Using knowledge and experience to learn something new, brainstorm, make associations, or write or tell what you know |
| Monitoring Comprehension | Being aware of how well a task is going, how well you understand what you are hearing or reading, or how well you are conveying ideas |
| Using/Making Rules | Applying a rule (phonics, decoding, grammar, linguistic, mathematical, scientific, and so on) to understand a text or complete a task; figuring out rules or patterns from examples |
| Taking Notes | Writing down key information in verbal, graphic, or numerical form, often as concept maps, word webs, timelines, or other graphic organizers |
| Visualizing | Creating mental pictures and using them to understand and appreciate descriptive writing |
| Cooperation | Working with classmates to complete a task or project, demonstrate a process or product, share knowledge, solve problems, give and receive feedback, and develop social skills |
| Making Inferences | Using the context of a text and your own knowledge to guess meanings of unfamiliar words or ideas |
| Substitution | Using a synonym or paraphrasing when you want to express an idea and do not know the word(s) |
| Using Resources | Using reference materials (books, dictionaries, encyclopedias, videos, computer programs, the Internet) to find information or complete a task |
| Classification | Grouping words, ideas, objects, or numbers according to their attributes; constructing graphic organizers to show classifications |
| Asking Questions | Negotiating meaning by asking for clarification, confirmation, rephrasing, or examples |
| Summarizing | Making a summary of something you listened to or read; retelling a text in your own words |
| Self-evaluation | After completing a task, judging how well you did, whether you reached your goal, and how effective your problem-solving procedures were |

# Grammar Handbook

In English there are eight **parts of speech**: nouns, pronouns, adjectives, verbs, adverbs, prepositions, conjunctions, and interjections.

### Nouns

**Nouns** name people, places, or things. There are two kinds of nouns: **common nouns** and **proper nouns**.

A **common noun** is a general person, place, or thing.

> person         thing       place
> The **student** brings a **notebook** to **class**.

A **proper noun** is a specific person, place, or thing. Proper nouns start with a capital letter.

> person       place        thing
> **Joseph** went to **Paris** and saw the **Eiffel Tower.**

A noun that is made up of two words is called a **compound noun**. A compound noun can be one word or two words. Some compound nouns have hyphens.

> One word: **newspaper, bathroom**
> Two words: **vice president, pet shop**
> Hyphens: **sister-in-law, grown-up**

**Articles** identify nouns. *A*, *an*, and *the* are articles.

*A* and *an* are called **indefinite articles**. Use the article *a* or *an* to talk about one general person, place, or thing.

Use *an* before a word that begins with a vowel sound.

> I have **an** idea.

Use *a* before a word that begins with a consonant sound.

> May I borrow **a** pen?

*The* is called a **definite article**. Use *the* to talk about one or more specific people, places, or things.

> Please bring me **the** box from your room.
> **The** books are in my backpack.

## Pronouns

**Pronouns** are words that take the place of nouns or proper nouns. In this example, the pronoun *she* replaces, or refers to, the proper noun *Angela*.

Pronouns can be subjects or objects. They can be singular or plural.

| | Subject Pronouns | Object Pronouns |
|---|---|---|
| **Singular** | I, you, he, she, it | me, you, him, her, it |
| **Plural** | we, you, they | us, you, them |

A **subject pronoun** replaces a noun or proper noun that is the subject of a sentence. A **subject** is who or what a sentence is about. In these sentences, *He* replaces *Daniel*.

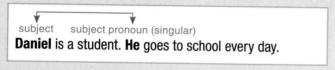

In these sentences, *We* replaces *Heather* and *I*.

An **object pronoun** replaces a noun or proper noun that is the object of a verb. A verb tells the action in a sentence. An **object** receives the action of a verb.

In these sentences the verb is *gave*. *Him* replaces *Ed*, which is the object of the verb.

> object        object pronoun (singular)
> Lauren gave **Ed** the notes. Lauren gave **him** the notes.

An object pronoun can also replace a noun or proper noun that is the **object of a preposition**. Prepositions are words like *for, to,* or *with*. In these sentences, the preposition is *with*. *Them* replaces *José* and *Yolanda*, which is the object of the preposition.

> object of a preposition        object pronoun (plural)
> I went to the mall with **José and Yolanda**. I went to the mall with **them**.

Pronouns can also be possessive. A **possessive pronoun** replaces a noun or proper noun. It shows who owns something.

| | Possessive Pronouns |
|---|---|
| **Singular** | mine, yours, hers, his |
| **Plural** | ours, yours, theirs |

In these sentences, *hers* replaces the words *Kyoko's coat*. It shows that Kyoko owns the coat.

> It is **Kyoko's coat**. It is **hers**.

408

## Adjectives

**Adjectives** describe nouns. An adjective usually comes before the noun it describes.

| | | |
|---|---|---|
| **tall** grass | **big** truck | **two** kittens |

An adjective can also come *after* the noun it describes.

The bag is **heavy**. The books are **new**.

Do not add *-s* to adjectives that describe plural nouns.

| | | |
|---|---|---|
| the **red** houses | the **funny** jokes | the **smart** teachers |

## Verbs

**Verbs** express an action or a state of being.

subject   verb                    subject   verb
Jackie **walks** to school. The school **is** near her house.

An **action verb** tells what someone or something does or did. You cannot always see the action of an action verb.

| Verbs That Tell Actions You Can See | | Verbs That Tell Actions You Cannot See | |
|---|---|---|---|
| dance | swim | know | sense |
| play | talk | remember | name |
| sit | write | think | understand |

A **linking verb** shows no action. It links the subject with another word that describes the subject.

| Linking Verbs | | |
|---|---|---|
| look | is | appear |
| smell | are | seem |
| sound | am | become |
| taste | were | |
| feel | | |

In this sentence, the adjective *tired* tells something about the subject, *dog*. *Seems* is the linking verb.

Our dog **seems** tired.

In this sentence, the noun *friend* tells something about the subject, *brother*. *Is* is the linking verb.

Your brother **is** my friend.

A **helping verb** comes before the main verb. It adds to the main verb's meaning. Helping verbs can be forms of the verbs *be*, *do*, or *have*.

| | Helping Verbs |
|---|---|
| Forms of *be* | am, was, is, were, are |
| Forms of *do* | do, did, does |
| Forms of *have* | have, had, has |
| Other helping verbs | can, must, could, have (to), should, may, will, would |

In this sentence, *am* is the helping verb; *walking* is the action verb.

helping action
verb     verb
I **am walking** to my science class.

In this sentence, *has* is the helping verb; *completed* is the action verb.

helping   action
verb     verb
He **has completed** his essay.

In questions, the subject comes between a helping verb and a main verb.

person
**Did** Liang **give** you the CD?

## Adverbs

**Adverbs** describe the action of verbs. They tell *how* an action happens. Adverbs answer the question *Where? When? How? How much?* or *How often?*

Many adverbs end in *-ly.*

| | | |
|---|---|---|
| easily | slowly | carefully |

Some adverbs do not end in *-ly.*

| | | |
|---|---|---|
| seldom | fast | very |

In this sentence, the adverb *everywhere* modifies the verb *looked.* It answers the question *Where?*

verb     adverb
Nicole looked **everywhere** for her cell phone.

In this sentence, the adverb *quickly* modifies the verb *walked.* It answers the question *How?*

verb     adverb
They walked home **quickly**.

Adverbs also modify adjectives. They answer the question *How much?* or *How little?*

In this sentence, the adjective *dangerous* modifies the noun *road.* The adverb *very* modifies the adjective *dangerous.*

adverb adjective  noun
This is a **very** dangerous road.

Adverbs can also modify other adverbs. In this sentence, the adverb *fast* modifies the verb *runs.* The adverb *quite* modifies the adverb *fast.*

verb adverb adverb
John runs **quite** fast.

## Prepositions

**Prepositions** can show time, place, and direction.

| Time | Place | Direction |
|---|---|---|
| after | above | across |
| before | below | down |
| during | in | into |
| since | near | to |
| until | under | up |

In this sentence, the preposition *above* shows where the bird flew. It shows place.

> preposition
> A bird flew **above** my head.

In this sentence, the preposition *across* shows direction.

> preposition
> The children walked **across** the street.

A **prepositional phrase** starts with a preposition and ends with a noun or pronoun.

In this sentence, the preposition is *near* and the noun is *school.*

> prepositional phrase
> The library is **near the new school**.

## Conjunctions

A **conjunction** joins words, groups of words, and whole sentences.

| Conjunctions | | | |
|---|---|---|---|
| and | for | or | yet |
| but | nor | so | |

In this sentence, the conjunction *and* joins two proper nouns: *Jonah and Teresa.*

> noun       noun
> Jonah **and** Teresa are in school.

In this sentence, the conjunction *or* joins two prepositional phrases: *to the movies* and *to the mall.*

> prepositional    prepositional
> ┌── phrase ──┐  ┌ phrase ┐
> They want to go to the movies **or** to the mall.

In this sentence, the conjunction *and* joins two independent clauses: *Amanda baked the cookies,* and *Eric made the lemonade.*

> ┌── independent clause ──┐    ┌─ independent clause ─┐
> Amanda baked the cookies, **and** Eric made the lemonade.

## Interjections

**Interjections** are words or phrases that express emotion.

Interjections that express strong emotion are followed by an exclamation point.

> **Wow!** Did you see that catch?
> **Hey!** Watch out for that ball.

Interjections that express mild emotion are followed by a comma.

> **Gee,** I'm sorry that your team lost.
> **Oh,** it's okay. We'll do better next time.

## CLAUSES

**Clauses** are groups of words with a subject and a verb. Some clauses form complete sentences; they tell a complete thought. Others do not.

This clause is a complete sentence. Clauses that form complete sentences are called **independent clauses**.

> subject   verb
> The dog's **tail wagged**.

This clause is not a complete sentence. Clauses that don't form complete sentences are called **dependent clauses**.

> subject   verb
> when the **boy patted** him.

Independent clauses can be combined with dependent clauses to form a sentence.

In this sentence, *The dog's tail wagged* is an independent clause. *When the boy patted him* is a dependent clause.

> ┌─independent clause─┐┌─independent clause─┐
> The dog's tail wagged when the boy patted him.

## SENTENCES

**Sentences** have a subject and a verb, and tell a complete thought. A sentence always begins with a capital letter. It always ends with a period, question mark, or exclamation point.

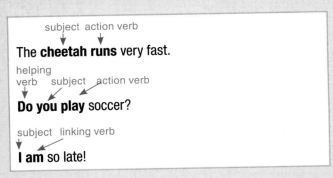

414

## Simple Sentences and Compound Sentences

Some sentences are called simple sentences. Others are called compound sentences. A **simple sentence** has one independent clause. Here is an example.

> ┌────── independent clause ──────┐
> The dog barked at the mail carrier.

**Compound sentences** are made up of two or more simple sentences, or independent clauses. They are joined together by a **conjunction** such as *and* or *but*.

> ┌───── independent clause ─────┐  ┌───── independent clause ─────┐
> The band has a lead singer, **but** they need a drummer.

## Sentence Types

Sentences have different purposes. There are four types of sentences: declarative, interrogative, imperative, and exclamatory.

**Declarative sentences** are statements. They end with a period.

> We are going to the beach on Saturday.

**Interrogative sentences** are questions. They end with a question mark.

> Will you come with us?

**Imperative sentences** are commands. They usually end with a period. If the command is strong, the sentence may end with an exclamation point.

> Put on your life jacket. Now jump into the water!

**Exclamatory sentences** express strong feeling. They end with an exclamation point.

> I swam all the way from the boat to the shore!

## End Marks

**End marks** come at the end of sentences. There are three kinds of end marks: periods, question marks, and exclamation points.

Use a **period** to end a statement (declarative sentence).

> The spacecraft *Magellan* took pictures of Jupiter.

Use a **period** to end a command or request (imperative sentence) that isn't strong enough to need an exclamation point.

> Please change the channel.

Use a **question mark** to end a sentence that asks a question. (interrogative sentence).

> Where does Mrs. Suarez live?

Use an **exclamation point** to end a sentence that expresses strong feeling (exclamatory sentence).

> That was a great party!
> Look at that huge house!

Use an **exclamation point** to end an imperative sentence that gives an urgent command.

> Get away from the edge of the pool!

**Periods** are also used after initials and many abbreviations.

Use a **period** after a person's initial or abbreviated title.

| | | |
|---|---|---|
| Ms. Susan Vargas | Mrs. Fiske | J. D. Salinger |
| Gov. Lise Crawford | Mr. Vargas | Dr. Sapirstein |

Use a **period** after the abbreviation of streets, roads, and so on.

| | | | |
|---|---|---|---|
| Avenue | Ave. | Road | Rd. |
| Highway | Hwy. | Street | St. |

Use a **period** after the abbreviation of many units of measurement. Abbreviations for metric measurements do *not* use periods.

| | | | |
|---|---|---|---|
| inch | in. | centimeter | cm |
| foot | ft. | meter | m |
| pound | lb. | kilogram | kg |
| gallon | gal. | liter | l |

## Commas

**Commas** separate, or set off, parts of a sentence, or phrase.

Use a comma to separate two independent clauses linked by a conjunction. In this sentence, the comma goes before the conjunction *but*.

┌── independent clause ──┐   ┌── independent clause ──┐
We went to the museum, **but** it is not open on Mondays.

Use commas to separate the parts in a series. A series is a group of three or more words, phrases, or very brief clauses.

| Commas in Series | |
|---|---|
| **To separate words** | Lucio's bike is red, white, and silver. |
| **To separate phrases** | Today, he rode all over the lawn, down the sidewalk, and up the hill. |
| **To separate clauses** | Lucio washed the bike, his dad washed the car, and his mom washed the dog. |

Use a comma to set off an introductory word, phrase, or clause.

| Commas with Introductory Words | |
|---|---|
| **To separate words** | Yes, Stacy likes to go swimming. |
| **To set off a phrase** | In a month, she may join the swim team again. |
| **To set off a clause** | If she joins the swim team, I'll miss her at softball practice. |

Use commas to set off an interrupting word, phrase, or clause.

| | Commas with Interrupting Words |
|---|---|
| **To set off a word** | We left, finally, to get some fresh air. |
| **To set off a phrase** | Carol's dog, a brown pug, shakes when he gets scared. |
| **To set off a clause** | The assignment, I'm sorry to say, was too hard for me. |

Use a comma to set off a speaker's quoted words in a sentence.

Jeanne asked, "Where is that book I just had?"
"I just saw it," said Billy, "on the kitchen counter."

In a direct address, one speaker talks directly to another. Use commas to set off the name of the person being addressed.

Thank you, Dee, for helping to put away the dishes.
Phil, why are you late again?

Use a comma between the day and the year.

My cousin was born on September 9, 2003.

If the date appears in the middle of a sentence, use a comma before and after the year.

Daria's mother was born on June 8, 1969, in New Jersey.

Use a comma between a city and a state and between a city and a nation.

My father grew up in Bakersfield, California.
We are traveling to Acapulco, Mexico.

If the names appear in the middle of a sentence, use a comma before *and* after the state or nation.

> My friend Carl went to Mumbai, India, last year.

Use a comma after the greeting in a friendly letter. Use a comma after the closing in both a friendly letter and formal letter. Do this in e-mail letters, too.

> Dear Margaret,          Sincerely,          Yours truly,

## Semicolons and Colons

**Semicolons** can connect two independent clauses. Use them when the clauses are closely related in meaning or structure.

> The team won again; it was their ninth victory.
> Ana usually studies right after school; Rita prefers to study in the evening.

**Colons** introduce a list of items or important information.

Use a colon after an independent clause to introduce a list of items. (The clause often includes the words *the following, these, those,* or *this*.)

> The following animals live in Costa Rica: monkeys, lemurs, toucans, and jaguars.

Use a colon to introduce important information. If the information is in an independent clause, use a capital letter to begin the first word after the colon.

> There is one main rule: Do not talk to anyone during the test.
> You must remember this: Stay away from the train tracks!

Use a colon to separate hours and minutes when writing the time.

> 1:30          7:45          11:08

## Quotation Marks

**Quotation Marks** set off direct quotations, dialogue, and some titles. A **direct quotation** is the exact words that somebody said, wrote, or thought.

Commas and periods *always* go inside quotation marks. If a question mark or exclamation point is part of the quotation, it is also placed *inside* the quotation marks.

> "Can you please get ready?" Mom asked.
> My sister shouted, "Look out for that bee!"

If a question mark or exclamation point is *not* part of the quotation, it goes *outside* the quotation marks. In these cases there is no punctuation before the end quotation marks.

> Did you say, "I can't do this"?

Conversation between two or more people is called **dialogue**. Use quotation marks to set off spoken words in dialogue.

> "What a great ride!" Pam said. "Let's go on it again."
> Julio shook his head and said, "No way. I'm feeling sick."

Use quotation marks around the titles of short works of writing or other art forms. The following kinds of titles take quotation marks:

| | |
|---|---|
| **Chapters** | "The Railroad in the West" |
| **Short Stories** | "The Perfect Cat" |
| **Articles** | "California in the 1920s" |
| **Songs** | "This Land Is Your Land" |
| **Single TV episodes** | "Charlie's New Idea" |
| **Short poems** | "The Bat" |

Titles of all other written work and artwork are underlined or set in italic type. These include books, magazines, newspapers, plays, movies, TV series, and paintings.

## Apostrophes

Apostrophes can be used with singular and plural nouns to show ownership or possession. To form the possessive, follow these rules:

For singular nouns, add an apostrophe and an *s*.

| | | |
|---|---|---|
| Maria's eyes | hamster's cage | the sun's warmth |

For singular nouns that end in *s*, add an apostrophe and an *s*.

| | | |
|---|---|---|
| her boss's office | Carlos's piano | the grass's length |

For plural nouns that do not end in *s*, add an apostrophe and an *s*.

| | | |
|---|---|---|
| women's clothes | men's shoes | children's books |

For plural nouns that end in *s*, add an apostrophe.

| | | |
|---|---|---|
| teachers' lounge | dogs' leashes | kids' playground |

Apostrophes are also used in **contractions**. A contraction is a shortened form of two words that have been combined. The apostrophe shows where a letter or letters have been taken away.

I will
**I'll** be home in one hour.
do not
We **don't** have any milk.

## Capitalization

There are five main reasons to use capital letters:

1. To begin a sentence and in a direct quotation
2. To write the word *I*
3. To write a proper noun (the name of a specific person, place, or thing)
4. To write a person's title
5. To write the title of a work (artwork, written work, magazine, newspaper, musical composition, organization)

Use a capital letter to begin the first word in a sentence.

Cows eat grass. They also eat hay.

Use a capital letter for the first word of a direct quotation. Use the capital letter even if the quotation is in the middle of a sentence.

Carlos said, "We need more lettuce for the sandwiches."

Use a capital letter for the word *I*.

How will I ever learn all these things? I guess I will learn them little by little.

Use a capital letter for a proper noun: the name of a specific person, place, or thing. Capitalize the important words in names.

Robert E. Lee          Morocco          Tuesday          Tropic of Cancer

| Capital Letters in Place Names | |
| --- | --- |
| Streets | Interstate 95, Center Street, Atwood Avenue |
| City Sections | Greenwich Village, Shaker Heights, East Side |
| Cities and Towns | Rome, Chicago, Fresno |
| States | California, North Dakota, Maryland |
| Regions | Pacific Northwest, Great Plains, Eastern Europe |
| Nations | China, Dominican Republic, Italy |
| Continents | North America, Africa, Asia |
| Mountains | Mount Shasta, Andes Mountains, Rocky Mountains |
| Deserts | Mojave Desert, Sahara Desert, Gobi Desert |
| Islands | Fiji Islands, Capri, Virgin Islands |
| Rivers | Amazon River, Nile River, Mississippi River |
| Lakes | Lake Superior, Great Bear Lake, Lake Tahoe |
| Bays | San Francisco Bay, Hudson Bay, Galveston Bay |
| Seas | Mediterranean Sea, Sea of Japan |
| Oceans | Pacific Ocean, Atlantic Ocean, Indian Ocean |

| Capital Letters for Specific Things | |
|---|---|
| **Historical Periods, Events** | Renaissance, Battle of Bull Run |
| **Historical Texts** | Constitution, Bill of Rights |
| **Days and Months** | Monday, October |
| **Holidays** | Thanksgiving, Labor Day |
| **Organizations, Schools** | Greenpeace, Central High School |
| **Government Bodies** | Congress, State Department |
| **Political Parties** | Republican Party, Democratic Party |
| **Ethnic Groups** | Chinese, Latinos |
| **Languages, Nationalities** | Spanish, Canadian |
| **Buildings** | Empire State Building, City Hall |
| **Monuments** | Lincoln Memorial, Washington Monument |
| **Religions** | Hinduism, Christianity, Judaism, Islam |
| **Special Events** | Boston Marathon, Ohio State Fair |

Use a capital letter for a person's title if the title comes before the name. In the second sentence below, a capital letter is not needed because the title does not come before a name.

I heard **S**enator Clinton's speech about jobs. The **s**enator may come to our school.

Use a capital letter for the first and last word and all other important words in titles of books, newspapers, magazines, short stories, plays, movies, songs, paintings, and sculptures.

Lucy wants to read The Lord of the Rings.
The newspaper my father reads is The New York Times.
Did you like the painting called Work in the Fields?
This poem is called "The Birch Tree."

# Reading Handbook

People often think of reading as a passive activity—that you don't have to do much, you just have to take in words—but that is not true. Good readers are active readers.

Reading comprehension involves these skills:

1. Understanding what you are reading.
2. Being part of what you are reading, or engaging with the text.
3. Evaluating what you are reading.
4. Making connections between what you are reading and what you already know.
5. Thinking about your response to what you have read.

## Understanding What You Are Reading

One of the first steps is to recognize letters and words. Remember that it does not matter if you do not recognize all the words. You can figure out their meanings later. Try to figure out the meaning of unfamiliar words from the context of the sentence or paragraph. If you cannot figure out the meaning of a word, look it up in a dictionary. Next, you activate the meaning of words as you read them. That is what you are doing now. If you find parts of a text difficult, stop and read them a second time.

## Engaging with the Text

Good readers use many different skills and strategies to help them understand and enjoy the text they are reading. When you read, think of it as a conversation between you and the writer. The writer wants to tell you something, and you want to understand his or her message.

Practice using these tips every time you read:

- Predict what will happen next in a story. Use clues you find in the text.
- Ask yourself questions about the main idea or message of the text.
- Monitor your understanding. Stop reading from time to time and think about what you have learned so far.

## Evaluating What You Are Reading

The next step is to think about what you are reading. First, think about the author's purpose for writing. What type of text are you reading? If it is an informational text, the author wants to give you information about a subject, for example, about science, social science, or math. If you are reading literature, the author's purpose is probably to entertain you.

When you have decided what the author's purpose is for writing the text, think about what you have learned. Use these questions to help you:

- Is the information useful?
- Have you changed your mind about the subject?
- Did you enjoy the story, poem, or play?

## Making Connections

Now connect the events or ideas in a text to your own knowledge or experience. Think about how your knowledge of a subject or your experience of the world can help you understand a text better.

- If the text has sections with headings, notice what these are. Do they give you clues about the main ideas in the text?
- Read the first paragraph. What is the main idea?
- Now read the paragraphs that follow. Make a note of the main ideas.
- Review your notes. How are the ideas connected?

## Thinking about Your Response to What You Have Read

You read for a reason, so it is a good idea to think about how the text has helped you. Ask yourself these questions after you read:

- What information have I learned? Can I use it in my other classes?
- How can I connect my own experience or knowledge to the text?
- Did I enjoy reading the text? Why or why not?
- Did I learn any new vocabulary? What was it? How can I use it in conversation or in writing?

## WHAT ARE READING STRATEGIES?

Reading strategies are specific things readers do to help them understand texts. Reading is like a conversation between an author and a reader. Authors make decisions about how to effectively communicate through a piece of writing. Readers use specific strategies to help them understand what authors are trying to communicate. Ten of the most common reading strategies are Previewing, Predicting, Skimming, Scanning, Comparing and Contrasting, Identifying Problems and Solutions, Recognizing Cause and Effect, Distinguishing Fact from Opinion, Identifying Main Idea and Details, and Identifying an Author's Purpose.

## HOW TO IMPROVE READING FLUENCY

### 1. What Is Reading Fluency?

Reading fluency is the ability to read smoothly and expressively with clear understanding. Fluent readers are better able to understand and enjoy what they read. Use the strategies that follow to build your fluency in these four key areas: accuracy and rate, phrasing, intonation, expression.

### 2. How to Improve Accuracy and Rate

Accuracy is the correctness of your reading. Rate is the speed of your reading.
- Use correct pronunciation.
- Emphasize correct syllables.
- Recognize most words.

### 3. How to Read with Proper Rate

- Match your reading speed to what you are reading. For example, if you are reading a mystery story, read slightly faster. If you are reading a science textbook, read slightly slower.
- Recognize and use punctuation.

### 4. Test Your Accuracy and Rate

- Choose a text you are familiar with, and practice reading it multiple times.
- Keep a dictionary with you while you read, and look up words you do not recognize.
- Use a watch or clock to time yourself while you read a passage.
- Ask a friend or family member to read a passage for you so you know what it should sound like.

### 5. How to Improve Intonation

Intonation is the rise and fall in the pitch of your voice as you read aloud. Pitch means the highness or lowness of the sound. Follow these steps:
- Change the sound of your voice to match what you are reading.
- Make your voice flow, or sound smooth, while you read.
- Make sure you are pronouncing words correctly.
- Raise the pitch of your voice for words that should be stressed, or emphasized.
- Use proper rhythm and meter.
- Use visual clues.

| Visual Clue and Meaning | Example | How to Read It |
|---|---|---|
| Italics: draw attention to a word to show special importance | He is *serious*. | Emphasize "serious." |
| Dash: shows a quick break in a sentence | He is—serious. | Pause before saying "serious." |
| Exclamation point: can represent energy, excitement, or anger | He is serious! | Make your voice louder at the end of the sentence. |
| All capital letters: can represent strong emphasis or yelling | HE IS SERIOUS. | Emphasize the whole sentence. |
| Boldfacing: draws attention to a word to show importance | He is **serious**. | Emphasize "serious." |
| Question mark: shows curiosity or confusion | Is he serious? | Raise the pitch of your voice slightly at the end of the sentence. |

## 6. How to Improve Phrasing

Phrasing is how you group words together. Follow these steps:
- Use correct rhythm and meter by not reading too fast or too slow.
- Pause for key words within the text.
- Make sure your sentences have proper flow and meter, so they sound smooth instead of choppy.
- Make sure you sound like you are reading a sentence instead of a list.
- Use punctuation to tell you when to stop, pause, or emphasize.

## 7. How to Improve Expression

Expression in reading is how you express feeling. Follow these steps:
- Match the sound of your voice to what you are reading. For example, read louder and faster to show strong feeling. Read slowly and more quietly to show sadness or seriousness.
- Match the sound of your voice to the genre. For example, read a fun, fictional story using a fun, friendly voice. Read an informative, nonfiction article using an even tone and a more serious voice.
- Avoid speaking in monotone, or using only one tone in your voice.
- Pause for emphasis and exaggerate letter sounds to match the mood or theme of what you are reading.

# Viewing and Representing

## WHAT ARE VIEWING AND REPRESENTING?

### Viewing

Viewing is something you do every day. Much of what you read and watch includes visuals that help you understand information. These visuals can be maps, charts, diagrams, graphs, photographs, illustrations, and so on. They can inform you, explain a topic or an idea, entertain you, or persuade you.

Websites use visuals, too. It is important for you to be able to view visuals critically in order to evaluate what you are seeing or reading.

### Representing

Representing is creating a visual to convey an idea. It is important for you to be able to create and use visuals in your own written work and presentations. You can use graphic organizers, diagrams, charts, posters, and artwork to illustrate and explain your ideas. Following are some examples of visuals.

## HOW TO READ MAPS AND DIAGRAMS

### Maps

Maps help us learn more about our world. They show the location of places such as countries, states, and cities. Some maps show where mountains, rivers, and lakes are located.

Many maps have helpful features. For example, a **compass rose** shows which way is north. A **scale** shows how miles or kilometers are represented on the map. A **key** shows what different colors or symbols represent.

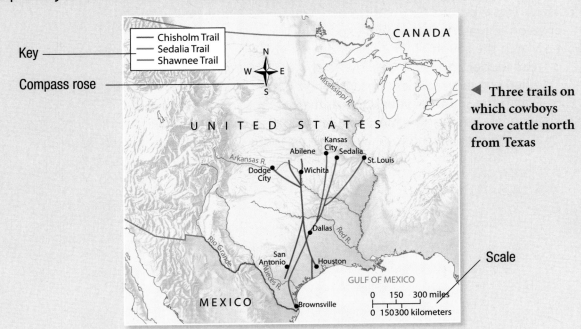

◀ Three trails on which cowboys drove cattle north from Texas

## Diagrams

Diagrams are drawings or plans used to explain things or show how things work. They are often used in social studies and science books. Some diagrams show pictures of how objects look on the outside or on the inside. Others show the different steps in a process.

This diagram shows what a kernel of corn looks like on the inside.

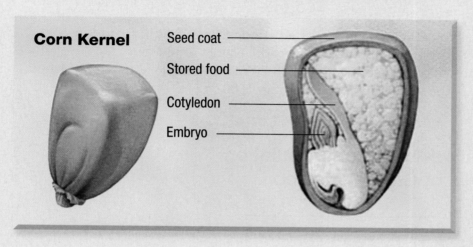

**Corn Kernel**

Seed coat

Stored food

Cotyledon

Embryo

A **flowchart** is a diagram that uses shapes and arrows to show a step-by-step process. The flowchart below shows the steps involved in baking chicken fingers. Each arrow points to the next step.

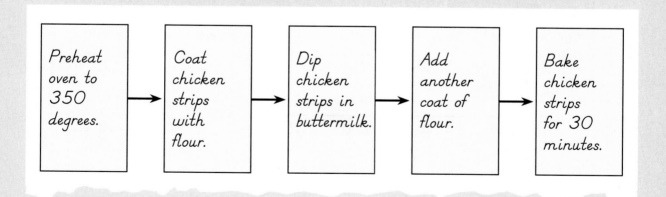

Preheat oven to 350 degrees. → Coat chicken strips with flour. → Dip chicken strips in buttermilk. → Add another coat of flour. → Bake chicken strips for 30 minutes.

## HOW TO READ GRAPHS

Graphs organize and explain information. They show how two or more kinds of information are related, or how they are alike. Graphs are often used in math, science, and social studies books. Three common kinds of graphs are **line graphs**, **bar graphs**, and **circle graphs**.

### Line Graphs

A line graph shows how information changes over a period of time. This line graph explains how, over a period of about 100 years, the Native-American population of Central Mexico decreased by more than 20 million people. Can you find the population in the year 1540? What was it in 1580?

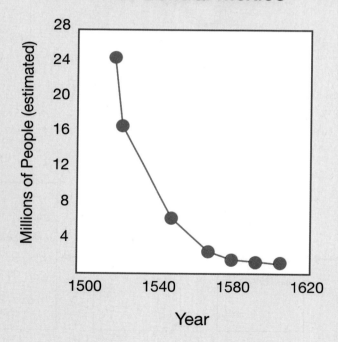

**Native-American Population of Central Mexico**

## Bar Graphs

We use bar graphs to compare information. For example, this bar graph compares the populations of the thirteen United States in 1790. It shows that, in 1790, Virginia had over ten times as many people as Delaware.

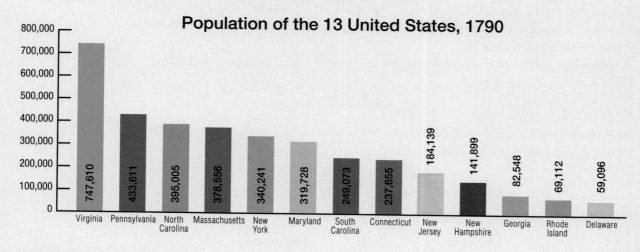

**Population of the 13 United States, 1790**

| State | Population |
| --- | --- |
| Virginia | 747,610 |
| Pennsylvania | 433,611 |
| North Carolina | 395,005 |
| Massachusetts | 378,556 |
| New York | 340,241 |
| Maryland | 319,728 |
| South Carolina | 249,073 |
| Connecticut | 237,655 |
| New Jersey | 184,139 |
| New Hampshire | 141,899 |
| Georgia | 82,548 |
| Rhode Island | 69,112 |
| Delaware | 59,096 |

## Circle Graphs

A circle graph is sometimes called a pie chart because it looks like a pie cut into slices. Circle graphs are used to show how different parts of a whole thing compare to one another. In a circle graph, all the "slices" add up to 100 percent. This circle graph shows that only 29 percent of the earth's surface is covered by land. It also shows that the continent of Asia takes up 30 percent of the earth's land.

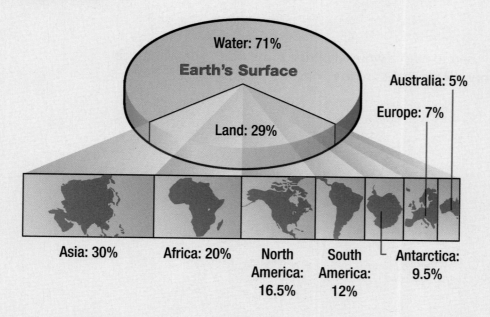

Water: 71%
Earth's Surface
Land: 29%
Australia: 5%
Europe: 7%
Asia: 30%  Africa: 20%  North America: 16.5%  South America: 12%  Antarctica: 9.5%

# HOW TO USE GRAPHIC ORGANIZERS

A graphic organizer is a diagram that helps you organize information and show relationships among ideas. Because the information is organized visually, a graphic organizer tells you—in a quick snapshot—how ideas are related. Before you make a graphic organizer, think about the information you want to organize. How are the ideas or details related? Choose a format that will show those relationships clearly.

**Venn diagrams** and **word webs** are commonly used graphic organizers. Here is an example of each.

## Venn Diagrams

A Venn diagram shows how two thing are alike and different. The diagram below compares oranges and bananas.

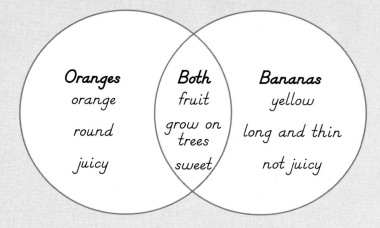

## Word Webs

A word web is often used to help a writer describe something. The word web below lists five sensory details that describe popcorn.

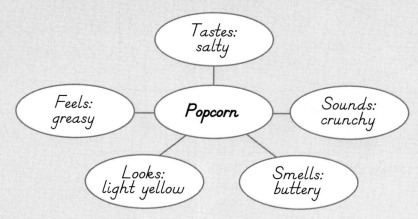

# Writing Handbook

## Narration

When writers tell a story, they use narration. There are many kinds of narration. Most include characters, a setting, and a sequence of events. Here are some types of narration.

A **short story** is a short, creative narrative. Most short stories have one or more characters, a setting, and a plot. A few types of short stories are realistic stories, fantasy stories, science-fiction stories, and adventure stories.

**Autobiographical writing** is a factual story of a writer's own life, told by the writer, usually in the first-person point of view. An autobiography may tell about the person's whole life or only a part of it.

**Biographical writing** is a factual story of a person's life told by another person. Most biographies are written about famous or admirable people.

## Description

Description, or descriptive writing, is writing that gives the reader a mental picture of whatever is being described. To do this, writers choose their words carefully. They use figurative language and include vivid sensory details.

## Persuasion

Writers use persuasion to try to persuade people to think or act in a certain way. Forms of persuasive writing include advertisements, essays, letters, editorials, speeches, and public-service announcements.

## Exposition

Exposition, or expository writing, is writing that gives information or explains something. The information that writers include in expository writing is factual. Here are some types of expository writing.

A **compare-and-contrast essay** analyzes the similarities and differences between or among things.

A **cause-and-effect essay** explains causes or effects of an event. For example, a writer might examine several causes of a single effect or several effects of a single cause.

Writers use a **problem-and-solution essay** to describe a problem and offer one or more solutions to it.

A **how-to essay** explains how to do or make something. The process is broken down into steps, which are explained in order.

A **summary** is a brief statement that gives the main ideas of an event or a piece of writing. One way to write a summary is to read a text and then reread each paragraph or section. Next put the text aside and write the main ideas in your own words in a sentence or two.

## Research Writing

Writers often use research to gather information about topics, including people, places, and things. Good research writing does not simply repeat information. It guides the readers through a topic, showing them why each fact matters and creating a complete picture of the topic. Here are some types of research writing.

**Research report** A research report presents information gathered from reference books, interviews, or other sources.

**Biographical report** A biographical report includes dates, details, and main events in a person's life. It can also include information about the time in which the person lived.

**Multimedia report** A multimedia report presents information through a variety of media, including text, slides, photographs, prerecorded music and sound effects, and digital imaging.

## Responses to Literature

A **literary essay** is one type of response to literature. In a literary essay, a writer discusses and interprets what is important in a book, short story, essay, article, or poem.

**Literary criticism** is another type of response to literature. Literary criticism is the result of a careful examination of one or more literary works. The writer makes a judgment by looking carefully and critically at various important elements in the work.

A book **critique** gives readers a summary of a book, encouraging the reader either to read it or to avoid reading it. A movie critique gives readers a summary of a movie, tells if the writer enjoyed the movie, and then explains the reasons why or why not.

A **comparison of works** compares the features of two or more works.

## Creative Writing

Creative writing blends imagination, ideas, and emotions, and allows the writer to present a unique view of the world. Poems, plays, short stories, dramas, and even some cartoons are examples of creative writing.

## Practical and Technical Documents

**Practical writing** is fact-based writing that people do in the workplace or in their day-to-day lives. A business letter, memo, school form, job application, and a letter of inquiry are a few examples of practical writing.

**Technical documents** are fact-based documents that identify a sequence of activities needed to design a system, operate machinery, follow a procedure, or explain the rules of an organization. You read technical writing every time you read a manual or a set of instructions.

In the following descriptions, you'll find tips for tackling several types of practical and technical writing.

**Business letters** are formal letters that follow one of several specific formats.

**News releases**, also called press releases, announce factual information about upcoming events. A writer might send a news release to a local newspaper, local radio station, TV station, or other media that will publicize the information.

**Guidelines** give information about how people should act or how to do something.

**Process explanations** are step-by-step explanations of how to do something. The explanation should be clear and specific and can include diagrams or other illustrations. Below is an example.

# KEYSTONE
## CD-ROM

**Usage Instructions**
1. Insert the *Keystone* CD-ROM into your CD drive.
2. Open "My Computer."
3. Double-click on your CD-ROM disk drive.
4. Click on the *Keystone* icon. This will launch the program.

## THE WRITING PROCESS

The **writing process** is a series of steps that can help you write effectively.

### Step 1: Prewrite

During **prewriting**, you collect topic ideas, choose a topic, plan your writing, and gather information.

A good way to get ideas for a topic is to **brainstorm**. Brainstorming means writing a list of all the topic ideas you can think of.

Look at your list of topic ideas. Choose the one that is the most interesting to you. This is your **topic**, the subject you will write about.

Plan your writing by following these steps:

- First, decide on the **type** of writing that works best with your topic. For example, you may want to write a description, a story, or an essay.
- The type of writing is called the **form** of writing.
- Then think about your **audience**. Identifying your audience will help you decide whether to write formally or informally.
- Finally, decide what your reason for writing is. This is your **purpose**. Is your purpose to inform your audience? To entertain them?

How you gather information depends on what you are writing. For example, for a report, you need to do research. For a description, you might list your ideas in a graphic organizer. A student named Becca listed her ideas for a description of her week at art camp in the graphic organizer below.

## Step 2: Draft

In this step, you start writing. Don't worry too much about spelling and punctuation. Just put your ideas into sentences.

Here is the first paragraph that Becca wrote for her first draft.

I saw an art contest advertised in the newspaper last spring. I entered my best drawing. I have always loved art. The prize was a week at an art camp in June with 9 other kids. I was very happy when I won.

## Step 3: Revise

Now it's time to revise, or make changes. Ask yourself these questions:
- Are my ideas presented in the order that makes the most sense?
- Does my draft have a beginning, a middle, and an end?
- Does each paragraph have a main idea and supporting details?

If you answered *no* to any of these questions, you need to revise. Revising can mean changing the order of paragraphs or sentences. It can mean changing general words for specific words. It can mean correcting errors.

Once you decide what to change, you can mark the corrections on your draft using editing marks. Here's how Becca marked up her first paragraph.

When ∧∧ I saw an art contest advertised in the newspaper last spring, I entered my best drawing. (I have always loved art.) The prize was a week at an art camp in June with nine 9 other kids. I was very excited happy when I won.

## Step 4: Edit and Proofread

In this step, you make a second draft that includes the changes you marked on your first draft. You can also add details you may have thought of since writing your first draft. Now you're ready to **proofread,** or check your work for errors and make final corrections.

Here's Becca's first draft after she finished proofreading.

### My Week at Art Camp

I have always loved art. When I saw an art contest advertised in the newspaper last spring, I entered my best drawing. The prize was a week at an art camp in June with nine other students. I was very excited when I won.

The camp was located at the Everson museum of art. On the first day, we looked at paintings by different artists. My favorite was by a painter named Monet. He painted colorful land scapes of boats and gardens. On the second day we began our own paintings. I choose to paint a picture of the duck pond on the campus. I worked hard on my painting because we were going to have an art show of all our work at the end of the week.

I learned alot about painting at camp. I especially liked learning to use watercolors. For example I found out that you can make interesting designs by sprinkling salt on a wet watercolor painting.

I had a great time at art camp. The show at the end of the week was a big success, and I made some new friends. I hope to go again next year.

## Step 5: Publish

Prepare a final copy of your writing to **publish**, or share with your audience. Here are some publishing tips.

- Photocopy and hand out your work to your classmates.
- Attach it to an e-mail and send it to friends.
- Send it to a school newspaper or magazine for possible publication.

Here is the final version of Becca's paper.

### My Week at Art Camp

I have always loved art. When I saw an art contest advertised in the newspaper last spring, I entered my best drawing. The prize was a week at an art camp in June with nine other students. I was very excited when I won.

The camp was located at the Everson Museum of Art. On the first day, we looked at paintings by different artists. My favorite was by a painter named Monet. He painted colorful landscapes of boats and gardens. On the second day, we began our own paintings. I chose to paint a picture of the duck pond on the campus. I worked hard on my painting because we were going to have an art show of all our work at the end of the week.

I learned a lot about painting at camp. I especially liked learning to use watercolors. For example, I found out that you can make interesting designs by sprinkling salt on a wet watercolor painting.

I had a great time at art camp. The show at the end of the week was a big success, and I made some new friends. I hope to go again next year.

Once you have shared your work with others, you may want to keep it in a **portfolio**, a folder or envelope with your other writing. Each time you write something, add it to your portfolio. Compare recent work with earlier work. See how your writing is improving.

## RUBRICS FOR WRITING

### What Is a Rubric?

A **rubric** is a tool, often in the form of a chart or a grid, that helps you assess your work. Rubrics are helpful for writing and speaking assignments.

To help you or others assess your work, a rubric offers several specific criteria to be applied to your work. Then the rubric helps you indicate your range of success or failure according to those specific criteria. Rubrics are often used to evaluate writing for standardized tests.

Using a rubric will save you time, focus your learning, and improve your work. When you know the rubric beforehand, you can keep the specific criteria for the writing in your mind as you write. As you evaluate the essay before giving it to your teacher, you can focus on the specific criteria that your teacher wants you to master—or on areas that you know present challenges for you. Instead of searching through your work randomly for any way to improve or correct it, you will have a clear and helpful focus.

### How Are Rubrics Structured?

Rubrics can be structured in several different ways:

1. Your teacher may assign a rubric for a specific assignment.
2. Your teacher may direct you to a rubric in your textbook.
3. Your teacher and your class may structure a rubric for a particular assignment together.
4. You and your classmates may structure a rubric together.
5. You can create your own rubric with your own specific criteria.

### How Will a Rubric Help Me?

A rubric will help you assess your work on a scale. Scales vary from rubric to rubric but usually range from 6 to 1, 5 to 1, or 4 to 1, with 6, 5, or 4 being the highest score and 1 being the lowest. If someone else is using the rubric to assess your work, the rubric will give your evaluator a clear range within which to place your work. If you are using the rubric yourself, it will help you improve your work.

### What Are the Types of Rubrics?

A **holistic rubric** has general criteria that can apply to a variety of assignments. An **analytic rubric** is specific to a particular assignment. The criteria for evaluation address the specific issues important in that assignment. The following pages show examples of both types of rubrics.

440

## Holistic Rubrics

**Holistic rubrics** such as this one are sometimes used to assess writing assignments on standardized tests. Notice that the criteria for evaluation are focus, organization, support, and use of conventions.

| Points | Criteria |
|---|---|
| **6 Points** | • The writing is focused and shows fresh insight into the writing task.<br>• The writing is marked by a sense of completeness and coherence and is organized with a logical progression of ideas.<br>• A main idea is fully developed, and support is specific and substantial.<br>• A mature command of the language is evident.<br>• Sentence structure is varied, and writing is free of fragments.<br>• Virtually no errors in writing conventions appear. |
| **5 Points** | • The writing is focused on the task.<br>• The writing is organized and has a logical progression of ideas, though there may be occasional lapses.<br>• A main idea is well developed and supported with relevant detail.<br>• Sentence structure is varied, and the writing is free of fragments.<br>• Writing conventions are followed correctly. |
| **4 Points** | • The writing is focused on the task, but unrelated material may intrude.<br>• Clear organizational pattern is present, though lapses occur.<br>• A main idea is adequately supported, but development may be uneven.<br>• Sentence structure is generally fragment free but shows little variation.<br>• Writing conventions are generally followed correctly. |
| **3 Points** | • Writing is focused on the task, but unrelated material intrudes.<br>• Organization is evident, but writing may lack a logical progression of ideas.<br>• Support for the main idea is present but is sometimes illogical.<br>• Sentence structure is free of fragments, but there is almost no variation.<br>• The work demonstrates a knowledge of conventions, with misspellings. |
| **2 Points** | • The writing is related to the task but generally lacks focus.<br>• There is little evidence of an organizational pattern.<br>• Support for the main idea is generally inadequate, illogical, or absent.<br>• Sentence structure is unvaried, and serious errors may occur.<br>• Errors in writing conventions and spellings are frequent. |
| **1 Point** | • The writing may have little connection to the task.<br>• There has been little attempt at organization or development.<br>• The paper seems fragmented, with no clear main idea.<br>• Sentence structure is unvaried, and serious errors appear.<br>• Poor diction and poor command of the language obscure meaning.<br>• Errors in writing conventions and spelling are frequent. |
| **Unscorable** | • The response is unrelated to the task or is simply a rewording of the prompt.<br>• The response has been copied from a published work.<br>• The student did not write a response.<br>• The response is illegible.<br>• The words in the response are arranged with no meaning.<br>• There is an insufficient amount of writing to score. |

## Analytic Rubrics

This analytic rubric is an example of a rubric to assess a persuasive essay. It will help you assess presentation, position, evidence, and arguments.

| Presentation | Position | Evidence | Arguments |
|---|---|---|---|
| **6 Points** Essay clearly and effectively addresses an issue with more than one side. | Essay clearly states a supportable position on the issue. | All evidence is logically organized, well presented, and supports the position. | All reader concerns and counterarguments are effectively addressed. |
| **5 Points** Most of essay addresses an issue that has more than one side. | Essay clearly states a position on the issue. | Most evidence is logically organized, well presented, and supports the position. | Most reader concerns and counterarguments are effectively addressed. |
| **4 Points** Essay adequately addresses issue that has more than one side. | Essay adequately states a position on the issue. | Many parts of evidence support the position; some evidence is out of order. | Many reader concerns and counterarguments are adequately addressed. |
| **3 Points** Essay addresses issue with two sides but does not present second side clearly. | Essay states a position on the issue, but the position is difficult to support. | Some evidence supports the position, but some evidence is out of order. | Some reader concerns and counterarguments are addressed. |
| **2 Points** Essay addresses issue with two sides but does not present second side. | Essay states a position on the issue, but the position is not supportable. | Not much evidence supports the position, and what is included is out of order. | A few reader concerns and counterarguments are addressed. |
| **1 Point** Essay does not address issue with more than one side. | Essay does not state a position on the issue. | No evidence supports the position. | No reader concerns or counterarguments are addressed. |

### Friendly Letters

A friendly letter is less formal than a business letter. It is a letter to a friend, a family member, or anyone with whom the writer wants to communicate in a personal, friendly way. Most friendly letters are made up of five parts: the **date**, the **greeting** (or salutation), the **body**, the **closing**, and the **signature**. The greeting is followed by a comma, and the paragraphs in the body are indented.

The purpose of a friendly letter is usually to share personal news and feelings, to send or to answer an invitation, or to express thanks.

In this letter, Maité tells her friend Julio about her new home.

**Greeting**

**Date**

March 2, 2009

Dear Julio,

   I was so happy to receive your letter today. I am feeling much better. My mom and I finally finished decorating my room. We painted the walls green and the ceiling pink. At first, my mom was nervous to paint the ceiling something other than white, but I knew it would look good. Now that my bedroom is finished, Manhattan is starting to feel more like home.

   Over the weekend I went to the Museum of Natural History. The whale exhibit made me think of back home and how you and I would spend hours at the beach. I am starting to adjust to city life, but I miss the smell of salt in the air and collecting sea glass on the shore.

   My parents said I can spend the summer with my grandparents at their beach house. They said I could invite you for a couple of weeks. We'll go swimming every day. I can't wait!

**Body**

Your friend,    **Closing**

Maité    **Signature**

## Business Letters

Business letters follow one of several formats. In **block format**, each part of the letter begins at the left margin. A double space is used between paragraphs. In **modified block format**, some parts of the letter are indented to the center of the page. No matter which format is used, all letters in business format have a date, an inside address, a greeting (or salutation), a body, a closing, and a signature. These parts are shown on the model business letter below, formatted in block style.

June 11, 2009 &larr; **Date**

Edward Sykes, Vice President
Animal Rights Group &larr; **Inside Address**
154 Denver Street
Syosset, NY 11791

Dear Mr. Sykes: &larr; **Greeting**

Many students at Bellevue High School would like to learn about animal rights for a project we're starting next fall. We've read about your program on your website and would like to know more about your activities.

**Body**

Would you send us some information about your organization? We're specifically interested in learning what we as students can do to help protect animals. About 75 students have expressed interest so far—I think we'll have the people power to make the project a success and have an impact.

Please help us get started. Thank you for your time and consideration.

Sincerely, &larr; **Closing**

*Pedro Rodriguez* &larr; **Signature**

Pedro Rodriguez

The **inside address** shows where the letter will be sent. The **greeting** is punctuated with a colon. The **body** of the letter states the writer's purpose. The **closing** "Sincerely" is common, but "Yours truly" or "Respectfully yours" are also acceptable. The writer types his or her name and writes a **signature**.

## FILLING IN FORMS

Forms are preprinted documents with spaces for the user to enter specific information. Some include directions; others assume that users will follow the labels and common conventions. Two common forms in the workplace are fax cover sheets and applications. When you fill out forms, it is important to do the following:

- Fill them out accurately and completely.
- Write neatly in blue or black ink.
- Include only information that is asked for on the form.

Forms usually have limited space in which to write. Because space is limited, you can use standard symbols and abbreviations, such as *$10/hr.* to mean "10 dollars per hour."

# FAX COVER SHEET

**To:** *Mr. Robert Thompson*

**Fax:** *(001) 921-9833*

**Date:** *12/04/09*

**Re:** *Job Application*

**From:** *Laura Rivas*

**Pages:** *2 (including cover sheet)*

**Message:**

*Dear Mr. Thompson:*

*Thank you for meeting with me today about the sales associate position at Story Land Bookshop. The following page is my completed application form.*

*Sincerely,*

*Laura Rivas*

## Filling in an Application for Employment

# Story Land Bookshop

**PRE-EMPLOYMENT QUESTIONNAIRE**
EQUAL OPPORTUNITY EMPLOYER
*Date:* 12/04/2009

## PERSONAL INFORMATION

**Name (last name first)**
Rivas, Laura

**Social Security No.**
145-53-6211

| **Present Address** | **City** | **State** | **Zip Code** |
|---|---|---|---|
| 351 Middleton Road | Osborne | TX | 78357 |

| **Permanent Address** | **City** | **State** | **Zip Code** |
|---|---|---|---|
| Same | | | |

**Phone No.**
(001) 661-1567

**Referred by**
Josh Logan

## EMPLOYMENT DESIRED

| **Position** | **Start Date** | **Salary Desired** |
|---|---|---|
| Sales associate | Immediately | $10/hr. |

Are you presently employed? ☐ Yes ☑ No
May we contact your former employer? ☑ Yes ☐ No
Were you ever employed by this company? ☐ Yes ☑ No

## EDUCATION

| **Name and Location of School** | **Yrs Attended** | **Did you graduate?** |
|---|---|---|
| Osborne High School, Osborne, TX | 3 | Expect to graduate 2010 |

## FORMER EMPLOYERS

| **Name and Address of Employer** | **Salary** | **Position** |
|---|---|---|
| Blue River Summer Camp<br>127 Horse Lane<br>Millwood, TX 78721 | $195 per week | Junior camp counselor |

| **Date Month and Year** | **Reason for Leaving** |
|---|---|
| 6/20/09 to 9/20/09 | Summer ended |

## CONDUCTING RESEARCH

### Reference Skills
There is a wide range of print and electronic references you can use to find many different kinds of information.

### Encyclopedias
Encyclopedias contain facts on a great many subjects. They provide basic information to help you start researching a topic. Use encyclopedias for basic facts, background information, and suggestions for additional research.

### Periodicals
Periodicals are magazines and journals. Once you've used a periodical index to identify the articles you want to read, ask a librarian to help you locate the periodicals. Often, past issues of magazines are stored electronically on microfilm, a database, or CD-ROMs. The librarian can help you use these resources. Use the table of contents, the titles, and other magazine features to help you find information.

### Biographical References
These books provide brief life histories of famous people in many different fields. Biographical references may offer short entries similar to those in dictionaries or longer articles more like those in encyclopedias. Most contain an index to help you locate entries.

### Nonfiction Books
Nonfiction books about your topic can also be useful reference tools. Use titles, tables of contents, prefaces, chapter headings, glossaries, indexes, and appendixes to locate the information you need.

### Almanacs
Almanacs are published annually. They contain facts and statistics about many subjects, including government, world history, geography, entertainment, business, and sports. To find a subject in a printed almanac, refer to the index in the front or back. In an electronic almanac, you can usually find information by typing a subject or key word.

### Electronic Databases
Available on CD-ROMs or online, electronic databases provide quick access to a wealth of information on a topic. Using a search feature, you can easily access any type of data, piece together related information, or look at the information in a different way.

## PROOFREADING

All forms of writing—from a letter to a friend to a research paper—are more effective when they are error-free. Once you are satisfied with the content of your writing, polish the grammar, usage, and mechanics.

Challenge yourself to learn and apply the skills of proofreading to everything you write. Review your writing carefully to find and correct all errors. Here are the broad categories that should direct your proofreading:

☑ **CHECK YOUR SPELLING:** Use a dictionary or an electronic spelling checker to check any spelling of which you are unsure.

☑ **CHECK YOUR GRAMMAR AND USAGE:** Use a writing handbook to correct problems in grammar or usage.

☑ **REVIEW CAPITALIZATION AND PUNCTUATION:** Review your draft to be sure you've begun each sentence with a capital letter and used proper end punctuation.

☑ **CHECK THE FACTS:** When your writing includes facts gathered from outside sources, confirm the accuracy of your work. Consult reference materials. Check names, dates, and statistics.

| Editing Marks | | |
|---|---|---|
| **To:** | **Use This Mark:** | **Example:** |
| add something | ∧ | We ate rice, bean and corn. |
| delete something | ℓ | We ate rice, beans, and corns. |
| start a new paragraph | ¶ | ¶We ate rice, beans, and corn. |
| add a comma | ⌄ | We ate rice, beans and corn. |
| add a period | ⊙ | We ate rice, beans, and corn⊙ |
| switch letters or words | ∼ | We ate rice, baens, and corn. |
| change to a capital letter | a̲ | we ate rice, beans, and corn. |
| change to a lowercase letter | ⁄ | WE ate rice, beans, and corn. |

## CITING SOURCES

### Proofreading and Preparing Manuscript

Before preparing a final copy, proofread your manuscript.

- Choose a standard, easy-to-read font.
- Type or print on one side of unlined 8 1/2" x 11" paper.
- Set the margins for the side, top, and bottom of your paper at approximately one inch. Most word-processing programs have a default setting that is appropriate.
- Double-space the document.
- Indent the first line of each paragraph.
- Number the pages in the upper right corner.

Follow your teacher's directions for formatting formal research papers. Most papers will have the following features: Title page, Table of Contents or Outline, Works Consulted List.

### Crediting Sources

When you credit a source, you acknowledge where you found your information and you give your readers the details necessary for locating the source themselves. Within the body of the paper, you provide a short citation, a footnote number linked to a footnote, or an endnote number linked to an endnote reference. These brief references show the page numbers on which you found the information. Prepare a reference list at the end of the paper to provide full bibliographic information on your sources. These are two common types of reference lists:

A **bibliography** provides a listing of all the resources you consulted during your research. A **works consulted list** lists the works you have referenced in your paper.

The chart on the next page shows the Modern Language Association format for crediting sources. This is the most common format for papers written in the content areas in middle school and high school. Unless instructed otherwise by your teacher, use this format for crediting sources.

## MLA Style for Listing Sources

| | |
|---|---|
| Book with one author | Pyles, Thomas. *The Origins and Development of the English Language*. 2nd ed. New York: Harcourt Brace Jovanovich, Inc., 1971. |
| Book with two or three authors | McCrum, Robert, William Cran, and Robert MacNeil. *The Story of English*. New York: Penguin Books, 1987. |
| Book with an editor | Truth, Sojourner. *Narrative of Sojourner Truth*. Ed. Margaret Washington. New York: Vintage Books, 1993. |
| Book with more than three authors or editors | Donald, Robert B., et al. *Writing Clear Essays*. Upper Saddle River, NJ: Prentice Hall, Inc., 1996. |
| Single work from an anthology | Hawthorne, Nathaniel. "Young Goodman Brown." *Literature: An Introduction to Reading and Writing*. Ed. Edgar V. Roberts and Henry E. Jacobs. Upper Saddle River, NJ: Prentice-Hall, Inc., 1998. 376–385. [Indicate pages for the entire selection.] |
| Introduction in a published edition | Washington, Margaret. Introduction. *Narrative of Sojourner Truth*. By Sojourner Truth. New York: Vintage Books, 1993, pp. v–xi. |
| Signed article in a weekly magazine | Wallace, Charles. "A Vodacious Deal." *Time* 14 Feb. 2000: 63. |
| Signed article in a monthly magazine | Gustaitis, Joseph. "The Sticky History of Chewing Gum." *American History* Oct. 1998: 30–38. |
| Unsigned editorial or story | "Selective Silence." Editorial. *Wall Street Journal* 11 Feb. 2000: A14. [If the editorial or story is signed, begin with the author's name.] |
| Signed pamphlet or brochure | [Treat the pamphlet as though it were a book.] |
| Pamphlet with no author, publisher, or date | *Are You at Risk of Heart Attack?* n.p. n.d. ["n.p. n.d." indicates that there is no known publisher or date.] |
| Filmstrips, slide programs, videocassettes, DVDs, and other audiovisual media | *The Diary of Anne Frank*. Dir. George Stevens. Perf. Millie Perkins, Shelly Winters, Joseph Schildkraut, Lou Jacobi, and Richard Beymer. Twentieth Century Fox, 1959. |
| Radio or television program transcript | "Nobel for Literature." Narr. Rick Karr. *All Things Considered*. National Public Radio. WNYC, New York. 10 Oct. 2002. Transcript. |
| Internet | *National Association of Chewing Gum Manufacturers*. 19 Dec. 1999 <http://www.nacgm.org/consumer/funfacts.html> [Indicate the date you accessed the information. Content and addresses at websites change frequently.] |
| Newspaper | Thurow, Roger. "South Africans Who Fought for Sanctions Now Scrap for Investors." *Wall Street Journal* 11 Feb. 2000: A1+ [For a multipage article, write only the first page number on which it appears, followed by a plus sign.] |
| Personal interview | Smith, Jane. Personal interview. 10 Feb. 2000. |
| CD (with multiple publishers) | Simms, James, ed. *Romeo and Juliet*. By William Shakespeare. CD-ROM. Oxford: Attica Cybernetics Ltd.; London: BBC Education; London: HarperCollins Publishers, 1995. |
| Signed article from an encyclopedia | Askeland, Donald R. "Welding." *World Book Encyclopedia*. 1991 ed. |

# Technology Handbook

## WHAT IS TECHNOLOGY?

Technology is a combination of resources that can help you do research, find information, and write. Good sources for research include the Internet and your local library. The library contains databases where you can find many forms of print and nonprint resources, including audio and video recordings.

### The Internet

The Internet is an international network, or connection, of computers that share information with each other. It is a popular source for research and finding information for academic, professional, and personal reasons. The World Wide Web is a part of the Internet that allows you to find, read, and organize information. Using the Web is a fast way to get the most current information about many topics.

Words or phrases can be typed into the "search" section of a search engine, and websites that contain those words will be listed for you to explore. You can then search a website for the information you need.

### Information Media

Media is all the organizations, such as television, radio, and newspapers that provide news and information for the public. Knowing the characteristics of various kinds of media will help you to spot them during your research. The following chart describes several forms of information media.

| Types of Information Media | |
|---|---|
| **Television News Program** | • Covers current news events<br>• Gives information objectively |
| **Documentary** | • Focuses on one topic of social interest<br>• Sometimes expresses controversial opinions |
| **Television Newsmagazine** | • Covers a variety of topics<br>• Entertains and informs |
| **Commercial** | • Presents products, people, or ideas<br>• Persuades people to buy or take action |

### Other Sources of Information

There are many other reliable print and nonprint sources of information to use in your research. For example: magazines, newspapers, professional or academic journal articles, experts, political speeches, press conferences.

Most of the information from these sources is also available on the Internet. Try to evaluate the information you find from various media sources. Be careful to choose the most reliable sources for this information.

451

## HOW TO USE THE INTERNET FOR RESEARCH

### Keyword Search

Before you begin a search, narrow your subject to a keyword or a group of **keywords**. These are your search terms, and they should be as specific as possible. For example, if you are looking for information about your favorite musical group, you might use the band's name as a keyword. You might locate such information as band member biographies, the group's history, fan reviews of concerts, and hundreds of sites with related names containing information that is irrelevant to your search. Depending on your research needs, you might need to narrow your search.

### How to Narrow Your Search

If you have a large group of keywords and still don't know which ones to use, write out a list of all the words you are considering. Then, delete the words that are least important to your search, and highlight those that are most important.

**Use search connectors to fine-tune your search:**

*AND:*   narrows a search by retrieving documents that include both terms. For example: *trumpets AND jazz*

*OR:*   broadens a search by retrieving documents including any of the terms. For example: *jazz OR music*

*NOT:*   narrows a search by excluding documents containing certain words. For example: *trumpets NOT drums*

### Good Search Tips

1. Search engines can be case-sensitive. If your first try at searching fails, check your search terms for misspellings and search again.
2. Use the most important keyword first, followed by the less important ones.
3. Do not open the link to every single page in your results list. Search engines show pages in order of how close it is to your keyword. The most useful pages will be located at the top of the list.
4. Some search engines provide helpful tips for narrowing your search.

## Respecting Copyrighted Material

The Internet is growing every day. Sometimes you are not allowed to access or reprint material you find on the Internet. For some text, photographs, music, and fine art, you must first get permission from the author or copyright owner. Also, be careful not to plagiarize while writing and researching. Plagiarism is presenting someone else's words, ideas, or work as your own. If the idea or words are not yours, be sure to give credit by citing the source in your work.

## HOW TO EVALUATE THE QUALITY OF INFORMATION

Since the media presents large amounts of information, it is important to learn how to analyze this information critically. Analyzing critically means you can evaluate the information for content, quality, and importance.

### How to Evaluate Information from Various Media

Sometimes the media tries to make you think a certain way instead of giving all the facts. These techniques will help you figure out if you can rely on information from the media.

- ☑ Ask yourself if you can trust the source, or if the information you find shows any bias. Is the information being given in a one-sided way?

- ☑ Discuss the information you find from different media with your classmates or teachers to figure out its reliability.

- ☑ Sort out facts from opinions. Make sure that any opinions given are backed up with facts. A fact is a statement that can be proved true. An opinion is a viewpoint that cannot be proved true.

- ☑ Be aware of any loaded language or images. Loaded language and images are emotional words and visuals used to persuade you.

- ☑ Check surprising or questionable information in other sources. Are there instances of faulty reasoning? Is the information adequately supported?

- ☑ Be aware of the kind of media you are watching. If it's a program, is it a documentary? A commercial? What is its purpose? Is it correct?

- ☑ Read the entire article or watch the whole program before reaching a conclusion. Then develop your own views on the issues, people, and information presented.

## How to Evaluate Information from the Internet

There is so much information available on the Internet that it can be hard to understand. It is important to be sure that the information you use as support or evidence is reliable and can be trusted. Use the following checklist to decide if a Web page you are reading is reliable and a credible source.

☑ The information is from a well-known and trusted website. For example, websites that end in **.edu** are part of an educational institution and usually can be trusted. Other cues for reliable websites are sites that end in **.org** for "organization" or **.gov** for "government." Sites with a **.com** ending are either owned by businesses or individuals.

☑ The people who write or are quoted on the website are experts, not just everyday people telling their ideas or opinions.

☑ The website gives facts, not just opinions.

☑ The website is free of grammatical and spelling errors. This is often a hint that the site was carefully made and will not have factual mistakes.

☑ The website is not trying to sell a product or persuade people. It is simply trying to give correct information.

☑ If you are not sure about using a website as a source, ask your teacher for advice. Once you become more aware of the different sites, you will become better at knowing which sources to trust.

## HOW TO USE TECHNOLOGY IN WRITING

### Personal Computers

A personal computer can be an excellent writing tool. It enables a writer to create, change, and save documents. The cut, copy, and paste features are especially useful when writing and revising.

### Organizing Information

Create a system to organize the research information you find from various forms of media, such as newspapers, books, and the Internet.

Using a computer and printer can help you in the writing process. You can change your drafts, see your changes clearly, and keep copies of all your work. Also, consider keeping an electronic portfolio. This way you can store and organize copies of your writing in several subject areas. You can review the works you have completed and see your improvement as a writer.

It is easy to organize electronic files on a computer. The desktop is the main screen, and holds folders that the user names. For example, a folder labeled "Writing Projects September" might contain all of the writing you do during that month. This will help you find your work quickly.

As you use your portfolio, you might think of better ways to organize it. You might find you have several drafts of a paper you wrote, and want to create a separate folder for these. Every month, take time to clean up your files.

### Computer Tips

1. Rename each of your revised drafts using the SAVE AS function. For example, if your first file is "essay," name the first revision "essay2" and the next one "essay3."
2. If you share your computer with others, label a folder with your name and keep your files separate by putting them there.
3. Always back up your portfolio on a server or a CD.

Personal computer ▶

455

# Glossary

**absorb** take in a liquid slowly

**access** a way of being able to use or do something

**achievement** something important that you succeed in doing through skill and hard work

**adapt** change your behavior or ideas to fit a new situation

**adjust** change or move something slightly in order to make it better or more effective

**affect** make someone feel strong emotions

**amplify** make something louder or stronger

**analyze** examine or think about something carefully in order to understand it

**anecdote** a short interesting story used to illustrate an important point

**appreciation** something you say or do to thank someone or show you are grateful

**archetype** an original model or pattern from which other things of the same type are copied

**aspect** one of the parts or features of a situation, idea, or problem

**assess** make a judgment about a person or situation after thinking carefully about it

**assistance** help or support

**association** an organization of people with a particular purpose or interest

**attitude** the opinions and feelings you usually have about a particular thing, idea, or person

**attribute** a good or useful quality that something has

**autonomy** independence

**awareness** knowledge or understanding of a particular subject or situation

**benefit** give an advantage or have a good effect

**blend** mix together

**boycott** a refusal to buy something, use something, or take part in something as a means of protest

**camouflage** hide something by making it look the same as the things around it

**category** a group of people or things that have the same qualities

**challenge** something exciting or difficult, requiring skill and effort

**characterization** description of imaginary persons in a way that makes them believable and lifelike

**character motivation** why a character in a book, play, or movie does something

**circulates** moves around in a system, or makes something do this

**climax** the most important or exciting events that come near the end of a story or experience

**colony** a group of the same kind of animals living together

**communicate** express thoughts or feelings

**community** the people who live in the same area, town, or city or who have something in common

**compensation** money paid to someone who has suffered injury, loss, or damage

**component** one part of something

**conclude** decide after considering all of the information

**conduct** the way someone behaves

**conflict** struggle between two opposing forces

**conform** act or think in a way similar to what is expected by the community

**consequence** something that happens as the result of a particular action

**consist** be made of

**constitute** combine to form something together

**contrast** compare two people, ideas, or things to show how they are different from each other

**contributes** gives

**control** make someone or something work in a particular way

**convey** communicate a message or information with or without using words

**convince** make someone feel certain that something is true

**cooperate** work together in order to get a job done

**create** make something exist or invent something new

**culture** art, beliefs, or behavior of a particular group of people

**currents** flow of water, air, or electricity

**cycle** a number of related events that happen again and again in the same order

**decline** gradual decrease in quality, quantity, or importance of something

**decrease** become less or fewer

**demand** the desire that people have for particular goods or services

**demonstrate** show or describe how to do something

**demonstration** an event at which many people meet to protest or support something in public

**deny** refuse to allow someone to have or do something

**depict** describe or show a character, situation, or event in writing or by using pictures

**depth** the distance from the top to the bottom of something

**design** the art of making drawings or plans for something

**dialogue** a conversation in a book, play, or movie

**dimensions** the measurements or size of something

**disaster** a sudden event that happens to many people and causes much damage or harm

**discrimination** the practice of treating one group of people differently from another in an unfair way

**displace** cause something to move, usually by force, from one place to another

**distinguish** see the difference between two things

**disturbance** something that interrupts normal conditions or the natural order of things

**diversity** variety; a state of being made up of different things or people

**domain** a particular place that is controlled by one person

**dominant** strongest, most important, or most notable

**drama** a play for the theater, television, or radio

**economy** the way that money and products are produced and used in a particular country, area, etc.

**emerge** appear after being hidden

**encounter** an unexpected meeting

**energy** power that produces heat and makes things work

**enforced** made people obey a rule or law

**entrepreneurs** people who start companies, arrange business deals, and take risks, usually in order to make a profit

457

environment  the land, water, and air in which people, animals, and plants live

equality  having the same opportunities and rights

erupts  explodes and sends out smoke, fire, and rocks, used about a volcano

establish  start something such as a company, system, situation, etc., especially one that will exist for a long time

evoke  produce a strong feeling or memory in someone

exceed  be more than a particular number or amount

exclude  not allow someone to enter a place or do something

extended metaphor  a comparison that continues for several lines or more in a poem, book, etc.

extract  remove an object or substance from the place where it comes from

factor  one of several things that influence or cause a situation

figurative language  writing or speech that is not meant to be read as fact

figure  a person in a picture

finance  provide money for something

focus  change the position of a lens on a camera, telescope, etc., in order to see something clearly

function  the natural purpose or action of a body part

generate  produce or make something

generation  all the people who are about the same age

geologists  scientists who study rocks and how they are made

geometric  having a regular pattern of shapes and lines

heredity  process of passing on a mental or physical quality from a parent to a child

humanitarian  a person concerned with improving bad living conditions and preventing unfair treatment of people

humidity  the amount of water that is contained in the air

identical  exactly the same

identify  recognize and name someone or something

illustrate  explain or make something clear by giving examples

image  a picture that you can see through a camera, on television, or in a mirror

imagery  use of words to create word pictures

impact  the effect that an event or situation has on someone or something

implement  if you implement a plan, process, etc., you begin to make it happen

impulses  signals sent along nerves

incompetent  not having the ability or skill to do something

individual  one person

influence  have an effect on the way someone develops, behaves or thinks

injury  damage or harm to someone or something

innovative  using new ideas, methods, or inventions

institution  a large organization that has a particular purpose, such as scientific, educational, or medical work

instructions  information or advice that tells you how to do something

insufficient  not enough

integrate  end the practice of separating people of different races in a place or institution interpret  explain the meaning of something, such as an event or a text

intervene  do something to try to stop an argument, problem, war, etc.

invest  give money to a company, bank, etc., in order to get a profit later

investigate  try to find out the truth

issue  a subject or problem that people think is important

legislation  a law or set of laws; the act of making laws

lithograph  a picture printed from something that has been cut into a piece of stone or metal

livelihoods  the way people earn money in order to live

longevity  long life

malnutrition  illness or weakness as a result of not eating enough food or of not eating good food

maturity  behaving in a sensible way, like an adult

maximum  the largest that is possible, allowed, or needed

medium  a way of communicating or expressing something

membrane  thin skin that covers or connects parts of the body

metaphor  an expression that compares two things without using the words *like* or *as*, for example, *a river of tears*

method  planned way of doing something

moisture  small amounts of water that are present in the air, in a substance, or on a surface

molecules  tiny particles too small to be seen

mood  general feeling created in a reader by a literary text

moral  a lesson about right and wrong ways to act

motivation  the reason why a person thinks, feels, or acts a certain way

multimedia  a mixture of sounds, words, pictures, etc., to give information, especially on a computer program

muscles  parts of your body under your skin that make you strong and help you to move

objective  something that you are working hard to achieve

obstacles  things that make it difficult for people to succeed

occur  happen, especially without being planned

offspring  an animal's baby or babies

onomatopoeia  the use of a word whose sound is related to the word's meaning

oppression  act of treating people unfairly or cruelly

organization  a group that has been formed for a particular purpose

organize  plan or arrange something

outcome  the final result

paradox  statement that appears to say two conflicting things

participation  the act of taking part in something

patterns  arrangements of shapes, lines, or colors

pension  money given to someone regularly by a company when he or she has stopped working

perceive  become aware of something through the senses

period  a particular length of time in history

personification  giving human qualities to nonhuman things

perspective  a way of thinking about something that is influenced by the type of person you are

phenomena  things that happen in nature

plentiful  more than enough in amount or number

plot  sequence of events in a narrative

point of view  the perspective from which a story is written

policy  a plan that has been agreed to by a political party, government, or organization

portrait  painting, drawing, or photograph of a person

portray  describe or represent something or someone

prejudice  an unfair opinion about something that is not based on facts or reason

pressure  the force produced by pressing on someone or something

principle  a moral rule or set of ideas that makes you behave in a particular way

proceed  begin and carry on an activity

process  a series of actions, developments, or changes that happen naturally

produced  made something happen or had a particular effect

production  the process of making something, or the amount that is made

prohibit  refuse to allow; forbid

project  cause something to fall upon a surface

promote  help something develop and succeed

raids  sudden attacks on a place

react  behave in a particular way because of what someone has done or said to you

recede  get farther and farther away

recovery  the process of returning to a normal condition after a period of trouble or difficulty

recycle  use something again instead of throwing it away

reflect  throw back light, heat, or an image off of a surface

reform  change that improves an organization or system

region  a fairly large area of a state, country, etc., usually without exact limits

regulate  control an activity or process, usually by having rules

release  let go or let loose

repetition  the use of a sound, word, or phrase more than once to emphasize an idea and create rhythm

research  serious study of a subject that is intended to discover new facts about it

reservoirs  special lakes where water is stored to be used by people in a city

resolve  firm purpose

resources  all the money, property, skills, etc., that you have available to use

respect  good opinion of or admiration for someone

reveal  make something known that was previously secret

reverse  undo the effect of something

rhythm  regular repeated pattern of sounds in music or speech

riot  violent behavior in a public place by an angry crowd of people

role  the position, job, or function someone or something has in a group

**sequence** a series of related events that have a particular result

**setting** time and place where the action of a story happens

**signals** sounds, actions, or movements that tell someone to do something

**significant** noticeable or important

**signify** express a wish, feeling, or opinion by doing something

**similar** almost the same, but not exactly the same

**simile** an expression that compares two things using the words *like* or *as*, for example, *as red as blood*

**specific** used when talking about a particular person, place, or thing

**status** a person's social position in relation to other people

**stimulate** encourage more of an activity or help a process develop faster

**stock** a share in a company

**strategy** a set of plans and skills used in order to gain success

**structure** the way a thing is made or the arrangement of its parts

**supply** amount of something you can use when needed

**support** give money, food, etc., for someone to live

**surface** the outside or top part of something

**surplus** more of something than is needed or used

**survival** the state of continuing to live or exist, especially after a difficult or dangerous situation

**suspense** feeling of uncertainty or tension

**symbol** a picture, person, object, etc. that represents a particular quality, idea, or organization

**tint** a small amount of a light color

**tone** the attitude of a writer or speaker toward his or her subject and audience

**torrents** large amounts of water moving very quickly in a particular direction

**tradition** a belief, custom, or way of doing something that has existed for a long time

**transform** change the nature, appearance, or character of something

**transmit** send a signal

**trigger** to make something happen

**turbulence** irregular and strong movements of air or water that are caused by the wind

**turmoil** a state of confusion, excitement, and trouble

**ultimately** at last; finally

**undertaking** an important job for which a person is responsible

**unemployment** the condition of not having a job, or the number of people who do not have a job

**unpredictable** changing so much that you do not know what to expect

**vary** be different from one another

**vitality** life and energy

**voice** a writer's unique sound or way of speaking on the page

**volume** the loudness or softness of a sound; the amount of space that something contains or fills

**volunteers** people who offer to do something without expecting to be paid

**wisdom** good judgment and knowledge gained through experience

461

# Index of Skills

# Index of Authors, Titles, Art, and Artists

# Acknowledgments

**UNIT 1**

"The Sounds of the City" by James Tuite. Published as "The Sounds of Manhattan" in *The New York Times*, August 6, 1966. Copyright © 1966 by The New York Times Company. Reprinted by permission.

"The Sounds of the Desert," excerpt from *Lazy B* by Sandra Day O'Connor and H. Alan Day. Copyright © 2002 by Sandra Day O'Connor and H. Alan Day. Used by permission of Random House, Inc.

"How We Hear" Copyright © Pearson Longman, 10 Bank Street, White Plains, NY 10606.

Excerpt from a *Girl with a Pearl Earring* by Tracy Chevalier. Copyright © 1999 by Tracy Chevalier. Used by permission of Plume, an Imprint of Penguin Group (U.S.A.) Inc.

"How We See" Copyright © Pearson Longman, 10 Bank Street, White Plains, NY 10606.

**UNIT 2**

"Mendel and the Laws of Heredity" from *Prentice Hall Science Explorer Life Science* by M.J. Padilla, Ph.D., I. Miaoulis, Ph.D., and M. Cyr, Ph.D. Copyright © 2002 by Pearson Education Inc., publishing as Prentice Hall. Used by permission.

"A Son Searches for His Father" by Daniel Comstock. Copyright © Pearson Longman, 10 Bank Street, White Plains, NY 10606.

"My Father and the Figtree" from *Different Ways to Pray* by Naomi Shihab Nye. Copyright © 1980 by Naomi Shihab Nye. Used by permission of the author.

"I Ask My Mother to Sing" by Li-Young Lee from *Rose*. Copyright © 1986 by Li-Young Lee. Reprinted with the permission of BOA Editions, Ltd.

"Mother to Son" by Langston Hughes from *Selected Poems of Langston Hughes*. Copyright © 1994 by The Estate of Langston Hughes. Reprinted by permission of Alfred A. Knopf, a Division of Random House, Inc. and Harold Ober Associates Incorporated.

"That Older Generation" by Barbara Weisburg. Copyright © Pearson Longman, 10 Bank Street, White Plains, NY 10606.

"An Hour with Abuelo" from *An Island Like You* by Judith Ortiz Cofer. Copyright © 1995 by Judith Ortiz Cofer. Reprinted by permission of Orchard Books, an Imprint of Scholastic Inc.

**UNIT 3**

"The Great Migration." Copyright © Pearson Longman, 10 Bank Street, White Plains, NY 10606.

Excerpt from *A Raisin in the Sun* by Lorraine Hansberry. Copyright © 1958 by Robert Nemiroff, as an unpublished work. Copyright © 1959, 1966, 1984 by Robert Nemiroff, copyright renewed 1986, 1987 by Robert Nemiroff. Used by permission of Random House, Inc. and A&C Black Publishers Ltd.

"The Savage, Beautiful World of Army Ants" by Alex Chadwick on National Public Radio, July 25, 2006. Copyright © 2007 by National Public Radio, Inc. Reprinted by permission.

Excerpt from an interview with Mawi Asgedom, from Hachette Book Group U.S.A. website. Used by permission of Little, Brown & Company.

Excerpt from *Of Beetles and Angels* by Mawi Asgedom. Copyright © 2001, 2002 by Mawi Asgedom. By permission of Little, Brown & Company.

**UNIT 4**

"Poogweese" from *Echoes of the Elders : The Stories and Paintings of Chief Lelooska*, edited by Christine Normandin. Copyright © 1997 by Don Lelooska Smith. Reprinted by permission of Callaway Arts & Entertainment.

"Tsunamis," excerpt from *Tsunami Alert!* by Niki Walker. Copyright © by Crabtree Publishing Company. Reprinted by permission of Crabtree Publishing Company.

# Credits

top-right, Jon Riley/Stone Allstock/Getty Images; 103 bottom, Courtesy of B. Weisberg; 105 right, Elie Bernager/ Stone Allstock/Getty Images; 107 right, © JupiterImages/ Thinkstock/Alamy; 109 bottom, Shutterstock; 110 bottom, Tom Stewart/Bettmann/CORBIS; 117 bottom, Rick O'Quinn/ The University of Georgia Press Z.Legacy.Corporate Digital Archive; 120 bottom, Photodisc/Getty Images; 121 right, Shutterstock.

UNIT 3: 132–133 background, First Light/Getty Images; 132 top-left, Joseph Solomon/The Granger Collection, New York; 132 top-center, Joan Marcus Photography; 132 top-right, Mark Moffett/Minden Pictures; 132 center, Courtesy of the Library of Congress; 132 bottom-left, Mark Moffett/Getty Images; 133 top, Jose Cendon/AP/Wide World Photos; 133 bottom, Photodisc/Getty Images; 135 right, Novastock/Stock Connection; 136 right, Dave King/Dorling Kindersley; 138 right, Dorothea Lange/Courtesy of the Library of Congress; 139 top-left, The Chicago Defender; 140 bottom, Culver Pictures, Inc.; 142–143 top-left, Frank Driggs Collection; 142 bottom, Joseph Solomon/The Granger Collection, New York; 143 top-right, Schomburg Center for Research in Black Culture/Art Resource; 144 top, © 2007 The Jacob and Gwendolyn Lawrence Foundation, Seattle /Artists Rights Society (ARS), New York; 147 right, Will Hart/PhotoEdit; 148 Joan Marcus Photography; 150 Myrleen Ferguson/PhotoEdit; 159 bottom, Bettmann/ CORBIS; 164 bottom, Mark Moffett Minden Pictures; 166 bottom, Mark Moffett/Minden Pictures; 167, Shutterstock; 168–171 background, © James P. Rowan/DRK Photo; 168 right, Mark Moffett/Minden Pictures; 168 bottom-left, Mark Moffett/Minden Pictures; 169 top, Mark Moffett/Minden Pictures; 170 bottom, Mark Moffett/Minden Pictures; 171 top Mark Moffett/Minden Pictures; 172 right, Mark Moffett/ Minden Pictures; 175 right, Noah Berger/AP/Wide World Photos; 178 bottom, Peter Bennett/Ambient Images; 180 bottom, Jose CendonAP/Wide World Photos; 182 bottom, Photo of Selamawi Asgedom courtesy of the author; 183 top, Photo of Selamawi Asgedom courtesy of the author/The Harvard News; 183 bottom, Photo courtesy of Selamawi Asgedom; 185 bottom, SW Productions/Photodisc/Getty Images; 187 right, Tony Freeman/PhotoEdit.

UNIT 4: 198–199 background, Jean Roche/Peter Arnold, Inc.; 198 top-left, David Falconer/SuperStock; 198 top-center, Bettmann/CORBIS; 198 top-right, JustASC/ Shutterstock; 198 bottom-left, Jim Watt/PacificStock.

com; 198–199 center, D. Sim/Getty Images; 199 top, Dave Fleetham/PacificStock.com; 200 bottom-right, David Falconer/SuperStock; 201 right, Alamy Images; 202 bottom, Dave Fleetham/PacificStock.com; 207 bottom, Ralph Norris; 209 bottom, Gunter Marx Photography/ CORBIS; 211 right, David Falconer/SuperStock; 212 bottom, CORBIS; 214 bottom, James A. Sugar/Bettmann/CORBIS; 216 bottom, Yuriko Nakao/Reuters America LLC/CORBIS; 217 top, James R. McGury/U.S. Navy/Getty Images; 218, Phil Mislinski/Omni-Photo Communications, Inc.; 219, Bettmann/CORBIS; 221 bottom, Jimin Lai/Agence France Presse/Getty Images; 224 left, Neuville, Alphonse Marie de (1835-85) (after) The Bridgeman Art Library International Private Collection/The Bridgeman Art Library; 224 right, Bettmann/CORBIS; 226 right, SPL/Photo Researchers, Inc.; 233 bottom, Lebrecht Music & Arts Photo Library; 237, JustASC/Shutterstock; 238 bottom, Mike Berceanu/ photolibrary.com; 241 right, Stuart Westmorland/CORBIS; 242 left, Doug Perrine/PacificStock.com; 242 center, Doug Perrine/Nature Picture Library; 242 right, Georgette Douwma/Nature Picture Library; 242–243 center, Doug Perrine/PacificStock.com; 244 bottom, Jurgen Freund/ Nature Picture Library; 244 center, Jan Hinsch/Photo Researchers, Inc.; 244 right, Roland Birke/Phototake NYC; 244 left, Jim Watt / PacificStock.com; 245 background, Jeff Rotman/Nature Picture Library; 245 left, Brandon D. Cole/ Bettmann/CORBIS; 245 right, Dave Fleetham/PacificStock. com; 246 top-right, © Norbert Wu/DRK Photo; 246 left, Frank Greenaway/Dorling Kindersley; 246 center, Frank Greenaway/Dorling Kindersley; 246 right, Doc White/Nature Picture Library; 247 background, © Mickey Gibson/Animals Animals/Earth Scenes; 247 inset, Mike Bacon/Tom Stack & Associates, Inc.; 249 bottom, Dave King/Dorling Kindersley; 251 top, Jan Hinsch/Photo Researchers, Inc.; 251 center, Doug Perrine/PacificStock.com; 251 bottom, Mike Bacon/ Tom Stack & Associates, Inc.

UNIT 5: 262–263 background, Burton Mcneely/Stone Allstock/Getty Images; 262 top-left, Brown Brothers; 262 top-center, Dorothea Lange/Courtesy of the Library of Congress; 262 top-right, Kent Wood/Photo Researchers, Inc.; 262 bottom, Paula Bronstein/Getty Images; 263 top Jacques M. Chenet/NWK/Getty Images; 263 bottom, Bettmann/CORBIS; 262–263, Archive Holdings Inc./Image Bank/Getty Images; 264 bottom, Bettmann/CORBIS; 266 bottom, Judi Bottoni/AP/Wide World Photos; 268, Cleve Bryant/PhotoEdit; 268 bottom, AP/Wide World Photos;

# Smithsonian American Art Museum
# List of Artworks

**UNIT 1 Technology's Impact on the Senses**
**Page 66**
Theodore Roszak
*Recording Sound,*
1932
plaster and oil on wood
32 x 48 x 6¾ in.
Smithsonian American Art Museum, Museum purchase

**Page 67**
David Hockney
*Snails Space with Vari-Lites, "Painting as Performance"*
1995–96
oil on two canvases, acrylic on canvas-covered masonite
84 x 260 x 135 in.
Smithsonian American Art Museum, Gift of Nan Tucker McEvoy
© 1995–96 David Hockney

**UNIT 2 Family Tales**
**Page 130**
Charles Willson Peale
*Mrs. James Smith and Grandson*
1776
oil on canvas
36⅜ x 29¼ in.
Smithsonian American Art Museum, Gift of Mr. and Mrs. Wilson Levering Smith Jr. and Museum purchase

**Page 131**
Velino Shije Herrera
*Story Teller*
about 1925–35
gouache and pencil on paperboard
10 x 15 in.
Smithsonian American Art Museum, Corbin-Henderson Collection, gift of Alice H. Rossin

**UNIT 3 Things Communities Share**
**Page 196**
Allan Rohan Crite
*School's Out*
1936
oil on canvas
30¼ x 36⅛ in.
Smithsonian American Art Museum, Transfer from The Museum of Modern Art

**UNIT 4 The Power of the Sea**
Page 260
Albert Pinkham Ryder
*Flying Dutchman*
completed by 1887
oil on canvas
14¼ x 17¼ in.
Smithsonian American Art Museum, Gift of John Gellatly

Page 261
Joseph Cornell
*Untitled*
about 1940–60
mixed media
2½ x 20⅝ x 9½ in.
Smithsonian American Art Museum, Gift of the Joseph and Robert Cornell Memorial Foundation

**UNIT 5 Showing the Strain**
Page 324
James E. Allen
*Prayer for Rain*
1938
lithograph on paper
10½ x 14⅛ in.
Smithsonian American Art Museum, Gift of the family of James E. Allen

Page 325
Alexandre Hogue
*Dust Bowl*
1933
oil on canvas
24 x 32⅝ in.
Smithsonian American Art Museum, Gift of International Business Machines Corporation

**UNIT 6 The Pursuit of Equality**
Page 392
L'Merchie Frazier
*From a Birmingham Jail: MLK*
1996
silk, photo transfer, gel medium, dyes, and beads
40 x 42 in.
Smithsonian American Art Museum, Gift of L'Merchie Frazier in memory of Watty
and Alberta Frazier and James and Merchie Dooley (grandparents)
© 1996 L'Merchie Frazier

**Page 393**
Sam Gilliam
*April 4*
1969
acrylic on canvas
110 x 179¾ in.
Smithsonian American Art Museum, Museum purchase

Roy DeCarava
*Mississippi Freedom Marcher, Washington, D.C.*
1963/printed 1982
gelatin silver print on paper
10⅞ x 13⅞ in.
Smithsonian American Art Museum, Museum purchase made possible by Henry L. Milmore
© 1982 Roy DeCarava